Inspired Prophetic Warnings

Book of Mormon and
Modern Prophecies
about America's Future

Inspired Prophetic Warnings

Book of Mormon and Modern Prophecies about America's Future

Duane S. Crowther

Horizon Publishers
An imprint of Cedar Fort, Inc.
Springville, Utah

ISBN 13: 978-0-88290-983-7

Published by Horizon Publishers, an imprint of Cedar Fort, Inc.
2373 W. 700 S., Springville, UT, 84663
Distributed by Cedar Fort, Inc., www.cedarfort.com

Cover design by Brian Halley

Printed in the United States of America

10 9 8 7 6 5 4 3 2 1

Contents

Section I
The Prophetic Warnings

Dedication

To my family,
whose love and companionship I cherish
and desire for the eternities.
May this book
strengthen them, guide them, and
stabilize their faith
during the trials of the last days.

Acknowledgments

Inspired Prophetic Warnings was not easily written. It required many months of work and effort, with time taken from a schedule which was already full to overflowing. Much was written beginning at four o'clock in the morning. During those long months of effort, I was blessed to have the love and support of my family. I was strengthened by all of them, and even the youngest ones prayed each day to their Heavenly Father, asking Him to "please help Daddy finish his book!"

During those busy months my wife, Jean, gave encouragement, read proofs, made constructive suggestions, and maintained a spirit of harmony in the home. She supported me in the effort, as she does in all things. How blessed I am to have her!

Deep appreciation is felt for the staff of Horizon Publishers who rendered effective service in helping this book towards completion. They devoted many weeks to the tasks of typesetting, proofreading, paste-up, stripping negatives, and making bluelines and plates in preparation for the press runs. Final production of the book was performed by Horizon's printing and bindery staff. Their efforts are appreciated on this project, as were those of the office, shipping and sales staffs, who joined in the effort to send this book across the nation as soon as it was completed.

But my greatest appreciation is for that Divine Being who guides and directs all our lives in this mortal existence. I often felt promptings and guidance as I wrote, and I know His influence has been manifested in what is written here. I readily confess His hand in all things, and express my deepest gratitude for His guidance, direction, and protection. May His blessings be upon us all.

Preface

I love America! It is my home, my native land. It has been great and good—a bastion of freedom and liberty. America has enjoyed the blessings and guidance of God, and her people have been protected through divine providence.

I have partaken of the liberties which she has granted to her citizens—privileges which are denied to people in many other lands. These liberties I value highly, and I regard them as priceless gems to be preserved at all costs. In the shadow of her freedoms I work, I plan, I dream, I hope, I build for the future. I seek America's well-being, her progress, and her protection, for my future is inseparably connected with hers. If she grows and prospers, I may progress also; if she endures trauma and agony, I also must suffer. I am an American citizen. Like every American—my future and fate is inextricably related to the future of this great country.

Seven Reasons Why This Book Was Written

During the past several years, as this book has moved from creative idea to researched notes to finished pages, I have carefully defined my motives for writing it. So that they may be clearly understood by those who read this volume, I have chosen to list those motives. They are as follows:

1. I love America, and seek the preservation of this land and of her liberties. There are many ways in which a citizen may work for his country. He may be active in political affairs, or work for the accomplishment of social goals. He may seek to improve the environment, or pursue better law enforcement methods, or render service through youth groups. Almost always he will serve in those capacities which give outlet for his best talents and abilities. By doing so, he gives the best of himself and accomplishes the greatest good.

I am no different. I am an author and publisher by profession. I seek to use my best skills as an expression of my patriotism and love of country. *Inspired Prophetic Warnings* is my way of contributing something of worth towards the betterment of this great nation.

2. I seek to warn of difficult times and loss of freedoms which are rapidly approaching. As I study the scriptures and the teachings of those whom I regard as the authorized servants of God today, I find clear warning of an epoch in these last days when "*there shall be a time of trouble, such as never was since there was a nation*."[1] This series of cataclysmic events will be worldwide in scope and devastating in its effect. It will bring much death, suffering, and desolation.

The Savior warned that "*as a snare shall it come on all them that dwell on the face of the whole earth*."[2] I have learned of the terrible suffering mankind must endure if its wickedness causes the prophesied events of this era to transpire. With this insight, I seek to warn others: we must labor with our might to turn the world towards righteousness in the hope that this great wrath and punishment might be withheld.

I approach the events of the future with the understanding of a person trained primarily in one important area. My study and background have been focused in particular aspects of religion and theology. This background includes an advanced degree in Old and New Testament, a thesis study which focused on latter-day eschatology, the authorship of more than a dozen books on the last days and other theological themes, and extensive study for more than two decades on the messages of the scriptures concerning future events. Like Peter of old, "Such as I have give I thee."[3] Though this book will comment on many national and world events, trends, and conditions, my approach will be theological rather than political.

3. I seek to fulfill the God-given commandments that such a warning be given. In Biblical times God revealed to Ezekiel that if a watchman failed to warn his people of impending danger, responsibility for the destruction of that people would be required of that man.[4] In modern times the Lord has commanded that "*the voice of warning shall be unto all people, by the mouths of my disciples,* whom I have chosen in these last days."[5] While warning of this

1. Dan. 12:1.
2. Lk. 21:35.
3. Acts 3:6.
4. See Ezek. 33:2-6.
5. *The Doctrine and Covenants of The Church of Jesus Christ of Latter-day Saints* (Salt Lake City, Utah: The Church of Jesus Christ of Latter-day Saints), section 1, verse 4. Further references to this volume of scripture will be shown as *D&C*, with sections and verses cited as: 1:4.

terrible period (known scripturally as the "desolation of abomination"), the Savior revealed that "*it becometh every man who hath been warned to warn his neighbor . . . and to prepare the saints for the hour of judgment which is to come;* that their souls may escape the wrath of God, the *desolation of abomination* which awaits the wicked, . . ."1

This warning responsibility belongs to every Latter-day Saint, not just to a few individuals. I am aware of the Lord's command to the priesthood of the Church to

> *. . . go ye forth as your circumstances shall permit, in your several callings, unto the great and notable cities and villages, reproving the world in righteousness of all their unrighteous and ungodly deeds, setting forth clearly and understandingly the desolation of abomination in the last days.*[2]

His commandment to all who preach the gospel is that

> . . . I send you out to reprove the world of all their unrighteous deeds, and *to teach them of a judgment which is to come.*[3]

Those who labor within the Church sometimes find that the Lord blesses them with talents, then prompts and uses them to fulfill particular responsibilities. If they fail to use the talents He gives them, He is angered.[4] I feel that I have been given some understanding and talent on the subject treated in this book. I feel it appropriate, and I feel prompted, that I express such warnings as this book contains. More important, I recognize that to fail to do so God might see fit to retract the talent with which He has blessed me.

4. I seek to assess the degree of danger which confronts this country and the members of the Church. In any endeavor norms must be set and evaluations conducted before trends and direction of movement can be established. No business can know if it is profitable until it carefully counts its assets and liabilities. No educational system can determine if learning is taking place until valid standards have been established and careful testing has been carried out.

1. D&C 88:81, 84-85. See also verses 87-89.
2. D&C 84:117.
3. D&C 84:87.
4. D&C 60:2-3, 12-13. See also Mt. 25:24-30.

The Lord has revealed very definite standards with which the people of this country must comply if they are going to escape His judgments and gain blessings and prosperity in the land. One effort of this book is to closely report those standards—those prophetic warnings. Another objective is to gather facts and statistics which would indicate whether Americans are turning to God or abandoning His ways.

5. I seek to clearly portray what God has revealed will happen unless the nation returns to righteousness. The Lord has revealed to the latter-day prophets much of what will transpire in America in the future if wickedness prevails. Patterns are also found in the histories of other civilizations as they broke divine laws and underwent the same judgments.

Over the years I have found that people soon separate into two schools of thought when they begin to consider the prophetic warnings concerning the last days. Some want to know, understand, and prepare. Others, however, adopt the classic "head-in-sand" pose of the ostrich—they don't want to know of the warnings God has revealed. They rationalize His words of warning as "pessimism," and say they are "not uplifting," rather than giving heed to the revealed words of God. The same problem existed in the days of Heber C. Kimball, counselor to Brigham Young. He said:

> . . . *if we do not take the right course, we are sure to see sorrow, and the greatest you have ever seen. Those who were never without bread, and clothing, and good houses to dwell in, murmur the worst; and those who never had any troubles and trials since they were in this Church, or since they have been on the earth, are the most ready to complain.*
>
> Go and read the prophets: They all say so. Don't be frightened; I tell you it will come; and *it would be better for you to believe it and go and make calculations accordingly.* Shall we ever be brought to want? I tell you, if we live our religion, we never shall.[1]

6. I seek to suggest possible solutions and appropriate actions. Over the years, many have proposed actions and policies which would help alleviate the nation's distress. I have assembled and sifted their proposals, and have attempted to suggest meaningful and realistic procedures which can serve to preserve and strengthen this country—

1. Heber C. Kimball, as quoted by Weston N. Nordgren, "Shall We Go Hungry?—A Vital Question Answered Nearly a Century Ago by a Prophet of the Lord—Heber C. Kimball," Salt Lake City, Utah: *Improvement Era*. Vol. 43, No. 11, Nov. 1940, p. 662.

policies which can be followed on an individual level for the betterment of this country.

7. I seek to make a contribution to the literature of the Church by assembling important materials and making them readily available to others.

In my profession as an author and publisher, I have learned that thoughts and materials must be available in usable form before they begin to have lasting impact upon large numbers of people.

In this book my role is that of reporter, compiler, and analyzer of teachings revealed in the scriptures and through modern prophets. I will assemble individual items together, point out relationships and trends, and draw such conclusions as would be appropriate for any editor or news analyst to make.

It should be understood that this book is a private endeavor; it is not an official publication of The Church of Jesus Christ of Latter-day Saints. From the beginning, the writing and compiling of Church-oriented books for commercial distribution has been left to individual authors who have functioned on their own initiative. Such books have been' privately published and are the responsibility of the individual authors, not the Church itself. Church authorities have been wisely refrained from regulation and censorship of the writings of individual members. Members write, often seeking and receiving revealed guidance, but without any official status. The Lord has said,

> . . . *It is not meet that I should command in all things;* for he that is compelled in all things, the same is a slothful and not a wise servant; wherefore he receiveth no reward.
>
> Verily I say, *men should be anxiously engaged in a good cause, and do many things of their own free will, and bring to pass much righteousness;*
>
> *For the power is in them, wherein they are agents unto themselves.* And inasmuch as men do good they shall in nowise lose their reward.[1]

A prominent LDS author once said to me, "You know, Duane, it's a blessing that there are members of the Church who write about Church history and doctrine on their own—*they are able to say a lot of important things that the Church can't say officially.*" His comment struck me with real force, and I am sure it is valid. There is definitely a place—an important place—for writings other than the manuals and

1. D&C 58:26-28.

instructions issued by the Church in its official capacity. The writings of individual Latter-day Saint members throughout the history of the Church illustrate his premise well. Such books soon find their own level. If their works furnish information and insights of real value, they are widely read; if they make little real contribution, they are soon discarded. The general Church readership does a far better job than any official regulation could do in determining true worth.

Pitfalls Avoided

There are several difficulties I have tried to avoid as I have written *Inspired Prophetic Warnings*.

First, I have sought to avoid political bias and party positions. You can rest assured that you won't know whether I am a Republican, a Democrat, or an Independent when you have finished the book. I have no political aspirations nor axe to grind.

Second, I have sought very carefully to *avoid extremism*—I am not a "right-winger," nor do I lean to the opposite extreme. I do not belong to any militant organization. I speak and write only as a deeply-concerned citizen.

If I have any bias, it is religious rather than political or ideological. This book is a theological book, which accepts the validity of Latter-day Saint scriptures and reveals my faith that the prophets who wrote them are inspired men who have expressed the Lord's will concerning America in their teachings. You who are not LDS may not accept the validity of this premise. I invite you, at least, to consider their messages as the words of wise men and evaluate them in the light of current world and national conditions. To do less than that would be foolishness on your part.

Third, I believe that propaganda and loose interpretation of documentation colors and falsifies truth. I have sought to *avoid propaganda and also to avoid the assertion of improper doctrinal or eschatological conclusions*. I have sought to quote the scriptures accurately and to interpret them with care, remembering well the words of the prophet Alma: "Behold, the scriptures are before you; *if ye will wrest them it shall be to your own destruction*."[1]

When one deals with prophecy, the future always stands as the final judge—erroneous data, improper conclusions, and incorrect interpretations are shown to be wrong with the passage of time.

1. Al. 13:20.

There is nothing to be accomplished by drawing an incorrect picture of the future.

It has been said that the two subjects one shouldn't discuss if he wishes to avoid controversy are religion and politics. *Inspired Prophetic Warnings* focuses on both of these areas. After having written other books on doctrinal themes, I am not so naive as to expect that this work will completely escape the barbs of a few self-appointed critics. Certainly a book with the message which this one carries will receive scrutiny by those who might oppose its warning voice. I only ask that their evaluation be honest, and that it be made with care and with a desire for the ultimate well-being of this great land.

Be there criticism or not, this message must go forth. The Spirit has prompted and instructed, and has not allowed me to turn aside. I am like Martin Luther: "Here I stand. I can do no other."

Concern Because of Wickedness and Indifference

While I love this country and work for its preservation, I cannot help but feel deep concern for its future. That concern is evident throughout much of this book. I fear we are losing the liberties we presently enjoy because of the wickedness which is engulfing our nation and because of governmental actions and decisions which are robbing us of our freedoms.

I find my feelings reflected in the attitudes of Moroni, a Book of Mormon patriot who rallied his people under a "title of liberty," on which he had inscribed the words

In memory of our God,
our religion, and freedom,
and our peace,
our wives, and our children.[1]

He was a good man, possessed with the qualities I greatly admire:

> And Moroni was *a strong and a mighty man; he was a man of a perfect understanding;* yea, a man that *did not delight in bloodshed;* a man *whose soul did joy in the liberty and the freedom of his country,* and his brethren from bondage and slavery;
>
> Yea, a man *whose heart did swell with thanksgiving to his God,* for the many privileges and blessings which he bestowed upon his people; a man who *did labor exceedingly for the welfare and safety of his people.*

1. Al. 46:12-14.

> Yea, and he was a man who was *firm in the faith of Christ,* and he had sworn with an oath to defend his people, his rights, and his country, and his religion, even to the loss of his blood.[1]

Yet, as Moroni fought against the invading Lamanites he was concerned and angry because of the wickedness and indifference of his own Nephite people and government:

> And now, when Moroni saw that the city of Nephihah was lost he was exceeding sorrowful, and *began to doubt, because of the wickedness of the people, whether they should not fall into the hands of their brethren.*
>
> Now this was the case with all his chief captains. *They doubted and marveled also because of the wickedness of the people,* and this because of the success of the Lamanites over them.
>
> And it came to pass that *Moroni was angry with the government, because of their indifference concerning the freedom of their country.*[2]

It is that same concern which motivates the writing of this book.

Constructive Criticism is Chastening with Love

A parent does not act in the best interests of his children by allowing their misdeeds to go uncorrected. A teacher does not give his best to his students unless he shows them their weaknesses and challenges them to improve. A citizen does not act in the best interests of his community unless he speaks out for correction of dangerous conditions. In each case, such individuals are motivated by love and concern for the well-being of others as they point out their weaknesses. God also chastens those He loves. Concerning the Nephites, for instance, Samuel the Lamanite observed,

> . . . they have been a chosen people of the Lord; yea, the people of Nephi hath he loved, and also hath he chastened them; yea, *in the days of their iniquities hath he chastened them because he loveth them.*[3]

When danger approaches, we call out with a warning voice to those we love. It is in that spirit that this book is written—it is an effort to warn and correct, so that we may be spared the terrible events which lie ahead if America continues on her present course. It is my sincere hope and prayer that its message will be heeded.

---

1. Al. 48:11-13.
2. Al. 59:11-13.
3. Hel. 15:3. See also D&C 95:1. 101:4-5

Though there may be some who resent the warning message, we are commanded by God to deliver it, and

> . . . notwithstanding their hardness, let us labor diligently; for *if we should cease to labor, we should be brought under condemnation; for we have a labor to perform whilst in this tabernacle of clay, that we may conquer the enemy of all righteousness, and rest our souls in the kingdom of God.*[1]

Duane S. Crowther

1. Moroni 9:6.

I

The Prophetic Warnings

I

First Warning: Those Who Do Not Believe In God Will Be Destroyed

The Conditional Nature of Book of Mormon Warnings

Many important warnings to last days inhabitants of America are recorded in the Book of Mormon. These warnings are usually given in conditional prophecies concerning future events. The Lord's promises made concerning this choice land are often based on alternatives—they contain an all-important *IF*. Implicit in each warning is a specific principle. The prophetic warnings describe what will happen *if* the people of America obey the principle in righteousness, they also warn what will transpire *if* the people choose to disobey that principle and work iniquity.

Each chapter in this section carefully considers one or more of these conditional warnings. The combined message is a matter of grave concern for all America, for it is a presentation of principles which must be obeyed if this nation is to survive.

While the chapters allude to many events which are prophesied to take place in the future, the chapters in this section are devoted to gaining an understanding of the principles upon which survival depends. Later chapters will consider the prophesied events to which the prophetic warnings allude.

Jacob's Warning: Unbelievers Will Be Destroyed by Fire, Tempest, Earthquakes, Bloodsheds, Pestilence, and Famine (2 Ne. 6:14-18)

The prophet Jacob, while preaching to the Nephites more than five centuries before the birth of Christ, made a sweeping prophecy concerning a period of conflict which is to occur in a time still future. Taking as his theme a passage from the prophet Isaiah,[1] Jacob tells how the people of Israel are to be gathered to the lands of their inheritance in the last days. He describes how God will pour out His judgments during the time of their gathering. He then sets forth the principle

1. Is. 49:22-23 (quoted by Jacob in 2 Ne. 6:6-7), and Is. 49:24-52:2 (quoted by Jacob in 2 Ne. 6:16-8:25). For interpretive comment on these chapters see the author's book, *Prophets and Prophecies of the Old Testament* (Bountiful, Utah: Horizon Publishers, 1973, 644 pp.) pp.351352, 356-357, 342.

which will determine who escapes the judgments which will be sent from God in that day. That principle, he says, is belief in the Messiah, the Holy One of Israel:

> And behold, according to the words of the prophet, the Messiah will set himself again the second time to recover them [Zion and the covenant people of the Lord]; wherefore, he will manifest himself unto them in power and great glory, unto *the destruction of their enemies,* when that day cometh when they shall believe in him; and *none will he destroy that believe in him.*
>
> *And they that believe not in him shall be destroyed,* both by *fire,* and by *tempest,* and by *earthquakes,* and by *bloodsheds,* and by *pestilence,* and by *famine.* And they shall know that the Lord is God, the Holy One of Israel.
>
> For shall the prey be taken from the mighty, or the lawful captive delivered?
>
> But thus saith the Lord: Even the captives of the mighty shall be taken away, and the prey of the terrible shall be delivered; for *the Mighty God shall deliver his covenant people.* For thus saith the Lord: *I will contend with them that contendeth with thee*
>
> *And I will feed them that oppress thee, with their own flesh; and they shall be drunken with their own blood* as with sweet wine; and all flesh shall know that I the Lord am thy Savior and thy Redeemer, the Mighty One of Jacob.[1]

Note that his prophecy is conditional: men will be able to escape destruction *if* they believe in God, but they will be destroyed by a series of judgments *if* they fail to meet the condition of belief in God.

Note also that the prophecy has a specific time of fulfillment: the unbelievers will be destroyed in the period when God moves to fulfill His covenants with Israel[2] by gathering and recovering her.[3] This event is clearly placed in the future in a chronological order of last days events set forth by the Savior Himself, as will be seen later in this book.[4]

Observe, too, that all people will not suffer the same fate: some will believe and escape while others who are unbelievers will be struck down. Thus the prophecy divides the people of that era into two distinct groups, believers and non-believers—a pattern established by many Book of Mormon prophecies.

---

1. 2 Ne. 6:14-18.
2. 2 Ne. 6:12.
3. 2 Ne. 6:11.
4. See p. 225.

The Savior's Warning: Unbelieving Gentiles Will Be Trodden Down by the House of Israel When They Sin Against the Gospel (3 Ne. 16:4-15)

Another conditional prophecy, which specifically concerns America in the last days, also places belief in God as the criterion for escape from future disaster. This prophecy is found in the words of Jesus Christ recorded in Third Nephi, chapter 16. The time of prophetic fulfillment is the same: the future era when the Savior will fulfill his covenant with Israel by gathering them from the four quarters of the earth.[1] This prophecy is directed specifically to the Gentiles—the Caucasian people of America.[2]

The preparatory verses (3 Ne. 16:4-13) paint the scenario. As in Jacob's prophecy, the criterion of belief in God divides the last days' people of America into two groups. One portion of the Gentiles believes, and receives the gospel:

> And *blessed are the Gentiles, because of their belief in me,* in and of the Holy Ghost, which witnesses unto them of me and of the Father.
>
> Behold, *because of their belief in me,* saith the Father, and because of the unbelief of you, O house of Israel, in the latter day shall the truth come unto the Gentiles, that the fulness of these things shall be made known unto them.[3]

The other portion of America's Gentiles does not believe, and "wo," says God, "*unto the unbelieving of the Gentiles.*"[4] This group will sin against the gospel and turn to gross wickedness. With the background clearly established by these preliminary verses, the Savior delivers His prophetic message. Like Jacob's, His warning is conditional—if the Gentiles of the last days reject the fulness of the gospel, they will lose their opportunity to hear it:

> . . . *At that day when the Gentiles shall sin against my gospel, and shall be lifted up in the pride of their hearts above all nations, and above all the people of the whole earth, and shall be filled with all manner of lyings, and of deceits, and of mischiefs, and all manner of hypocrisy, and*

1. 3 Ne. 16:5.
2. Note that these Gentiles are the descendants (the fulness) of the American Gentiles who received the Book of Mormon (3 Ne. 16:4; compare with 1 Ne. 13:14-39, which clearly identifies the Gentiles of America as those who receive the Book of Mormon in the last days).
3. 3 Ne 16:6-7.
4. 3 Ne. 16:8.

> *murders, and priestcrafts, and whoredoms, and of secret abominations;* and *if* they shall do all those things, and shall reject the fulness of my gospel, behold, saith the Father, *I will bring the fulness of my gospel from among them.*[1]

The conditional nature of the prediction continues to be seen throughout the warning portion of prophecy: *if* these wicked American Gentiles will repent they will be numbered among Israel and won't be trodden down,[2] but the Lord warns what will happen if they don't repent:

> But if they will not turn unto me, and hearken unto my voice, *I will suffer them, yea, I will suffer my people, O house of Israel, that they shall go through among them, and shall tread them down,* and they shall be as salt that hath lost its savor, which is thenceforth good for nothing but *to be cast out, and to be trodden under foot of my people,* O house of Israel.
>
> Verily, verily, I say unto you, thus hath the Father commanded me that I should give unto this people this land for their inheritance [3]

Belief in God is again stated as the principle which will determine the difference between safety and destruction in this future event.

The Savior's Warning: Unbelieving Gentiles Will Be Cut Off By a Remnant of Jacob (3 Ne. 21:1-14)

The Lord presents a similar prophecy in a different context, but again sets belief in God as the criterion which will allow some to escape destruction in America in the last days. Christ is speaking of the same time and place as in His former prophetic warning: He speaks of an event in connection with the future gathering of Israel[4] which takes place *"in this land"* where the Gentiles are "*set up as a free people* by the power of the Father."[5] He describes, once again, two groups who are differentiated by the belief in God. He tells of the righteous portion of the Gentiles, who are willing to believe in God. that the Father

---

1. 3 Ne. 16:10 Note that this verse intimates a separating of the righteous from the wicked as the fulness of the gospel is taken from the unbelieving Gentiles. Whether this is a gathering out of the righteous, or a cessation of missionary work among the wicked, or both, is not indicated.
2. 3 Ne. 16:13-14.
3. 3 Ne. 16:15-16. Note that verse 16 clearly places this prophecy in the Americas. See also D&C 103:5-11 .
4. 3 Ne. 21:1.
5. 3 Ne. 21:4.

> . . . may show forth his power unto the Gentiles, for this cause that *the Gentiles, if they will not harden their hearts, that they may repent and come unto me* and be baptized in my name and know of the true points of my doctrine, that they may be numbered among my people, O house of Israel;[1]

These believing Gentiles are contrasted with the unbelieving who will reap destruction as the Savior gives His prophetic warning. According to the Master, the unbelieving Gentiles will be destroyed by a remnant of Jacob which will cut them off:

> Therefore it shall come to pass that *whosoever will not believe in my words, who am Jesus Christ,* which the Father shall cause him to bring forth unto the Gentiles, and shall give unto him power that he shall bring them forth unto the Gentiles, (it shall be done even as Moses said) *they shall be cut off from among my people who are of the covenant.*
>
> *And my people who are a remnant of Jacob shall be among the Gentiles, yea, in the midst of them as a lion among the beasts of the forest, as a young lion among the flocks of sheep, who, if he go through both treadeth down and teareth in pieces, and none can deliver.*
>
> Their hand shall be lifted up upon their adversaries, and all *their enemies shall be cut off.*
>
> Yea, wo be unto the Gentiles except they repent; . . .[2]

Mormon's Warning: The Sword of Vengeance for the Blood of the Saints Hangs Over the Unbelieving (Morm. 8:27-9:6)

The prophet Mormon also presents belief in God as the principle which will separate those who will suffer God's vengeance in the last days from those who will be spared. He describes the day when *"the blood of the saints shall cry unto the Lord, because of secret combinations,"*[3] when *"the power of God shall be denied,"*[4] and there will be *wars* and *earthquakes,*[5] and "*persecutions, and all manner of iniquities,*"[6] and "*secret abominations to get gain.*"[7]

1. 3 Ne. 21:6.
2. 3 Ne. 21:11-14 His prophecy continues in detail, describing the great destruction which will be brought upon the Gentiles. The remainder of this prophecy is considered later in the book.
3. Morm. 8:27.
4. Morm. 8:28
5. Morm. 8:30.
6. Morm. 8:36.
7. Morm. 8:40.

Then he warns:

> Behold, *the sword of vengeance hangeth over you;* and the time soon cometh that *he avengeth the blood of the saints* upon you, for he will not suffer their cries any longer.1

Speaking "concerning those who do not believe in Christ,"[2] he warns.

> Behold, *will ye believe* in the day of your visitation—behold, when the Lord shall come, yea, even that great day when the *earth shall be rolled together as a scroll, and the elements shall melt with fervent heat,* yea, in that great day when *ye shall be brought to stand before the Lamb of God*—then will ye say that there is no God?[3]

Then he shows that his prophecy is conditional—he contrasts the scene he has depicted with the state of those who will repent and believe in God:

> *O then ye unbelieving, turn ye unto the Lord;* cry mightily unto the Father in the name of Jesus, that *perhaps ye may be found spotless, pure, fair, and white,* having been cleansed by the blood of the Lamb, at that great and last day.[4]

Nephi's Warning: God Will Cause a Great Division Among the People and Will Destroy the Wicked (2 Ne. 30:1-10)

Yet other Book of Mormon passages present belief in God as the criterion which will distinguish between those who are to be spared and those who are to be destroyed in a last days period of destruction connected with the gathering of Israel. Nephi spoke of the Gentiles in the last days, telling how some of them through belief in God might be among the covenant people:

> For behold, I say unto you that *as many of the Gentiles as will repent are the covenant people of the Lord; and as many of the Jews as will not repent shall be cast off; for the Lord covenanteth with none save it be with them that repent and believe in his Son,* who is the Holy One of Israel.[5]

1. Morm. 8:41.
2. Morm. 9:1.
3. Morm. 9:2.
4. Morm. 9:6.
5. 2 Ne. 30:2.

Then, after talking of the gathering of Israel[1] when God will cause a great division among the people and will destroy those who are not His people, he said:

> For the time speedily cometh that *the Lord God shall cause a great division among the people, and the wicked will he destroy;* and he will spare his people, yea, even if it so be that he must destroy the wicked by fire.

Moroni's Warning: Those Who Deny the Word of the Lord Shall Be Accursed and Destroyed By Fire (Eth. 4:6-18)

Moroni, writing to the Gentiles in the last days, cited the Lord's warning to unbelievers among both the Gentiles and among Israel in the last days. As he did so, he told of the portion of the revelation given to the brother of Jared which has not yet been given to the Church in the last days. He explained that it, and other revelation, is to be restored to the Saints. Some of the Gentiles will believe it, while others will deny the Lord's word and will be destroyed:

> . . . I have written upon these plates the very things which the brother of Jared saw; and there never were greater things made manifest than those which were made manifest unto the brother of Jared. . . .
>
> . . . *They shall not go forth unto the Gentiles until the day that they shall repent of their iniquity, and become clean before the Lord.*
>
> And in that day that they shall exercise faith in me, saith the Lord, even as the brother of Jared did, that they may become sanctified in me *then will I manifest unto them the things which the brother of Jared saw, even to the unfolding unto them all my revelations*, saith Jesus Christ, the Son of God, the Father of the heavens and of the earth, and all things that in them are.
>
> *And he that will contend against the word of the Lord, let him be accursed; and he that shall deny these things, let him be accursed; for unto them will I show no greater things,* saith Jesus Christ; for I am he who speaketh.
>
> *And at my command the heavens are opened and are shut; and at my word the earth shall shake; and at my command the inhabitants thereof shall pass away, even so as by fire.*[3]

---

1. 2 Ne. 30:3-8.
2. 2 Ne. 30:10.
3. Eth. 4:4, 6-9. Then there followed this beautiful explanation of belief:

   And he that believeth not my words believeth not my disciples; and if it so be that I do not speak, judge ye; for ye shall know that it is I that speaketh, at the last day.

   But he that believeth these things which I have spoken, him will I visit with the manifestations of my Spirit, and he shall know and bear

After promising rich blessings to those who would believe during the future period (when the gathering process will be the sign God has remembered His covenant with Israel and has commenced His work), Moroni repeated the Lord's prophetic warning that believers would be saved while unbelievers would be damned:

> *Behold, when ye shall rend that veil of unbelief which doth cause you to remain in your awful state of wickedness, and hardness of heart, and blindness of mind,* then shall the great and marvelous things which have been hid up from the foundation of the world from you—yea, when ye shall call upon the Father in my name, with a broken heart and a contrite spirit, *then shall ye know that the Father hath remembered the covenant which he made unto your fathers, O house of Israel.*
>
> *And then shall my revelations which I have caused to be written by my servant John be unfolded in the eyes of all the people. Remember, when ye see these things, ye shall know that the time is at hand that they shall be made manifest in very deed.*
>
> Therefore, when ye shall receive this record ye may know that the work of the Father has commenced upon all the face of the land.
>
> Therefore, repent all ye ends of the earth, and *come unto me, and believe in my gospel, and be baptized in my name; for he that believeth and is baptized shall be saved; but he that believeth not shall be damned;* and signs shall follow them that believe in my name.

Summary

1. The Book of Mormon contains important warnings to the last days' inhabitants of the Americas. These warnings are usually found in conditional prophecies concerning last days events.

---

1. Eth. 4:15–18. Note that the revelation written by John is the final book of the New Testament. "The Revelation of St. John the Divine." This verse is telling when the last day's events it prophecies will find fulfillment.

> *record.* For because of my Spirit he shall know that these things are true; for it persuadeth men to do good.
>
> *And whatsoever thing persuadeth men to do good is of me*; for good cometh of none save it be of me. I am the same that leadeth men to all good; *he that will not believe my words will not believe me—that I am*; and he that will not believe me will not believe the Father who sent me. For behold, I am the Father, I am the light, and the life, and the truth of the world.
>
> *Come unto me, O ye Gentiles, and I will show unto you the greater things, the knowledge which is hid up because of unbelief* (Eth. 4:10-13)

2. Many of the conditional warnings state a specific gospel principle. They say what blessings will be reaped by those who obey the principle, then warn of destruction which will come upon those who are disobedient to that law.

3. The chapters in section I are devoted to gaining an understanding of the principles upon which survival depends. Later chapters will consider the prophesied events to which the prophetic warnings allude.

4. The people of America must believe in God or they will be destroyed in a future period of God-sent judgments. This is the first of the principles for survival cited and the central theme of this chapter.

5. Six key prophetic warnings are cited to demonstrate this principle. They are prophecies made by:

A. Jacob (2 Ne. 6:14-18)
B. the Savior (3 Ne. 16:4-15)
C. the Savior (3 Ne. 21:1-14)
D. Mormon (Morm. 8:27-9:6)
E. Nephi (2 Ne. 30:1-10)
F. Moroni (Eth. 4:6-18)

6. A major theme of the prophecies is that the people of the Americas will be divided into two factions, one righteous and the other wicked. They will be separated; the righteous will be spared while the wicked are destroyed.

7. The prophecies generally refer to a specific time of fulfillment: a time of future conflict during which God will fulfill His covenant with Israel by gathering that people to the lands of their inheritance. Some of the prophecies, however, may have reference to the destruction of the wicked to take place at the time of Christ's coming in glory to begin His millennial reign.

8. The prophecies are usually directed to the "Gentiles," or Caucasian inhabitants who settled in the Americas following the coming of Columbus. According to the Book of Mormon, the gospel is restored to and through the Gentiles. It appears that Church members may be found among both the "believing" and "unbelieving" categories of the Gentiles in the last days.

9. The prophecies allude to unrighteous conditions which will exist in America as the time of conflict and destruction draws near

A. The Gentiles will sin against the gospel (3 Ne. 16:10)
B. The Gentiles will be lifted up in pride above all people of the whole earth (3 Ne. 16:10)
C. The Gentiles will be filled with lyings, deceits, mischiefs, hypocrisy, murder, priestcrafts, whoredoms, and secret abominations (3 Ne. 16:10)
D. The blood of the Saints will cry unto the Lord because of secret combinations (Morm. 8:27)
E. The power of God shall be denied (Morm. 8:28)
F. There will be persecutions (Morm. 8:36)
G. There will be secret abominations to get gain (Morm. 8:40)
H. The people will be unbelieving (Morm. 9:6)
I. Some will contend against the word of the Lord (Eth. 4:8)
J. Some will deny the validity of newly-revealed revelations (Eth. 4:7-8)
K. People will be in an awful state of wickedness (Eth. 4:15)

The degree in which these conditions exist at present may be some indication as to how close this future period of conflict and destruction is in time.

10. The warnings allude to specific events which will transpire as the prophecies are fulfilled:

A. God will begin to recover and gather Israel (2 Ne. 6:12-14; 3 Ne. 16:5; 21:1)
B. Those who don't believe in God will be destroyed by fire, tempest earthquakes, bloodsheds, pestilence, and famine (2 Ne. 6:15)
C. People will contend with Israel and oppress her (2 Ne. 6:17-18)
D. Israel (or some of Israel) will be captive to a mighty enemy but will be delivered from it (2 Ne. 6:16-18)
E. God will deliver His covenant people (2 Ne. 6:17)
F. Believers will be spared from destruction (2 Ne. 6:14-15)
G. Enemies of Israel will fight among themselves (2 Ne. 6:18)

H. Some Gentiles will receive the gospel (3 Ne. 16:6-7; 21:6)
I. The gospel will be taken away from the wicked Gentiles (3 Ne. 16:10, 21:11)
J. Members of the House of Israel (the remnant of Jacob) will tear and tread down the Gentiles (3 Ne. 16:15; 21:12-13)
K. There will be wars and earthquakes (Morm. 8:30)
L. God will avenge the blood of the Saints upon the Gentiles (Morm. 8:41)
M. God shall cause a great division among the people (2 Ne. 30:10)
N. God will destroy the wicked by fire (2 Ne. 30:10; Eth. 4:9)
O. Things shown to the Brother of Jared, plus other revelations, will be manifested to righteous Gentiles (Eth. 4:7)
P. Men will contend against these new revelations and deny them (Eth. 4:8)
Q. The revelations given to John [the Revelator] will be unfolded (Eth. 4:16)
R. The Lord will come. The elements will melt with fervent heat (Morm. 9:2)

II

Second Warning: Those Who Will Not Serve God Will Be Destroyed

Failure to serve God is also cited as a cause for past and future destruction of the inhabitants of the promised land in Book of Mormon warnings. It stands as the second of the principles which must be obeyed if the peoples of the Americas are to escape God's judgments.

Moroni's Warning: Nations Not Serving God Will Be Swept Off When the Fulness of God's Wrath Comes Upon Them (Eth. 2:7-12)

Moroni, while referring to "the land of promise, which was choice above all other lands, which the Lord God had preserved for a righteous people,"[1] told of God's everlasting decree and promise to the brother of Jared:

> And *he had sworn* in his wrath unto the brother of Jared, that *whoso should possess this land of promise, from that time henceforth and forever, should serve him, the true and only God, or they should be swept off when the fulness of his wrath should come upon them.*
>
> And now, we can behold the decrees of God concerning this land, that it is a land of promise; and *whatsoever nation shall possess it shall serve God, or they shall be swept off when the fulness of his wrath shall come upon them.* And the fulness of his wrath cometh upon them when they are ripened in iniquity.
>
> For behold, this is a land which is choice above all other lands; wherefore *he that doth possess it shall serve God or shall be swept off; for it is the everlasting decree of God.* And it is not until the fulness of iniquity among the children of the land, that they are swept off.[2]

He then directed his writing to the American Gentiles of the last days, whom he knew would eventually read his words in the Book of Mormon. He knew that iniquity would come among them, and warned that they must repent and not allow their wickedness to reach a "fulness:"

---

1. Eth. 2:7.
2. Eth. 2:8-10.

> And this cometh unto you, O ye Gentiles, *that ye may know the decrees of God—that ye may repent, and not continue in your iniquities until the fulness come,* that ye may not bring down the fulness of the wrath of God upon you as the inhabitants of the land have hitherto done.
>
> Behold, *this is a choice land, and whatsoever nation shall possess it shall be free from bondage, and from captivity, and from all other nations under heaven, if they will but serve the God of the land, who is Jesus Christ,* who hath been manifested by the things which we have written [1]

Lehi's Warning: If Iniquity Abounds, the Land Will Be Cursed (2 Ne. 1:5-7)

Lehi, in his prophecy concerning "the land of promise, a land which is choice above all other lands,"[2] saw that *if* the people brought here by God would serve Him, then this would be a land of liberty unto them. But if they turned to wickedness they might be brought into captivity and the land would be cursed for their sakes

> Wherefore, I, Lehi, prophesy according to the workings of the Spirit which is in me, that *there shall none come into this land save they shall be brought by the hand of the Lord.*
>
> Wherefore, this land is consecrated unto him whom he shall bring. And *if it so be that they shall serve him* according to the commandments which he hath given, it shall be a land of liberty unto them; wherefore, they shall never be brought down into captivity; *if so, it shall be because of iniquity; for if iniquity shall abound cursed shall be the land for their sakes,* but unto the righteous it shall be blessed forever.[3]

Thus Lehi, like Moroni, foresaw that serving God would be a criterion which would determine whether the people of this land would enjoy liberty and divine blessings or would be cursed and destroyed.

King Limhi's Warning: If the People Sow Filthiness They Shall Reap Immediate Destruction (Mos. 7:29-33)

Past situations in the Book of Mormon indicate the importance of serving God as being the key to retaining liberty and escaping from divine judgments. King Limhi (leader of the people of Lehi-Nephi

---

1. Ether 2:11-12.
2. 2 Ne. 1:5.
3. 2 Ne. 1:6-7. Note that Lehi, in his prophecy, also follows the procedure of dividing the people into two groups: those iniquitous ones for whom the land will remain blessed forever. This is the pattern of prophecies in the preceding section.

who were in bondage to the Lamanites) assembled his people and taught them that serving God would be the only way they could escape from captivity. After telling how their wickedness led to their being conquered, he warned that[1]

> . . . the Lord hath said: *I will not succor my people in the day of their transgression, but I will hedge up their ways that they prosper not;* and their doings shall be as a stumbling block before them.
>
> And again, he saith: *If my people shall sow filthiness they shall reap the chaff* thereof in the whirlwind; and *the effect thereof is poison.*
>
> And again he saith: *If my people shall sow filthiness they shall reap the east wind, which bringeth immediate destruction.*
>
> And now, behold, the promise of the Lord is fulfilled, and ye are smitten and afflicted.
>
> But if ye will *turn to the Lord* with full purpose of heart, and *put your trust in him,* and *serve him with all diligence of mind,* if ye do this, he will, according to his own will and pleasure, deliver you out of bondage.[2]

Serving God the Key to Escaping Divine Retribution: Examples from Book of Mormon History

A Famine Sent to Stir Up Warring People in Remembrance of Their God

An important example of how serving God is the key to enjoying blessings from God and escaping divine retribution occurred in the period shortly before the birth of Christ. During the days of the Prophet Nephi,[3] the people had become so wicked that God sent His prophet to them with the message that "*Except ye repent ye shall be smitten, even unto destruction.*"[4]

---

1. Concerning the cause of their downfall, he said:

   > . . . Great are the reasons which we have to mourn; for behold how many of our brethren have been slain, and their blood has been spilt in vain, and all because of iniquity.
   >
   > For if this people had not fallen into transgression the Lord would not have suffered that this great evil should come upon them. But behold, they would not hearken unto his words; but there arose contentions among them, even so much that they did shed blood among themselves.
   >
   > And a prophet of the Lord have they slain; yea, a chosen man of God, who told them of their wickedness and abominations, and prophesied of many things which are to come, yea, even the coming of Christ. (Mos. 7:24-26)

2. Mos. 7:29-33.
3. The Son of Helaman II. See Hel. 3:37.
4. Hel. 10:1.

Wars were raging throughout the land because of the inroads made by the Gadianton robbers. Rather than allow all his people to be destroyed, Nephi pled with the Lord to send a famine to stir them up in remembrance of their God. Drought and famine came, and *"they did perish by thousands in the more wicked parts of the land."*[1] Then Nephi beseeched the Lord that the famine might end and that the people might again be tested whether they would serve God:

> And now, O Lord, wilt thou turn away thine anger, and *try again if they will serve thee?* And if so, O Lord, thou canst bless them according to thy words which thou hast said.[2]

After three years of drought-caused famine, the rains fell once again. The people now were sufficiently ready to serve God. Because of their repentant attitude, the Church spread throughout the land and they lived in peace.[3]

War and Siege Humble Wicked Nephites Until They Serve God

Another prophet named Nephi[4] saw his people endure terrible war and bloodshed until they were willing to serve God with diligence. The people saw the new star which was the sign of Christ's birth,[5] yet so many of them were corrupted and led astray by the "secret society of Gadianton"[6] that they engaged in the war which brought the greatest slaughter among the people of Lehi since that prophet came to the promised land.[7] It was not until the Nephites had endured a harsh siege that God delivered them out of the hands of their enemies "and *they knew it was because of their repentance and their humility that they had been delivered from an everlasting destruction*."[8] What did they then do?

> . . . They did forsake all their sins, and their abominations, and their whoredoms, and *did serve God with all diligence day and night*.[9]

Again, service to God was linked with escape from destruction.

---

1. Hel. 11:6.
2. Hel. 11:16.
3. Hel. 11:17-21.
4. The son of the above Nephi and grandson of Helaman (II). See 3 Ne. 1:10.
5. 3 Ne. 1:19-21. This was the sign prophesied by Samuel the Lamanite. See Hel. 14:1-6.
6. 3 Ne. 3:9. See all of 3 Ne. 3 and 4
7. 3 Ne. 4:11 .
8. 3 Ne. 4:33.
9. 3 Ne. 5:3.

Moroni's Warning to Last Days' Unbelievers: Despisers of God's Works Shall Wonder and Perish (Morm. 9:26-28)

Moroni, in his address to the unbelievers who would read his words in the last days, warned that those who will rise up against the power of the Lord will perish. His admonition was that the Gentiles follow the course of wisdom by serving God:

> *. . . Who can stand against the works of the Lord ? Who can deny his sayings? Who will rise up against the almighty power of the Lord ? Who will despise the works of the Lord ? Who will despise the children of Christ? Behold, all ye who are despisers of the works of the Lord, for ye shall wonder and perish.*
>
> O then despise not, and wonder not, but hearken unto the words of the Lord, and ask the Father in the name of Jesus for what things soever ye shall stand in need. Doubt not, but be believing, and begin as in times of old, and come unto the Lord with all your heart, and work out your own salvation with fear and trembling before him.
>
> Be wise in the days of your probation; strip yourselves of all uncleanness; ask not, that ye may consume it on your lusts, but ask with a firmness unshaken, that ye will yield to no temptation, but that *ye will serve the true and living God.*[1]

Service to God thus stands as a second important criterion for America's survival in the perilous last days' scene. In warning after warning, inspired prophets have held this principle as a vital key to the receiving of divine blessings and the avoiding of Godsent judgments.

There can be no compromise nor mixed allegiance. As the Savior taught:

> *No man can serve two masters;* for either he will hate the one and love the other, or else he will hold to the one and despise the other. *Ye cannot serve God and Mammon.*[2]

Summary

1. Prophetic warnings concerning the Americas as a land of promise show service to God as a necessary criterion for escaping

---

1. Morm. 9:26-28.
2. 3 Ne. 13:24. Nor is there room for discouragement among God's people. The Savior, while among the Nephites, quoted them His former revelation to Malachi in which he observed their diminished faithfulness: "Ye have said: It is vain to serve God, and what doth it profit that we have kept his ordinances and that we have walked mournfully before the Lord of Hosts?" (3 Ne. 24:14).

God's judgments. If the people serve God, they will be blessed and protected. If they do not serve God, His judgments will come upon them

2. Four prophetic warnings on this theme are cited in this chapter:

A. Moroni (Eth. 2:8-12)
B. Lehi(2Ne.1:5-7)
C. King Limhi (Mos. 7:29-33)
D. Moroni (Morm. 9:26-28)

3. With the warnings are promises of blessings if the people of the land will truly serve God:

A. Whatever nation possesses the "choice land" of America shall be free from bondage and captivity, and from all other nations if they will serve Jesus Christ (Eth. 2:12).
B. The people brought to this "consecrated" land will enjoy liberty and shall never be brought into captivity if they will serve the Lord by keeping His commandments (2 Ne. 1:7).
C. If people will turn to the Lord, trust Him, and serve Him with all diligence, He will deliver them out of bondage (Mos. 7:33).

4. God's actions when wickedness prevails are also described in the prophetic warnings:

A. The fulness of the wrath of God comes upon those who continue in iniquities until the fulness comes (Eth. 2:11).
B. If iniquity abounds, the people may go into captivity and the land will be cursed because of the wicked people (2 Ne. 1:7).
C. The Lord won't succor His people if they transgress. He will hedge up their ways so they won't prosper and their doings will be their stumbling blocks (Mos. 7:29).
D. Those who rise up against the Lord's power and despise His works will wonder and perish (Morm. 9:26).

5. According to the prophet Lehi, "there shall none come into this land save they be brought by the hand of the Lord"(2 Ne. 1:6). This

does not necessarily mean that no enemies can ever come here, but rather that if they were to come, they would be brought by God (as often happened in both Biblical and Book of Mormon accounts when the people became wicked).

6. People have been humbled so that they would serve God through bondage, famines, and wars. The examples of the Lehi-Nephi colony captivity to the Lamanites (Mos. 7), the famine sought by the prophet Nephi (Hel. 11), and the Nephite war against the Gadianton robbers (3 Ne. 3-5) were cited.

7. Moroni's address to unbelievers in the last days indicates another aspect of last days conditions: men will stand against the work of God, deny His sayings, and despise both His works and His children [followers] (Morm. 9:26).

III

Third Warning: If the People Turn to Wickedness, They and the Land Will Be Cursed

Alma's Warning: The Land is Cursed Unto Destruction Unto Every People Which Do Wickedly (Al. 45:16)

The Lord has set high standards for the inhabitants of America—the land "choice above all other lands." He expects them to believe in Him, He expects them to serve Him, and He expects them to refrain from wicked deeds. Though many are aware of the promises of blessings He has made if the people are righteous, relatively few seem to know of the curses He has pronounced on the land if the inhabitants choose wickedness.

Alma, while giving a father's blessing to his sons, taught them of this conditional curse:

> . . . Thus saith the Lord God—*Cursed shall be the land, yea, this land, unto every nation, kindred, tongue, and people, unto destruction, which do wickedly, when they are fully ripe;* and as I have said so shall it be; for this is the cursing and the blessing of God upon the land, for the Lord cannot look upon sin with the least degree of allowance

He taught his son that

> . . . *There is a curse upon all this land, that destruction shall come upon all those workers of darkness,* according to the power of God, when they are fully ripe; therefore I desire that this people might not be destroyed.[2]

Lehi's Warning: If Iniquity Abounds, Cursed Shall be the Land (2 Ne. 1:7)

Lehi, it will be remembered, taught the same principle, saying that "*if iniquity shall abound, cursed shall be the land* for their sakes. . . ."[3] He taught his sons that God had said that

> . . . Inasmuch as ye shall keep my commandments ye shall prosper in the land; but *inasmuch as ye will not keep my commandments ye shall be cut off from my presence*.

---

1. Al. 45:16. See also D&C 1:31.
2. Al. 37:28. See also verse 31.
3. 2 Ne. 1:7.

And now that my soul might have joy in you, and that my heart might leave this world with gladness because of you, that I might not be brought down with grief and sorrow to the grave, *arise from the dust, my sons, and be men, and be determined in one mind and in one heart, united in all things, that ye may not come down into captivity;*

That ye may not be cursed with a sore cursing; and also, that ye may not incur the displeasure of a just God upon you, unto the destruction, yea, the eternal destruction of both soul and body.[1]

He also described the nature and extent of such a curse:

My heart hath been weighed down with sorrow from time to time, for I have feared, lest for the hardness of your hearts the Lord your God should come out in the fulness of his wrath upon you, that ye be cut off and destroyed forever;

Or, that a cursing should come upon you for the space of many generations; and ye are visited by sword, and by famine, and are hated, and are led according to the will and captivity of the devil.[2]

Instances of God's Curse Upon the Land: Book of Mormon Examples

The Book of Mormon gives striking examples of what takes place when the Lord's curse becomes operative. Five-and-a-half centuries after Lehi's warning, the people of Nephi witnessed the effects of the Lord's curse:

And they did prosper exceedingly, and they became exceedingly rich; yea, and they did multiply and were strong in the land.

And thus we see how merciful and just are all the dealings of the Lord, to the fulfilling of all his words unto the children of men; yea, we can behold that his words are verified, even at this time, which he spake unto Lehi, saying:

Blessed art thou and thy children; and they shall be blessed, inasmuch as they shall keep my commandments they shall prosper in the land. *But remember, inasmuch as they will not keep the commandments they shall be cut off from the presence of the Lord.*

And we see that *these promises have been verified to the people of Nephi;* for it has been their *quarrelings* and their *contentions,* yea, their *murderings,* and their *plunderings,* their *idolatry,* their *whoredoms,* and their *abominations,* which were among themselves, *which brought upon them their wars and their destructions.*

And *those who were faithful in keeping the commandments of the Lord were delivered* at all times, whilst *thousands of their wicked brethren have been consigned to bondage, or to perish by the sword, or to dwindle in unbelief, and mingle with the Lamanites.*[3]

1. 2 Ne 1:20-22.
2. 2Ne. 1:17-18.
3. Al. 50:18-22.

A thousand years after Lehi's day, Mormon saw that God no longer would send His word to the wicked Nephites and, because of the hardness of their hearts, the land again was cursed:

> And I did endeavor to preach unto this people, but my mouth was shut, and I was forbidden that I should preach unto them; for behold *they had wilfully rebelled against their God;* and the beloved *disciples were taken away out of the land,* because of their iniquity.
>
> But I did remain among them, but I was forbidden to preach unto them, because of the hardness of their hearts;and *because of the hardness of their hearts the land was cursed for their sake.*
>
> And these Gadianton robbers, who were among the Lamanites, did infest the land, insomuch that the inhabitants thereof began to hide up their treasures in the earth; and *they became slippery, because the Lord had cursed the land, that they could not hold them, nor retain them again.*[1]

The curse continued until a quarter-of-a-million Nephite warriors, plus their women and children, were slain in a single day. The entire nation was destroyed.[2]

Jacob's Warning: The People Must Keep the Lord's Commandments, or Cursed Be the Land (Jac. 1:29; 3:3)

The prophet Jacob, on several occasions, warned of the Lord's curse. When his people became unchaste, he proclaimed that "*this people shall keep my commandments, saith the Lord of Hosts, or cursed be the land for their sakes.*"[3] His warning cry was "Wo, wo unto you that are not pure in heart, that are filthy this day before God; for *except ye repent the land is cursed for your sakes. . . .*"[4]

Nephi's Warning: The Lord Destroys the Wicked, and Curses the Land for Their Sakes (1 Ne. 17:36-38)

The words of Nephi summarize this principle or warning:

> Behold, the Lord hath created the earth that it should be inhabited; and he hath created his children that they should possess it.
>
> And he raiseth up a righteous nation, and *destroyeth the nations of the wicked.*
>
> And he leadeth away the righteous into precious lands, and *the wicked he destroyeth, and curseth the land unto them for their sakes.*[5]

1. Morm. 1:16-18.
2. See Morm. 6:10-15.
3. Jac. 2:29.
4. Jac. 3:3. He alluded to the Lord's cursing of the wicked in the last days. See Jac. 6:2-3.
5. 1 Ne. 17:36-38.

What more need be added? Just three brief observations from the scriptures. First, Alma the Younger's comment:

> Now I would that ye should see that *they brought upon themselves the curse; and even so doth every man that is cursed bring upon him self his own condemnation.*[1]

Second, the same prophet's observation concerning who might receive the greatest cursing:

> And now, how much *more cursed is he that knoweth the will of God and doeth it not,* than he that only believeth, or only hath cause to believe, and falleth into transgression?[2]

And finally, an observation by Mormon:

> But, behold, the judgments of God will overtake the wicked; and *it is by the wicked that the wicked are punished;* for it is the wicked that stir up the hearts of the children of men unto bloodshed.[3]

Summary

1. The third principle which must be obeyed, if America is to escape future destruction, is that wickedness must not become commonplace. The prophets have repeatedly warned that the promised land will be cursed if wickedness abounds and prevails.

2. Prophetic warnings on this theme are cited in this chapter from four prophets:

   A. Alma (Al. 45:16, 37:28)
   B. Lehi (2 Ne. 1:7, 17-18, 20-22)
   C. Jacob (Jac. 2:29, 3:3)
   D. Nephi (1 Ne. 17:36-38)

3. Book of Mormon examples indicate that the threatened cursing of the land comes in varying degrees. As people move toward national wickedness their economy is affected, and they can't retain their riches (Morm. 1:18; Hel. 13:30-36). If iniquity progresses until it is

---

1. Al. 3:19.
2. Al. 32:19.
3. Morm 4:5

fully "ripe," the people are visited with God's judgments by famine, sword, and pestilence.

4. Every man that is cursed by God brings upon himself his own condemnation

5. Those who know but do not obey the will of God are more cursed than those with lesser belief and knowledge.

IV

Fourth Warning: If The People Do Not Repent, They Will Be Destroyed

Book of Mormon prophecies repeatedly warn of a last days' period when there will be great wickedness among the people of America. At that day, according to the prophecies, the people must repent or they will be destroyed. If they do repent, however, they will be spared and blessed.

Alma's Warning: Unless Nations That Possess the Promised Land Repent, They Will Be Destroyed (Al. 37:22-25)

Repentance from wickedness has been required by the Lord from every nation that has possessed this land throughout its history, and that principle stands as a fundamental requirement to national survival. Alma explained this great truth to his son, Helaman, as he spoke of the previous destruction of the Jaredite nation and of the records of their downfall:

> . . . the Lord saw that his people began to work in darkness, yea, work secret murders and abominations; therefore the Lord said, *if they did not repent they should be destroyed* from off the face of the earth.
>
> And the Lord said: I will prepare unto my servant Gazelem, a stone, which shall shine forth in darkness unto light, that *I may discover unto my people who serve me, that I may discover unto them the works of their brethren, yea, their secret works, their works of darkness, and their wickedness and abominations*
>
> And now, my son, these interpreters were prepared that the word of God might be fulfilled, which he spake, saying:
>
> I will bring forth out of darkness unto light all their secret works and their abominations; and *except they repent I will destroy them from off the face of the earth;* and I will bring to light all their secrets and abominations, *unto every nation that shall hereafter possess the land.*[1]

1. Al. 37:22-25. Alma made this observation concerning the Jaredites: "And now, my son, we see that they did not repent; therefore they have been destroyed, and thus far the word of God has been fulfilled;"... (Al. 37:26).

Thus repentance, or the lack of it, becomes another criterion for the survival of America as the Book of Mormon prophecies foretell the future of this nation. As with the previous prophetic warnings, the prophecies are conditional.

Nephi's Warning: In the Day the Earth's Inhabitants are Fully Ripe in Iniquity, They Shall Perish (2 Ne. 28:16-17)

For instance, Nephi prophesied concerning the people of the last days, observing that they will all have "*gone astray save it be a few, who are the humble followers of Christ,*"[1] and that there will come a time when they will "*turn aside the just for a thing of naught*" and that the devil will "*stir them up to anger against that which is good.*"[2] In close chronological proximity to the fall of the great and abominable church[3] and a period of great wickedness and apathy in Zion,[4] he gives this warning concerning the necessity of repentance:

> Wo unto them that turn aside the just for a thing of naught and revile against that which is good, and say that is of no worth! For the day shall come that *the Lord God will speedily visit the inhabitants of the earth; and in that day that they are fully ripe in iniquity they shall perish.*
>
> But behold, *if the inhabitants of the earth shall repent of their wicked ness and abominations they shall not be destroyed,* saith the Lord of Hosts.[5]

His prophetic utterance contains the Lord's warning that the Gentiles of the last days will deny Him, but also holds the promise of God's love if the people will repent:

> Wo be unto the Gentiles, saith the Lord God of Hosts! For notwithstanding I shall lengthen out mine arm unto them from day to day, *they will deny me; nevertheless, I will be merciful unto them, saith the Lord God, if they will repent and come unto me;* for mine arm is lengthened out all the day long, saith the Lord God of Hosts.[6]

---

1. 2 Ne. 28:14.
2. 2 Ne. 28:16, 20. See 1 Ne. 14:7 and 2 Ne. 30:10.
3. 2 Ne. 28:18. See pp. 71-97.
4. 2 Ne. 28:21-31. See pp. 1_7-1.58
5. 2 Ne. 28:16-17.
6. 2 Ne. 28:32.

Nephi's Warning: Whoso Repenteth Not Must Perish (1 Ne. 14:5-6)

In earlier prophecy, Nephi had warned of the future dominion, power and wickedness of the great and abominable church.[1] He spoke of the Gentiles as two factions, the repentant and the wicked:

> And it came to pass that the angel spake unto me, Nephi, saying: Thou hast beheld that *if the Gentiles repent it shall be well with them;* and thou also knowest concerning the covenants of the Lord unto the house of Israel; and thou also hast heard that *whoso repenteth not must perish.*
>
> Therefore, *wo be unto the Gentiles if it so be that they harden their hearts against the Lamb of God.*[2]

The Savior's Warning: The Gentiles Shall Not Have Power Over The House of Israel (3 Ne. 16:12-14)

In the vivid prophecies concerning events yet future made by the resurrected Christ, repentance plays the determining role concerning the escape or fall of the Gentiles. In the approaching era of great wickedness,[3] as the Gentiles are about to suffer the wrath of the remnant of Jacob,[4] the great need for repentance among the Gentiles is described:

> . . . *I will show unto thee, O house of Israel, that the Gentiles shall not have power over you;* but I will remember my covenant unto you, O house of Israel, and ye shall come unto the knowledge of the fulness of my gospel.
>
> But *if the Gentiles will repent and return unto me,* saith the Father, *behold they shall be numbered among my people,* O house of Israel.
>
> *And I will not suffer my people, who are of the house of Israel, to go through among them, and tread them down,* saith the Father.[5]

The Savior's Warning: A Remnant of Jacob Will Tread Down and Tear the Unrepentant Gentiles (3 Ne. 20:14-16)

In the second of His three great prophecies describing this future event, the Lord portrays the necessity of repentance even more vivid-

1. 1 Ne. 14:9-17. Note the chronological relationship of verse 17: it is in the era that judgments are to be poured out upon this great church that the major period of the gathering of Israel begins (see 3 Ne. 20:22, 27-46; 21:1-29).
2. 1 Ne. 14:5-6. Note that the next verse alludes to some important but undefined future event which will clearly separate the people into these two groups, the repentant and unrepentant.
3. See 3 Ne.16:10.
4. See 3 Ne. 16:15, 20:16-17, 21:12-19.
5. 3 Ne. 16:12-14.

ly. While speaking unto the Book of Mormon descendants of the House of Israel He warned that

> . . . The Father hath commanded me that I should give unto you this land, for your inheritance.
>
> And I say unto you, that *if the Gentiles do not repent after the blessing which they shall receive,* after they have scattered my people
>
> *Then shall ye, who are a remnant of the house of Jacob, go forth among them; and ye shall be in the midst of them who shall be many;* and ye shall be among them as a lion among the beasts of the forest, and *as a young lion among the flocks of sheep, who, if he goeth through both treadeth down and teareth in pieces, and none can deliver. . . .*
>
> And it shall come to pass, saith the Father, that *the sword of my justice shall hang over them at that day; and except they repent it shall fall upon them,* saith the Father, yea, even upon all the nations of the Gentiles.[1]

The Savior then foretold that blessings to the Gentiles would make them "mighty above all," but warned that "when they shall have received the fulness of my gospel, then *if they shall harden their hearts against me I will return their iniquities upon their own heads,* saith the Father."[2]

The Savior's Warning: He Will Cut Off the Unrepentant and Execute Vengeance and Fury Upon Them (3 Ne. 21:20-22)

Again, in His third prophecy depicting this great series of future events, the Master emphasized the need for repentance among the Gentiles in the era when the remnant of Jacob will move against them. He warned that ". . . *wo be unto the Gentiles except they repent;* for it shall come to pass in that day, saith the Father, that *I will cut off thy horses out of the midst of thee, and I will destroy thy chariots; . . .*"[3] Yet repentance will provide the means of bringing some of the Gentiles to dwell among the Saints:

> For it shall come to pass, saith the Father, that at that day *whosoever will not repent and come unto my Beloved Son, them will I cut off from among my people, O house of Israel;*

---

1. 3 Ne. 20:14-16, 20. Note that in this passage, as in 1 Ne. 14:5-17, the need for repentance and the impending judgments pertain to "all the nations of the Gentiles." Though much of this chapter pertains specifically to the inhabitants of the Americas, the international scope of this warning should not be overlooked.
2. 3 Ne. 20:27-28.
3. 3 Ne. 21:14. See also verse 6.

> *And I will execute vengeance and fury upon them,* even as upon the heathen, such as they have not heard.
>
> But *if they will repent and hearken unto my words, and harden not their hearts, I will establish my church among them,* and they shall come in unto the covenant and be numbered among this the remnant of Jacob. unto whom I have given this land for their inheritance; . . .[1]

Mormon's Admonition to Last Days' Gentiles: Repent of Your Evil Doings (3 Ne. 30:2)

After receiving revealed insights concerning the Gentiles in the last days, the prophet Mormon responded in this manner to God's command that he admonish them to repent in his writings:

> *Turn, all ye Gentiles, from your wicked ways; and repent of your evil doings,* of your *lyings* and *deceivings,* and of your *whoredoms,* and of your *secret abominations,* and your *idolatries,* and of your *murders,* and your *priestcrafts,* and your *envyings,* and your *strifes,* and from all your *wickedness* and *abominations,* and come unto me, and be baptized in my name, that ye may receive a remission of your sins, and be filled with the Holy Ghost, that ye may be numbered with my people who are of the house of Israel.[2]

Repentance Necessary to Escape Destruction: Book of Mormon Examples

Examples of repentance being necessary to escape destruction constitute a major message of the Book of Mormon. The inhabitants of Jerusalem were warned that they must repent or suffer the destruction of their city.[3] Nephi's wicked brothers found that "the judgments of God were upon them, and that they must perish save they should

---

1. 3 Ne. 21:20-22. Note Nephi's prediction that "as many of the Gentiles as will repent are the covenant people of the Lord." (See 2 Ne. 30:1-2.) In Alma's day only the repentant were numbered among the people (Mos. 26:30-32. See Al. 6:3.).
2. 3 Ne. 30:2. The prophet Alma had previously warned of the danger of procrastinating repentance. He wrote:

   > . . . I beseech of you that ye do not procrastinate the day of your repentance until the end; . . .
   >
   > Ye cannot say, when ye are brought to that awful crisis, that I will repent, that I will return to my God....
   >
   > For behold, if ye have procrastinated the day of your repentance even until death, behold, ye have become subjected to the spirit of the devil, and he doth seal you his; . . . (Al. 34:33-35).
3. 1 Ne. 1:4.

repent of their iniquities"[1] when they bound Nephi during their ocean crossing. Jacob warned the Nephites that "except ye repent the land is cursed for your sakes," and prophesied that the Lamanites would scourge them "even unto destruction."[2] Abinadi warned the priests of the wicked King Noah that "except they repent in sackcloth and ashes, and cry mightily to the Lord their God" the Lord would deliver them into the hands of their enemies and would not hear their prayers nor deliver them from their afflictions.[3] Alma was sent by an angel to warn the people of the city of Ammonihah that "except they repent the Lord God will destroy them."[4]

Near the time of the birth of Christ, the missionaries, Nephi and Lehi, preached and prophesied to the people "what should come unto them if they did not repent of their sins."[5] Later Nephi returned to the land of Zarahemla and observed the great wickedness of the people even there at the center of the church. With the cry, "O repent ye, repent ye! Why will ye die?"[6] he warned that they would be utterly destroyed unless they repent:

> . . . *Wo shall come unto you except ye shall repent*. For if ye will not repent, behold, this great city, and also all those great cities which are round about, which are in the land of our possession, shall be taken away that ye shall have no place in them; for behold, *the Lord will not grant unto you strength, as he has hitherto done, to withstand against your enemies*.
>
> For behold, thus saith the Lord: *I will not show unto the wicked of my strength, to one more than the other, save it be unto those who repent of their sins, and hearken unto my words*. Now therefore, I would that ye should behold, my brethren, that it shall be better for the Lamanites than for you except ye shall repent.
>
> For behold, they are more righteous than you, for they have not sinned against that great knowledge which ye have received; therefore the Lord will be merciful unto them; yea, he will lengthen out their days and increase their seed, even when thou shalt be utterly destroyed except thou shalt repent.[7]

1. 1 Ne. 18:15
2. Jac. 3:3-4.
3. Mos 11:20-21, 25. He warned them, in even harsher terms, of famine, pestilence, hail, insects, and complete destruction. See Mos. 12:1-8
4. Al. 8:15-16. The reason for the warning is significant: "They do study at this time that they may destroy the liberty of thy people. (verse 17.) See also Al. 8:29.
5. Hel. 4:14. Because of his warning, the people repented and began to prosper.
6. He l. 7:17. See verses 19 - 21.
7. Hel. 7:22-24. See verses 25-29; 9:22, 10 11-12, 14; 15:17.

Samuel the Lamanite looked four hundred years into the future and warned that only repentance would save the Nephites from utter destruction;

> . . . the sword of justice hangeth over this people; and four hundred years pass not away save the sword of justice falleth upon this people.
>
> Yea, heavy destruction awaiteth this people, and it surely cometh unto this people, and *nothing can save this people save it be repentance and faith on the Lord Jesus Christ, . . .*[1]

When the time for the fulfillment of Samuel's prophecy drew near, Mormon recorded that "*notwithstanding the great destruction which hung over my people, they did not repent* of their evil doings; *therefore there was blood and carnage* spread throughout all the face of the land."[2]

These examples should suffice to indicate that God has required repentance of the inhabitants of the Americas throughout Book of Mormon history. When the people have abandoned their wickedness, they have been preserved and blessed. When they have not repented, God has visited them in His wrath with bondage, suffering, and even with total destruction. When these prophetic warnings speak so clearly of the need for repentance in the last days, recognition of the need for repentance as a criterion for the preservation of this nation is an absolute necessity.

Summary

1. Book of Mormon prophecies repeatedly warn of a last days period when there will be great wickedness among the people of America. At that day, according to the prophecies, the people must repent or

---

1. Hel. 13:5-6. See also verses 8-10. He made a similar warning to those of his day. See verses 11-13 and 3 Ne.9:1-2.
2. Morm. 2:8. He wrote to his son concerning the effects of his preaching upon the unrepentant Nephites:

   > . . . I fear lest the Lamanites shall destroy this people; for they do not repent, and Satan stirreth them up continually to anger one with another.
   >
   > Behold, I am laboring with them continually; and when I speak the word of God with sharpness they tremble and anger against me; and when I use no sharpness they harden their hearts against it; wherefore, I fear lest the Spirit of the Lord hath ceased striving with them.
   >
   > For so exceedingly do they anger that it seemeth me that they have no fear of death; and they have lost their love, one towards another; and they thirst after blood and revenge continually. (Moro. 9:3-5).

they will be destroyed. If they do repent, however, they will be spared and blessed.

2. Prophetic warnings concerning a need for repentance to avert judgments from God in the last days were cited from:

A. Alma (Al. 37:22-25).
B. Nephi (2 Ne. 28:16-17).
C. Nephi (1 Ne. 14:5-6).
D. The Savior (3 Ne. 16:12-14).
E. The Savior (3 Ne. 20:14-16).
F. The Savior (3 Ne. 21:20-22).

3. The scriptures frequently indicate that there will be great wickedness among the Gentiles in the last days, and give details concerning the nature and extent of their wickedness:

A. Secret works of darkness, wickedness and abominations (Al. 37:22).
B. All have gone astray save a few humble followers of Christ (2 Ne. 28:14).
C. They turn aside the just for a thing of naught (2 Ne. 28:16).
D. They revile against good, saying it has no worth (2 Ne. 28:16).
E. In the day they are fully ripe in iniquity, they shall perish (2 Ne. 28:16).
F. The Gentiles will deny Christ (2 Ne. 28:32).
G. Gentiles may harden their hearts (3 Ne. 20:28; 21:22).
H. The Gentiles wicked ways: lyings, deceivings, whoredoms, secret abominations, idolatries, murders, priestcrafts, envyings, strifes (3 Ne. 30:2).

4. The Savior, in three separate passages, warns that a remnant of Jacob [the Lamanite] will tread down and tear the unrepentant Gentiles in the last days, and none can deliver them (3 Ne. 16:12-14; 20:14-16, 20; 21:12-21).

5. The Gentiles will not have power over the House of Israel in the day that God remembers His covenant with Israel (3 Ne. 16:12-14).

6. The impending last days' judgments pertain to all the nations of the Gentiles, not just to the Gentiles in the Americas (3 Ne. 20:20; 1 Ne. 14:5-17).

7. Mormon admonished the Gentiles of the last days to turn from their wicked ways by coming unto Christ, being baptized, receiving a remission of sins and the Holy Ghost, and being numbered among the house of Israel (3 Ne. 30:2).

8. There is a danger in procrastinating repentance, for Satan may seal you his as death approaches (Al. 34:33-35).

9. Examples of repentance being necessary to escape destruction were cited from the Book of Mormon:

A. The inhabitants of Jerusalem (1 Ne. 1:4).
B. Laman and Lemuel (1 Ne. 18:15).
C. The wicked Nephites (Jac. 3:3-4).
D. The city of Ammonihah (Al. 8:15-16).
E. Nephites shortly before the birth of Christ (Hel. 4:14).
F. The city of Zarahemla (Hel. 7:17-24).
G. The final generation of Nephites (Hel. 13:5-6; Morm. 2:8).

10. One reason the unrepentant reap God's judgments is that they seek to destroy the liberty of His people (Al. 8:17).

11. The nearness of destruction does not necessarily cause people to repent. The wicked tend to be angry, hard of heart, lack fear of death, have no love, and seek for blood and revenge (Moro. 9:3-5).

12. When people become wicked, God withholds His strength from them (Hel. 7:22-23), withdraws His Spirit (Moro. 9:4), and prevents His prophets from preaching to them (Morm. 1:16-17).

V

Fifth Warning: If the People Fight Against Zion, They Will Be Destroyed

Jacob's Warning: Gentiles Who Fight Against Zion Shall be Destroyed (2 Ne. 6:12-15)

The prophet Jacob added another important item to the list of prophetic warnings found in the Book of Mormon concerning the future. He warned that in the last days, in the era of the return of the House of Israel to the lands of their inheritance,[1] there would be those who would fight against the Lord's people. He foresaw the destruction that would come upon those who would fight against Zion, and described it in this manner. Again, his words are in the nature of conditional prophecy: *if* the people don't fight against Zion, they'll be saved; *if* they do, they will be destroyed:

> And *blessed are the Gentiles,* they of whom the prophet has written; for behold, *if it so be that they shall repent and fight not against Zion,* and do not unite themselves to that great and abominable church, they shall be saved; for the Lord God will fulfill his covenants which he has made unto his children; and for this cause the prophet has written these things.
>
> Wherefore, *they that fight against Zion and the covenant people of the Lord shall lick up the dust of their feet;and the people of the Lord shall not be ashamed.* For the people of the Lord are they who wait for him; for they still wait for the coming of the Messiah.
>
> And behold, according to the words of the prophet, the Messiah will set himself again the second time to recover them; wherefore, he will manifest himself unto them in power and great glory, *unto the destruction of their enemies,* when that day cometh when they shall believe in him; and none will he destroy that believe in him.
>
> And *they that believe not in him shall be destroyed, both by fire, and by tempest, and by earthquakes, and by bloodsheds, and by pestilence, and by famine.* And they shall know that the Lord is God, the Holy One of Israel.[2]

1. 2 Ne. 6:11 .
2. 2 Ne. 6:12-15.

Nephi's Warning: All that Fight Against Zion Shall Be Destroyed (1 Ne. 22:14, 19)

Nephi also taught this principle concerning the last days, saying that "*all that fight against Zion shall be destroyed,*"[1] and teaching that "the righteous shall not perish; for the time surely must come that *all they who fight against Zion shall be cut off.*"[2]

And who, or what, or where, is Zion? The scriptures speak of three Zions which are to exist in the last days:

1. The city of Jerusalem, in Israel,
2. The city of the New Jerusalem, to be built in Jackson County, Missouri.
3. The Lord's people who are pure in heart.

Zion—the City of Jerusalem

When Bible and Book of Mormon passages speak of Zion, they almost always have reference to the city of Jerusalem in Israel and the area which surrounds it. Zion was the name of the Jebusite fortress which David conquered and made his capital in Old Testament times, as is described in Second Samuel, chapter 5:

> David was thirty years old when he began to reign and he reigned forty years.
>
> In Hebron he reigned over Judah seven years and six months: and in Jerusalem he reigned thirty and three years over all Israel and Judah.
>
> And *the king and his men went to Jerusalem unto the Jebusites, the inhabitants of the land:* which spake unto David, saying, Except thou take away the blind and the lame, thou shalt not come in hither; thinking, David cannot come in hither.
>
> Nevertheless *David took the stronghold of Zion: the same is the city of David.*[3]

---

1. 1 Ne. 22:14. Note that this destruction is related to the fall of the great and abominable church. This relationship is considered further in the chapter.
2. 1 Ne. 22:19.
3. 2 Sam. 5:4-7. There is no question among Bible scholars that Zion is a synonym for Jerusalem. For instance, the listing for *Zion* in the *Dictionary of the Bible* (ed. by James Hastings, revised ed. by Frederick C. Grant and H. H. Rowley; New York: Charles Scribner's Sons, 1963, p. 1058), says: "ZION (AV Sion in NT).—The name of the fortress of the pre-israelite city of Jerusalem (2 S 57), which was conquered by David and made his capital. The name is frequently used in the Psalms and the Prophets as a synonym for Jerusalem."

   Merrill Unger, in *Unger's Bible Handbook* (Chicago: Moody Press, 1966, p. 202) explains further: "The towns of Jerusalem had been taken in the time of the judges (Jud. 1:8), but not the stronghold of the Jebusites.

This was the southeast hill, later called the city of David or Zion. Zion is closely connected with David's being made king over all Israel."

The Bible Dictionary of the *Cambridge Bible* (specially bound for The Church of Jesus Christ of Latter-day Saints, 1950) in its article says:

Zion, or 'the city of David ' (2 S. 5. 7-9), one of the hills of Jerusalem on which the Temple stood. The sanctity of Z. may be accounted for by the fact that it was for many years the resting place of the Ark; *Z. thus became the sacred name for the whole city,* and on the return from Exile may have been specially applied to the Temple Mount, though this was not the original Zion.

The Westminster Historical Atlas to the Bible, by George Ernest Wright and Floyd Vivian Filson (Philadelphia:The Westminster Press, 1946, p. 97), describes the topography of early Jerusalem in this manner:

The location of the water supply determined that the earliest settlements should be located on the Eastern Hill, south of the Temple area and above the Gihon spring. In ancient times this hill was called, in its northern part at least, Ophel (XVII:A D-E 5; Micah 4:8, R.V. marg.; II Chron. 27:3, 33:14; Neh. 3:26f; 11:21). *This was also the site of the City of David, or Zion, and of the Jebusite city before it.* This part of the Eastern Hill is not formidable in appearance, and since the fourth century A.D. tradition has associated Zion with the southern part of the Western Hill, where guides still show tourists the traditional Tomb of David (XVII:D, C-6). Archaeological investigation, however, has proved that Zion was south of the Temple area, as indeed it had to be in order to be near its water supply. In Old Testament times it was higher than at present, the Hasmonaeans in the second century B.C. removed the top of the Eastern Hill in order that it might not rival the Temple in height.

A recent work by an LDS author, LaMar C. Berrett, *Discovering the World of the Bible* (Provo, Utah: Brigham Young University Press, 1973, p. 281), adds other insights:

Mount Zion ("fortress"). Zion was the name of the citadel of the Jebusite city of Jerusalem, captured by David. Today, tradition (probably in error) says this was on the southwest hill of the city. Zion was also a title applied to the temple area. The present traditional site of Mount Zion is on a hill close to the southwest corner of the old walled city. In A.D. 340, a large basilica, called Hagia Zion, was built on the mount and it was probably from this building that the mount received its name. The basilica was destroyed by the Persians in 614. This area was once within the city wall, and is very sacred to the Jews because they believe David is buried here. On the slope of Mount Zion is a Protestant cemetery in which Sir Flinders Petrie, the noted archaeologist, is buried.

He then cites Biblical references pertaining to Zion:

The ark was carried from here to the temple (1 Kings 8:1; 2 Chron 5:2).

"Out of Zion shall go forth the law" (Isa. 2:3).

Mount Zion was spoken of as Temple Hill (Isa. 8:18; Jer. 31:6; Mic. 4:7)

Zion was the name of the whole city (Ps. 102:21; Mic. 3:10-12).

Here Jesus was taken before Annas and Caiaphas (Matt. 26:3-5, 57-75, John 18:12-24).

Here Peter denied Jesus at the palace of Caiaphas (Matt. 26:59-75; Luke 22:54-62).

Solomon expanded Jerusalem to the north and encompassed Mt. Moriah, the area where Solomon's temple was built. He moved the ark of the covenant from Zion to the new temple location in the city (1 Ki. 8:1, 2 Chron. 5:2) but the term Zion remained a synonym for Jerusalem and was frequently used in that manner (see Ps. 51:18;147:12;Is.2:3;33:20; 40:9; 41:27; 51:16-17; 52:1, 7-9; 62:1; 64:10; Jer. 4:6, 14; 26:18; 51:35; Lam. 1:17; Amos 1:2; Mi. 3:10, 12; 4:2; Zech. 1:14, 17; 8 3).1 In many other passages, the term Zion is used in a historical or a prophetic sense which clearly applies to Jerusalem.[2]

Zion—the New Jerusalem

Passages referring to Zion in the Doctrine and Covenants usually have reference to the city to be known as the New Jerusalem, which is to be built in Jackson County, Missouri in the last days.

3 Ne. 21:14-29 clearly establishes the building of this city in close chronological proximity to the destruction of many of the Gentiles by the remnant of Jacob and just prior to the major period of the gathering of Israel worldwide.

As He described the New Jerusalem in the last days, the Lord said that

---

1. In almost all of these references, the passages have been examples of Synonymous Parallelism, a characteristic form of Hebrew poetry. In this poetic style,

   The second line restates the first, not merely by repetition, however, as in many of the Near Eastern liturgies, but by enriching, deepening, and even transforming it with new words, by adding fresh nuances, and by giving it a symmetry and balance, as in

   O Lord, who shall sojourn in thy tent?
   Who shall dwell on thy holy hill?—(Ps 151)

   or

   The heavens are telling the glory of God; and the firmament proclaims his handiwork.—(Ps 191) (Hastings, Dictionary of the Bible, op. cit., p. 779.)

2. Many biblical references cited or repeated in the Book of Mormon fall into these categories: 1 Ne. 21:14-21, for instance, refers to Jerusalem in its desolate state prior to the gathering of Israel, as does 2 Ne. 8:3, 11, 16-17. Zion (Jerusalem) putting on her strength (2 Ne. 8:24; 3 Ne. 20:36) is interpreted in a last days setting in D&C 113:7-10 in relation to the redemption of Israel, etc.

. . . it shall be called the New Jerusalem, a land of peace, *a city of refuge, a place of safety for the saints of the Most high God;*

And the glory of the Lord shall be there, and the terror of the Lord also shall be there, insomuch that *the wicked will Not come unto it, and it shall be called Zion*.[1]

In 1831 the Lord revealed that Independence, Missouri was the exact place for the city to be built, and designated that location as an "everlasting inheritance."[2]

Some of the early saints moved to this area but were subsequently driven out by mobs. The Lord rebuked the saints for disobedience.[3] and said that

. . . in consequence of the transgressions of my people, it is expedient in me that *mine elders should wait for a little season for the redemption of Zion—*

That they themselves may *be prepared,* and that my people may *be taught more perfectly,* and *have experience,* and *know more perfectly concerning their duty,* and the things which I require at their hands [4]

Further instruction from the Lord has led the Saints to believe that the New Jerusalem will be regained in a time of conflict and unrest. The Savior has said:

For behold, I do not require at their hands to fight the battles of Zion; for, as I said in a former commandment, even so will I fulfil—*I will fight your battles*.

Behold, *the destroyer I have sent forth to destroy and lay waste mine enemies; and not many years hence they shall not be left to pollute mine heritage,* and to blaspheme my name upon the lands which I have consecrated for the gathering together of my saints.[5]

And also:

Behold, I say unto you, *the redemption of Zion must needs come by power;*

Therefore, I will raise up unto my people a man, who shall lead them like as Moses led the children of Israel.

For ye are the children of Israel, and of the seed of Abraham, and *ye must needs be led out of bondage by power, and with a stretched out arm.*

And as your fathers were led at the first, *even so shall the redemption of Zion be*.[6]

1. D&C 45:66-67.
2. D&C 57:1-5. See D&C 84:2-5
3. D&C 105:1-8.
4. D&C 105:9 -10.
5. D&C 105:14-15.
6. D&C 103:15-18.

And concerning the New Jerusalem when it is finally established:

> And *it shall come to pass among the wicked, that every man that will not take his sword against his neighbor must needs flee unto Zion for safety.*
>
> *And there shall be gathered unto it out of every nation under heaven; and it shall be the only people that shall not be at war one with another.*
>
> *And it shall be said among the wicked: Let us not go up to battle against Zion,* for the inhabitants of Zion are terrible; wherefore we cannot stand.
>
> And it shall come to pass that *the righteous shall be gathered out from among all nations, and shall come to Zion,* singing with songs of everlasting joy. . . .
>
> For when the Lord shall appear he shall be terrible unto them, that fear may seize upon them, and they shall stand afar off and tremble.
>
> And *all nations shall be afraid because of the terror of the Lord,* and the power of his might.[1]

Zion—the Pure in Heart

A revelation in 1833 indicated that Zion was not only a name for geographical places, but also a name for people. This revelation also indicated that the Zion people would exist in the last days' era of terrible calamities:

> Therefore, verily, thus saith the Lord, let Zion rejoice, for *this is Zion—THE PURE IN HEART;* therefore, let Zion rejoice, while *all the wicked shall mourn.*
>
> For behold, and lo, *vengeance cometh speedily upon the ungodly* as the whirlwind; and who shall escape it?
>
> *The Lord's scourge shall pass over by night and by day,* and the report thereof shall vex all people; yea, it shall not be stayed until the Lord come;
>
> *For the indignation of the Lord is kindled against their abominations and all their wicked works.*[2]

Fight Against Zion, a Worldwide Conflict Against the House of Israel and the Church

To which of these Zions do the Book of Mormon warnings refer? It appears that all three, God's people and both places of gathering, are

1. D&C 45:68-71, 74-75. See also D&C 97:18-20.
2. D&C 97:21-24. Biblical passages occasionally use the term "Zion" in reference to the Lord's people, as in Zech. 2:6-8.

involved in the period of this great conflict. Jacob, in 2 Ne. 6:13-14, seems to refer to Zion as the covenant people of the Lord who are being recovered for the second time and "gathered again to the lands of their inheritance."[1] Nephi, in connection with his warning that all that fight against Zion will be destroyed, observes that "*every nation which shall war against thee, O house of Israel,* shall be turned one against another, and they shall fall into the pit which they digged to ensnare the people of the Lord."[2] He links the fall of these nations with the collapse of the great and abominable church in the same verse. His description of this event is of the wrath of God being poured out upon the earth by blood, smoke, and fire:

> For behold, saith the prophet, the time cometh speedily that Satan shall have no more power over the hearts of the children of men; for the day soon cometh that all the proud and they who do wickedly shall be as stubble; and the day cometh that they must be burned.
>
> For the time soon cometh that *the fulness of the wrath of God shall be poured out upon all the children of men; for he will not suffer that the wicked shall destroy the righteous.*
>
> Wherefore, *he will preserve the righteous by his power,* even if it so be that the fulness of his wrath must come, and the righteous be preserved, *even unto the destruction of their enemies by fire.* Wherefore, the righteous need not fear; for thus saith the prophet, they shall be saved, even if it so be as by fire.
>
> Behold, my brethren, I say unto you, that these things must shortly come; *yea, even blood, and fire, and vapor of smoke must come;* and it must needs be upon the face of this earth; and it cometh unto men according to the flesh if it so be that they will harden their hearts against the Holy One of Israel.
>
> For behold, *the righteous shall not perish; for the time surely must come that all they who fight against Zion shall be cut off.*[3]

This account bears similarities to Nephi's earlier description of the "wars and rumors of wars among all the nations which belonged to the mother of abominations."[4] These wars, it appears, will result from the actions of the "great mother of abominations" who will "*gather together multitudes upon the face of all the earth, among all the nations of the Gentiles, to fight against the Lamb of God.*"[5] At that time, according to Nephi's vision, there will be two groups who will be granted protective power from God: "the saints of the church of the

---

1. 2 Ne. 6:13-14, and also verse 1].
2. 1 Ne. 22:14.
3. 1 Ne. 22:15-19.
4. 1 Ne. 17:16. See 14:10-17.
5. 1 Ne. 14:13.

Lamb," and "the covenant people who were scattered upon all the face of the earth."1 It appears that both the Lord's Church and the entire house of Israel, both scattered throughout the world, will bear the onslaught of Satan's forces fighting against Zion.

Jacob's Warning: The Whore of the Earth that Fights Against Zion Shall Perish (2 Ne. 10:11-16)

Jacob locates some of this conflict in the Americas, and associates it with the influence of "the whore of all the earth:"

> . . . This land shall be a land of liberty unto the Gentiles, and there shall be no kings upon the land, who shall raise up unto the Gentiles.
>
> *And I will fortify this land against all other nations.*
>
> *And he that fighteth against Zion shall perish,* saith God.
>
> For he that raiseth up a king against me shall perish, for I, the Lord, the king of heaven, will be their king, and I will be a light unto them forever, that hear my words.
>
> Wherefore, for this cause, that my covenants may be fulfilled which I have made unto the children of men, that I will do unto them while they are in the flesh, *I must needs destroy the secret works of darkness, and of murders, and of abominations.*
>
> *Wherefore, he that fighteth against Zion, both Jew and Gentile, both bond and free, both male and female, shall perish; for they are they who are the whore of all the earth; for they who are not for me are against me, saith our God.*[2]

Nephi's Warning: The Nations that Fight Against Zion Will Be Visited with Earthquake, Storm, and Devouring Fire (2 Ne. 27:1-5)

Nephi saw that the wickedness and judgments of this era will involve "those who shall come upon this land and those who shall be upon other lands, yea, even upon all the lands of the earth," and that the judgments will involve "all the nations that fight against Zion:"

> But behold, *in the last days, or in the days of the Gentiles*—yea, behold all the nations of the Gentiles and also the Jews, *both those who shall come upon this land and those who shall be upon other lands, yea, even upon all the lands of the earth, behold, they will be drunken with iniquity and all manner of abominations*—

1. 1 Ne. 14:14.
2. 2 Ne. 10:11-16.

And when that day shall come they shall be visited of the Lord of Hosts, with *thunder* and with *earthquake,* and with a *great noise,* and with *storm,* and with tempest, and with the *flame of devouring fire*.

And all the nations that fight against Zion, and that distress her, shall be as a dream of a night vision; yea, it shall be unto them, even as unto a hungry man which dreameth, and behold he eateth but he awaketh and his soul is empty; or like unto a thirsty man which dreameth, and behold he drinketh but he awaketh and behold he is faint, and his soul hath appetite; *yea, even so shall the multitude of all the nations be that fight against Mount Zion.*

For behold, all ye that doeth iniquity, stay yourselves and wonder, for ye shall cry out, and cry; yea, ye shall be drunken but not with wine, ye shall stagger but not with strong drink.

For behold, the Lord hath poured out upon you the spirit of deep sleep. For behold, ye have closed your eyes, and *ye have rejected the prophets;and your rulers, and the seers hath he covered because of your iniquity.*[1]

Nephi's Warning: Those Who Fight Against His People Israel will be Shown the Lord is God (2 Ne. 29:12-14)

Nephi's predictions show that the future conflict will involve a fight against God's word and God's people, and will come in a period when other sacred records will have come to light:

For behold, I shall speak unto the *Jews* and they shall write it; and I shall also speak unto the *Nephites* and they shall write it; and I shall also speak unto *the other tribes of the house of Israel, which I have led away,* and they shall write it; and I shall also speak unto *all nations of the earth* and they shall write it.

And it shall come to pass that the Jews shall have the words of the Nephites, and the Nephites shall have the words of the Jews; and the Nephites and the Jews shall have the words of the lost tribes of Israel; and the lost tribes of Israel shall have the words of the Nephites and the Jews.

And it shall come to pass that *my people, which are of the house of Israel, shall be gathered home unto the lands of their possessions; and my word also shall be gathered in one. And I will show unto them that fight against my word and against my people, who are of the house of Israel, that I am God,* and that I covenanted with Abraham that I would remember his seed forever.[2]

1. 2 Ne. 27:1-5.
2. 2 Ne. 29:12-14

Thus it appears that the future conflict in which many will fight against Zion will be international in scope. It will involve the tribes of Israel as they gather home to the lands of their inheritance.

It will involve the Church. It will involve the saints who participate in the return to the New Jerusalem. It will be Satan-inspired with a vast evil church leading much of the onslaught against the Lord's people. The conflict will culminate with the collapse of this great and abominable church, which is the subject of the next chapter.

Summary

1. A fifth principle which must be obeyed if America and the other Gentile nations are to escape future destruction is that they must not fight against Zion. Again, the principle is conditional: if the people don't fight against Zion, they will be saved; if they do, they will be destroyed.

2. Prophetic warnings on this theme are cited in this chapter:

A. Jacob (2 Ne. 6:12-15)
B. Nephi (1 Ne. 22:14, 19)
C. Jacob (2 Ne. 10:11-16)
D. Nephi (2 Ne. 27:1-5)
E. Nephi (2 Ne. 29:12-14)

3. The destruction of those who fight against Zion will come by a variety of judgments: fire, tempest, earthquakes, bloodsheds, pestilence, famine, and nations warring among themselves (2 Ne. 6:12-15; 1 Ne. 22:14-19; D&C 45:68-69).

4. As the judgments are poured out, God will preserve the righteous while He destroys the wicked (2 Ne. 6:14; 1 Ne. 22:16, 19) and will fight the battles for the righteous (D&C 105:14-15; 45:74-75)

5. The fight against Zion will be instigated by the great and abominable church which is called the whore of all the earth (2 Ne. 6:12; 1 Ne. 22:14; 1 Ne. 14:13).

6. The conflict will be worldwide in scope, involving a multitude of nations including America (D&C 45:69; 1 Ne. 22:14; 1 Ne. 14:13, 16; 2 Ne. 27:1-4; 2 Ne. 10:11-16).

7. The scriptures speak of three Zions which will be in existence at the time of the great conflict:

A. The city of Jerusalem, in Israel.

B. The city of the New Jerusalem, in Jackson County, Missouri.
C. The Lord's people who are pure in heart.

The great conflict will involve all three of them.

8. Zion is the name of the fortress of the pre-Israelite city of Jerusalem which David conquered from the Jebusites and made his capital, the "city of David." The term Zion has remained a synonym for Jerusalem and is frequently used in that manner in the Bible (particularly in instances of synonymous parallelism, a common Hebrew poetic form).

9. The city of the New Jerusalem, to be built in Jackson County, Missouri, will be

A. A land of peace (D&C 45:66).
B. A city of refuge (D&C 45:66).
C. A place of safety for the saints (D&C 45:66).
D. Protected from the wicked by the glory and terror of God which will be there (D&C 45:67).
E. Consecrated for the gathering of the saints (D&C 105:15).
F. Redeemed by power through a man God will raise up to lead the saints out of bondage (D&C 103:15-18).
G. A gathering place for those who won't fight against their neighbors (D&C 45:68).
H. A gathering place for righteous people of every nation (D&C 45:69, 71).
I. The only people not at war with one another (D&C 45:69).
J. A source of fear to the wicked (D&C 45:70, 74-75).

10. Zion also refers to people who are pure in heart as well as to the two geographical places mentioned above (D&C 97:21). This, apparently, embraces both righteous Church members and righteous members of the scattered House of Israel.

11. The Lord has revealed that a terrible scourge will come upon the wicked in the last days which will vex all people and which will continue until He comes (D&C 97:21-24).

12. As is seen in this chapter and later in this book, the fight against Zion will be so far-reaching that it will involve all three of the Zions

mentioned. The New Jerusalem Zion, apparently, will rise to power and will be strong enough to resist enemy onslaught. Both the Church and the House of Israel will be subjected to distress and Jerusalem will see much strife which will culminate in the Battle of Armageddon.

VI

Sixth Warning: The Great and Abominable Church Will Persecute the Saints

Jacob's Warning: To Be Saved, the Gentiles Must Not Unite with the Great and Abominable Church (2 Ne. 6:12)

In the same passage in which he warned of the fate of those who would fight against Zion in the last days, the prophet Jacob cautioned the Gentiles of the danger of affiliating with a great and abominable church. Avoiding unity with or participation in that body was one of the criteria he specified as being necessary for the Gentiles to be saved from God's judgments:

> And blessed are the Gentiles, they of whom the prophet has written;for behold, *if it so be that they shall repent and fight not against Zion, and do not unite themselves to that great and abominable church, they shall be saved;* for the Lord God will fulfill his covenants which he has made unto his children; and for this cause the prophet has written these things.[1]

Numerous scriptural passages foretell the existence in the last days of this great and abominable church which is depicted as being opposed to the true work of Christ. The identity of this organization is subject to many different interpretations—indeed, it has been the source of much controversy throughout the entire Christian world since the time of the Reformation. Its identity is especially of vital concern to Latter-day Saints, however, because of the numerous prophetic warnings concerning it found in the Book of Mormon.

Important to Be Forewarned of Future Danger to the Saints

In recent years some Latter-day Saints have been content to ignore the numerous scriptural warnings of the persecutions which this great world-wide organization will bring upon them. Yet signs of the times indicate that the prophesied conflict involving this great church is

1. 2 Ne. 6:12

approaching. The time must soon come when the passive attitudes of yesterday must give way to the alertness necessary to preserve God's people. God, through His prophets, has revealed His warning of the oppressive role this abominable church will play in a broad scriptural pattern based on dozens of passages.l To refuse to ponder those revealed warnings, as to refuse to consider any pattern of revealed scripture, is a serious matter before the Lord.

This author does not seek to bring criticism nor create animosity towards any existing church or sect. Indeed, this chapter will contain no statement by the author which labels any existing church as being the fulfillment of the prophecies reported, nor will it advocate any action or procedure against any existing religious organization. If any sects impute offense against themselves from what is written herein, let them recall the proverb that "the wicked flee when no man pursueth."[2]

Past Activities of the Great and Abominable Church Recorded in Scriptures

The scriptures describe both the past and future activities of the great and abominable church in considerable detail. Nephi told of being visited by an angel who showed him its origin. The vision was part of a chronological overview which indicated that the time of the foundation of the church was to be following the ministry of Christ,[3] yet preceding the discovery and settling of America by Columbus and European Gentiles:[4]

---

1. In such a case, the Lord's warning through Ezekiel must be heeded:

> Son of man, speak to the children of thy people, and say unto them, When I bring the sword upon a land, if the people of the land take a man of their coasts, and set him for their watchman:
>
> If when he seeth the sword come upon the land, he blow the trumpet, and warn the people;
>
> Then whosoever heareth the sound of the trumpet, and taketh not warning; if the sword come, and take him away, his blood shall be upon his own head.
>
> He heard the sound of the trumpet, and took not warning; his blood shall be upon him. But he that taketh warning shall deliver his soul. (Ezek. 33:2-5)

2. Prov. 28:1. See also Lev. 26:17, 36-37.
3. See 1 Ne. 11:15-33;12:6-10.
4. See 1 Ne. 13:10-14.

And it came to pass that I saw *among the nations of the Gentiles the foundation of a great church*

And the angel said unto me: Behold the foundation of a church which *is most abominable above all other churches, which slayeth the saints of God,* yea, and *tortureth them* and *bindeth them down,* and yoketh them with a yoke of iron, and *bringeth them down into captivity.*

And it came to pass that I beheld this great and abominable church; and I saw the devil that he was the foundation of it.

And I also saw gold, and silver, and silks, and scarlets, and fine-twined linen, and all manner of precious clothing; and I saw many harlots

And the angel spake unto me, saying: Behold the gold, and the silver, and the silks, and the scarlets, and the fine-twined linen, and the precious clothing, and the harlots, are the desires of this great and abominable church.

And also for the praise of the world do *they destroy the saints of God, and bring them down into captivity.*[1]

The above passage is meaningful in its rich detail. It locates the foundation of the church as being centered in the nations of the Gentiles,[2] or European nations. It clearly identifies the organization as actually being a church and not just general wickedness, and specifies that in the era prior to the settling of America it is "most abominable above all other churches."[3] The passage characterizes the church as using fine and precious clothing,[4] being involved with harlotry,[1] and

---

1. 1 Ne. 13:4-9.
2. It is from these Gentile nations that America is settled (1 Ne. 13:10-19). Hence the conclusion that the Gentile nations are the nations of Europe. Orson Pratt equated the Gentile nations with "the nations of Christendom." (See JD, 7:186.) In prophetic terminology the Gentile nations are contrasted with the heathen, or non-Christian nations.
3. Note the approximate dates of the formation of some of the earliest "other churches" in Christianity:

Mennonites	(1525)	(Swiss brethren)
Evangelical Lutherans	(1526)	(Luther, Melanchthon)
Church of England	(1533)	(Henry VIII)
Anabaptist	(1534)	(Phillips, Simons)
Reformed Churches	(1536)	(Calvin, Zwingle, Knox)
Presbyterians	(1559)	(Calvin, Zwingle, Bucer)
Congregationalists	(1560)	(English brethren)
Quakers	(1666)	(Fox)
Methodists	(1739)	(Wesley, Whitefield)

4. How expensive is clerical garb? A 1967 AP News dispatch gives some indication of the expense involved for one denomination:

   ROME (AP)—The ecclesiastical tailors of Rome were busy Saturday making final adjustments on the new scarlet garments for 27 new cardinals being elevated by Pope Paul VI in consistory Monday.

begins the warning theme that this church would eventually slay the saints, torture them, bind them, bring them into captivity, and destroy many of them.[2] These evil deeds will be done in a world climate of antagonism against the the Lord's people, when persecuting the saints will bring "the praise of the world."[3] Nephi leaves no doubt about the origin of this church: the devil is its founder.[4]

Nephi's vision contained other insights concerning the identity of the great and abominable church. He saw the writings which were to be the Bible come forth from the Jews[5] and that they were carried forth in purity by the Savior's twelve apostles.[6] The vision then indicated that that period immediately following the labors of the twelve in the meridian of time would be the time of the great church's beginning,[7] and that the church would take away many portions of both Christ's gospel8 and the book that was to become the Bible.[9] According to the vision, the great and abominable church would take away these truths before the Bible would go forth to the Gentile nations and before the Bible would be brought to the Americas:[10]

> Wherefore, *these things go forth from the Jews in purity unto the Gentiles,* according to the truth which is in God.
>
> And *after they go forth by the hand of the twelve apostles* of the Lamb, from the Jews unto the Gentiles, *thou seest the foundation of a great and abominable church, which is most abominable above all other churches;*

> What does it cost to dress a cardinal in the rich red cassock and cape and buckled shoes that go with his princely rank in the Roman Catholic Church?
>
> At least $1,400 is the figure given by one of Rome's best ecclesiastical outfitters—and that's only for a minimum wardrobe of 23 items, exclusive of ring and pectoral cross.
>
> Most expensive item on the typical price list is the three-yard long scarlet silk "Capa Magna" or Great Cape. It goes for $176. Least costly is a Roman collar of red silk with square white cutout in front. They cost 80 cents.
>
> The new cardinals are saving at least $448 thanks to papal-ordered changes just put into effect for simplifying the dress and protocol for all cardinals. ("Beau Cardinal Costs Less," *Salt Lake Tribune,* June 25, 1967)

---

1. 1 Ne. 13:7.
2. 1 Ne. 13:5, 9.
3. 1 Ne. 13:9.
4. 1 Ne. 13:6
5. 1 Ne. 13:20-24.
6. 1 Ne. 13:25-26.
7. 1 Ne. 13:26.
8. 1 Ne. 13:26.
9. 1 Ne. 13:28.
10. 1 Ne. 13:29.

for behold, *they have taken away from the gospel of the Lamb many parts which are plain and most precious; and also many covenants of the Lord have they taken away.*

And all this have they done that they might pervert the right ways of the Lord, that they might blind the eyes and harden the hearts of the children of men.

Wherefore, thou seest that after the book hath gone forth through the hands of the great and abominable church, that *there are many plain and precious things taken away from the book,* which is the book of the Lamb of God.

And after these plain and precious things were taken away it goeth forth unto all the nations of the Gentiles; and after it goeth forth unto all the nations of the Gentiles, yea, even across the many waters which thou hast seen with the Gentiles which have gone forth out of captivity, thou seest—because of the many plain and precious things which have been taken out of the book, which were plain unto the understanding of the children of men, according to the plainness which is in the Lamb of God—because of these things which are taken away out of the gospel of the Lamb, an exceeding great many do stumble, yea, insomuch that Satan hath great power over them.[1]

Nephi observes repeatedly that the withholding of gospel and scriptural truths by this great church would cause many to "stumble exceedingly[2] and be in an "awful state of blindness"[3] and be subject to Satan's power,[4] and that this effect would be manifest even before the Lord would bring forth His gospel and the Book of Mormon in the Americas.[5]

A "Great and a Marvelous Work" and the Lord's "Strange Act"—A Future Event Causing Men to Join Either the Church of God or the Church of the Devil

As the chronological prophetic picture left by Nephi sweeps from the past into the future,[6] a highly-significant change is to be noted concerning the identity of the great and abominable church. Nephi prophesies that some undefined event will cause men to move into two distinct factions which cause them to align themselves with either the church of the lamb of God or with the church of the devil. This

1. 1 Ne. 13:25-29.
2. 1 Ne. 13:29, 34.
3. 1 Ne. 13:32.
4. 1 Ne . 13:29.
5. 1 Ne. 13:34-35.
6. Note that the chronological account moves past Gentile persecution of the American Indians (1 Ne. 13:30-31), the restoration of the gospel (1 Ne. 13:34), the coming forth of the book of Mormon (1 Ne. 13:35-36, 39-41), and the preaching of the gospel to the Lamanites (1 Ne.13:38).

divisive event, when *the Lord God shall cause a great division among the people, and the wicked shall he destroy,*"[1] is called by an angel "a great and a marvelous work."[2] As a result of this event, men will no longer be lukewarm "fence-sitters," but will be moved to take a definite position either for or against the Lord's people. When this situation aligns men into opposing camps of good and evil, then "*whoso belongeth not to the church of the Lamb of God belongeth to that great church, which is the mother of abominations.*"[3] This is the angel's prophecy recorded by Nephi:

> For *the time cometh,* saith the Lamb of God, that *I will work a great and a marvelous work among the children of men; a work which shall be everlasting, either on the one hand or on the other either to the convincing of them unto peace and life eternal, or unto the deliverance of them to the hardness of their hearts* and the blindness of their minds unto their being *brought down into captivity, and also into destruction, both temporally and spiritually,* according to the captivity of the devil, of which I have spoken.
>
> And it came to pass that when the angel had spoken these words, he said unto me: Rememberest thou the covenants of the Father unto the house of Israel? I said unto him, Yea.
>
> And it came to pass that he said unto me: *Look, and behold that great and abominable church, which is the mother of abominations, whose foundation is the devil.*
>
> And he said unto me: *Behold there are save two churches only; the one is the church of the Lamb of God, and the other is the church of the devil; wherefore, whoso belongeth not to the church of the Lamb of God belongeth to that great church, which is the mother of abominations; and she is the whore of all the earth.*[4]

The term "marvelous work and a wonder" has sometimes been assumed to mean the restoration of the gospel,[5] but careful study of passages which use the term indicates the full meaning involves a

1. 2 Ne. 30:10.
2. 1 Ne 14:7.
3. 1 Ne. 14:10.
4. 1 Ne. 14:7-10.
5. For instance, Elder LeGrand Richards, in his useful and widely read missionary volume entitled *A Marvelous Work and A Wonder,* assumes that the term refers to the "conundrum of Joseph Smith and the work he established," hut offers no interpretational substantiation to justify his assumption, only a question after citing Isaiah 29:13-14: "How could this prediction possibly be more literally fulfilled than in the case of Joseph Smith and the work the Lord established through him?" (LeGrand Richards, *A Marvelous Work and A Wonder* (Salt Lake City, Utah: Deseret Book Company, 1953), pp. 364-365.)

future latter-day event related to the cataclysmic era surrounding the restoration of Israel.

The term "a marvelous work and a wonder" is rarely used in scripture. Its most frequently cited source is the 29th chapter of Isaiah, a chapter with clear allusions to at least three different periods of time.

Verses 1-6 seem to be a comparison of destruction in Jerusalem ("Ariel, the city where David dwelt," Is. 29:1) to the fall of the Nephites about 385 A.D. This comparison becomes clear when Is. 29:1-6 is considered in the light of 2 Ne. 26:14-18 and the fulfillment of the prophecy recorded in Mormon 6.[1]

Isaiah 29:11-13 apparently refers to the coming forth of the Book of Mormon to Joseph Smith, and the delivery of words from that manuscript to a scholar by the name of Charles Anthon. A comparison of Is. 29:11-13 with 2 Ne. 27:15-22 and Joseph Smith History 1:64-65 will give understanding of these verses.[2]

A third event is also prophesied in Isaiah 29: a future campaign against Mount Zion by many nations. It is to this event that the term "marvelous work and a wonder" appears to be related. This event is to take place in an era when the love of God will be diminished upon the earth and the righteous will be persecuted by the wicked. Note the message of these verses selected from Isaiah 29:

> And *the multitude of all the nations that fight against Ariel [Jerusalem],* even all that fight against her and her munition, and that distress her, shall be as a dream of a night vision.
>
> It shall even be as when an hungry man dreameth, and, behold, he eateth; but he awaketh, and his soul is empty: or as when a thirsty man dreameth, and, behold, he drinketh; but he awaketh, and, behold, he is faint, and his soul hath appetite: *so shall the multitude of all the nations be, that fight against mount Zion.*
>
> Stay yourselves, and wonder; cry ye out, and cry: they are drunken, but not with wine; they stagger, but not with strong drink.
>
> For the Lord hath poured out upon you the spirit of deep sleep, and hath closed your eyes: *the prophets and your rulers, the seers hath he covered. . . .*
>
> Wherefore the Lord said, Forasmuch as this people draw near me with their mouth, and with their lips do honour me, but have removed their heart far from me, and their fear toward me is taught by the precept of men:
>
> Therefore, behold, *I will proceed to do a marvellous work among this people, even a marvellous work and a wonder: for the wisdom of their wise men shall perish, and the understanding of their prudent men shall be hid.*

---

1. For a discussion of these passages see the author s book, *The Prophecies of Joseph Smith* (Bountiful, Utah: Horizon Publishers, 1983), pp. 174-179.
2. See *The Prophecies of Joseph Smith,* pp. 76-86.

> Woe unto them that seek deep to hide their counsel from the Lord, and their works are in the dark, and they say, Who seeth us? and who knoweth us?
>
> Surely your *turning of things upside down* shall be esteemed as the potter's clay: for shall the work say of him that made it, He made me not? or shall the thing framed say of him that framed it, He had no understanding?. . .
>
> *For the terrible one is brought to nought, and the scorner is consumed, and all that watch for iniquity are cut off:*
>
> That make a man an offender for a word, and lay a snare for him that reproveth in the gate, and turn aside the just for a thing of nought.[1]

In this context, the marvelous work and a wonder does not appear to be the restoration of the gospel, but rather a later last days event which leads to the fall of those who have persecuted the Lord's people.

Passages related to "a marvelous work and a wonder" or to a "marvelous work" in the Book of Mormon consistently link those phrases to the cataclysmic events of the last days which will involve the restoration of Israel. In addition to 1 Nephi 14:6-17, which is under consideration in this section, other passages carry the same intent.

In 1 Nephi 22:8-19, Nephi prophesies that the Lord will do a "marvelous work" among the Gentiles, which he links with the message that the Lord will bring "the house of Israel . . . out of captivity, and they shall be gathered together to the lands of their inheritance."[2] In the passage he prophesies that members of the great and abominable church "*shall war among themselves*,"[3] and that "*every nation which shall war against thee, O house of Israel, shall be turned one against another,*"[4] and that "*all that fight against Zion shall be destroyed*."[5] In the series of events which he describes, people are clearly divided into two opposing factions, and Nephi prophesies that "*the wicked shall not destroy the righteous,*"[6] and that *the righteous will "be preserved, even unto the destruction of their enemies by fire*."[7] Surely the "marvelous work" of this passage refers to a last days era far later than the 1820-1830 restoration of the gospel—it focuses on the results of that future divisive event when men will "harden their hearts against the holy one of Israel."[8]

1. Is. 29:7-10, 13-16, 20-21.
2. 1 Ne. 22:11-12
3. 1 Ne. 22:13.
4. 1 Ne. 22:14.
5. *Ibid.*
6. 1 Ne. 22:16.
7. 1 Ne. 22:17.
8. 1 Ne. 22:18.

2 Nephi 25:15-18 also links "a marvelous work and a wonder"[1] to the gathering of Israel when "the Lord will set his hand again the second time to restore his people from their last and fallen state."[2] This passage may give a clue to the nature of the divisive event under discussion, for it alludes to "a false Messiah which should deceive the people."[3]

2 Nephi 27 is a commentary and paraphrase of Isaiah 29 and subject to the same analysis as that suggested for Isaiah 29 above. But the context stated in the beginning of 2 Nephi 27 places the fulfillment "in the last days, or in the days of the Gentiles," when the people of America ("this land") and other lands "*will be drunken with iniquity and all manner of abominations*."[4] This will be the era when the "*multitude of all the nations* " will "*fight against Mount Zion*."[5] The divisive event will have taken place, for the people will have "*rejected the prophets*."[6] That day when the Lord will "do a marvelous work among this people, yea, a marvelous work and a wonder,"[7] will be the time when scorners and those who "watch for iniquity"[8] will "*make a man an offender for a word, and lay a snare for him that reproveth in the gate, and turn aside the just for a thing of naught*."[9] Certainly the "marvelous work" of this passage refers to an era later than the time of the restoration of the gospel through Joseph Smith.

2 Nephi 28:32 through 2 Ne. 29:14 bears the same message. In the last days era when the Gentiles will deny Christ,[10] the Lord will "do a marvelous work among them,"[11] and set his hand again "to recover my people, which are of the house of Israel."[12] As he gathers Israel, the Savior will deal with "*them that fight against my word and against my people*."[13] Again evidence that a divisive event will have occurred is presented in a marvelous work prophecy.

---

1. 2 Ne.25:17.
2. *Ibid*.
3. 2 Ne. 25:18.
4. 2 Ne. 27:1. Compare 2 Ne. 27:1-5, 25-32 with Is. 29:7-10, 13-16, 20-21.
5. 2 Ne. 27:3.
6. 2 Ne. 27:5.
7. 2 Ne. 27:26.
8. 2 Ne. 27:31.
9. 2 Ne. 27:32.
10. 2 Ne. 28:32.
11. 2 Ne. 29:1.
12. *Ibid*.
13. 2 Ne. 29:14.

In 3 Nephi 21:7-29, in the era when the Lamanites have already begun to hear the gospel and "know these things"[1] and when the Lord has already commenced fulfilling his covenant to the house of Israel,[2] the Lord prophesies that his "servant" or representative will declare God's word to "those who will not believe it,"[3] and that servant will be "marred because of them,"[4] and then healed. Perhaps the ministry of this last days servant is closely connected with the divisive event, for after he brings forth the words of Christ "unto the Gentiles,"[5] the Savior says that the unbelieving Gentiles "shall be cut off from among my people who are of the covenant"[6] and great destruction will be worked by the remnant of Jacob upon the cities of the Gentiles and God will "*execute vengeance and fury upon them, even as upon the heathen*."[7] This is the era described when the Lord says that the Father shall "work a work, which shall be a great and a marvelous work among them."[8]

In 3 Ne. 28:25-32, Mormon prophesies of the role of the three Nephite apostles in the last days. The lives of these three Nephites were extended so they could minister unto the earth until the second coming of the Lord. Mormon prophesies that they shall be "among the Gentiles" and "among the Jews," in the last days, and that the Lord will eventually send them to "minister unto all the scattered tribes of Israel, and unto all nations, kindreds, tongues and people."[9] In that era "before the great and coming day when all people must surely stand before the judgment-seat of Christ"[10] they will "bring out of them unto Jesus many souls."[11] Mormon says that "great and marvelous works shall be wrought by them"[12] in that era when they will be separating the righteous from the nations (and doesn't the "bring out" process indicate that the dividing and separating process will be underway at that time?)

---

1. 3 Ne. 21:7.
2. *Ibid.*
3. 3 Ne. 21:9.
4. 3 Ne. 21:10.
5. 3 Ne. 21:11 .
6. *Ibid.*
7. 3 Ne. 21 12-21. Note that the context indicates that this will occur before the building of the New Jerusalem. (See 3 Ne. 21:22-24, which follow in chronological order.
8. 3 Ne. 21:9.
9. 3 Ne. 28:27-29.
10. 3 Ne. 28:31.
11. 3 Ne. 28:29.
12. 3 Ne. 28:31

Thus all the major scriptural passages dealing with a"marvelous work" or "a marvelous work and a wonder" relate to a future era—the time of the major gathering of Israel, persecution of the Lord's people, and the pouring out of God's judgments. Those who might still hold to the theory that the "marvelous work" of 1 Ne. 14:7 refers only to the 1820-1830 restoration and the missionary labor which has followed it, should recall that the restored gospel has been preached for a century-and-a-half, and many have either accepted or rejected it. Those who have rejected it may even have reaped captivity by the devil in hell when they died—but it was an eventual thing, and a spiritual rather than an immediate temporal result. More preaching of the gospel, in the way it has been done previously, does not appear to fulfill the criteria of Nephi's prophecy of delivering men into captivity and destruction, *both temporally and spiritually.*

This future event of which Nephi speaks is different! On the basis of Nephi's prophecy in 1 Ne. 14:7, it appears that when this future "marvelous work" transpires, all men will be obliged to take a stand for or against the Lord's work, and those who unite themselves with the great and abominable church will reap actual, temporal destruction! No, this is more than missionary work, in a sense the saints have known it in the past.

The nature of this event that will divide men into opposing factions is not clearly defined in the scriptures, but some clues may shed light on it. While prophesying of the fall of the great and abominable church, Nephi warned that there will be those at that day who will "*turn aside the just for a thing of naught and revile against that which is good, and say that is of no worth!*"[1] He also taught that at that day Satan will "rage in the hearts of the children of men, and *stir them up to anger against that which is good.*"[2] Can this be a cryptic explanation of what will happen as men divide themselves into two opposing camps—one following the Lord and one following Lucifer?

In a revelation given in 1833, the Lord said that a time would come when he would proceed to "*bring to pass my act, my strange act, and perform my work, my strange work.*"[3] This strange act will have the same result as the "great and a marvelous work" prophesied by Nephi: it will cause that "*men may discern between the righteous and the wicked.*"[4] In the revelation, the Master related the parable of a "woman

1. 2 Ne. 28:16.
2. 2 Ne 28:20.
3. D&C 101:95.
4. *Ibid.*

and the unjust judge,"[1] in which he likened the future Zion to a woman who sought and finally received vengeance on her adversary. He then revealed that a time will come when, because of the unwillingness of governmental officials to heed the requests of the saints (for relief from the offenses of their adversaries), the Lord will "arise and come forth out of his hiding place, and *in his fury vex the nation,*"[2] and "*cut off those wicked, unfaithful, and unjust stewards.*"[3] This is his prophetic utterance:

> Thus will I liken the children of Zion.
> Let them importune at the feet of the judge;
> And if he heed them not, let them importune at the feet of the governor;
> And if the governor heed them not, let them importune at the feet of the president;
> *And if the president heed them not, then will the Lord arise and come forth out of his hiding place, and in his fury vex the nation;*
> *And in his hot displeasure, and in his fierce anger, in his time, will cut off those wicked, unfaithful, and unjust stewards, and appoint them their portion among hypocrites and unbelievers;*
> Even in outer darkness, where there is weeping, and wailing, and gnashing of teeth.
> Pray ye, therefore, that their ears may be opened unto your cries, that I may be merciful unto them, that these things may not come upon them.
> What I have said unto you must needs be, that all men may be left without excuse;
> That wise men and rulers may hear and know that which they have never considered;
> *That I may proceed to bring to pass my act, my strange act, and perform my work, my strange work that men may discern between the righteous and the wicked, saith your God.*[4]

Again, the passage does not say what the specific situation is that will cause the oppression against the saints and bring God's wrath upon the nation. Yet there appears to be obvious relationships between the "great and a marvelous work" prophesied by Nephi, the time when

1. D&C 101:81-85.
2. D&C 101:89.
3. Note that they are to be consigned to hell ["outer darkness"—see Al. 40:13-14], just as are the evil ones who choose to follow Satan at the time of the "marvelous work" of 1 Ne. 14:7.
4. D&C 101:85-95. This revelation was given in a time when the saints were undergoing persecution, yet the prophetic warning was not fulfilled in that era. Presumably fulfillment is yet future.

men will "turn aside the just for a thing of naught," the Lord's "strange act" and "strange work," and the time when "the Lord God shall cause a great division among the people ."

What issue will serve to focus adverse attention upon the church and bring intense pressure and persecution upon the saints? Is it the Negro and the priesthood? the ERA and women's rights? abortion? taxation of church properties? released time religious education? Or is it some other issue which is not yet visible? Certainly when Satan stirs men to anger, he will be able to provide them with some excuse to "revile against that which is good."

The important thing to understand in this context is that until this change takes place, the great and abominable church is neither fully functioning in its antagonistic role, nor truly discernible as the great church which is to be the "whore of all the earth."

Paul's Warning: Some Will Heed Doctrines of Devils and Speak Lies in Hypocrisy (1 Tim. 4:1-3)

Others besides Nephi have warned of the great and abominable church in the last days. Paul identified it as one which would teach Satan-inspired doctrines, speak lies, function without conscience, forbid marriage and which would command abstention from meats:

> Now the Spirit speaketh expressly, that in the latter times some shall depart from the faith, *giving heed to seducing spirits, and doctrines of devils;*
>
> *Speaking lies in hypocrisy;* having their conscience seared with a hot iron;
>
> *Forbidding to marry, and commanding to abstain from meats,* which God hath created to be received with thanksgiving of them which believe and know the truth.[1]

John's Warning: The Dragon Will Make War With the Remnant (Rev. 12:17-13:18)

John the Revelator also saw the role that Satan and his followers would play in this last days sequence.[2] He pictured Satan

1. 1 Tim. 4:1-3.
2. Note the guidance to understanding the chronology of the Book of Revelation found in D&C section 77. The sequence of events from Revelation, chapters 8-19, lead up to the coming of the Savior in glory and the beginning of the millennium. D&C 77:12 indicates that these events take place after the beginning of the seventh thousand years (a time yet future, but drawing near).

as a dragon,[1] the Lord's church as a woman, and Jesus Christ as a man child, and saw that "the dragon . . . persecuted the woman which brought forth the man child."[2] From his vision John reported that "the dragon was wroth with the woman, and *went to make war with the remnant of her seed,* which keep the commandments of God, and have the testimony of Jesus Christ.[3]

In symbolic form John described Satan's followers (functioning in political as well as religious roles) as beasts. He spoke of one of them, saying that "the dragon (Satan) gave him his power, and his seat, and great authority."[4] John warned of the power this "beast" will wield when the time comes for the conflict with the saints to take place:

> And it was given unto him to make war with the saints, *and to over come them: and power was given him over all kindreds, and tongues, and nations.*
>
> And all that dwell upon the earth *shall worship him,* whose names are not written in the book of life of the Lamb slain from the foundation of the world.[5]

John spoke of another "beast" which would arise in this period, and foretold the great power he would exert:

> . . . *he exerciseth all the power of the first beast before him, and causeth the earth and them which d well therein to worship the first beast,* whose deadly wound was healed.
>
> And he *doeth great wonders,* so that he maketh fire come down from heaven on the earth in the sight of men,
>
> And *deceiveth them* that dwell on the earth by the means of those miracles which he had power to do in the sight of the beast;saying to them that dwell on the earth, that they should make an image to the beast, which had the wound by a sword, and did live.

---

1. Rev. 12:9.
2. Rev. 12:13.
3. Rev. 12:17.
4. Rev. 13:2.
5. Rev. 13:7-8. Verse 8 does not appear to indicate a universal alignment with Satan when this period transpires, but rather warns that those who follow him at that day will not have their names recorded in the Lamb's book of life. (See D&C 88:2; 76:68; Heb. 12:23; Rev. 21:24-27; Phil. 4:3; Rev. 3:5; Dan. 12:1-2; D&C 128:8; 132:19; Ex. 32:33.)

And he had power to give life unto the image of the beast, that the image of the beast should both speak, and *cause that as many as would not worship the image of the beast should be killed.*

And he causeth all, both small and great, rich and poor, free and bond, to receive a mark in their right hands, or in their foreheads:

And that no man might buy or sell, save he that had the mark, or the name of the beast, or the number of his name.

Here is wisdom Let him that hath understanding count the number of the beast: for it is the number of a man; and his number is *Six hundred threescore and six.*[1]

---

1. Rev. 13:12-18. Note that the Savior also warned of deception in the last days through miracles that "shall deceive the very elect." (Mt. 24:24, Mk. 13:22, J.S.1:22. Compare with 2 Ne. 25:18, D&C 64:37-39; Mos. 15:13;Rev. 2:2).

The number 666 has provided an interpretational field day for Bible commentators, who since the reformation have devised a continually growing list of numerical explanations. Protestants asserted that the number referred to the Roman Catholic Pope, drawing the Roman numeral equivalents from the title on the papal crown: VICARIVS/FILII/ DEI.

A second Protestant interpretation is based on the word Lateinos, which also contains numerical letters totaling 666—the assertion being that the church of Rome is the Latin church because of its origin and language. A corollary to this interpretation is that the Hebrew word for Lateinos is Romiith, which also produces numerical letters totaling 666 in the Hebrew language.

Athird interpretation is that the prophecy was filled in Roman times by Nero redivivus. The name Neron Caesar is translated into Hebrew letters, which give the numerical equivalent of 666.

An interpretation based on the Preterist interpretational viewpoint of the book of Revelation is similar to the above. It goes into Pythagorean numerology, seeing 666 as a triangular number being the sum of numbers 1-36 inclusive; 36 is the sum of numbers 1-8, so 666 is resolved into the number 8, connected with Rev. 17:11, and comes out with the conclusion that the Antichrist is Nero redivivus.

A fifth interpretation is aimed against the founder of the Seventh-day Adventists, Helen Harmon White. Her name, in Greek numerology, also yields 666.

Hitler becomes 666 in a numbering system that assumes A is 100, B is lO1, C is lO2, etc.

Stalin is 666 when his Russian name Dzugashvili is used in a system that assumes that A is 49, B is 50, C is 51, etc.

The author has even seen in print a numbering system in which 'Church of Jesus Christ of Latter-day Saints" is asserted to total 666.

Latest in the interpretational assertions to come to the author's attention is reference to a giant computer at the headquarters of the Common Market Confederacy. It is asserted that computer experts are working on a plan to computerize all world trade, assigning a number to every human on earth which would be invisibly laser-tattooed on the forehead or back of the hand. The number would show up under infra-red scanners at all check-

Daniel's Warning: The Horn Will Wear Out the Saints and They Shall Be Given Into His Hand (Dan. 7:21-27)

The prophet Daniel also saw key events of the last days in vision. He described a great power as a "beast" and a "horn," warning that the horn would make war against the saints. Like John, he saw that the saints would fare poorly in this conflict:

> I beheld, and the *same horn made war with the saints, and prevailed against them;*
>
> *Until the Ancient of Days came,* and judgment was given to the Saints of the most High; and the time came that the saints possessed the kingdom.
>
> Thus he said, The fourth beast shall be the fourth kingdom upon earth, which shall be diverse from all kingdoms, and shall devour the whole earth, and shall tread it down, and break it in pieces.
>
> And the ten horns out of this kingdom are ten kings that shall arise: and another shall rise after them; and *he shall be diverse from The first,* and he shall subdue three kings.
>
> And *he shall speak great words against the most High, and shall wear out the saints of the most High, and think to change times and laws: and they shall be given into his hand* until a time and times and the dividing of time.
>
> But the judgment shall sit, and they shall take away his dominion, to consume and to destroy it unto the end.
>
> And the kingdom and dominion, and the greatness of the kingdom under the whole heaven, shall be given to the people of the saints of the most High, whose kingdom is an everlasting kingdom, and all dominions shall serve and obey him.[1]

---

out counters and places of business. Without his assigned number, no one would be able to buy or sell. The program is being devised as a restoration plan to be implemented in the aftermath of world chaos.

---

1. Dan.7:21-27. These passages from John and Daniel have proved controversial throughout Christianity and, indeed, within Mormondom. Early LDS leaders expressed varying opinions concerning how they should be used and interpreted. Joseph Smith, for instance, expounded at length on the images and beasts of both the book of Daniel and the Revelation of St John, (Apr. 8, 1843: TPJS pp. 287-294; HC 5:339-345), and in doing so expressed his opinion that "It is not very essential for the elders to have knowledge in relation to the meaning of beasts, and heads and horns, and other figures made use of in the revelations; still, it ma., be necessary, to prevent contention and division and do away with suspense " (TPJS p. 287) He regarded the persecution of the saints prophesied by Daniel as an actual event which will occur in the last days scenario, for he commented that "The 'Horn' made war with the Saints and overcame them, until the Ancient of Days came; judgment was given to the Saints of the Most High from the Ancient of Days;.. . " (HC 3:389. This prophecy is linked with an extensive prophetic statement warning the church of future suffering the saints must endure. See HC 3:389-391.)

While these passages are difficult to interpret with exactness, their major messages are clear, and in harmony with Nephi's visions, and interpretative wrangling must not be allowed to obscure them:[1]

1. There will be conflict between the church of the devil and the saints of the Lamb of God in the last days.

2. The conflict, for a time, will go badly for the saints. Satan will prevail over them and overcome them to a degree. This will be a period of great distress.

3. The turning point will be the arrival of the Ancient of Days, when judgment is given to the Saints.

Nephi's Warning: Multitudes Will Gather Among Gentile Nations to Fight Against the Lord's Church (1 Ne. 14:11-13)

Nephi's continuing prophecy describes what will happen after the future "marvelous work" a divisive event which will cause people to muster into two distinct factions. He describes the buildup of the antagonism and locates it primarily among the Gentile (Caucasian) nations. He also emphasizes that the wickedness of the abominable church will have restricted the size and growth of the Lord's church:

> And it came to pass that I looked and beheld the whore of all the earth, and *she sat upon many waters; and she had dominion over all the earth, among all nations, kindreds, tongues, and people.*
>
> And it came to pass that I beheld the *church of the lamb of God, and its numbers* were few, because of the wickedness and abominations of the whore who sat upon many waters; nevertheless, I beheld that *the church of the Lamb, who were the saints of God, were also upon all the face of the earth;* and their dominions upon the face of the earth were small, because of the wickedness of the great whore whom I saw.
>
> And it came to pass that I beheld that *the great mother of abominations did gather together multitudes upon the face of all the earth, among all the nations of the Gentiles, to fight against the Lamb of God.*[2]

Nephi's prophecy continues by describing the fall of the great and abominable church, as do several other prophetic passages. A significant aspect of these passages, however, is that they contain clues to

---

1. For comment on portions of this chapter pertaining to the Council at Adam-ondi-Ahman see the author's book, *Prophecy—Key to the Future* (Salt Lake City, Utah: Bookcraft, 1962), pp. 167-176. See also Duane S. Crowther, "Daniel," *Prophets and Prophecies of the Old Testament,* (Bountiful, Utah: Horizon Publishers, 1973), pp. 496-527.
2. 1 Ne. 14:11-13.

what the saints must endure during this period of tribulation. These clues will be considered in this chapter in the form of prophetic warnings before the prophesied fall of the great and abominable church is described.

Nephi's Warning: Nations Shall Dig a Pit to Ensnare the People of the Lord and Pervert the Lord's Ways (1 Ne. 22:14)

As he tells how the great and abominable church will be destroyed by nations warring among themselves in a far-reaching world war, Nephi indites the wicked with three prophetic accusations. According to his prophecy, they will:

1. fight as nations against the house of Israel,
2. dig a pit to ensnare the people of the Lord, and
3. pervert the right ways of the Lord.

This is his prophetic utterance:

> *Every nation which shall war against thee,* O house of Israel, shall be turned one against another, and they shall fall into *the pit which they digged to ensnare the people of the Lord.* And all that *fight against Zion* shall be destroyed, and that great whore, who hath *perverted the right ways of the Lord,* yea, that great and abominable church, shall tumble to the dust and great shall be the fall of it.l

The nature of the pit, or entrapment, which the unrighteous will attempt to use against the people of the Lord is not described in the passage. However, the possibility that it is related to the "marvelous work" which will divide people into "save two churches only"[2] is great.

Nephi's Warning: The Wicked Will Turn Aside the Just and Revile Against Good (2 Ne. 28:16)

As he prophesies of the wickedness of organized religion in the last days[3] and foretells the fall of the great and abominable church,[4] Nephi again indites the wicked for their persecution of the saints. He warns:

---

1. 1 Ne. 22:14
2. Review 1 Ne 14:7-10.
3. 2 Ne. 28:1 -17.
4. 2 Ne. 28:18.

> Wo unto them that *turn aside the just for a thing of naught and revile against that which is good, and say it is of no worth!* For the day shall come that the Lord God will speedily visit the inhabitants of the earth; and in that day they that are fully ripe in iniquity they shall perish.[1]

He adds that at that day Satan will "rage in the hearts of the children of men, and *stir them up to anger against that which is good.*"[2]

Again the picture is portrayed: anger against the saints for doing good while others are committed to evil.

Jacob's Warning: The Lord's People Shall Be Oppressed, Prey, and Captives of the Mighty (2 Ne. 6:17-18)

Yet another passage which will be considered as the fall of the great and abominable church is described and yields clues as to what the Lord's people must first endure. Jacob describes the saints as being:

1. captives of the mighty,
2. prey of the terrible,
3. contended with, and
4. oppressed by their enemies.

His prophecy, which details the fall of the great and abominable church,[3] ends with this warning to the wicked:

> But thus saith the Lord: Even the *captives of the mighty* shall be taken away, and the *prey of the terrible* shall be delivered; for the Mighty God shall deliver his covenant people. For thus saith the Lord: I will contend with *them that contendeth with thee*—
>
> And I will feed *them that oppress thee,* with their own flesh; and they shall be drunken with their own blood as with sweet wine; and all flesh shall know that I the Lord am thy Savior and thy Redeemer, the Mighty One of Jacob.[4]

John's Warning: The Woman Will Be Drunken with Blood of the Saints and Martyrs (Rev. 17:6)

John the Revelator characterizes the capital city of the great and abominable church as a "great city. which reigneth over the kings of

1. 2 Ne. 28:16.
2. 2 Ne. 28:20.
3. 2 Ne. 6:12-18.
4. 2 Ne. 6:17-18.

the earth."[1] As he begins to describe the fall of the great and abominable church, he gives grim reminder of the death and slaughter she will have brought upon the Lord's people:

> And I saw the woman *drunken with the blood of the saints, and with the blood of the martyrs of Jesus:* and when I saw her, I wondered with great admiration [2]

John's Warning: Ten Kings Will Make War with the Lamb (Rev. 17:12-14)

As John the Revelator described the woman, or capital city of the great and abominable church, he indicated that the city had "ten horns," or control over ten kings or nations which would function for a short interval in the last days scenario. He indicated that these nations would give their strength to the beast and wage war against the Lord's people:

> And the *ten horns which thou sawest are ten kings,* which have received no kingdom as yet; but *receive power as kings one hour with the beast.*
>
> These have one mind, and shall give their power and strength unto the beast
>
> These shall make war with the Lamb, and the Lamb shall overcome them.[3]

Though we do not yet know who these nations will be, John's warning is similar to those of the other prophets previously cited, that the Lord's people will have to endure war with the forces of Antichrist—war on a large, multi-nation scale—world war!

Prophecies of World War as the Great and Abominable Church is Destroyed

Nephi, in his great chronological prophecy of 1 Nephi 11-14, describes the disunity and chaos which will come upon the great and abominable church as it prepares to wage war against the saints After foretelling how the mother of abominations will gather among all the Gentile nations to fight against the Lamb of God, he describes the power of God which will be with the saints and also the divine wrath

1. Rev. 17:18.
2. Rev 17:6.
3. Rev. 1 7:12-14

which will cause the nations dominated by the mother of abominations to fight among themselves:

> And it came to pass that I, Nephi, beheld *the power of the Lamb of God, that it descended upon the saints of the church of the Lamb, and upon the covenant people of the Lord,* who were scattered upon all the face of the earth; and they were armed with righteousness and with the power of God in great glory.
>
> And it came to pass that I beheld that *the wrath of God was poured out upon the great and abominable church, insomuch that there were wars and rumors of wars among all the nations and kindreds of the earth.*
>
> And as there began to be wars and rumors of wars among all the nations which belonged to the mother of abominations, the angel spake unto me, saying: Behold, the wrath of God is upon the mother of harlots; and behold, thou seest all these things—
>
> *And when the day cometh that the wrath of God is poured out upon the mother of harlots, which is the great and abominable church of all the earth, whose foundation is The devil, then, at that day, the work of the Father shall commence, in preparing the way for the fulfilling of his covenants, which he hath made to his people who are of the house of Israel.*[1]

In another prophecy made by Nephi, the fall of the great and abominable church is also described. Again the event is linked to the time of the gathering of Israel.[2] Again the description is one of international war, with nations who had been warring against the Lord's people suddenly turning on one another and wreaking great destruction:

> *And the blood of that great and abominable church, which is the whore of all the earth, shall turn upon their own heads; for they shall war among themselves, and the sword of their own hands shall fall upon their own heads, and they shall be drunken with their own blood.*
>
> *And every nation which shall war against thee, O house of Israel, shall be turned one against another,* and they shall fall into the pit which they digged to ensnare the people of the Lord.
>
> *And all that fight against Zion shall be destroyed, and that great whore, who hath perverted the right ways of the Lord, yea, that great and*

---

1. 1 Ne 14:14-17. Verse 17 provides an important chronological clue, when linked with verses 27-29 of the Lord's prophetic panorama of 3 Nephi, chapter 21 This relationship indicates that the fall of the great and abominable church will not occur until after internal warfare in the Americas (3 Ne 21:12-22), the building of the New Jerusalem (3 Ne 21:23), the gathering to the New Jerusalem of the Lamanites (3 Ne. 21:24), an appearance of Christ there (3 Ne. 21:25), and the preaching of the gospel among the dispersed of Israel, including the lost tribes (3 Ne. 21:26).
2. 1 Ne 22:9-11.

> *abominable church, shall tumble to the dust* and great shall be the fall of it.
>
> For behold, saith the prophet, the time cometh speedily that Satan shall have no more power over the hearts of the children of men; for the day soon cometh that all the proud and they who do wickedly shall be as stubble; and the day cometh that they must be burned.
>
> For the time soon cometh that the fulness of the wrath of God shall be poured out upon all the children of men; for *he will not suffer that the wicked shall destroy the righteous.*
>
> Wherefore, he will preserve the righteous by his power, even if it so be that the fulness of his wrath must come, and *the righteous be preserved, even unto the destruction of their enemies by fire.* Wherefore, the righteous need not fear; for thus saith the prophet, they shall be saved, even if it so be as by fire.
>
> Behold, my brethren, I say unto you, that these things must shortly come; yea, even *blood, and fire, and vapor of smoke must come;* and it must needs be upon the face of this earth; and it cometh unto men according to the flesh if it so be that they will harden their hearts against the Holy One of Israel.
>
> For behold, *the righteous shall not perish; for the time surely must come that all they who fight against Zion shall be cut off.*[1]

That the fall of the evil church is an event of major significance was emphasized by Nephi, who in yet another prophetic context taught that the "great and abominable church, the whore of *all the earth,* must tumble to the earth, and *great must be the fall thereof.*[2]

As John the Revelator described "the judgment of the great whore that sitteth upon many waters,"[3] he told of the destruction which would come upon the "woman," or capital city of the great and abominable church. He identified this city as being "arrayed in purple and scarlet colour, and decked with gold and precious stones and pearls,"[4] and being full of abominations, filthiness and fornication.[5] The city will be situated on seven mountains,[6] and be a large or "great" city which reigns over kings[7] and which is noted for its trade.[8] It will be sufficiently near to the ocean that men on ships will be able to see "the smoke of her burning."[9]

John sees that the great city is suddenly destroyed, "in one hour,"[10] by the ten kings or nations who had previously supported it and made war[11] against the Lamb of God:

---

1. 1 Ne. 22:13-19.
2. 2 Ne. 28:18.
3. Rev. 17:1.
4. Rev. 17:4.
5. *Ibid.*
6. Rev. 17:9.
7. Rev. 17:18.
8. Rev. 18:3, 11-16.
9. Rev. 18:17-18.
10. Rev. 18:17. And what instrument of war has modern man devised that can instantly destroy a huge, sprawling city, leaving smoke billowing high into the sky above the mountains?
11. See again Rev. 17:12-14.

> *And the ten horns which thou sawest upon the beast, these shall hate the whore, and shall make her desolate and naked, and shall eat her flesh, and burn her with fire.*[1]

John saw and described her downfall:

> And I heard another voice from heaven, saying, *Come out of her, my people, that ye be not partakers of her sins, and that ye receive not of her plagues.*
>
> For her sins have reached unto heaven, and God hath remembered her iniquities.
>
> *Reward her even as she rewarded you,* and double unto her double according to her works: in the cup which she hath filled fill to her double.
>
> How much she hath glorified herself, and lived deliciously, so much torment and sorrow give her: for she saith in her heart, I sit a queen, and am no widow, and shall see no sorrow.
>
> *Therefore shall her plagues come in one day, death, and mourning, and famine; and she shall be utterly burned with fire:* for strong is the Lord God who judgeth her.
>
> And the kings of the earth, who have committed fornication and lived deliciously with her, shall bewail her, and lament for her, when they shall see the smoke of her burning,
>
> Standing afar off for the fear of her torment, saying, Alas, alas, that great city Babylon, that mighty city! *for in one hour is thy judgment come.*[2]

Its downfall will serve to avenge the saints for the many losses they will have suffered at her hands:

> Rejoice over her, thou heaven, and *ye holy apostles and prophets;* for God hath avenged you on her. . . .
>
> *And in her was found the blood of prophets, and of saints, and of all that were slain upon the earth.*[3]

Summary

1. Both Book of Mormon and Biblical passages warn of the existence of a great and abominable church. The message of these passages is that this church will persecute and make war upon the saints, but will collapse and fall when nations previously under its control war among themselves and then destroy the church's capital city.

---

1. Rev. 17:16.
2. Rev. 18:4-10.
3. Rev. 18:20, 24.

2. Numerous clues from,-the scriptures help to identify the great and abominable church:

A. The church was founded shortly after the ministry of Christ in the meridian of time (1 Ne.13:26; compare the chronological relationship of 1 Ne. 13:5-9 with 1 Ne.11:15-23,12:6-10).
B. The church was founded prior to the voyage of Columbus and the settling of America by the European Gentiles (compare the chronological relationship of 1 Ne. 13:5-9 with 1 Ne.13:12-13).
C. The church is founded across the waters from America among the nations and kingdoms of the Gentiles (1 Ne.13:3-4, 10).
D. The church is abominable above all other churches (1 Ne. 13:5), so it is a church, and not "general wickedness" or a combination of churches.
E. The church slays, tortures, binds, and imprisons the saints of God (1 Ne.13:5).
F. The devil is its foundation (1 Ne.13:6).
G. The church has gold, silver, silks, scarlets, fine linen and precious clothing (1 Ne.13:7).
H. The church has many harlots (1 Ne.13:7).
I. The church desires riches (1 Ne.13:8).
J. The church destroys and imprisons the saints for the praise of the world (1 Ne.13:9).
K. The church receives the gospel from Christ's apostles and the Jews, but takes away many plain and precious parts and many covenants (1 Ne.13:26-27).
L. The church takes away many plain and precious things from the book of the Lamb of God—the Bible (1 Ne. 13:28).
M. The church removes portions of the Bible before that book goes to the nations of the Gentiles or is brought to America (1 Ne.13:29).
N. The church removes portions of the Bible, which causes many to stumble, prior to the restoration of the gospel (1 Ne.13:34).
O. The capital city of the church sits on seven mountains (Rev.17:9).
P. The capital city of the church is a great city which reigns over the kings of the earth (Rev. 17:18).

Q. The capital city of the church is a great center of commerce which has made many merchants rich (Rev. 18:3, 11-15).
R. The capital city is located close enough to the sea that people on ships will be able to see smoke rising from it as it burns (Rev. 18:17-18).

3. Book of Mormon prophecies indicate that in the future God will do a "marvelous work," by bringing to pass some event which will divide people into two distinct groups, the righteous and the wicked. After this event there will be "two churches only." (1 Ne. 14:7-10.)

4. The "marvelous work" which is also mentioned in 1 Ne. 22:8-19; 2 Ne. 25:17-18; 2 Ne. 27:1-5, 25-32; 2 Ne. 28:32-29:14; 3 Ne. 21:9-29; and 3 Ne. 28:25-32, is continually linked in the scriptures with future last days events and is therefore regarded as being an event other than the restoration of the gospel through Joseph Smith. It may be the same as the Lord's "strange act" mentioned in D&C 101:85-95, in which the saints are depicted as importuning before judges, governors, and the president just before the Lord in his fury vexes the nation.

5. Prophetic warnings concerning the tribulations which will come to the saints and the house of Israel because of the great and abominable church in the last days were cited from:

A. Jacob (2 Ne. 6:12).
B. Paul (1 Tim. 4:1-3).
C. John (Rev. 12:17-13:18).
D. Daniel (Dan. 7:21-27).
E. Nephi (1 Ne. 14:11-13).
F. Nephi (1 Ne. 22:14).
G. Nephi (2 Ne. 28:16).
H. Jacob (2 Ne. 6:17-18).
I. John (Rev. 17:6).
J. John (Rev. 17:12-14).

6. Several of the prophetic warnings indicate that the Lord's people will be the recipients of false charges and evil allegations brought by the great and abominable church as the last days conflict takes shape:

A. Nephi: Satan will stir them to anger against that which is good (2 Ne. 28:20).
B. Paul: They will speak lies in hypocrisy, without conscience (1 Tim. 4:2).
C. Daniel: The horn shall speak great words against the most High (Dan. 7:25).
D. Nephi: The nations will dig a pit to ensnare the people of the Lord (1 Ne. 22:14).
E. Nephi: The whore shall pervert the right ways of the Lord (1 Ne. 22:14).
F. Nephi: They will turn aside the just for a thing of naught (2 Ne. 28:16).
G. Nephi: They will revile against that which is good, and say it is of no worth (2 Ne. 28:16).
H. Jacob: They will contend with the covenant people (2 Ne. 6:17).

7. The prophecies warn that the great and abominable church will exercise great control over the saints during the period of persecution and tribulation:

A. John: The beast will make war with the saints and overcome them. Power is given him over all kindreds, tongues, and nations (Rev. 13:7-8).
B. John: Another beast has power to cause that as many as would not worship the image of the beast should be killed (Rev. 13:15).
C. John: The beast causes all to receive a number in their right hands or foreheads; they cannot buy or sell without it (Rev. 13:16-17).
D. Daniel: The horn made war with the saints, and prevailed against them (Dan. 7:21).
E. Daniel: The horn shall wear out the saints, and they shall be given into his hand (Dan. 7:25).
F. Jacob: The captives of the mighty shall be taken away, for God shall deliver his covenant people (2 Ne. 6:17).

8. The great and abominable church will wield international political power.

A. Nephi: She had dominion over all nations, kindreds, tongues, and people (1 Ne. 14:11).

B. Nephi: The mother of abominations did gather multitudes upon the face of all the earth, among all the nations of the Gentiles (1 Ne. 14:13).
C. John: Ten kings receive power one hour, and shall give their power and strength unto the beast (Rev. 17:12-13).
D. John: The "woman," or capital city, reigns over kings (Rev. 17:18).

9. The effort to fight against the saints will disintegrate into world war—international war in which the Gentile nations do battle with one another and finally destroy the capital city of the great and abominable church:

A. Nephi: Every nation which shall war against the house of Israel shall be turned one against another (1 Ne. 22:14).
B. Jacob: I will feed them that oppress thee with their own flesh (2 Ne. 6:18).
C. Nephi: There were wars and rumors of wars among all the nations and kindreds of the earth (1 Ne. 14:15).
D. Nephi: The great and abominable church shall war among themselves (1 Ne. 22:13).
E. John: The ten horns shall hate the whore and shall burn her with fire (Rev. 17:16).
F. John: Her plagues shall come in one day: death, famine, and fire (Rev. 18:8).

10. Though many of the saints will be slain by the great and abominable church (Rev. 13:15; 17:6), the righteous will ultimately be preserved while they who fight against Zion will be cut off and destroyed (1 Ne. 22:16-19).

VII

Seventh Warning: If Secret Combinations Are Allowed To Spread, the Nation Will Be Destroyed

Moroni's Warning: If a Nation Allows Secret Combinations to Spread Over It, the Nation Will Be Destroyed (Eth. 8:21)

The Book of Mormon bears strong and compelling testimony concerning one of man's most corrupt practices: the organizing of secret combinations to obtain power and wealth through evil deeds. The message of the scriptures is that such a "*combination is most abominable and wicked above all, in the sight of God; For the Lord worketh not in secret combinations,* neither doth he will that man should shed blood, but in all things hath forbidden it."[1]

A powerful warning was given by Moroni to the last days inhabitants of the Americas as he wrote concerning the danger of secret combinations. After warning that secret combinations had caused the destruction of two great cultures, the Jaredites and the Nephites,[2] the last Book of Mormon prophet wrote a warning which may have far-reaching significance during the great panorama of last days events:

> . . . *whatsoever nation shall uphold such secret combinations, to get power and gain, until they shall spread over the nation, behold, they shall be destroyed;* for the Lord will not suffer that the blood of his saints, which shall be shed by them, shall always cry unto him from the ground for vengeance upon them and yet he avenge them not.[3]

His admonition was specifically addressed to the latter-day Gentiles, or inhabitants of America, as a preliminary to a second, and more specific warning concerning a last days secret combination which he saw would be international in scope and objectives:

Moroni's Warning: A Secret Combination Will Seek to Overthrow the Freedom of All Nations (Eth.8:23-26)

As he prophesied to the "Gentiles" who would read his words in the last days, he not only warned of a specific secret combination of

1. Eth. 8:18-19. 2. Eth. 8:21. 3. Eth. 8:22.

international proportions which would come, hut commanded the inhabitants of America that they must awake to the sense of their awful situation because of the presence of the combination among them:

> Wherefore, O ye Gentiles, it is wisdom in God that these things should be shown unto you, that thereby ye may repent of your sins, *and suffer not that these murderous combinations shall get above you, which are built up to get power and gain—and the work, yea, even the work of destruction come upon you, yea, even the sword of the justice of the Eternal God shall fall upon you, to your overthrow and destruction if ye shall suffer these things to be.*
>
> Wherefore, the Lord *commandeth you, when ye shall see these things come among you that ye shall awake to a sense of your awful situation, because of this secret combination which shall be among you;* or wo be unto it, because of the blood of them who have been slain; for they cry from the dust for vengeance upon it, and also upon those who built it up.
>
> For it cometh to pass that *whoso buildeth it up seeketh to overthrow the freedom of all lands, nations, and countries; and it bringeth to pass the destruction of all people,* for it is built up by the devil, who is the father of all lies; even that same liar who beguiled our first parents, yea, even that same liar who hath caused man to commit murder from the beginning; who hath hardened the hearts of men that they have murdered the prophets, and stoned them, and cast them out from the beginning.
>
> *Wherefore, I, Moroni, am commanded to write these things that evil may be d one away,* and that the time may come that Satan may have no power upon the hearts of the children of men, but that they may be persuaded to do good continually, that they may come unto the fountain of all righteousness and be saved.[1]

His prophecy was not only concerned with the danger from the secret combination, but was a warning that if a nation allowed the spread of such an organization in its midst, it would be so corrupt that God's justice would soon cause the fall and overthrow of that nation a sobering thought!

Nephi's Warning: Satan Will Bind Secret Combinations With His Strong Cords Forever (2 Ne. 26:20-23)

Moroni wasn't alone in his prophetic warning of secret combinations among the latter-day Gentiles—Nephi also foresaw the last days existence of such combinations and the danger they would bring:

1. Eth. 8:23-26.

> *And the Gentiles are lifted up in the pride of their eyes, and have stumbled,* because of the greatness of their stumbling block, that they have built up many churches; nevertheless, they put down the power and miracles of God, and preach up unto themselves their own wisdom and their own learning, that they may get gain and grind upon the face of the poor.
>
> And there are many churches built up which cause envyings, and strifes, and malice.
>
> And *there are also secret combinations, even as in times of old, according to the combinations of the devil, for he is the foundation of all these things; yea, the foundation of murder, and works of darkness;* yea, and he leadeth them by the neck with a flaxen cord, until *he bindeth them with his strong cords forever.*
>
> For behold, my beloved brethren I say unto you that the Lord God worketh not in darkness.[1]

Nephi's Warning: God Must Destroy Secret Works of darkness (2 Ne. 10:15)

Nephi had previously warned of the danger of secret combinations in a context that had international implications. After prophesying that God would "fortify this land against all other nations,"[2] he warned that "he that fighteth against Zion shall perish, saith God,"[3] and then cited the Lord's prophetic promise that "*I must needs destroy the secret works of darkness, and of murders, and of abominations.*"[4]

Alma's Warning: Cursed Be the Land Forever to Secret Combinations, Even Unto Destruction (Al. 37:28, 31)

Alma also warned that the land would be cursed and destroyed unless the inhabitants repent of the influence of secret combinations. He was instructing his son, Helaman, concerning the secret oaths and evil plans found in the twenty-four plates of the Jaredite records. He reiterated that the Jaredites had been destroyed because they embraced the workings of the secret combinations, asserted that such secret works would be brought to light, and told his son not to pass on the details of the secret oaths, covenants, and abominations:

> And now, I will speak unto you concerning those twenty-four plates, that ye keep them, that the mysteries and the works of darkness, and their

1. 2 Ne. 26:20-23.
2. 2 Ne. 10:12.
3. 2 Ne. 10:13.
4. 2 Ne. 10:15.

secret works, or the secret works of those people who have beer destroyed, may be made manifest unto this people; yea, *all their murders and robbings, and their plunderings, and all their wickedness and abominations, may be made manifest unto this people;* yea, and that ye preserve these interpreters.

For behold, the Lord saw that his people began to work in darkness yea, work secret murders and abominations; therefore the Lord said, if they did not repent they should be destroyed from off the face of the earth.

And the Lord said: I will prepare unto my servant Gazelem, a stone which shall shine forth in darkness unto light, that I may discover unto my people who serve me, that I may discover unto them the works of their brethren, yea, their secret works, their works of darkness, and their wickedness and abominations.

And now, my son, these interpreters were prepared that the word of God might be fulfilled, which he spake, saying:

I will bring forth out of darkness unto light all their secret works and their abominations;and except they repent I will destroy them from off the face of the earth; and I will bring to light all their secrets and abominations, unto every nation that shall hereafter possess the land.

And now, my son, we see that *they did not repent; therefore they have been destroyed,* and thus far the word of God has been fulfilled yea, their secret abominations have been brought out of darkness and made known unto us.

And now, my son, I command you that ye retain all their oaths, and their covenants, and their agreements in their secret abominations; yea, and *all their signs and their wonders ye shall keep from this people, that they know them not,* lest peradventure they should fall into darkness also and be destroyed.[1]

Then Alma stated the first of his warnings of the curse that hangs over this land if the people embrace the works of secret combinations:

For behold, there is a curse upon all this land, that destruction shall come upon all those workers of darkness, according to the power of God, when they are fully ripe; therefore I desire that this people might not be destroyed.[2]

He explained to Helaman what the people should be taught concerning secret combinations:

Therefore ye shall *keep these secret plans of their oaths and their covenants from this people,* and only their wickedness and their murders and their abominations shall ye make known unto them; and ye shall

1. Al. 37:21-27.
2. Al. 37:28.

> teach them to abhor such wickedness and abominations and murders; and ye shall also *teach them that these people were destroyed on account of their wickedness and abominations and their murders.*
>
> *For behold, they murdered all the prophets of the Lord who came among them to declare unto them concerning their iniquities;* and the blood of those whom they murdered did cry unto the Lord their God for vengeance upon those who were their murderers; and thus the judgments of God did come upon these workers of darkness and secret combinations.

And then Alma repeated his prophetic warning concerning secret combinations in America that spans all eras of time:

> Yea, and *cursed be the land forever and ever unto those workers of darkness and secret combinations, even unto destruction,* except they repent before they are fully ripe.[2]

Secret Combinations Prior to the Savior's Mortal Advent: A Chronicle of the Rapid Growth of Evil in Government

The record of the rapid rise of secret combinations in Book of Mormon days shows the great power which such groups can rapidly acquire. One such combination was formed when Gadianton became leader of a robber band about 50 B.C.[3] His network of evil doers began to grow "in the more settled parts of the land."[4] At that time they were "*not known unto those who were at the head o f government;* therefore they were not destroyed out of the land. "[5]

In this era the Nephite society had become soft and corrupt, "For behold, the Lord had blessed them so long with the riches of the world that they had not been stirred up to anger, to wars, nor to bloodshed; therefore they began to set their hearts upon their riches; yea, *they began to seek to get gain that they might be lifted up one above another; therefore they began to commit secret murders, and to rob and to plunder, that they might get gain.*"[6] With the people in this condition, they were ripe for Satan's influence to be manifested on a national level, and

> . . . behold, *Satan did stir up the hearts of the more part of the Nephites, insomuch that they did unite with those bands of robbers, and*

1. Al. 37:29-30.
2. Al. 37:31.
3. Hel 2:2-11. This was in the 42nd year of the reign of the judges
4. Hel 3:23. This was in the 49th year Or the reign of the judges.
5. *Ibid.*
6. Hel. 6:17.

> *did enter into Their covenants and their oaths, that they would protect and preserve one another* in whatsoever difficult circumstances they should be placed, that they should not suffer for their murders, and their plunderings, and their stealings.
>
> And it came to pass that *they did have their signs, yea, their secret signs, and their secret words;* and this that they might distinguish a brother who had entered into the covenant, that whatsoever wickedness his brother should do he should not be injured by his brother, nor by those who did belong to his band, who had taken this covenant.
>
> *And thus they might murder, and plunder, and steal, and commit whoredoms and all manner of wickedness, contrary to the laws of their country and also the laws of Their God.*
>
> And whosoever of those who belonged to their band should reveal unto the world of their wickedness and their abominations, should be tried, not according to the laws of their country, but according to the laws of their wickedness, which had been given by Gadianton and Kishkumen.[1]

It wasn't long until Satan "got great hold upon the hearts of the Nephites; yea, insomuch that they had become exceedingly wicked; yea, *the more part of them had turned out of the way of righteousness.*"[2]

Only a short period transpired from the formation of the secret combination to the day when the majority of the Nephite population had joined it—only eighteen years.[3] In one more year their infiltration was so extensive that "*they did obtain the sole management of the government.*"[4] When in full governmental control they began to persecute the righteous, "Insomuch that they did trample under their feet and smite and rend and turn their backs upon the poor and the meek, and the humble followers of God. "[5] These few verses not only chronicle the rise of a secret combination, but describe the characteristics which make them such an abomination in the sight of God. Note them:

1. The members make covenants to protect each other so they won't have to pay for their crimes.
2. They have signs and passwords.

---

1. Hel 6:21-24.
2. Hel. 6:31.
3. Compare Hel. 3:22-24 [the 49th year...] when the people were righteous and only a handful of Gadiantons were functioning, still unknown to the government, and Hel. 6:31-32 [the 67th year. . .], when the majority had turned to wickedness.
4. Hel. 6:38-39.
5. Hel. 6:39.

3. They are willing to murder and steal to accomplish their ends.

4. If their members betray them, they are disciplined according to their own special code.

5. They flourish in a society which is dulled to the needs of social justice and which is devoted to seeking riches and power.

6. They strive to infiltrate and gain control of government, usurping the power and authority of the land.

7. They control the courts and judicial systems. Under their rule the righteous are condemned and the wicked go unpunished.

8. They grow rapidly and can gain control of a nation within two decades.

9. When in control, they persecute the poor and the righteous.

And then, with the people in such a wicked condition, the Lord revealed through Nephi the inevitable warning:

> *And except ye repent ye shall perish; yea, even your lands shall be taken from you, and ye shall be destroyed from off the face of the earth.*
>
> Behold now, I do not say that these things shall be, of myself, because it is not of myself that I know these things; but behold, *I know that these things are true because the Lord God has made them known unto me, therefore I testify that they shall be.*[1]

How did the people receive his prophetic warning in their wickedness? The judges raised their voices against Nephi, accusing him of reviling against the people and against their law:

> *Therefore they did cry unto the people, saying: Why do you suffer this man to revile against us? For behold he doth condemn all this people, even unto destruction;* yea, and also that these our cities shall be taken from us, that we shall have no place in them.
>
> And now we know that this is impossible, for behold, we are powerful, and our cities great, therefore our enemies can have no power over us,
>
> And it came to pass that *thus they did stir up the people to anger against Nephi . . .*[2]

Within three more years "the contentions did increase, insomuch that *there were wars throughout all the land among all the people of*

---

1. Hel. 7:28-29.
2. Hel. 8:5-7. See also verses 1-4. It was only Nephi's popularity among the people that saved him in this instance. Some of them recognized him as "a good man" and as a prophet. (See verses 7-10.)

Nephi. And it was this secret band of robbers who did carry on this work of destruction and wickedness."[1]

After three years of civil war the prophet Nephi pled with God that the people might not be completely destroyed by the sword. In answer to his prayer, God sent a famine to stir them up to repentance. Finally, after "*they did perish by thousands in the more wicked parts of the land*,"[2] they "began to remember the Lord their God."[3] The people repented and humbled themselves in sackcloth, and "swept away the band of Gadianton from among them" until the secret combination had "become extinct."[4]

But secret combinations, like pernicious weeds, keep springing up again and again, once they are established. How long did the newly-won period of freedom and righteousness last? Only five years! Then dissenters again united and formed the secret band, the robbers of Gadianton:

> *And they did commit murder and plunder; and then they would retreat back into the mountains*, and into the wilderness and secret places, hiding themselves that they could not be discovered, receiving daily an addition to their numbers, inasmuch as *there were dissenters that went forth unto them*.
>
> And thus in time, yea, even *in the space of not many years, they became an exceeding great band of robbers;* and they did search out all the secret plans of Gadianton; and thus they became robbers of Gadianton.
>
> Now behold, these robbers did make great havoc, yea, even great destruction among the people of Nephi, and also among the people of the Lamanites.[5]

The Gadianton forces grew so strong that even the whole armies of the Nephites and Lamanites could not stop them.[6] As the years passed, social unrest and discontent among the Nephites fed their ranks,[7] and they "had become so numerous, and *did slay so many of the people, and did lay waste so many cities, and did spread so much death and carnage throughout the land*."[8] that all the Nephites and Lamanites had to take up arms against them "*to maintain their rights, and the privileges of their church and of their worship, and their freedom and*

1. Hel. 11:1-2. This was the 72nd year of the reign of the judges.
2. Hel.11:6.
3. Hel 11:7.
4. Hel.11:10. This was the 75th year of the reign of the judges.
5. Hel 11:25-27. The Gadianton band was reformed in the 80th year of the reign of the judges.
6. Hel 11:28-33.
7. 3 Ne 1 27-28.
8. 3 Ne.2:11.

their liberty."[1] It was only after eight years of war,[2] in which the Nephites and Lamanites were forced to abandon their homes and to unite in one central place, living for many months from stored provisions without being able to farm their lands, and enduring the most savage warfare that the Nephites had ever known, that they were finally able to conquer the secret combination after slaying its armies by the tens of thousands.[3]

But once again, like the recurring malignancy of cancer, the secret combinations were organized. In less than ten years of peace, Satan again extended his influence and, through secret combinations, brought about the assassination of the chief judge and the destruction of national government.[4] Through whom did Satan work this time? Through a combination of church leaders (high priests), judges, and lawyers who plotted to destroy the governor and establish a king in the land.[5]

It was not until the great destruction at the time of Christ's death that a lasting end came to the long series of secret combinations.

---

1. 3 Ne. 2:12. This was the 104th year since the beginning of the reign of the judges, which was called the 13th year (after the birth of Christ) in the new Nephite numbering system (see 3 Ne. 2:5-8).
2. 3 Ne. 2:13; 3 Ne. 4:16. During this era the pressure on the righteous Nephites and Lamanites to defect to the Gadianton band was intense. A letter from Giddianhi, leader of the secret combination, to the Nephite governor, Lachoneus, is evidence of this pressure:

   I write unto you, desiring that ye would yield up unto this my people, your cities, your lands, and your possessions, rather than that they should visit you with the sword and that destruction should come upon you.

   Or in other words, yield yourselves up unto us, and unite with us and become acquainted with our secret works, and become our brethren that ye may be like unto us—not our slaves, but our brethren and partners of all our substance.

   And behold, I swear unto you, if ye will do this, with an oath, ye shall not be destroyed; but if ye will not do this, I swear unto you with An oath, that on the morrow month I will command that my armies shall come down against you, and they shall not stay their hand and shall spare not, hut shall slay you, and shall let fall the sword upon you even until ye shall become extinct.

   And behold, l am Giddianhi; and I am the governor of this the secret society of Gadianton; which society and the works thereof I know to be good; and they are of ancient date and they have been handed down unto us. (3 Ne. 3:6-9.)
3. 3 Ne. 4, 5:3-6.
4. 3 Ne. 7:1-2
5. 3 Ne. 6:10-30

Secret Combinations Caused Final Destruction of the Nephites

Two hundred years of peace and righteousness passed after the coming of the Savior to the Americas.[1] Then, as the Nephite society began to decay, secret combinations appeared once again. In just forty years, they "spread over all the face of the land:"

> And it came to pass that the wicked part of the people began again to build up the secret oaths and combinations of Gadianton.
>
> And also the people who were called *the people of Nephi began to be proud in their hearts, because of their exceeding riches, and become vain* like unto their brethren, the Lamanites.
>
> And from this time the disciples began to sorrow for the sins of the world.
>
> And it came to pass that when three hundred years had passed away, both the people of Nephi and the Lamanites had become exceeding wicked one like unto another.
>
> And it came to pass *that the robbers of Gadianton did spread over all the face of the land; and there were none that were righteous save it were the disciples of Jesus*. And gold and silver did they lay up in store in abundance, and did traffic in all manner of traffic.[2]

As the final destruction of the Nephites approached,

> . . . these Gadianton robbers, who were among the Lamanites, did infest the land, insomuch that *the inhabitants thereof began to hide up their treasures in the earth; and they became slippery, because the Lord had cursed the land, that they could not hold them, nor retain them again.*
>
> And it came to pass that there were sorceries, and witchcrafts, and magics; and the power of the evil one was wrought upon all the face of the land. . . .[3]

---

1. The Book of Mormon describes these choice years in this beautiful passage:

   > And it came to pass that there was no contention in the land, because of the love of God which did dwell in the hearts of the people.
   >
   > And there were no envyings, nor strifes, nor tumults, nor whoredoms, not Iyings, nor murders, nor any manner of lasciviousness; and surely there could not be a happier people among all the people who had been created by the hand of God.
   >
   > There were no robbers, nor murderers, neither were there Lamanites, not any manner of -ites; but they were in one, the children of Christ, and heirs to the kingdom of God.
   >
   > And how blessed were they! For the Lord did bless them in all their doings; yea, even they were blessed and prospered until an hundred and ten years had passed away; and the first generation from Christ had passed away, and there was no contention in all the land. (4 Ne. 15-18.)

2. 4 Ne. 42-46
3. Morm. 1:18-19. The record says ". . . no man could keep that which was his own, for the thieves, and the robbers, and the murderers, and the magic art, and the witchcraft which was in the land." (Morm. 2:10.)

"The land was filled with robbers and with Lamanites . . . and it was one complete revolution throughout all the face of the land."[1] This great wickedness eventually led through a long succession of battles to the final destruction of the Nephites at the Hill Cumorah, when almost a quarter of a million Nephite men, plus their women and children, were slain in one day.[2]

Secret Combinations Among the Jaredites

The Jaredites, an earlier Book of Mormon culture, also knew the effect of secret combinations. Prince Jared and his daughter enticed Akish to begin a secret combination in order to assassinate Jared's father, Omer, and usurp the kingdom:

> And it came to pass that Akish gathered in unto the house of Jared all his kinsfolk, and said unto them: Will ye swear unto me that ye will be faithful unto me in the thing which I shall desire of you?
>
> And it came to pass that they all sware unto him, by the God of heaven, and also by the heavens, and also by the earth, and by their heads, that whoso should vary from the assistance which Akish desired should lose his head; and whoso should divulge whatsoever thing Akish made known unto them, the same should lose his life.
>
> And it came to pass that thus they did agree with Akish. And *Akish did administer unto them the oaths which were given by them of old who also sought power, which had been handed down even from Cain, who was a murderer from the beginning.*
>
> *And they were kept up by the power of the devil to administer these oaths unto the people, to keep them in darkness, to help such as sought power to gain power, and to murder, and to plunder, and to lie, and to commit all manner of wickedness and whoredoms.*
>
> And it was the daughter of Jared who put it into his heart to search up these things of old; and Jared put it into the heart of Akish; wherefore, Akish administered it unto his kindred and friends, leading them away by fair promises to do whatsoever thing he desired.
>
> And it came to pass that *they formed a secret combination, even as they of old; which combination is most abominable and wicked above all, in the sight of God.*
>
> *For the Lord worketh not in secret combinations,* neither doth he will that man should shed blood, but in all things hath forbidden it, from the beginning of man [3]

In just one generation, "*So great had been the spreading of this wicked and secret society that it had corrupted the hearts of all the*

1. Morm 2:8.
2. Morm. 6:1-15.
3. Eth 8:13-19 See Eth. 9:1-6. It was this evil act which caused Moroni to write his prophetic warning cited at the beginning of this chapter.

people."[1] The wickedness soon led to war "which lasted for the space of many years, yea, unto the destruction of nearly all the people of the kingdom, yea, even all, save it were thirty souls."[2]

The Jaredite populace began to grow and multiply from this tiny remnant, but five generations later, "Heth began to embrace the secret plans again of old, to destroy his father."[3] Prophets were sent to warn of impending destruction from famine, and then many of the people died from that great dearth and from poisonous serpents, in fulfillment of their prophetic warnings.[4]

Generations later, near the end of the Jaredite civilization, secret combinations were again established. The Book of Mormon records that

> In the days of Com there began to be robbers in the land; and they adopted the old plans, and administered oaths after the manner of the ancients, and *sought again to destroy the kingdom*.[5]

These combinations caused the people to reject the word of God and to rise in rebellion:

> *And they hearkened not unto the voice of the Lord, because of their wicked combinations; wherefore, there began to be wars and contentions in all the land, and also many famines and pestilences, insomuch that there was a great destruction, such as one as never had been known upon the face of the earth;* and all this came to pass in the days of Shiblom. . . .
>
> And it came to pass that *there arose a rebellion among the people, because of that secret combination which was built up to get power and gain;* and there arose a mighty man among them in iniquity, and gave battle unto Moron, in which he did overthrow the half of the kingdom; and he did maintain the half of the kingdom for many years
>
> And in the days of Coriantor there also came many prophets, and prophesied of great and marvelous things, and cried repentance unto the people, and *except they should repent the Lord God would execute judgment against them to their utter destruction;*
>
> And that the Lord God would send or bring forth another people to possess the land, by his power, after the manner by which he brought their fathers
>
> And *they did reject all the words of the prophets, because of their secret society and wicked abominations*.[6]

As the end of the Jaredite civilization drew near, the prophet, Ether, watched from his hiding place and saw that "there were many people

1. Eth. 9:6.
2. Eth. 9:12.
3. Eth. 9:26.
4. Eth. 9:28-32.
5. Eth. 10:33
6. Eth. 11:7, 15, 20-22

who were slain by the sword of these secret combinations, fighting against Coriantumr that they might obtain the kingdom."[1] Again, in that era, a curse was placed upon the land:

> And now there began to be *a great curse upon all the land because of the iniquity of the people, in which, if a man should lay his tool or his sword upon his shelf, or upon the place whither he would keep it, behold, upon the morrow, he could not find it, so great was the curse upon the land.*
>
> Wherefore every man did cleave unto that which was his own, with his hands, and would not borrow neither would he lend; and every man kept the hilt of his sword in his right hand, in the defence of his property and his own life and of his wives and children.[2]

As the ultimate conflict approached, members of the secret combinations committed murders in their own ranks as they sought to gain power and position.[3]

Lib became the leader of the secret combination and the final battle was fought between Lib (and Shiz, his brother), with his secret combination forces, and the legitimate Jaredite king, Coriantumr. Prior to that battle more than two million men, plus their wives and children, had already been slain.[4]

Summary

1. Secret combinations which are organized to obtain power and wealth through evil deeds are the most abominable and wicked above all in the sight of God. The Lord does not work in secret combinations

2. Secret combinations caused the decline and collapse of two great Book of Mormon cultures: the Jaredites and the Nephites.

3. The Lord has warned that if a nation upholds secret combinations and allows them to spread over the nation, that nation shall be destroyed.

4. Prophetic warnings concerning secret combinations were given by

A. Moroni (Eth. 8:21).
B. Moroni (Eth. 8:23-26).

---

1. Eth. 13:18.
2. Eth. 14:1-2.
3. Eth. 14:8-10.
4. Eth. 15:2

C. Nephi (2 Ne. 26:20-23).
D. Nephi (2 Ne. 10:15).
E. Alma (Al. 37:28, 31).

5. Moroni wrote to the American Gentiles of the last days, warning of a secret combination which will seek to overthrow the freedom of all nations and countries. He commanded the Gentiles to awake to a sense of their awful situation when they see the secret combination among them.

6. The Lord prepared the way so that the abominations of the secret combinations would be made manifest to other people.

7. Alma taught his son Helaman that the details of the secret oaths, signs, and plans of the wicked combinations should not be preserved in the histories or records of the people. He instructed that the people should bc taught to abhor such wickcdncss and abominations, and that the members of evil combinations were destroyed because of their wickedness.

8. According to the prophet, Alma, there is a curse upon the Americas, that destruction will come upon workers of darkness when they are fully ripe, except they repent.

9. Nephi prophesied that there would be secret combinations among the latter-day Gentiles and warned that the Lord would destroy them.

10. An examination of secret combinations described in the Book of Mormon reveals some of their characteristics:

A. They make secret covenants to protect each other. B. They have signs, passwords, and secret means of member identification.
C. They are willing to murder and steal to accomplish their ends.
D. They severely discipline members who betray them.
E. They flourish in societies dulled to social justice and devoted to seeking riches.
F. They strive to infiltrate and gain control of government and to usurp political power and authority.
G. They seek to control the courts and judicial systems.

H. They condemn the righteous and let the wicked go unpunished.
I. They grow rapidly and can gain control of a nation in two decades.
J. When in control they persecute the poor and the righteous .
K. When attacked or criticized, they seek to ostracize and condemn their critics.

11. A technique used by secret combinations to gain new members is to offer the individuals the alternatives of partnership and a share in the profits from their evil doings, or death.

12. The experiences of both the Nephites and the Jaredites indicate that secret combinations, once they are established, are not easily destroyed. Like a malignant cancer, they spread rapidly—if one portion of their evil doing is stopped, their evil activities break out in another direction. Even though the total secret combination would be defeated, new combinations would spring up within a few years.

13. Secret combinations can grow beyond the level of small, hidden crime activities. They can become large robber bands and full-fledged armies. In these latter stages, they attract dissenters, malcontents, and revolutionaries to their ranks.

VIII

Eighth Warning: If The People Choose Iniquity, Judgments Will Come Upon Them

King Mosiah's Warning: If the Voice of the People Chooses Iniquity, God Will Visit Them With Great Destruction (Mos. 29:26-27)

King Mosiah, a righteous leader of the Nephites in the land of Zarahemla, reached the end of his long reign in 91 B.C. He had led his people in righteousness, as did his father, King Benjamin. In his wisdom, Mosiah recognized the danger of continuing their present form of government, and regarded the danger of an unjust king leading the people into unrighteousness as very real.[1] He wanted his people to continue to enjoy the benefits of freedom and peace, and expressed his wish forcefully to his people:

> *I desire that this land be a land of liberty, and every man may enjoy his rights and privileges alike, so long as the Lord sees fit that we may live and inherit the land, . . .*[2]

He proposed a new democratic form of government, in which the people would be ruled by judges whom they would elect:

> Let us appoint judges, to judge this people according to our law; and we will newly arrange the affairs of this people, for we will appoint wise men to be judges, that will judge this people according to the commandments of God.[3]

His plan contained checks and balances to control the judges who would rule. If necessary, higher judges would review the decisions of lower judges, while a group of lower judges would have power to evaluate the conduct of the higher judges.[4]

---

1. Mos 29:31. See also verses 16-24.
2. Mos. 29:32.
3. Mos. 28:11. He continued with the observation that "it is better that a man should be judged of God than of man, for the judgments of God are always just, but the judgments of man are not always just. (Mos. 29:12)
4. Mos. 29:28-29.

Mosiah instructed his people to choose righteous judges who would rule by correct laws. Then he expressed his confidence that the majority of the people would choose the right, although a minority might seek improper ends. His observation was followed with a prophetic warning—if the majority of the people chooses wickedness, then is the time God will visit them with judgments and destruction:

> Now it is not common that the voice of the people desireth anything contrary to that which is right; but it is common for the lesser part of the people to desire that which is not right; therefore *this shall ye observe and make it your law to do your business by the voice of the people.*
>
> *And if the time comes that the voice of the people doth choose iniquity, then is the time that the judgments of God will come upon you; yea, then is the time he will visit you with great destruction even as he has hitherto visited this land.*[1]

Thus King Mosiah stated a principle which has been proven true throughout Book of Mormon history, and which remains equally true today: if the majority of the populace of a nation chooses unrighteousness, that nation will soon be destroyed because of its wickedness.

Amulek's Warning: If the Righteous Are Cast Out, Destruction Comes by Famine, Pestilence and Sword (Al. 10:22-23)

Ten years later, Amulek, while performing his missionary labors, cited the prophetic warning of King Mosiah as a rebuke to wicked lawyers who were trying to entrap him:

> O ye wicked and perverse generation, ye lawyers and hypocrites, for ye are laying the foundations of the devil; for ye are laying traps and snares to catch the holy ones of God.
>
> Ye are laying plans to pervert the ways of the righteous, and *to bring down the wrath of God upon your heads, even to the utter destruction of this people.*
>
> Yea, well did Mosiah say, who was our last king, when he was about to deliver up the kingdom, having no one to confer it upon, causing that this people should be governed by their own voices—yea, well did he say that *if the time should come that the voice of this people should choose iniquity, that Is, if the time should come that this people should fall into transgression, they would be ripe for destruction.*

1. Mos. 29:26-27

> And now I say unto you that well doth the Lord judge of your iniquities; well doth he cry unto this people, by the voice of his angels: *Repent ye, repent, for the kingdom of heaven is at hand.*[1]
>
> Yea, well doth he cry, by the voice of his angels that:
>
> I will come down among my people, with equity and justice in my hands.[2]

He taught that even when wickedness prevails in a land, the prayers of the remaining righteous inhabitants can stave off impending destruction. But if the righteous inhabitants are cast out, then the Lord will no longer stay his hand. This is his prophetic warning:

> Yea, and I say unto you that *if it were not for the prayers of the righteous, who are now in the land, that ye would even now be visited with utter destruction;* yet it would not be by flood, as were the people in the days of Noah, but *it would be by famine, and by pestilence, and the sword.*
>
> *But it is by the prayers of the righteous that ye are spared; now therefore, if ye will cast out the righteous from among you then will not the Lord stay his hand;* but in his fierce anger he will come out against you; then ye shall be smitten by famine, and by pestilence, and by the sword; and the time is soon at hand except ye repent.[3]

Just as the secret combinations later heaped epithets and abuse upon the prophet Nephi, who rebuked them,[4] Amulek's wicked audience accused him of speaking against their laws and the men they had chosen as their leaders. Amulek countered their hue and cry, however, showing that he had not spoken against their law. He reminded them that "I have spoken in favor of your law, to your condemnation."[5] And then he warned of what happens when the majority of the people choose unrighteous leaders:

---

1. Note the meaning of the phrase "the kingdom of heaven is at hand," as used in this context. It does not refer to available blessings but is a warning of impending destruction. It is used similarly in other passages. See Mt. 3:1-3;4:17;11:11-12.
2. Al. 10:17-21.
3. Al. 10:22-23. This principle was demonstrated early in Old Testament times at the destruction of Sodom. The Lord promised Abraham that the city wouldn't be destroyed if even ten righteous inhabitants remained (Gen. 18:20-32). But when Lot and his family, the remaining righteous, left the city, destruction sent by God was immediate (Gen. 19:1-25; see also 2 Pet. 2:6-9).
4. See Hel. 8:1-7.
5. Al. 10:26 See verses 24-30.

> Behold, I say unto you, that *the foundation of the destruction of this people is beginning to be laid by the unrighteous of your lawyers and your judges.*[1]

Samuel's Warning: When You Cast Out the Righteous, You Are Ripe for Destruction (Hel. 13:12-14)

The theme that even a righteous minority of inhabitants of a city or nation can save it from destruction recurs several times throughout the ancient scriptures and appears to be a principle applicable to all times and places. Its corollary, that destruction is imminent when the righteous are cast out, also is found in these passages.

Samuel the Lamanite, for instance, sounded both concepts when he spoke of the impending destruction of Zarahemla:

> Yea, wo unto this great city of Zarahemla; for behold, *it is because of those who are righteous that it is saved;* yea, wo unto this great city, for I perceive, saith the Lord, that there are many, yea, even the more part of this great city, that will harden their hearts against me, saith the Lord.
>
> *But blessed are they who will repent, for them will I spare. But behold, if it were not for the righteous who are in this great city, behold, I would cause that fire should come down out of heaven and destroy it.*
>
> But behold, it is for the righteous' sake that it is spared. But behold, *the time cometh, saith the Lord, that when ye shall cast out the righteous from among you, then shall ye be ripe for destruction;* yea, wo be unto this great city, because of the wickedness and abominations which are in her.[2]

Samuel the Lamanite warned the wicked Nephites that their land was already cursed because they had cast out the prophets and were willing to accept the words of evil men who spoke flattering words to them:

> Yea, wo unto this people, because of this time which has arrived, that *ye do cast out the prophets, and do mock them, and cast stones at them, and do slay them, and do all manner of iniquity unto them,* even as they did of old time.
>
> And now when ye talk, ye say: If our days had been in the days of our fathers of old, we would not have slain the prophets; we would not have stoned them, and cast them out.
>
> Behold ye are worse than they; for as the Lord liveth, *if a prophet come among you and declareth unto you the word of the Lord, which testifieth of*

1. Al. 10:27. The wicked practices of these lawyers and judges is explained in Al. 10:13-32.
2. Hel 13:12-14

your sins and iniquities, ye are angry with him, and cast him out and seek all manner of ways to destroy him; yea, you will say that he is a false prophet, and that he is a sinner, and of the devil, because he testifieth that your deeds are evil.

But behold, if a man shall come among you and shall say: Do this, and there is no iniquity; do that and ye shall not suffer; yea, he will say: Walk after the pride of your own hearts; yea, walk after the pride of your eyes, and do whatsoever your heart desireth—and if a man shall come among you and say this, ye will receive him, and say that he is a prophet.

Yea, ye will lift him up, and ye will give unto him of your substance; ye will give unto him of your gold, and of your silver, and ye will clothe him with costly apparel; and because he speaketh flattering words unto you, and he saith that all is well, then ye will not find fault with him.

O ye wicked and ye perverse generation; ye hardened and ye stiffnecked people, how long will ye suppose that the Lord will suffer you? Yea, how long will ye suffer yourselves to be led by foolish and blind guides? Yea, how long will ye choose darkness rather than light?

Yea, behold, the anger of the Lord is already kindled against you; behold, he hath cursed the land because of your iniquity.

And behold, *the time cometh that he curseth your riches, that they become slippery, that ye cannot hold them; and in the days of your poverty ye cannot retain them.*

And in the days of your poverty ye shall cry unto the Lord; and *in vain shall ye cry, for your desolation is already come upon you, and your destruction is made sure;* and then shall ye weep and howl in that day. saith the Lord of Hosts.[1]

Nephi's Warning: Destruction Comes to Those Who Kill the Prophets and the Saints (2 Ne. 26:3-8)

Five-and-a-half centuries earlier, the prophet Nephi had foretold the destruction which would occur at the time of the Savior's death. In his prophecy he clearly foresaw that their casting out the prophets and the saints, and slaying them, would be the reason the people would reap God's wrath:

And after the Messiah shall come there shall be signs given unto my people of his birth, and also of his death and resurrection; and great and terrible shall that day be unto the wicked, for they shall perish; and *they perish because they cast out the prophets, and the saints, and stone them, and slay them; wherefore the cry of the blood of the saints shall ascend up to God from the ground against them.*

Wherefore, all those who are proud, and that do wickedly, the day that cometh shall burn them up, saith the Lord of Hosts, for they shall be as stubble.

---

1. Hel. 13:24-32. Casting out the prophets is a wicked practice frequently recorded in the Book of Mormon. See Mos. 17:3; Al. 8:13, 24-25, 29; 15:1; 26:29; Hel. 14:10; 3 Ne. 7:14; Eth. 13:13-15.

> *And they that kill the prophets, and the saints, the depths of the earth shall swallow them up, saith the Lord of Hosts;* and mountains shall cover them, and whirlwinds shall carry them away, and buildings shall fall upon them and crush them to pieces and grind them to powder.
>
> *And they shall be visited with thunderings, and lightnings, and earthquakes, and all manner of destructions, for the fire of the anger of the Lord shall be kindled against them,* and they shall be as stubble, and the day that cometh shall consume them, saith the Lord of Hosts.
>
> O the pain, and the anguish of my soul for the loss of the slain of my people! For I, Nephi, have seen it, and it well nigh consumeth me before the presence of the Lord; but I must cry unto my God: Thy ways are just.
>
> But behold, the *righteous that hearken unto the words of the prophets, and destroy them not, but look forward unto Christ with steadfastness for the signs which are given, notwithstanding all persecution—behold, they are they which shall not perish.*[1]

The scriptures tell the fulfillment of his prophecy, and record the Savior's statement that casting out the righteous was the specific reason why the cities of Laman, Josh, Gad, and Kishkumen were burned by fire at the time of his death:

> And behold, the city of Laman, and the city of Josh, and the city of Gad, and the city of Kishkumen, have I caused to be burned with fire, and the inhabitants thereof, *because of their wickedness in casting out the prophets, and stoning those whom I did send to declare unto them concerning their wickedness and their abominations.*
>
> And because they *did cast them all out, that there were none righteous among them,* I did send down fire and destroy them, that their wickedness and abominations might be hid from before my face, that *the blood of the prophets and the saints whom I sent among them might not cry unto me from the ground against them.*
>
> And many great destructions have I caused to come upon this land, and upon this people, because of their wickedness and their abominations.[2]

Nephi's Warning: Speedy Destruction Comes to a People If They Choose Darkness (2 Ne. 26:10-11)

Nephi also prophesied the final destruction of the Nephite civilization, and stated the eternal principle that speedy destruction comes upon a people if they yield unto the devil and choose works of darkness rather than light for that is the time the Spirit ceases to strive with man. His prophecy begins with the appearance of the Savior to the Nephites following his resurrection:

---

1. 2 Ne. 26:3-8.
2. 3 Ne. 9:10-12.

But the Son of righteousness shall appear unto them; and he shall heal them, and they shall have peace with him, until three generations shall have passed away, and many of the fourth generation shall have passed away in righteousness.

And when these things have passed away *a speedy destruction cometh unto my people;* for, notwithstanding the pains of my soul, I have seen it; wherefore, I know that it shall come to pass; and they sell themselves for naught; for, for the reward of their pride and their foolishness they shall reap destruction; for because *they yield unto the devil and choose works of darkness rather than light, therefore they must go down to hell.*

For the Spirit of the Lord will not always strive with man. *And when the Spirit ceaseth to strive with man then cometh speedy destruction,* and this grieveth my soul.[1]

Jaredite History: Famine Because Prophets Were Cast Out (Eth. 9:28-30)

Many centuries before the time of Christ, the Jaredites suffered a destructive famine because they cast out the prophets. The nation had begun to turn to wickedness by adopting the evil plans of secret combinations:

And there came prophets in the land again, crying repentance unto them—that they must prepare the way of the Lord or there should come a curse upon the face of the land; yea, even *there should be a great famine, in which they should be destroyed if they did not repent.*

But the people believed not the words of the prophets, but they cast them out; and some of them they cast into pits and left them to perish. And it came to pass that they did all these things according to the commandment of the king, Heth.

And it came to pass that there began to be a great dearth upon the land, and the inhabitants began to be *destroyed exceeding fast because of the dearth, for there was no rain upon the face of the earth.*[2]

Their suffering continued until the people repented and humbled themselves:

. . . Now when the people saw that they must perish they began to repent of their iniquities and cry unto the Lord.

And it came to pass that *when they had humbled themselves sufficiently before the Lord he did send rain* upon the face of the earth; and the

---

1. 2 Ne. 26:9-11.
2. Eth. 9.28-30. Several generations earlier, when the people began to mock and revile against the prophets who were warning of an approaching curse upon the land, their righteous king protected the prophets by law, which caused the people to repent. "The Lord did spare them." (See Eth. 7:23-26.)

people began to revive again, and there began to be fruit in the north countries, and in all the countries round about. *And the Lord did show forth his power unto them in preserving them from famine.*[1]

Jaredite History: Wars, Famines and Pestilences When Prophets Are Slain (Eth. 11:1-7, 12-13)

Several generations after the above famine was abated, many prophets were sent by the Lord to warn the Jaredites that ultimate destruction faced their civilization because of its great wickedness. They put some of the prophets to death, which brought famines and pestilences upon them, and caused the other prophets to cease their labors among them:

> And there came also in the days of Com *many prophets, and prophesied of the destruction of that great people except they should repent,* and turn unto the Lord, and forsake their murders and wickedness
>
> And it came to pass that the prophets were rejected by the people, and they fled unto Com for protection, for the people sought to destroy them.
>
> And they prophesied unto Com many things; and he was blessed in all the remainder of his days.
>
> And he lived to a good old age, and begat Shiblom; and Shiblom reigned in his stead And the brother of Shiblom rebelled against him, and there began to be an exceeding great war in all the land.
>
> And it came to pass that the brother of Shiblom caused that all the prophets who prophesied of the destruction of the people should be put to death;
>
> And there was *great calamity in all the land, for they had testified that a great curse should come upon the land, and also upon the people, and that there should be a great destruction among them, such an one as never had been upon the face of the earth, and their bones should become as heaps of earth upon the face of the land except they should repent of their wickedness*
>
> And they hearkened not unto the voice of the Lord, because of their wicked combinations; wherefore, *there began to be wars and contentions in all the land, and also many famines and pestilences, insomuch that there was a great destruction,* such an one as never had been known upon the face of the earth; and all this came to pass in the days of Shiblom. . . .
>
> And it came to pass that in the days of Ethem there came *many prophets, and prophesied again unto the people; yea, they did prophesy that the Lord would utterly destroy them from off the face of the earth except they repented of their iniquities.*
>
> And it came to pass that the people hardened their hearts, and would not hearken unto their words;and the *prophets mourned and withdrew from among the people.*[2]

---

1. Eth. 9:34-35
2. Eth. 11:1-7, 12-13.

While a wicked people may hasten their own destruction by casting out the righteous, they may also discover that the Lord can direct His followers to cease working among them, leaving them without the uplifting influence of the saints. In the days of Mormon, for instance,

> Wickedness did prevail upon the face of the whole land, insomuch that the Lord did take away His beloved disciples, and the work of miracles and of healing did cease because of all the iniquity of the people.
>
> And there were no gifts from the Lord, and the Holy Ghost did not come upon any, because of their wickedness and unbelief.[1]

Such will be the result when the saints are gathered out from among the wicked in anticipation of the great judgments which will be poured out[2]—there will be no leavening influence to lift and protect the wicked who remain.

The message of the scriptures is clear: God-sent destruction comes rapidly upon a people or nation if they reject and slay the prophets and the Lord's people.

Nephite History: Corrupt Laws and Political Leaders Bring Destruction (Helaman 5:2-3)

Nephi records another principle upon which the well-being of a nation depends: if the majority of a people choose to be governed by evil and corrupt laws, that nation will be ripening for destruction. He also stated a corollary to this principle: if the people refuse to be governed by law or by justice, their destruction is also near.

> For as their laws and their governments were established by the voice of the people, and *they who chose evil were more numerous than they who chose good, therefore they were ripening for destruction, for the laws had become corrupted.*
>
> Yea, and this was not all; they were a stiffnecked people, insomuch that *they could not be governed by the law nor justice,* save it were to their destruction.[3]

The people in Nephi's day, just three decades before the birth of the Savior, had allowed their laws to be corrupted. They found that governmental corruption was a sign of their general wickedness, that the

1. Morm. 1:13-14. See also 2 Ne. 26:10-11.
2. See D&C 133:8-14, Rev. 18:4, etc. 3. Hel 5:2-3.

church was dwindling in their midst, that they no longer were being preserved by the Spirit of the Lord, and that judgments and destruction appeared imminent:

> They had altered and trampled under their feet the laws of Mosiah, or that which the Lord commanded him to give unto the people; and *they saw that their laws had become corrupted, and that they had become a wicked people,* insomuch that they were wicked even like unto the Lamanites.
>
> *And because of their iniquity the church had begun to dwindle;* and they began to disbelieve in the spirit of prophecy and in the spirit of revelation; and the judgments of God did stare them in the face.
>
> And they saw that they had become weak, like unto their brethren, the Lamanites, and that *the Spirit of the Lord did no more preserve them; yea, it had withdrawn from them* because the Spirit of the Lord doth not dwell in unholy temples
>
> *Therefore the Lord did cease to preserve them by his miraculous and matchless power,* for they had fallen into a state of unbelief and awful wickedness; and they saw that the Lamanites were exceedingly more numerous than they, and *except they should cleave unto the Lord their God they must unavoidably perish.*[1]

Nephi saw that when men inspired from heaven came testifying boldly of the sins of the people,[2] these men were taken and "put to death secretly by the judges."[3] When these corrupt judges were brought to trial, the judicial leadership of the country formed a secret covenant to protect them, "*And they did set at defiance the law and the rights of their country; and they did covenant one with another to destroy the governor, and to establish a king over the land, that the land should no more be at liberty. . . .*[4] And

> All this iniquity had come upon the people because they did yield themselves unto the power of Satan.
>
> And the regulations of the government were destroyed, because of the secret combination of the friends and kindreds of those who murdered the prophets.[5]

The problem of governmental corruption had existed among the Nephites a generation earlier. In that previous era, a righteous general gave vent to his displeasure concerning his nation's leadership: "Moroni was angry with the government, because of their indifference concerning the freedom of their country."[6] He challenged the govern-

---

1. Hel 4:22-25.
2. 3 Ne. 6:20.
3. 3 Ne. 6:23.
4. 3 Ne, 6:30,
5. 3 Ne, 7:5-6,
6. Al, 59:13

ment, telling them that "it is because of your iniquity that we have suffered so much loss."[1]

And then Moroni warned that the Lord would not allow a corrupt government to destroy a righteous people, but would inspire the people to rise against them:

> *The Lord will not suffer that ye shall live and wax strong in your iniquities to destroy his righteous people.*
>
> Behold, can you suppose that the Lord will spare you and come out in judgment against the Lamanites, when it is the tradition of their fathers that has caused their hatred, yea, and it has been redoubled by those who have dissented from us, while *your iniquity is for the cause of your love of glory and the vain things of the world?*
>
> Ye know that ye do transgress the laws of God, and ye do know that ye do trample them under your feet. Behold, *the Lord saith unto me: If those whom ye have appointed your governors do not repent of their sins and iniquities, ye shall go up to battle against them.*[2]

The Lord summed up the danger of corrupt leaders and how they can be avoided with this modern revelation:

> *When the wicked rule the people mourn.*
>
> Wherefore, honest men and wise men should be sought for diligently, and good men and wise men ye should observe to uphold; whatsoever is less than these cometh of evil.[3]

Nephi's Warning: If People Forget God Because of Their Riches, He Will Chasten Them with Terror, Famine and Pestilence (Hel. 12:2-3)

In no area of human endeavor is the effect of choosing wickedness more apparent than in the deliberate choice of temporal riches over service to God. Nephi warned that when people who have been blessed by God harden their hearts because of their prosperity,

> . . . We may see at the very time when he doth prosper his people, yea, in the increase of their fields, their flocks and their herds, and in gold, and

---

1. Al. 60:28.
2. Al. 60:31-33. Moroni received a reply to his threat from Pahoran, the chief governor, in which he learned that the government had become so weak that a corrupt faction had risen in rebellion against the free man and was attempting to overrun the nation from within while it was struggling to defend itself from outside attack. See Al. 61. Concerning the principle of rising up against wicked leaders and enemies, see D&C 98.
3. D&C 98:9-10.

> in silver, and in all manner of precious things of every kind and art; *sparing their lives, and delivering them out of the hands of their enemies; softening the hearts of their enemies that they should not declare wars against them;* yea, and in fine, doing all things for the welfare and happiness of his people; yea, *then is the time that they do harden their hearts, and do forget the Lord their God,* and do trample under their feet the Holy One—yea, and this because of their ease, and their exceedingly great prosperity.
>
> And thus we see that *except the Lord doth chasten his people with many afflictions, yea, except he doth visit them with death and with terror, and with famine and with all manner of pestilence, they will not remember him.*[1]

It can thus be clearly seen that Book of Mormon prophets warn that judgment will come upon a nation if its people choose iniquity and yield themselves to Satan's temptations. Well did the prophet Lehi say that

> Men are free according to the flesh; and all things are given them which are expedient unto man. And they are *free to choose liberty and eternal life,* through the great mediation of all men, or to *choose captivity and death, according to the captivity and power of the devil;* for he seeketh that all men might be miserable like unto himself [2]

Summary

1. Book of Mormon prophets have warned that if the people of a nation deliberately choose iniquity rather than righteousness, then they are ripe for destruction and the judgments of God will soon come upon them.

2. King Mosiah observed that it is not common that the majority of a people choose unrighteousness, though a minority commonly choose wickedness. Judgments come when the wicked minority grows to become the majority.

3. Prophetic and historical warnings concerning the danger of people choosing wickedness and/or casting out the righteous were given by

A. King Mosiah (Mos. 29:26-27)
B. Amulek (Al. 10:22-23)

---

1. Hel. 12:2-3.
2. 2 Ne. 2:27

C. Samuel the Lamanite (Hel. 13:12-14)
D. Nephi (2 Ne. 26:3-8)
E. Nephi (2 Ne. 26:10-11)
F. Jaredite History (Eth. 9:28-30)
G. Jaredite History (Eth. 11:1-7, 12-13)
H. Nephi (Hel. 12:2-3)

4. The prayers of the righteous can save a land from being "visited with utter destruction," but if the righteous leave or are cast out, then the Lord will no longer stay his hand and withhold punishment.

5. Unrighteous laws, judges, and lawyers can lay the foundation for the destruction of a people. A nation cannot afford to allow or tolerate corruption in government.

6. The wicked cast out the prophets, mocking and slaying them. But if false prophets tell them their actions are not sinful and that they won't be held accountable for them, the wicked people receive those false prophets as their leaders.

7. The Lord promises to spare the righteous and repentant when he destroys the wicked. (2 Ne. 26:8)

8. The prophetic warnings indicate many ways in which God sends his judgments upon the wicked, including

A. famine (Al. 10:22-23;Eth. 9:28-30, 35; 11:7)
B. pestilence (Al. 10:22-23; Eth. 11:7)
C. war and the sword (Al. 10:22-23; Eth. 11:7)
D. fire coming down from heaven (Gen. 19:24; Hel. 13:13; 3 Ne. 9:11)
E. cursing their riches, so they become slippery (Hel. 13:31-32)
F. refusing to hear their cry (Hel. 13:32)
G. fire (2 Ne. 26:4)
H. earth swallow them up (2 Ne. 26:5)
I. mountains cover them (2 Ne. 26:5)
J. whirlwinds carry them away (2 Ne. 26:5)
K. buildings fall and crush them (2 Ne. 26:5)
L. thunder and lightning (2 Ne. 26:6)
M. earthquakes (2 Ne. 26:6)
N. no rain (Eth. 9:30)
O. terror (Hel. 12:3)

8. The Lord destroys the wicked to hide their wickedness and abominations from before his face, and to stop the blood of slain prophets and saints from crying from the ground unto him against them. (3 Ne. 9:11)

9. Righteous leaders have saved their people from destruction by passing laws protecting the prophets from harm and abuse. (Eth. 7:23-26; Al. 23:2. See also Al. 1:2-27)

10. When a wicked people repents and humbles itself, God moderates or ends the judgments which he is sending upon them.

11. When the wicked rule, the people mourn. Citizens should diligently seek for honest and wise leaders, and then uphold them in their leadership decisions.

12. Casting out the righteous and slaying the prophets brought destruction upon the Jaredites, and upon the Nephites both following the death of the Savior and three-and-a-half centuries later when the Nephite civilization was destroyed.

13. God blesses those who trust and serve him by prospering them, delivering them out of the hands of their enemies, and softening the hearts of their enemies so they won't declare war against them.

14. It is when people are living in ease and great prosperity that they tend to forget God and harden their hearts. When they forget him, God chastens them with death, terror, famine and pestilence.

15. Men are free to choose liberty and eternal life through obedience to Christ, or captivity and death according to the power of the devil.

IX

Ninth Warning: Conflict and Apostasy

A final series of prophetic warnings found in the scriptures is related to the future of the Lord's church. These warnings are penetrating in their implications, for they indicate the far-reaching extent to which Satan will exert his influence in his efforts to thwart the Lord's work prior to the millennial era of the Savior's earthly reign. Most of these prophetic warnings appear to relate chronologically to the early period of the New Jerusalem.

Scriptural prophecies of future conflict within the church are not pleasant for Latter-day Saints to consider. Indeed, they are not pleasant to write about. The author would prefer to avoid them, but cannot do so with integrity, for they truly exist, and it is impossible to give an accurate portrayal of future events without giving them due consideration.

It is probable that some will attempt to explain them away, rationalizing that the prophecies refer to the "great apostasy" which commenced following the New Testament era. Such a rationalization would fly in the face of basic principles of scriptural interpretation, ignoring the many internal and contextual indications that the passages focus on a future era. Such rationalizations would also assume that the prophesied events have already come to pass, though no specific events can be cited as literal fulfillment.

There may also be some who would challenge the propriety of a "lay member" pointing out the existence of such a prophetic pattern, and somehow believe that their challenge would negate the scriptures cited. They, of course, would overlook the Lord's express commandment that

> . . . *every man, both elder, priest, teacher, and also member,* go to with his might, with the labor of his hands, to prepare and accomplish the things which I have commanded.
>
> And *let your preaching be the warning voice, every man to his neighbor,* in mildness and in meekness.[1]

1. D&C 38:40-41.

Such individuals would also forget the scriptural admonition that "*every man* should take righteousness in his hands and faithfulness upon his loins, and *lift a warning voice* unto the inhabitants of the earth; and declare both by word and by flight that *desolation shall come upon the wicked*."[1] Indeed, "it becometh *every man who hath been warned to warn his neighbor . . . and to prepare the saints* for the hour of judgment which is to come."[2]

Certainly I find no pleasure in these prophecies of future difficulties within the church. Nor do I want to see them come to pass, for I recognize the problems, sorrow, strife and confusion their fulfillment would inevitably bring. I write to avert or soften their fulfillment, in the spirit of a priesthood bearer functioning in the universal calling to "watch over the church always, and be with and strengthen them; and see there is no iniquity in the church. "[3]

God's Kingdom Shall Never Be Destroyed

These prophetic warnings should be viewed, I believe, in the context of what God has revealed concerning His kingdom and authority in this last dispensation. Daniel prophesied of the permanent nature of the restored kingdom of God as he interpreted the prophetic dream received by the Babylonian king, Nebuchadnezzar. He foresaw that the God of heaven would

> . . . set up a kingdom, which *shall never be destroyed:* and the *kingdom shall not be left to other people,* but it shall break in pieces and consume all these kingdoms, and *it shall stand for ever.*[4]

A modern revelation alludes to Daniel's interpretation of Nebuchadnezzar's vision, proclaiming that "the keys of the kingdom of God are committed unto man on the earth, and from thence shall the gospel roll forth unto the ends of the earth, as the stone which is cut out of the mountain without hands shall roll forth, *until it has filled the whole earth*."[5]

1. D&C 63:37.
2. D&C 88:81, 84. See also D&C 84:87, 117.
3. D&C 20:53-54.
4. Dan. 2:44. For a discussion of Nebuchadnezzar's dream see the author's book, The Prophecies of Joseph Smith, pp. 197-199. Concerning other interpretational views of a political nature see Prophecy—Key to the Future pp. 67-81.
5. D&C 65:2.

That this kingdom will endure was repeatedly emphasized by the Savior, who revealed to the Church in the days of Joseph Smith that "the kingdom is yours, and *the enemy shall not overcome,*"[1] and "Fear not, little flock, *the kingdom is yours until I come.*"[2] It was revealed to the saints that "the kingdom is given you of the Father, and *power to overcome all things which are not ordained of him*—"[3] The prophet Joseph was told by revelation that the "kingdom is coming forth *for the last time*"[4] and the saints believe that the Savior "shall deliver up the kingdom, and present it unto the Father, spotless," when "Christ shall have subdued all enemies under his feet, and shall have perfected his work."[5]

The priesthood power restored in the last days is also established with permanence, for John the Baptist proclaimed that the priesthood of Aaron "*shall never be taken again from the earth,* until the sons of Levi do offer again an offering unto the Lord in righteousness."[6] And the Lord has revealed that "the power of this priesthood [is] given, *for the last days and for the last time,* in the which is the dispensation of the fulness of times."[7]

Thus, though apostasy and strife may come among the saints in fulfillment of the prophecies, it is expected that the Church and priesthood will remain and fulfill the roles to which they have been called and appointed.

Though scriptural prophecies warn of difficult times ahead for the Lord's Church, the message of the scriptures is that the Church will survive the problems it must endure and will eventually come off victorious in the latter-days panorama.

Isaiah's Warning: The Earth Shall Be Left Desolate Because They Have Broken the Everlasting Covenant (Isaiah 24:5-6)

As has been seen, the scriptures speak repeatedly of a period in the last days called the "desolation of abomination"[8]—a time when the judgments of God will come upon the wicked and greatly reduce the population of the earth. Prophecies relating to this period refer to it as

1. D&C 38:9.
2. D&C 35:27. See also 62:9; 64:4; 78:18; 82:24.
3. D&C 50:35.
4. D&C 90:2.
5. D&C 76:106-107.
6. D&C 13:1. See D&C 84:18.
7. D&C 112:30.
8. See D&C 88:85, 84 117.

a time of "desolation," when the wicked will be destroyed "and their house shall be left unto them desolate."[1] The prophet Isaiah speaks of this future event. He prophesies that "*the Lord maketh the earth empty, and maketh it waste,* and turneth it upside down, and scattereth abroad the inhabitants thereof. . . . The land shall be utterly emptied, and utterly spoiled: for the Lord hath spoken this word."[2] As he prophesies of the future cleansing, Isaiah reveals the reason why it will come upon the earth—the earth's inhabitants will have "transgressed the laws, changed the ordinance, broken the everlasting covenant." This is his prophetic warning:

> The earth also is defiled under the inhabitants thereof: because *they have transgressed the laws, changed the ordinance, broken the everlasting covenant.*
>
> Therefore hath the curse devoured the earth and *they that dwell Therein are desolate: therefore the inhabitants of the earth are burned, and few men left.*[3]

The prophecy continues by describing the people of the earth who will remain following this destruction:

> The new wine mourneth, the vine languisheth, all the merryhearted do sigh.
>
> The mirth of tabrets ceaseth, the noise of them that rejoice endeth, the joys of the harp ceaseth.
>
> They shall not drink wine with a song; strong drink shall be bitter to them that drink it.
>
> *The city of confusion is broken down: every house is shut up, that no man may come in.*
>
> There is a crying for wine in the streets; all joy is darkened, *the mirth of the land is gone.*
>
> *In the city is left desolation, and the gate is smitten with destruction.*[4]

It is the immediate cause of this desolating destruction that makes it appropriate for the prophecy to be cited in this context—Isaiah's warning that men will change the ordinance, and break the everlasting

1. D&C 84:115.
2. Is. 24:1, 3.
3. Is. 24:5-6.
4. Is. 24:7-12. This description is indication that the burning of verse 6 is not the cleansing of the earth at Christ's coming in glory, for the prophesied situation differs markedly from the millennial era when "the former shall not be remembered, nor come into mind" and, as the Lord says, "I create Jerusalem a rejoicing, and her people a joy." See Is. 65:17-25.

covenant. To do so would seem to require Church membership, for can one change something which he does not already have, or break a covenant which he has not made?

What is the everlasting covenant of which Isaiah speaks? It is the gospel of Jesus Christ. As a modern revelation states, "Blessed are you for receiving mine *everlasting covenant, even the fulness of my gospel,* sent forth unto the children of men, that they might have life and be made partakers of the glories which are to be revealed in the last days."[1] The Savior refers to the process of joining the Church "When men are *called unto mine everlasting gospel, and covenant with an everlasting covenant*. . . ."[2] He speaks of "a new and everlasting covenant, . . ." and says that "I have caused *this last covenant and this church* to be built up unto me."[3] It is by making the everlasting covenant that saints are received into fellowship in the church.[4] Those who don't receive the gospel do not receive the everlasting covenant,[5] and he who enters into the new and everlasting covenant "must and shall abide the law, or he shall be damned. "[6] The everlasting covenant, like the Church itself, is to be a standard for the nations.[7]

Isaiah's warning, then, is that judgments will come because Church members will transgress gospel laws, change gospel ordinances, and break the everlasting covenant by which they became members of the Church. His prophecy is very similar to a prophetic warning found in the Lord's "Preface" to the Doctrine and Covenants, which is considered next.

The Lord's Warning: Those Who Will Not Heed the Lord Nor His Prophets Shall Be Cut Off (D&C 1:14-16)

The Master has warned his people to prepare for the time to come when his anger shall fall upon the inhabitants of the earth.[8] It will come in a time when apostates who have strayed from his ordinances and broken his everlasting covenant will be cut off from among the people:

1. D&C 66:2.
2. D&C 101:39.
3. D&C 22:1-4.
4. D&C 88:133.
5. D&C 76:101.
6. D&C 132:6.
7. Compare D&C 45:9 with D&C 115:4-6.
8. D&C 1:12-13.

> . . . The arm of the Lord shall be revealed; and the day cometh that they who will *not hear the voice of the Lord, neither the voice of his servants, neither give heed to the words of the prophets and apostles, shall be cut off from among the people;*
>
> *For they have strayed from mine ordinances, and have broken mine everlasting covenant;*
>
> They seek not the Lord to establish his righteousness, but every man walketh in his own way, and after the image of his own God, whose image is in the likeness of the world, and whose substance is that of an idol. . . .[1]

Here, then, is one of a series of prophecies warning of a future time when saints will be "cut off." It has similarities to 3 Ne. 21:20, which talks about the unrepentant being cut off in the context of internal destruction in America at the time of the establishment of the New Jerusalem.[2] Other prophecies considered in this chapter will give greater insight into possible reasons for the future saints to refuse to heed the word of the Lord.

The Lord's Warning: The Rebellious Shall Be Cut Off from Zion and False Apostles and Prophets Shall Be Known (D&C 64:35-40)

A prophecy concerning the saints in the New Jerusalem indicates that there will be a rebellious faction in that day which will be cut off, and shows that the apostasy may even reach the highest councils, for the saints "will judge all things pertaining to Zion," and "they who are not apostles and prophets shall be known:"

> . . . *The rebellious shall be cut off out of the land of Zion, and shall be sent away, and shall not inherit the land.*
>
> For, verily I say that the rebellious are not of the blood of Ephraim, wherefore *they shall be plucked out.*
>
> Behold, I, the Lord, have made my church in these last days like unto a judge sitting on a hill, or in a high place, to judge the nations.
>
> For it shall come to pass that *the inhabitants of Zion shall judge all things pertaining to Zion.*
>
> *And liars and hypocrites shall be proved by them, and they who are not apostles and prophets shall be known.*

---

1. D&C 1:14-16. Note the similarities to the wording of Isaiah's prophecy (compare Is. 24:5 with D&C 1:15), also that the D&C passage is future (the day cometh ...). The Lord then says that he, "Knowing the calamity which should come upon the inhabitants of the earth, " called upon Joseph Smith and gave him commandments (D&C 1:17).
2. See 3 Ne. 21:12-24;D&C 63:63.

> And even the bishop, who is a judge, and his counselors, if they are not faithful in their stewardships *shall be condemned, and others shall be planted in their stead*.[1]

The Church has had to contend with false apostles and prophets in other dispensations. John the Revelator wrote to the saints in Ephesus, for instance, and commented that "I know thy works, and thy labour, and thy patience, and how thou canst not bear them which are evil: and *thou hast tried them which say they are apostles, and are not, and hast found them liars*."[2] King Mosiah, in the Book of Mormon, alluded to prophets which had "fallen into transgression."[3] And many Old Testament passages tell of problems caused by false prophets who were the accepted leaders of the Church in their day.[4]

The Lord's Warning: False Christs and False Prophets Shall Deceive the Elect (Matthew 24:24)

In his great prophecy given on the Mount of Olives, Jesus warned of the last days "abomination of desolation"[5] which will come upon the earth. He described the period vividly, saying that

> . . . *Then shall be great tribulation, such as was not since the beginning of the world to this time, no, nor ever shall be.*
>
> And except those days should be shortened, there should no flesh be saved: but for the elect's sake those days shall be shortened.[6]

At that juncture in the world's future will come false leaders who will seek to deceive the saints:

---

1. D&C 64:35-40. Note the context (verses 41-43) which indicates that the time of fulfillment for this passage is yet future, and not during the brief interlude in the first decade of the Church's existence when the saints lived in Jackson County, Missouri.
2. Rev. 2:2.
3. Mos. 15:13.
4. See, for instance,Zeph. 3:4;Jer. 2:8;5:31;10:21;12:10-11;14:13-16; 23:1-2, 11, 13, 16-17, 21-22, 25-40; 27:9-10, 14-18; 29:8-9; Ezek 13:2-4;22:25-28;34:2-4;Zech. 10:2;Mal. 2:7-8;etc.
5. Mt. 24:15. see Dan. 9:26-27. Note that Mt. 24 speaks of two periods shortly after the time of Christ (around 70 A.D., when the temple in Jerusalem was destroyed by the Romans), and the last days. The inspired translation of Mt. 24, found in the Writings of Joseph Smith 1, shows that there was to be two periods of "abomination of desolation": one in 70 A.D. and another in the last days (see J.S. 1 12 and 1:32).
6. Mt. 24:21-22 Compare Mk. 13:19-20.

> Then, if any man shall say unto you, Lo, here is Christ, or there believe it not.
>
> *For there shall arise false Christs, and false prophets,* and shall shew great signs and wonders; insomuch that, if it were possible, *they shall deceive the very elect.*[1]

In his inspired translation of Matthew 24, Joseph Smith clarifies the identity of the "elect," indicating that they are Church members, or "the very elect, who are the elect according to the covenant":

> If any man shall say unto you, Lo, here is Christ, or there, believe him not;
>
> For in those days there shall also arise *false Christs, and false prophets,* and shall show great signs and wonders, insomuch, that if possible, *They shall deceive the very elect, who are the elect according to the covenant.*[2]

Jesus, in his prophecy, describes his future coming to where the saints [the eagles] will be assembled following the false Christ experience:

> . . . If they shall say unto you, Behold, he is in the desert; go not forth: behold, he is in the secret chambers; believe it not.
>
> For as the lightning cometh out of the east, and shineth even unto the west; so shall also the coming of the Son of man be.
>
> For wheresoever the carcass is, there will the eagles be gathered together.[3]

He explains that his final coming in glory will be later than this appearance, following other signs in the heavens.[4]

Another prophet, Nephi, also mentioned a false Christ situation in a last days context. In his explanation of future events, Nephi alluded to a false Messiah who would work deception among the unwary. He prophesied that the Jews, in the last days, will receive the words of Christ. These words are to convince them "that they need not look forward any more for a Messiah to come, for there should not any come, *save it should be a false Messiah which should deceive the people. . . .*"[5]

In Summary: Jesus, himself, warned of false Christs and false prophets who, if possible, will deceive the very elect, or members

---

1. Mt. 24:23-24.
2. J.S. 1:21-22. See p. 131 concerning the "everlasting covenant."
3. Mt. 24:26-28. See Lk. 17:21-37.
4. Mt. 24:29-31.
5. 2 Ne. 25:18.

of the Church. This will precede an appearance he will make to where the saints are gathered together which will be prior to his final coming in glory. A Book of Mormon prophet, Nephi, was also aware of a false Christ who will appear. These prophetic warnings relate closely with D&C 64:35-40, which reveals that false apostles and prophets will be found in the early days of the New Jerusalem.

Paul's Warning: A Son of Perdition Will Show Himself As God in the Temple (2 Thess. 2:3-12)

The apostle Paul also prophesied of one who would attempt to deceive the saints and warned of a future "falling away." In his ministry he had taught the saints in Thessalonica about the coming of Christ. Some of them apparently misunderstood and believed that the second coming was imminent. To clarify his teachings, Paul wrote his epistle to them in which he gave them a sign. He carefully described a last days event which would precede Christ's coming, and taught them that the Savior would not appear until the event given as a sign had taken place. This is his prophetic warning:

> *Let no man deceive you by any means:* for that day [Christ's coming in glory] shall not come, except *there come a falling away first, and that man of sin be revealed, The son of perdition;*
>
> Who opposeth and exalteth himself above all that is called God, or that is worshipped; so that *he as God sitteth in the temple of God, shewing himself that he is God.*
>
> Remember ye not, that, when I was yet with you, I told you these things?
>
> And now ye know what withholdeth that he might be revealed in his time.
>
> For the mystery of iniquity doth already work: only he who now letteth will let, until he be taken out of the way.
>
> And then shall that Wicked be revealed, *whom the Lord shall consume with the spirit of his mouth, and shall destroy with the brightness of his coming:*
>
> *Even him, whose coming is after the workings of Satan* with all power and signs and lying wonders,
>
> And with all *deceivableness of unrighteousness* in them that perish, because they received not the love of the truth, that they might be saved.
>
> And for this cause God shall send them strong delusion, that they should believe a lie:

That all might be damned who believed not the truth, but had pleasure in unrighteousness.1

Paul's prophecy has several elements which require detailed comment:

1. There will be a falling away of unrighteous saints who will be deceived, before the coming of Christ (2:3, 10-12).
2. A son of perdition will be revealed whose coming is after the working of Satan (2:3, 9).
3. The son of perdition will sit in the temple of God, representing himself as being God (2:4).
4. Christ will destroy the son of perdition with the brightness of his coming (2:8).

1. *There will be a falling away of unrighteous saints who will be deceived, before the coming of Christ*. Other passages make reference to such an apostasy in the period of the New Jerusalem. 3 Ne. 21:20 describes a group of unrepentant individuals who will be cut off from among the Lord's people as the gathering to the New Jerusalem is taking place.[2] Nephi also tells of a group who will be "cut off" because they won't heed the words of Christ, while the righteous "shall not be confounded." This is to happen in the days of the New Jerusalem, for the passage speaks of those who will "fight against Zion" during this time.[3] D&C 64:35 tells how "the rebellious shall be cut off out of the land of Zion,"[4] while D&C 85:11 proclaims that those who "have apostatized" or have been "cut off from the church" will be excluded from the New Jerusalem.5 D&C 45:57 also alludes to those who will have been "deceived" among the church in the last days.[6] Thus there is a definite pattern of prophecy warning of apostacy and cleansing of the church in the last days, and specifically in the early days of the New Jerusalem period. This prophecy of Paul is a harmonious part of that pattern.

2. *A son of perdition will be revealed whose coming is after the working of Satan*. In the pre-mortal conflict in heaven, Satan stood in

1. 2 Thess. 2:3-12.
2. See 3 Ne. 21:12-25.
3. 1 Ne. 22:14-22.
4. D&C 64:35. See 64:33-43.
5. D&C 85:11. See 85:3-12.
6. D&C 45:57. See 45:56-7.

opposition to God. He was "thrust down from the presence of God and the Son, And was called Perdition, for the heavens wept over him—he was Lucifer, a son of the morning.[1] Members of the Church who succumb to Satan's temptations, after having full preparation and a firm testimony, become "sons of perdition":

> . . . We beheld Satan, that old serpent, even the devil, who rebelled against God, and sought to take the kingdom of our God and his Christ—
>
> *Wherefore, he maketh war with the saints of God, and encompasseth them round about.*
>
> And we saw a vision of the sufferings of those with whom he made war and overcame, for thus came the voice of the Lord unto us:
>
> Thus saith the Lord concerning *all those who know my power. and have been made partakers thereof, and suffered themselves through the power of the devil to be overcome, and to deny the truth and defy my power*
>
> *These are they who are the sons of perdition,* of whom I say that it had been better for them never to have been born;
>
> For they are vessels of wrath, doomed to suffer the wrath of God, with the devil and his angels in eternity;
>
> Concerning whom I have said there is no forgiveness in this world nor in the world to come
>
> *Having denied the Holy Spirit after having received it, and having denied the Only Begotten Son of the Father, having crucified him unto themselves and put him to an open shame.*[2]

Latter-day Saint understanding has been that only members of The Church of Jesus Christ of Latter-day Saints can have sufficient preparation to become sons of perdition if they yield to Satan's wiles.[3] President Joseph Fielding Smith, for instance, taught the following in general conference:

> I think I am safe in saying that *no man can become a Son of Perdition until he has known the light: Those who have never received the light are not to become Sons of Perdition*. They will be punished if they rebel against God. They will have to pay the price of their sinning, but *it is only those who have the light through the priesthood and through the power of God and through their membership in the Church* who will be banished forever from his influence into outer darkness to dwell with the devil and his angels. *That is a pun-*

1. D&C 76:25-26. Perdition means "Lost."
2. D&C 76:28-35. For further explanation on the sons of perdition-their sin and their fate—see the author's book Life Everlasting, pp. 289308. D&C 76 also indicates that the sons of perdition are those who "deny the Son after the Father has revealed him" (76:43), and that there will be many who will suffer this fate f 76:45-48).
3. See again D&C 76:29, 32

> *ishment that will not come to those who have never known the truth.* Bad as they may suffer, and awful as their punishment may be, they are not among that group which is to suffer the eternal death and banishment from all influence concerning the power of God.[1]

In the same conference, President Stephen L. Richards alluded to President Smith's statement and said.

> I wish all of you—perhaps all did not—had heard what President Joseph Fielding Smith told us yesterday, something I have long believed, and I was glad to have sanction for my belief. He said in substance that *there will be no Sons of Perdition who do not hold the Priesthood.* I have believed that for years because I do not think that the Lord in his mercy would ever condemn a man to that indescribable penalty of being put out entirely from the Kingdom and from all grace *unless that man knew that Jesus was the Christ, unless he knew the power of the Christ, and he could only know that, I think, by holding the Priesthood.* I believe that in the main that can be said to be true—*that only men who hold the Priesthood of God stand in danger of that terrible penalty of being classed as outcasts.*[2]

If one must hold Church membership to be a son of perdition, then it becomes obvious that this false Christ cannot be a Catholic pope, nor a Protestant minister, nor some traveling evangelist. He will have to be an apostate Mormon, not some unknown outsider. This would explain how he may be able to "deceive the very elect," and how he will have temple access. He will appear to have priesthood power, and will per-

---

1. Joseph Fielding Smith, President of the Council of the Twelve Apostles, CR, October, 1958, p. 21.
2. President Stephen L. Richards, First Counselor in the First Presidency, CR, October, 1958, p. 86.
3. 2 Thess. 2:9. Note that the false Christ will not be Satan himself—he will be a "son of perdition" and his power will be "after the working of Satan. " He will be "destroyed" with the brightness of Christ's coming, but Satan will remain on the earth and finally be bound a thousand years. (See Rev. 20:2-3.) Concerning false apostles who function with Satanic power, the apostle Paul wrote:

    > But what I do, that will I do, that I may cut off occasion from them which desire occasion; that wherein they glory, they may be found even as we.
    >
    > For such are *false apostles, deceitful workers, transforming themselves into the apostles of Christ.*
    >
    > And no marvel; for Satan himself is transformed into an angel of light. Therefore it is no great thing if his ministers also be transformed as the ministers of righteousness; whose end shall be according to their works. (2 Cor. 11:12-15. See also Al. 30-53.)

form "signs and lying wonders," but his power will be counterfeit, "after the working of Satan."[3]

3. *The son of perdition will sit in the temple of God, presenting himself as being God.* The existence of a temple is an integral part of this prophetic warning, and the tangible existence of this building is a requisite for the literal fulfillment of the prophecy.

Paul visited Thessalonica during his second missionary journey,[1] then journeyed to Athens and on to Corinth. While in Corinth he wrote both his epistles to the Thessalonian saints. Bible scholars place the date of these epistles about 50 or 51 A.D. A temple existed at that time in Jerusalem. This temple, known as the temple of Herod, stood until 70 A.D., when it was destroyed by Roman legions under the command of Titus. No temple was then found on the earth until such sacred temples were again constructed in the last days, beginning with the Kirtland temple in the mid1830s.

Since the son of perdition must sit in a temple to fulfill the prophecy, he would have to do so in a time when a temple exists upon the earth. This helps to determine the time of fulfillment of the prophecy. If it was fulfilled in ancient times, then the fulfillment would have had to take place in the two decades between the time of Paul's epistle and the fall of the temple, from 50 to 70 A.D.

But those who believe this prophecy was fulfilled in ancient times, as part of the "great apostasy," can offer no historical incident during that period which could be a possible fulfillment. Indeed, 70 A.D. would be an extremely early dating—an untenable dating—for the time of the "great apostasy" to have occurred.

If fulfillment wasn't accomplished before 70 A.D., then it must be in the last days era commencing with the Kirtland temple in 1836. Certainly no fulfillment is known from that date to the present, so it must be concluded that fulfillment is yet future.

The son of perdition will actually represent himself as being the Christ, exalting himself above all that is worshipped. He will occupy a place in God's temple (in the New Jerusalem?) and shew himself that he is God, deceiving the unrighteous who lack the spirit of discernment[2] through lying wonders, and causing their downfall.[3]

---

1. See Acts 17:1-14.
2. See D&C 50:1-34;45:56-57.
3. 2 Thess. 2:9-12.

4. *Christ will destroy the son of perdition with the brightness of his coming*. Again, an element of the prophecy aids in its interpretation. Did Christ come in ancient times and destroy an apostate representing himself to be God, or is that event still future? The answer is obvious—history records no event that would fulfill the prophetic warning.[1] The event is yet future.

Here, then, is a prophecy of extreme importance to Latter-day Saints. It warns of a false Christ who will have profound influence upon the course of the Church in a future era, and will be able to deceive an unrighteous faction, leading them away into strong delusion and damnation. He must be a Church member to be able to be a son of perdition, and one who enjoys ready access to a temple in the last days. The ultimate message to future Church members was aptly stated by Paul: "Let no man deceive you by any means. . . .

The Lord's Warning: Those Who Have Been Deceived Will Be Cast Into the Fire (D&C 45:56-57)

As part of his prophetic sermon on the Mount of Olives, Jesus told his disciples the parable of the ten virgins. The parable concerned ten virgins who went out to meet the bridegroom with their lamps. But the bridegroom tarried, and five of the virgins ran out of oil for their lamps. When the bridegroom came, he allowed only the five wise virgins who were properly prepared to enter into the marriage chamber with him.

Passages in the Doctrine and Covenants add insights to the interpretation of the parable, and indicate that the virgins represent the members of the Church in the last days. Some of the members, it is prophesied, will be wicked:

> These things are the things ye must look for; and, speaking after the manner of the Lord, they are nigh at hand, and in a time to come, even in the day of the coming of the Son of Man.

---

1. If there are those who would persist in the assertion that this prophecy was fulfilled long ago as part of the "great apostasy," they should be prepared to explain:
   A. Who was the son of perdition?
   B. In what temple did he manifest himself as God?
   C. When and how Christ destroyed him by the brightness of his coming?
   D. What historical records lend credence to such an interpretation?

2, 2 Thess. 2:3

> *And until that hour there will be foolish virgins among the wise; and at that hour cometh an entire separation of the righteous and the wicked;* and in that day will I send mine angels to pluck out the wicked and cast them into unquenchable fire.[1]

According to the Lord's prophetic warning, the saints will need to take the Holy Spirit for their guide or they will be deceived and cast into the fire:

> And at that day, when I shall come in my glory, shall the parable be fulfilled which I spake concerning the ten virgins.
>
> For they that are wise and have received the truth, and *have taken the Holy Spirit for their guide, and have not been deceived*—verily I say unto you they shall not be hewn down and cast into the fire, but shall abide the day.[2]

Nephi's Warning: Satan Will Lull the Inhabitants of Zion Into Carnal Security and Lead Them Down to Hell (2 Nephi 28:21-31)

The prophet Nephi warned of an event of serious consequence to the saints in the last days. He placed it in a future period when churches of men will deny the Holy Ghost[3] and revile against the just,[4] and in the era of the fall of the great and abominable church.[5] It was also linked with God's "marvelous work"[6] and the period in which God will set his hand to recover Israel.[7] He warned that in that period, Satan's work will have a double thrust—on one hand he will "*rage in the hearts of the children of men, and stir them up to anger against that which is good.*"[8] The second part of his attack will be directed towards the saints themselves, whom he will attempt to lull into a false security.

It is clear that this second portion of his plan will actually concern the church members, both in the Americas and in Israel. Who else could be "at ease in Zion,"[9] have already "received the word

---

1. D&C 63:53-54. concerning the things the saints are to look for, see 63:24-52.
2. D&C 45:56-57.
3. 2 Ne. 28:4.
4. 2 Ne. 28:16.
5. 2 Ne. 28:18.
6. see 2 Ne. 29:1.
7. *Ibid.*
8. 2 Ne. 28:20.
9. 2 Ne. 28:24.

of God,"[1] and have been taught "line upon line, precept upon precept"?[2]

This is Nephi's prophetic warning:

> *And others will he pacify, and lull them away into carnal security, that they will say: All is well in Zion; yea, Zion prospereth, all is well-and thus the devil cheateth their souls, and leadeth them away carefully down to hell.*
>
> And behold, others he flattereth away, and telleth them there is no hell; and he saith unto them: I am no devil, for there is none and thus he whispereth in their ears, until he grasps them with his awful chains, from whence there is no deliverance.
>
> Yea, they are grasped with death, and hell; and death, and hell, and the devil, and all that have been seized therewith must stand before the throne of God, and be judged according to their works, from whence they must go into the place prepared for them, even a lake of fire and brimstone, which is endless torment.
>
> *Therefore, wo be unto him that is at ease in Zion!*
>
> *Wo be unto him that crieth: All is well!*
>
> *Yea, wo be unto him that hearkeneth unto the precepts of men, and denieth the power of God, and the gift of the Holy Ghost!*
>
> *Yea, wo be unto him that saith: We have received, and we need no more!*
>
> *And in fine, wo unto all those who tremble, and are angry because of the truth of God !* For behold, he that is built upon the rock receiveth it with gladness; and he that is built upon a sandy foundation trembleth lest he shall fall.
>
> Wo be unto him that shall say: We have received the word of God, and we need no more of the word of God, for we have enough!
>
> For behold, thus saith the Lord God: I will give unto the children of men line upon line, precept upon precept, here a little and there a little; and blessed are those who hearken unto my precepts, and lend an ear unto my counsel, for they shall learn wisdom; for unto him that receiveth I will give more; and *from them that shall say, We have enough, from them shall be taken away even that which they have.*
>
> *Cursed is he that putteth his trust in man, or maketh flesh his arm, or shall hearken unto the precepts of men, save their precepts shall be given by the power of the Holy Ghost.*[3]

What will be the nature of the conflict in that day? According to the prophetic warning, they will have received new revelation and be unwilling to accept it. Lacking the gift of the Holy Ghost, they will say, "We have received and we need no more!" "We have enough!" There will be "those who tremble, and are angry because of the truth of God!"

---

1. 2 Ne. 28:29.
2. 2 Ne. 28:30. See D&C 128:21, Is. 28:10, 13.
3. 2 Ne. 28:21-31.

As indicated in the prophecy, there will be those who will trust in man and hearken unto the precepts of man instead of following the promptings of the Holy Ghost. This indicates a conflict will exist in which the saints will be receiving direction from at least two different sources and will be uncertain who to follow. Will this be a result of the teachings of the false Christ?[1] Or of saints refusing to accept and heed the Savior when he appears?[2] Or of conflict between the "one mighty and strong" and the man who "putteth forth his hand to steady the ark of God"?[3]

The Lord's Warning: Those Who Won't Hear Christ When He Appears Shall Be Cut Off (3 Nephi 20:22-23)

The Savior himself, while ministering among the Nephites in the meridian of time, spoke of the future era of the New Jerusalem. He spoke of a time when the remnant of the house of Jacob will ravage the land and tread down their enemies,[4] and when the sword of God's justice will fall "upon all the nations of the Gentiles."[5] He will gather his people together,[6] establish the New Jerusalem,[7] and appear to his people there.[8] But he foresees that some will reject him and be cut off:

> And behold, this people will I establish in this land, unto the fulfilling of the covenant which I made with your father Jacob; and it shall be a *New Jerusalem. And the powers of heaven shall be in the midst of this people; yea, even I will be in the midst of you.*
>
> Behold, I am he of whom Moses spake, saying: Aprophet shall the Lord your God rise up unto you of your brethren, like unto me; him shall ye hear in all things whatsoever he shall say unto you. *And it shall come to pass that every soul who will not hear that prophet shall be cut off from among the people.*[9]

He then spoke of the Gentile converts to the Church, saying that "when they shall have received the fulness of my gospel, *then if they*

1. See pp. 133-140.
2. See pp. 131-132,144.
3. See pp. 144-147.
4. 3 Ne. 20:15-17 Compare with 3 Ne. 16:14-16 and 3 Ne. 21:14-25.
5. 3 Ne. 20:20.
6. 3 Ne. 20:18.
7. 3 Ne. 20-22.
8. 3 Ne. 20:22-23.
9. Ibid. Deut. 18:15, 18-19 is where Moses' original prophecy is recorded. Peter quoted the prophecy in Acts 3:22-23, and Moroni said that Christ would be the one to fulfill the prophecy in a time yet future (J.S. 2:40).

shall harden their hearts against me I will return their iniquities upon their own heads, . . ."[1]

Here then, is prophetic indication that when the Savior appears to the saints in the New Jerusalem, some of them will harden their hearts and refuse to hear the Lord. According to the Master, they will be "cut off from among the people." Is it possible that they will have placed their confidence in the "arm of flesh"[2] of the false Christ[3] and will he deceived so they won't acknowledge the true Christ when he appears?

Nephi's Warning: Those Who Won't Hear the Prophet, Shall Be Cut Off (1 Nephi 22:20-22)

Nephi also cited the prophecy of Moses concerning the coming of Christ, which Jesus later explained. Like the Savior, he placed the prophecy in the chronological context of the gathering of Israel,[4] the fall of the great and abominable church,[5] the time of the New Jerusalem when men would be fighting against Zion,[6] and the pouring out of the wrath of God upon the wicked so they are destroyed by fire.[7] He said,

> . . . The Lord will surely prepare a way for his people, unto the fulfilling of the words of Moses, which he spake, saying: A prophet shall the Lord your God raise up unto you, like unto me; him shall ye hear in all things whatsoever he shall say unto you. And it shall come to pass that *all those who will not hear that prophet shall be cut off from among the people*.
>
> And now I, Nephi, declare unto you, that this prophet of whom Moses spake was the Holy One of Israel; wherefore, *he shall execute judgment in righteousness*.
>
> And the righteous need not fear, for *they are those who shall not be confounded*.[8]

Once again the pattern emerges: when the Lord appears in the New Jerusalem, there will be confusion and apostasy. Some will be confounded and refuse to heed the Lord, and they will be cut off, or excommunicated.

The Lord's Warning: Apostates Will Be Cut Off When One Mighty and Strong Sets In Order the House of God (D&C 85:7-12)

Joseph Smith described the strong physical impact he felt when he received one particular revelation which is recorded in the Doctrine

1. 3 Ne. 20:28.
2. See 2 Ne. 28:31.
3. 2 Thess. 2:3-4.
4. See 1 Ne. 22:8-12.
5. See 1 Ne. 22:13.
6. See 1 Ne. 22:14, 19
7. See 1 Ne. 22:15-17.
8. 1 Ne. 22:20-22

and Covenants. His recording of his feelings was unusual, and not characteristic of other revelations he recorded. Yet it served to underscore the important prophecy which followed. He wrote,

> Yea, thus saith the still small voice, which whispereth through and pierceth all things, and *often times it maketh my bones to quake while it maketh manifest,* saying. . . .[1]

The revelation he recorded is also unusual, for it tells of the coming of "one mighty and strong," who will come in the days of the New Jerusalem. He will set in order the house of God and arrange the inheritance of the righteous saints. At that time there will be apostates who will be cut off from the Church and denied a place to live among the saints:

> And it shall come to pass that I, the Lord God, *will send one mighty and strong,* holding the scepter of power in his hand, clothed with light for a covering, whose mouth shall utter words, eternal words; while his bowels shall be a fountain of truth, *to set in order the house of God, and to arrange by lot the inheritances of the saints* whose names are found, and the names of their fathers, and of their children, enrolled in the book of the law of God;
>
> *While that man, who was called of God and appointed, that putteth forth his hand to steady the ark of God, shall fall by the shaft of death, like as a tree that is smitten by the vivid shaft of lightning.*
>
> And all they who are not found written in the book of remembrance shall find none inheritance in that day, but they shall be cut asunder, and their portion shall be appointed them among unbelievers, where are wailing and gnashing of teeth.
>
> These things I say not of myself; therefore, as the Lord speaketh, he will also fulfil.
>
> *And they who are of the High Priesthood, whose names are not found written in the book of the law, or that are found to have apostatized, or to have been cut off from the church, as well as the lesser priesthood, or the members, in that day shall not find an inheritance among the saints of the Most High.*
>
> Therefore, it shall be done unto them as unto the children of the priest, as will be found recorded in the second chapter and sixty-first and second verses of Ezra.[2]

Several observations are appropriate concerning the prophecy. First, who is the "one mighty and strong"? It most probably is the Lord himself. Just as he is the prophet whom Moses said would come, can

---

1. D&C 85:6. Joseph also emphasized that this is not his own statement but a message from the Lord which will certainly be fulfilled. (D&C 85:10.)
2. D&C 85:7-12.

he not also be the fulfillment of this prophecy? That he will come in the days of the New Jerusalem has already been clearly established, as is the teaching that unrighteous saints will be cut off when the Lord makes his appearance. And note the phrases which describe the one mighty and strong, which are used in other contexts to describe the Lord Jehovah, who is Jesus Christ. He is *mighty*,[1] *strong*,[2] holds the *sceptre* of power,[3] and is clothed with *light*.[4]

Over the years, various apostates have claimed to be the one mighty and strong, yet they have not come in the time, nor the place, specified by the revelation; neither have they performed the dual mission of setting in order the house of God and arranging by lot the inheritances of the saints as stipulated in the revelation. Furthermore, they have not been opposed by one who was struck down, nor have they uttered "eternal words," nor have they shown themselves to have "bowels" that are "a fountain of truth." They have not functioned in a situation where there was a "book of the law of God" kept, nor in a situation when apostates have been prohibited from finding an inheritance among the saints. The prophecy refers to a time and situation which are yet future, and no "one mighty and strong" has been sent by the Lord to date.

The one mighty and strong is to set in order the house of God. Can this be action taken to correct the wrongs of the son of perdition who will sit in the temple?[5]

Note that the "one mighty and strong" will utter "eternal words." Are these the words that will cause those who are "at ease in Zion" to be "angry because of the truth of God" and say "we need no more of the word of God, for we have enough!" as prophesied in 2 Nephi 28?

---

1. Compare Ps. 24:8 (the Lord strong and mighty), Ps. 89:13 (Thou hast a mighty arm: strong is thy hand), Is. 63:1 (the greatness Of his strength, mighty to save), Jer. 32:18-19 (the Mighty God, mighty in work), Is 1:24 (the mighty One Of Israel), Is. 49:26; 60:16 (the mighty One Of Jacob), etc.
2. See again Ps. 24:8, 89:13; 1 Ki. 8:42, Neh. 1 10 (thy strong hand), Ps. 31:2 (be thou my strong rock), Ps. 71:7 (my strong refuge), Ps. 89:8 (who is a strong Lord like unto thee?), etc.
3. Ps. 45:6 (the sceptre of thy kingdom); Heb. 1 8 (a sceptre of righteousness); Num. 24:17 (a Sceptre shall rise out of Israel).
4. Ps. 4:6 (the light Of thy countenance); Ps. 27:1 (the Lord is my light); Ps. 104:2 (coverest thyself with light as with a garment); Dan. 2:22 (light dwelleth with him); Hab. 3:4 (his brightness was as the light); etc
5. 2 Thess. 2:3-4.

It appears that there will be conflict between the "one mighty and strong" and the man that "putteth forth his hand to steady the ark of God." Will this be the time in which "they who are not apostles and prophets shall be known," as prophesied in D&C 64? According to the prophecy, people are to be cut off, and not allowed an inheritance with the saints. Is this the same "cutting off" as described in 3 Ne. 20:23 and 3 Ne. 21:20? And could this relationship indicate that the "one mighty and strong" is actually the Lord Jesus Christ himself?

Certainly the prophecy describes an important future event, and its message is one that cannot be ignored.

Isaiah's Warning: A Mighty and Strong One Shall Come, An Overflowing Scourge Shall Pass Through, and the Lord Will Bring to Pass His Strange Act (Isaiah 28:1-22)

An intriguing prophecy by Isaiah links key last days phrases that correlate with other prophetic warnings:

> Woe to the crown of pride, to the drunkards of Ephraim whose glorious beauty is a fading flower, which are on the head of the fat valleys of them that are overcome with wine!
>
> *Behold, the Lord hath a mighty and strong one, which as a tempest of hail and a destroying storm, as a flood of mighty waters overflowing, shall cast down to the earth with the hand.*
>
> The crown of pride, the drunkards of Ephraim, shall be trodden under feet:
>
> And the glorious beauty, which is on the head of the fat valley, shall be a fading flower, and as the hasty fruit before the summer; which when he that looketh upon it seeth, while it is yet in his hand he eateth it up.
>
> *In that day shall the Lord of hosts be for a crown of glory, and for a diadem of beauty, unto the residue of his people,*
>
> *And for a spirit of judgment to him that sitteth in judgment, and for strength to them that turn the battle to the gate.*
>
> But they also have erred through wine, and through strong drink are out of the way; *the priest and the prophet have erred through strong drink, they are swallowed up of wine, they are out of the way through strong d rink; they err in vision, they stumble in judgment.*
>
> For all tables are full of vomit and filthiness, so that there is no place clean.
>
> Whom shall he teach knowledge? and whom shall he make to understand doctrine? them that are weaned from the milk, and drawn from the breasts.
>
> *For precept must be upon precept, precept upon precept; line upon line, line upon line; here a little, and there a little:*
>
> *For with stammering lips and another tongue will he speak to this people.*

To whom he said, This is the rest wherewith ye may cause the weary to rest; and this is the refreshing: yet they would not hear.

But the word of the Lord was unto them precept upon precept, precept upon precept; Line upon line, line upon line; here a little, and there a little; that they might go, and fall backward, and be broken, and snared, and taken.

Wherewith hear the word of the Lord, ye scornful men, that rule this people which is in Jerusalem.

Because ye have said, We have made a covenant with death, and with hell are we at agreement; *when the overflowing scourge shall pass through, it shall not come unto us: for we have made lies our refuge, and under falsehood have we hid ourselves:*

Therefore thus saith the Lord God, *Behold, I lay in Zion for a foundation a stone, a tried stone, a precious corner stone, a sure foundation: he that believeth shall not make haste.*

Judgment also will I lay to the line, and righteousness to the plummet: and the *hail shall sweep away the refuge of lies, and the waters shall overflow the hiding place.*

And your covenant with death shall be disannulled, and your agreement with hell shall not stand; *when the overflowing scourge shall pass through, then ye shall be trodden down by it.*

From the time that it goeth forth it shall take you: for morning by morning shall it pass over, by day and by night: and it shall be a vexation only to understand the report.

For the bed is shorter than that a man can stretch himself on it: and the covering narrower than that he can wrap himself in it.

For the Lord shall rise up as in mount Perazim, he shall be wroth as in the valley of Gibeon, *that he may do his work, his strange work; and bring to pass his act, his strange act.*

Now therefore be ye not mockers, lest your bands be made strong: for I have heard from the Lord God of hosts *a consumption, even determined upon the whole earth.*[1]

The key phrases deserve special comment:

1. *"The Lord hath a mighty and Strong One"* (Is. 28:2). Note the relationship with D&C 85:7, which foretells the coming of "one mighty and strong" to set in order the house of God and to arrange the inheritance of the saints in the New Jerusalem. His appearance is described as being accompanied by hail, a destroying storm, and a flood.[2] Does verse 5 ("In that day shall the Lord of hosts be for a crown of glory . . .") and verse 16 ("Behold, I lay in Zion for a foundation a stone, a tried stone, a precious corner

---

1. Is. 28:1-22.
2. Is. 28:2, 17. Is this prophecy linked to D&C 29:14-21, which associates a hailstorm, a terrible disease, and the fall of the great and abominable church?

stone,[1] a sure foundation . . .") indicate that Christ himself is the "mighty and strong one"?

2. In that day the Lord will be a *"spirit of judgment to him that sitteth in judgment and for strength to them that turn the battle to the gate"* (Is. 28:6). This will be the era when the church will judge the nations (D&C 64:37-38) and during the period when those in Zion will be the only ones not as war (D&C 45:66-71).

3. *"The overflowing scourge shall pass through"* (Is. 28:15, 18-19). Though the people think they will be able to escape this terrible last days plague (through a false "covenant with death"[2]), it will still come upon them. They will be "trodden down by it,"[3] and "it shall be a vexation only to understand the report."[4] This scourge is also prophesied in D&C 84:58,96-97; 97:22-26,5:19; and 45:31. Isaiah warns that there will be *"a consumption, even determined upon the whole earth"* (Is. 28:22).

4. The Lord will *"do his work, his strange work; and bring to pass his act, his strange act"* (Is. 28:21). As prophesied in D&C 95:89-95, the Lord will vex the nation, and perform a strange act "that men may discern between the righteous and the wicked."[5] The relationship of this "strange act" and the "marvellous work and a wonder" were previously discussed.[6]

Yet the prophecy of Isaiah 28 does not appear to be directed only to the saints in America, but also to "scornful men, that rule this people which is in Jerusalem."[7] They are depicted as "the drunkards of Ephraim, whose glorious beauty is a fading flower,"[8] and they are described by Isaiah as erring in vision and being troubled by drunkenness:

> But they also have erred through wine, and through strong drink are out of the way; *the priest and the prophet have erred through strong drink,*

---

1. Christ is the cornerstone and foundation. See Eph. 2:20, 1 Cor. 3:11, Ps. 118:22 and Mt. 21:42-44.
2. Is. 28:15, 18.
3. Is. 28:18.
4. Compare with D&C 97:23.
5. D&C 101:95.
6. See pp 75-83. Note also the Close proximity of Is. 28:21 and Is. 29:14 which links the two terms together. Both chapters of Isaiah are showing last days relationships between America and Israel.
7. Is. 28:14.
8. Is. 28:1.

> *they are swallowed up of wine. they are out of the way through strong drink; they err in vision, they stumble in judgment.*[1]

While the relationship of Isaiah 28 to the other prophetic warnings of the last days is not fully apparent, it is obvious that this prophecy makes pointed reference to key phrases found in modern scripture which can only be understood in a future context.

The Lord's Warning: A Scourge and Judgment Upon the Children of Zion Unless They Repent and Obey the Commandments (D&C 84:54-59)

In 1832 the Lord spoke with the voice of warning to the Church. and told them,

> And your minds in times past have been darkened because of unbelief, and because you have treated lightly the things you have received—
>
> *Which vanity and unbelief have brought the whole church under condemnation.*
>
> *And this condemnation resteth upon the children of Zion, even all.*
>
> And they shall remain under this condemnation until they *repent and remember the new covenant, even the Book of Mormon and the former commandments* which I have given them, not only to say, but to do according to that which I have written—
>
> That they may bring forth fruit meet for their Father's kingdom; *otherwise there remaineth a scourge and judgment to be poured out upon the children of Zion.*
>
> For shall the children of the kingdom pollute my holy land? Verily, I say unto you, Nay.[2]

The Master then instructed the Church members on how they should preach, saying, "Behold, I send you out to reprove the world of all their unrighteous deeds, and to teach them of a judgment which is to come."[3] And then he explained what that judgment would be:

> . . . *Wo unto that house, or that village or city that rejecteth you, or your words, or your testimony concerning me.*
>
> Wo, I say again, unto that house, or that village or city that rejecteth you, or your words, or your testimony of me;

1. Is. 28:7.
2. D&C 84:54-59. See D&C 63:63.
3. D&C 84:87. See also verse 117.

For I, the Almighty, have laid my hands upon the nations, to *scourge them for their wickedness.*

And plagues shall go forth, and they shall not be taken from the earth until I have completed my work, which shall be cut short in righteousness—

Until all shall know me, *who remain,* even from the least unto the greatest, and shall be filled with the knowledge of the Lord, and shall see eye to eye, . . .[1]

The Lord's Warning: Zion Will Be Visited With Scourge, Pestilence, Plague, Sword, and Fire If She Fails to Obey Commandments (D&C 97:21-26)

Another passage warns of the desolating scourge which will come upon the earth in the last days, and gives a conditional warning to the latter-day Zion and its inhabitants. The saints are promised that they can escape from the judgments *if* they do *"all things"* that God commands, but they are warned that severe judgments will come upon them if they fail to render complete obedience:

Therefore, verily, thus saith the Lord, *let Zion rejoice, for this is Zion—THE PURE IN HEART; therefore, let Zion rejoice, while all the wicked shall mourn.*

For behold, and lo, vengeance cometh speedily upon the ungodly as the whirlwind; and who shall escape it?

The Lord's scourge shall pass over by night and by day, and the report thereof shall vex all people; yea, it shall not be stayed until the Lord come;

For the indignation of the Lord is kindled against their abominations and all their wicked works.

Nevertheless, Zion shall escape if she observe to do all things whatsoever I have commanded her.

But if she observe not to do whatsoever I have commanded her, I will visit her according to all her works, with sore affliction, with pestilence, with plague, with sword, with vengeance, with devouring fire.[2]

---

1. D&C 84:94-98. Later in the revelation, speaking of Albany, Boston, and New York, the Savior alluded to "the desolation and utter abolishment which await them if they do reject these things. For if they do reject these things the hour of their judgment is nigh, and their house shall be left unto them desolate. " (D&C 84:114-115.)
2. D&C 97:21-26. Yet the Lord emphasizes that he seeks to bless Zion rather than punish her, and promises that these judgments will be averted "if she sin no more":

   Nevertheless, let it be read this once to her ears, that I, the Lord, have accepted of her offering; and is she sin no more none of these things shall come upon her;

   And I will bless her with blessings, and multiply a multiplicity of blessings upon her and upon her generations forever and ever, saith the Lord your God. Amen. (D&C 97:27-28.)

Coupled with this prophetic warning is a prophecy of the glory of the latter-day Zion, or New Jerusalem. But even that prophecy is conditioned upon righteousness, and expresses the danger that the New Jerusalem temple may be defiled:

> And inasmuch as my people build a house unto me in the name of the Lord, and *do not suffer any unclean thing to come into it, that it be not defiled,* my glory shall rest upon it;
>
> Yea, and my presence shall be there, for I will come into it, and all the pure in heart that shall come into it shall see God.
>
> *But if it be defiled I will not come into it, and my glory shall not be there; for I will not come into unholy temples.*
>
> And, now, behold, if Zion do these things she shall prosper, and spread herself and become very glorious, very great, and very terrible.
>
> And the nations of the earth shall honor her, and shall say: Surely Zion is the city of our God, and surely Zion cannot fall, neither be moved out of her place, for God is there, and the hand of the Lord is there;
>
> And he hath sworn by the power of his might to be her salvation and her hi h tower.[1]

The Lord's Warning: A Desolating Sickness, and Men Will Kill One Another With the Sword (D&C 45:31-33)

The Lord has spoken more concerning a future desolation of the earth in the 45th section of the Doctrine and Covenants. In the generation in which the time of the Gentiles are fulfilled,[2] God will pour out his "overflowing scourge"—a "desolating sickness." This will be the period that men will "harden their hearts" and "take up the sword, one against another":

> And there shall be men standing in that generation, that shall not pass until they shall *see an overflowing scourge; for a desolating sickness shall cover the land.*

---

1. D&C 97:15-20. Note again the prophetic pattern of scripture warning of false Christs and a son of perdition who will sit in the temple of God. The danger of the temple being defiled is real, and the subject of repeated scriptural warnings.
2. The "times of the Gentiles" are discussed in detail in the author's book Prophecy Key to the Future, pp. 17-34. Briefly, the "times of the Gentiles" is the present era when the gospel is to be preached to the people of the Gentile (Caucasian) nations. The "fulfilling of the times of the Gentiles" is the end of the period of missionary labors to them. That end will be identified by the withdrawing of missionaries from among them and an increase in the judgments of God being poured out upon the world. The times of the Gentiles will be fulfilled before the saints return to establish the New Jerusalem in Jackson County, Missouri.

> *But my disciples shall stand in holy places, and shall not be moved;* but among the wicked, men shall lift up their voices and curse God and die.
> And there shall be earthquakes in divers places, and *many desolations; yet men will harden their hearts against me, and they will take up the sword, one against another, and they will kill one another.*[1]

The Savior has characterized this period (after the times of the Gentiles are fulfilled) as the time when the scattered remnant of Israel will be gathered[2] again to their promised land, and a time of world-wide wars and commotion:

> And in that day shall be heard of wars and rumors of wars, and the whole earth shall be in commotion, and men's hearts shall fail them, and they shall say that Christ delayeth his coming until the end of the earth.
> And the love of men shall wax cold, and iniquity shall abound.[3]

The Lord's Warning: A Desolating Scourge Shall Be Poured Out Until the Earth is Empty, If They Repent Not (D&C 5:18-19)

The warning of a last days desolation of the earth was revealed to Joseph Smith even before the Church was restored. Like so many of the other prophetic warnings, it was conditional. It describes what will happen if the people "harden their hearts" and if "they repent not":

> And their testimony shall also go forth unto the condemnation of this generation if they harden their hearts against them;
> For a desolating scourge shall go forth among the inhabitants of the earth, and shall continue to be poured out from time to time, if they repent not, until the *earth is empty, and the inhabitants thereof are consumed away and utterly destroyed by the brightness of my coming.*[4]

After giving the prophetic warning, the Master asserted the literal nature of the prophecy by comparing it with the destruction of Jerusalem (in 70 A.D.) and proclaiming that "my word *shall be verified* at this time as it hath hitherto been verified."[5]

---

1. D&C 45:31-33. Observe the pattern reported repeatedly throughout this book: people will clearly fall into two distinct categories at this time the righteous (in this case the "disciples"), and the wicked who will reap God's judgments.
2. D&C 45:24-25. See also 3 Ne. 21:24-29.
3. D&C 45:26-27
4. D&C 5:18-19.
5. D&C 5:20. See also D&C 1:7, 37-39.

The Lord's Warning: God's Wrath Will Begin Among Those Who Blaspheme In His House (D&C 112:24-26)

Much has been said in this chapter about future problems which are to arise in the Church, primarily in the early days of the New Jerusalem. This final passage also focuses on that theme, and warns that there will be those who will blaspheme against God in his holy house. The Lord's vengeance will be poured out upon those apostates, and shall go forth from there:

> Behold, vengeance cometh speedily upon the inhabitants of the earth, *a day of wrath, a day of burning, a day of desolation, of weeping, of mourning, and of lamentation;* and as a whirlwind it shall come upon all the face of the earth, saith the Lord.
>
> *And upon my house shall it begin,* and from my house shall it go forth, saith the Lord;
>
> First among those among you, saith the Lord, *who have professed to know my name and have not known me, and have blasphemed against me in the midst of my house,* saith the Lord.1

That judgments would begin at the house of God was foreknown by the apostle Peter in Biblical days, and the passage in I Peter has important parallels[2] with D&C 112:24-26 and D&C 63:34. He saw that it would be a "fiery trial"[3] and warned that the righteous would "scarcely be saved."[4] This is his prophecy:

---

1. D&C 112:24-26. In the context of this prophecy the Lord describes the wickedness of the earth's inhabitants during this period with the observation that "darkness covereth the earth, and gross darkness the minds of the people, and all flesh has become corrupt before my face." (D&C 112:23.)
2. It is interesting to note how the time of fulfillment has been altered by translators' insertions in the I Peter passage. These insertions, rendered in italic type in the King James version, change the meaning of I Pet. 4:17 with the words is come and of I Pet. 4:18 with begin. These changes make the passage appear to have application only to that era, which is not clearly established as Peter's intent. Could it not be that he knew of the last days judgments which were to begin at the house of God? Was he attempting to compare that future event with circumstances in his day? (He made a comparison of this type in Acts 2 17-21. Compare that passage with Joel 2, which places this prophecy afterward [Joel 2:28] of the future Battle of Armageddon, and see Moroni's explanation that the event had not yet transpired in Joseph Smith's day [JS. 2:41].)
3. Compare I Pet. 4:12 and I Pet.1:7 with D&C 112:24's day of burning and D&C 63:34's unquenchable fire.
4. Compare I Pet. 4:18 with D&C 63:34's "the saints also shall hardly escape."

> *For the time is come that judgment must begin at the house of God:* and if it first begin at us, what shall the end be of them that obey not the gospel of God?
>
> *And if the righteous scarcely be saved,* where shall the ungodly and sinner appear?
>
> Wherefore let them that suffer according to the will of God *commit the keeping of their souls to him in well doing, as unto a faithful Creator.*[1]

Both D&C 112:24-26 and Peter's prophecy are ominous warnings for ungodly sinners who will blaspheme against God. They will do well to heed Peter's counsel to "*commit the keeping of their souls to him in well doing,* as unto a faithful Creator."[2]

Summary

1. The scriptures contain numerous prophetic warnings of a future period of conflict and apostasy within the Church. Chronological clues in these passages and their contexts indicate that the apostasy will primarily occur in the early period of the New Jerusalem.

2. The Lord has revealed that it is the responsibility of every man and every Church member to warn others of coming judgments. They are to warn the inhabitants of the earth that "desolation shall come upon the wicked." They are also commanded to "prepare the saints for the hour of judgment which is to come.

3. Though the possibility of future difficulties within the Church is unpleasant to contemplate, discuss, or write about, it is a subject which cannot be avoided by those attempting to obey all the commandments. Priesthood bearers have the responsibility to "watch over the Church always, and be with and strengthen them; and see there is no iniquity in the Church."

4. Though it must endure future strife and apostasy, the kingdom of God shall "never be destroyed" nor "left to other people." It is to continue to grow, in spite of the difficulties it must endure, until "it has filled the whole earth." The kingdom has come forth "for the last time" and the saints have been given the divine promise that "the enemy shall not overcome."

---

1. 1 Pet. 4:17-19.
2. 1 Pet. 4:19.

5. Sixteen prophetic warnings are cited in this chapter. They are prophecies made by

A. Isaiah (Is. 24:5-6).
B. The Lord (D&C 1:14-16).
C. The Lord (D&C 64:36-40).
D. The Lord (Mt. 24:24).
E. Paul (2 Thess. 2:3-12).
F. The Lord (D&C 45:56-57).
G. Nephi (2 Ne. 28:21-31).
H. The Lord (3 Ne. 20:22-23).
I. Nephi (1 Ne. 20:20-22).
J. The Lord (D&C 85:7-12).
K. Isaiah (Is. 28:1-22).
L. The Lord (D&C 84:54-59).
M. The Lord (D&C 97:21-26).
N. The Lord (D&C 45:31-33).
O. The Lord (D&C 5:18-19).
P. The Lord (D&C 112:24-26).

6. Many of the prophecies are related to the last days period called the "desolation of abomination." This is a time when the judgments of God will come upon the wicked and greatly reduce the population of the earth, leaving portions of it desolate.

7. Isaiah prophesied that the Lord's curse will leave the earth desolate because the inhabitants will transgress the laws, change the ordinance, and break the everlasting covenant. The everlasting covenant is the fulness of the gospel. Since one can only break a covenant if he has made the covenant, and can only change an ordinance if he already has the ordinance, it appears that it will be transgression among the future saints which will occasion the judgments Isaiah foresees. This interpretation is reinforced by the Lord's prophecy concerning future saints who "shall be cut off"-he reveals that they will stray from his ordinances and break his everlasting covenant (D&C 1:14-16).

8. The saints to be "cut off" will "not hear the voice of the Lord, neither the voice of his servants." It appears that confusion will exist because of a false Christ, false prophets, false apostles, and other church leaders who will be unmasked in the days of the New Jerusalem. If possible, they will "deceive the very elect," or members of the Church. The inhabitants of Zion shall judge all things pertaining to Zion, and shall prove those who are liars and hypocrites.

9. The rebellious apostates shall be cut off out of the land of Zion, and shall be sent away, and shall not inherit the land.

10. There is to come a period of tribulation more severe than any the earth has ever seen or endured. Unless the period is shortened, no flesh shall be saved. The Lord has revealed the time will be shortened for the elect's sake.

11. A son of perdition will sit in the temple of God, showing himself to be God. He will show signs and wonders, and deceive the unrighteous. When Christ appears, he will destroy the son of perdition. (It is assumed that this will be Christ's appearance in the New Jerusalem, prior to his final coming in glory.)

12. Church leaders have taught that one must be a Church member to be able to be a son of perdition. Sons of perdition are those who know God's power and who have received the Holy Ghost, then denied the truth and defied God's power. According to D&C 76:45-48, there will be many sons of perdition.

13. Fire is repeatedly mentioned in the prophecies concerning the desolation of abomination. According to the prophecies, many of the wicked will be destroyed by fire. This is not the fire which will accompany Christ's final coming in glory.

14. In order to avoid being deceived during this period of apostasy, it will be necessary for the saints to take the Holy Spirit for their guide. That Spirit is the spirit of discernment.

15. Satan will lull some of the inhabitants of Zion into carnal security and will lead them down to hell. It appears they will trust in the precepts of men and will refuse to receive new revelation when it is given to them. Of specific concern are the prophetic warnings that they will refuse to accept and heed the Savior when he appears among the saints in the New Jerusalem. Those who refuse to hear him will be cut off.

16. "One mighty and strong," probably the Savior himself, will come to the New Jerusalem to set in order the house of God and to arrange by lot the inheritances of the saints. He may be counteracting the influence of the son of perdition who will sit in the temple of God. One called of God will put forth his hand "to steady the ark of God" and be struck down. Apostates will be denied inheritances in the new

Zion, which seems to indicate that these events will transpire relatively early in the New Jerusalem era.

17. God's vengeance in the last days shall begin at his house and from there it will go forth. It will begin with men who will have blasphemed in the midst of his house.

18. Repeated prophecies are recorded in the scriptures of an "overflowing scourge" or "desolating sickness" which will be poured out and will continue until the Lord comes. It will be "a consumption, even determined upon the whole earth." The children of Zion can escape it only if they repent, remember the new covenant (found in the Book of Mormon), live God's commandments, and bring forth fruit suitable for their Father's kingdom. Zion is specifically warned that if the saints fail to do "all things" the Lord has commanded, they will be visited with "sore affliction, with pestilence, with plague, with sword, with vengeance, with devouring fire."

19. The Lord has warned that if the New Jerusalem temple is defiled, he will not come into it, and his glory shall not be there, for he will not come to unholy temples.

20. As the overflowing scourge is poured out, the wicked will harden their hearts, then take up the sword and kill one another. God's disciples shall stand in holy places, and shall not be moved.

II

Famine, Sword, and Pestilence

Instruments of God's Judgments

X

Prophecies of Future Famine

Judgments by Famine, Sword, and Pestilence

On September 21, 1823, Joseph Smith received three visits from Moroni, an angelic representative of the Lord. Moroni taught the prophet, giving comment on a series of Biblical prophecies which foretell significant events of the last days. While relating the words of his angelic visitor, Joseph recorded that

> . . . He informed me of *great judgments which were coming upon the earth, with great desolations by famine, sword, and pestilence;* and that these grievous judgments would come on the earth in this generation.[1]

Famine! Sword! Pestilence! These three terms have been used repeatedly in the scriptures to symbolize the full extent of God's judgments. Though they are used together, each represents a different aspect of the suffering which man can bring upon himself through disobedience to God's commandments.

Examples of these terms being used together in the scriptures are both numerous and varied. The Hebrews in the days of Moses pleaded with the Egyptian Pharaoh to permit them to offer sacrifices to God so they wouldn't be smitten with pestilence or the sword.[2] When Israel sinned in King David's day, they were given the choice of seven years of famine, three months of war, or three days of pestilence. Pestilence was chosen and 70,000 men died before the pestilence abated.[3] King Solomon spoke of famine, pestilence, and enemies besieging Israel as he dedicated the great temple he had constructed.[4] Jehoshaphat, king of Judah, prayed God would prevent the evils of "the sword, judgment, or pestilence, or famine"[5] from coming upon his people. By the days of Jeremiah, Judah had become so wicked that God promised that his threefold judgments would come upon them, and even forbid Jeremiah from praying in their behalf:

1. J.S. 2:45.
2. Ex. 5:3.
3. 2 Sam. 24:13-16.
4. 1 Ki. 8:37-38; 2 Chron. 6:28-29.
5. 2 Chron. 20:19.

> Then said the Lord unto me, *Pray not for this people for their good. When they fast, I will not hear their cry;* and when they offer burnt offering and an oblation, I will not accept them: but *I will consume them by the sword, and by the famine, and by the pestilence.*[1]

Jeremiah warned repeatedly of the famine, sword, and pestilence which would come upon his people for their wickedness.[2] The prophet Ezekiel issued numerous warnings concerning the people of Jerusalem, always linking the three aspects of God's judgments together.[3]

Famine, sword and pestilence are repeatedly linked in the Book of Mormon also. Lehi warned his people that they would be cursed for many generations, and that they would be "visited by sword, and by famine, and are hated."[4] Abinadi cursed King Noah, telling him his people would be driven by men and be smitten with famine and pestilence.[5] Amulek warned the people of Ammonihah of impending judgments by famine, pestilence, and sword.[6] Nephi was given power to smite the earth with famine, pestilence, and destruction a few years before the birth of the Savior.[7] Concerning the final Nephite generation the Lord revealed, through Samuel the Lamanite, that "I will visit them with the sword and with famine and with pestilence."[8]

Both the Bible and the Book of Mormon, then, contain ample evidence that famine, sword, and pestilence are combined tools of God's judgments upon the wicked. Not only are they instruments of divine retribution, they also serve as God's method for awakening his people

1. Jer. 14:11-12. False prophets had been telling the people no famine nor war would come upon them. Concerning them the Lord warned,

> . . . Thus saith the Lord concerning the prophets that prophesy in my name, and I sent them not, yet they say, Sword and famine shall not be in this land; By sword and famine shall those prophets be consumed.
>
> And the people to whom they prophesy shall be cast out in the streets of Jerusalem because of the famine and the sword; and they shall have none to bury them, them, their wives, nor their sons, nor their daughters; for I will pour their wickedness upon them. (Jer. 14:15-16. See also verses 17-22.)

2. See Jer. 21:4-9;24:10; 27:8, 13; 29:17-18; 32:24, 36; 34:17; 38:2.
3. See Ezek. 5:2, 12; 6:11-12; 7:15; 12:16. In Ezek. 14:21 a fourth judgment is added: "the noisome beast."
4. 2 Ne. 1:1 8.
5. Mos. 12:1-8.
6. Al. 10:22-23.
7. Hel. 10:6.
8. Hel. 13:9.

to righteousness as it begins to slip away from them. As Nephi observed,

> We see that except the Lord doth chasten his people with many afflictions, yea, *except he doth visit them with death and with terror, and with famine and with all manner of pestilence, they will not remember him*.[1]

Future Judgments by Famine, Sword and Pestilence Predicted

The scriptures also speak of the future, and warn that famine, sword and pestilence will be combined in last days judgments which will be poured out upon the earth. The Lord has revealed his warning that

> . . . *With the sword and by bloodshed the inhabitants of the earth shall mourn; and with famine, and plague,* and earthquake, and the thunder of heaven, and the fierce and vivid lightning also, shall the inhabitants of the earth be made to feel the wrath, and indignation, and chastening hand of an Almighty God, *until the consumption decreed hath made a full end of all nations;*
>
> That the cry of the saints, and of the blood of the saints, shall cease to come up into the ears of the Lord of Sabaoth, from the earth, to be avenged of their enemies.
>
> *Wherefore, stand ye in holy places, and be not moved,* until the day of the Lord come; for behold, *it cometh quickly,* saith the Lord.[2]

Christ, in his great panoramic prophecy on the Mount of Olives, taught that

> . . . *Nation shall rise against nation, and kingdom against kingdom: and there shall be famines, and pestilences, and earthquakes, in diverse places.*
>
> All these are the *beginning of sorrows*.[3]

It is the intent of these next three chapters to examine each of these instruments of God's judgment as they pertain to the future.

Famine—Examples from the Past

Few people realize the number and severity of famines which have occurred in the earth's history. Most famines have taken place in areas lacking adequate communication with the outside world.

---

1. Hel. 12:3.
2. D&C 87:6-8.
3. Mt. 24:7-8.

Most have been poorly documented. The most complete published list includes 370 famines up to 1940,[1] but many local famines are excluded from it. The most serious famines include the following:

1333-37	China—a great famine, with 4,000,000 reported dead in one region only; it may have been the source of Europe's Black Death.
1600	Russia—500,000 dead; also plague.
1769-70	India, Bengal—death estimates range from 3,000,000 (1/10 of population to 10,000,000 (1/3 of population).
1837-38	Northwest India—800,000 dead.
1846-51	Ireland—great potato famines; 1,000,000 died from starvation and disease, even more immigrated.
1866	India, Bengal & Orissa—1,500,000 deaths.
1876-78	India—over 36,000,000 affected; deaths estimated at 5,000,000.
1876-79	North China—9,000,000-13,000,000 estimated deaths.
1892-94	China—1,000,000 deaths estimated.
1896-97	India—5,000,000 deaths estimated.
1899-1900	India—3,250,000 affected, 1,250,000 deaths estimated.
1920-21	North China—20,000,000 affected; 500,000 deaths.
1921-22	U.S.S.R.—20,000,000-24,000,000 affected; death estimates 1,250,000-5,000,000.
1928-29	China, Shensi, Honan, & Kansu—in Shensi alone an estimated 3,000,000 died.
1932-34	U.S.S.R.—an estimated 5,000,000 died.
1941-43	Greece—losses estimated at 450,000.
1943-44	India, Bengal—1,500,000 died.[2]

The most severe of the past famines have killed as much as one-third of the population of the affected areas. What causes famines? Several reasons are given:

---

1. "Famine," *Encyclopaedia Britannica* (Chicago. Encyclopaedia Britannica, Inc., 1971), Vol. 9, p. 58A. To indicate the incompleteness of the above list the article adds:

> Adetailed study by Ping-ti Ho of the local histories of Hupei Province of China indicates that 62 famines occurred between 1644 and 1911; not one is included in the list of 370. W. H. Mallory refers to a study made at the University of Nanking reporting 1,828 famines in China between 108 B.C. and A.D. 1911. (Ibid.)

2. Adapted from *Ibid*.. pp. 58-58A.

Crop Failure. Drought is the usual cause, with almost no rain falling in affected areas for from three to seven years. Other climatic factors include cold during the planting and early growing season; excess rain, often resulting in flooding; insects, plant diseases, and early frosts or snowfalls which shorten the growing season.

War and Civil Disturbances. Blockades and sieges of cities have caused many famines. Invading armies may prevent crops from being planted or harvested. Food has often been used as a weapon.

Natural Catastrophes. Hurricanes, floods, earthquakes, and volcanic eruptions can result in destruction of crops, food stores, and means of earning a living.

What happens to individuals when famine strikes? The immediate effect, of course, is a loss of body weight. After two to three months on a daily diet of 1,600 calories, weight loss will be about 25%. Activity will be reduced. General lethargy will occur. The mind becomes dominated by a desire for food. Other emotions are dulled. Birthrates fall and stillbirths increase. There is constant diarrhea, which often is the immediate cause of death. The belly becomes bloated, arms and legs become very thin, the hair turns grey, the eyes become piercing. Infectious diseases spread: cholera, malaria, smallpox, typhus, and influenza often accompany famine.

People search for food. They eat grass, sawdust, the bark of trees. They chew pieces of leather. Prices skyrocket, till food becomes impossible to buy. Moral values disintegrate. People rob and steal. Parents sell their children. Some turn to murder and cannibalism.

Consider the terrible effects of famine, as described in the Bible:

> And there was a great famine in *Samaria: and, behold, they besieged it, until an ass's head was sold for fourscore pieces of silver, and the fourth part of a cab of dove's dung for five pieces of silver.*
>
> And as the king of Israel was passing by upon the wall, there cried a woman unto him, saying, Help, my lord, O king.
>
> And he said, If the Lord do not help thee, whence shall I help thee? out of the barnfloor, or out of the winepress?
>
> And the king said unto her, What aileth thee? And she answered, *This woman said unto me, Give thy son, that we may eat him to day, and we will eat my son to morrow.*
>
> *So we boiled my son, and did eat him: and I said unto her on the next day, Give thy son, that we may eat him: and she hath hid her son.*

And it came to pass, when the king heard the words of the woman, that he rent his clothes; and he passed by upon the wall, and the people looked, and, behold, he had sackcloth within upon his flesh.[1]

The prophet Jeremiah described a famine in his day:

How is the gold become dim! how is the most fine gold changed! the stones of the sanctuary are poured out in the top of every street,

The precious sons of Zion, comparable to fine gold, how are they esteemed as earthen pitchers, the work of the hands of the potter!

Even the sea monsters draw out the breast, they give suck to their young ones: *the daughter of my people is become cruel, like the ostriches in the wilderness.*

The tongue of the sucking child cleaveth to the roof of his mouth for thirst: the young children ask bread, and no man breaketh it unto them.

They that did feed delicately are desolate in the streets: they that were brought up in scarlet embrace dunghills.

For the punishment of the iniquity of the daughter of my people is greater than the punishment of the sin of Sodom, that was overthrown as in a moment, and no hands stayed on her.

Her Nazarites were purer than snow, they were whiter than milk, they were more ruddy in body than rubies, their polishing was of sapphire:

Their visage is blacker than a coal; they are not known in the streets: *their skin cleaveth to their bones; it is withered, it is become like a stick.*

They that be slain with the sword are better than they that be slain with hunger: for *these pine away, stricken through for want of the fruits of the field.*

The hands of the pitiful women have sodden their own children: they were their meat in the destruction of the daughter of my people.

The Lord hath accomplished his fury; he hath poured out his fierce anger, and hath kindled a fire in Zion, and it hath devoured the foundations thereof.[2]

But the degenerating morality that comes with widespread famine is perhaps best described by the historian Josephus, who related the events which took place in Jerusalem as that city was besieged by the Romans in 70 A.D.:

. . . *The madness of the seditious did also increase together with their famine, and both those miseries were every day inflamed more and more;*

---

1. 2 Ki. 6:25-30. This famine occurred during the Syrian siege of Samaria. Fourscore pieces of silver, for purchasing an ass's head, amounted to about $50; a pint (the fourth part of a cab) of dove excrement cost about $3. 2 Ki. 7 tells how God brought a miraculous end to the famines (See also Ezek. 5:10; Deut. 28:53-57.)
2. Lam. 4:1-11. This famine occurred as Jerusalem fell to Babylonia. See also Jer. 14:1-6;

for there was no corn which any where appeared publicly, *but the robbers came running into, and searched men's private houses; and then, if they found any, they tormented them, because they had denied they had any;* and if they found none, they tormented them worse, because they supposed they had more carefully concealed it. *The indication they made use of whether they had any or not was taken from the bodies of these miserable wretches; which, if they were in good case, they supposed they were in no want at all of food; but if they were wasted away, they walked off without searching any further;* nor did they think it proper to kill such as these, because they saw they would very soon die of themselves for want of food. *Many there were indeed who sold what they had for one measure; it was of wheat, if they were of the richer sort; but of barley, if they were poorer.* When these had so done, they shut themselves up in the inmost rooms of their houses, and ate the corn they had gotten; some did it without grinding it, by reason of the extremity of the want they were in, and others baked bread of it, according as necessity and fear dictated to them: a table was no where laid for a distinct meal, but they snatched the bread out of the fire, half-baked, and ate it very hastily.

It was not a miserable case, and a sight that would justly bring tears into our eyes, how men stood as to their food, while *the more powerful had more than enough, and the weaker were lamenting* [for want of it]. *But the famine was too hard for all other passions, and it is destructive to nothing so much as to modesty;* for what was otherwise worthy of reverence was in this case despised; insomuch that *children pulled the very morsels that their fathers were eating out of their very mouths, and what was still more to be pitied, so did the mothers do as to their infants; and when those that were most dear were perishing under their hands, they were not ashamed to take from them the very last drops that might preserve their lives:* and while they ate after this manner, yet were they not concealed in so doing; but the seditious every where came upon them immediately, and snatched away from them what they had gotten from others; for *when they saw any house shut up, this was to them a signal that the people within had gotten some food;* whereupon they broke open the doors, and ran in, and took pieces of what they were eating almost up out of their very throats, and this by force: the old men, who held their food fast, were beaten; and if the women hid what they had within their hands, their hair was torn for so doing; nor was there any commiseration shown either to the aged or to the infants, but they lifted up children from the ground as they hung upon the morsels they had gotten, and shook them down upon the floor. *But still they were more barbarously cruel to those that had prevented their coming in, and had actually swallowed down what they were going to seize upon, as if they had been unjustly defrauded of their right.* They also invented terrible methods of torments to discover where any food was, and they were these: to stop up the passages of the privy parts of the miserable wretches, and to drive sharp stakes up their fundaments; and a man was forced to bear what it is terrible even to hear, in order to make him confess that he had but one loaf of bread, or that he might discover a handful of barley-meal that was concealed; and this was done when these tormentors were not themselves hungry; for the thing had been less barbarous had necessity forced them to it; but this was done to keep their madness in exercise, and as making preparation of provisions for themselves for the following days. These men went also to meet those that had crept out of the city by night, as far as the Roman guards, to gather some plants and herbs that grew wild; and *when those people thought they had got clear of the enemy, they snatched from them what they had brought with them,* even while they had frequently entreated them, and that by calling upon the tremendous name of God, to give them back some part of what they had brought; though these would not give them the least crumb, and they were to be well contented that they were only spoiled. and not slain at the same time [1]

Seven Years of Famine

When God sends a famine, how long does it last? Though famines recorded in the scriptures and in secular history have continued for varying periods of time, one interval has been specified by scripture and modern-day prophets so many times that it cannot be overlooked. *Seven* years has been the duration proclaimed by God's prophets. That term is frightening, for it far exceeds the length of major famines which have claimed the lives of millions in years past. If a widespread famine of seven years' duration came upon the earth in the future, it would truly leave much of the earth desolate.

Probably the best-known instance of famine in the scriptures is the seven years of dearth that came in the days of Joseph, who was sold into Egypt. God favored the Egyptian Pharaoh with two prophetic dreams,[2] which warned that seven good years would be followed by seven years of famine. Joseph interpreted the dreams, telling the ruler that "God hath shewed Pharaoh what he is about to do:"

> The seven good kine are seven years; and the seven good ears are seven years; the dream is one.

---

1. Flavius Josephus, The Life and Works of Flavius Josephus (New York: Holt, Rinehart and Winston, n.d.), Wars of the Jews, Bk V, chpt. X, pp. 798-799.
2. See Gen. 41:1-7. Note that the revelation was given to a secular leader, not through God's prophet, as was also the case with King Nebuchadnezzar's visions of the future (see Dan. chpts. 2 & 4). These and other instances from the scriptures and religious history demonstrate that God, in his wisdom, grants valid prophetic insights to many others besides his prophets. Though such revelations do not constitute "doctrine" or "commandment" to God's church, they are nevertheless revealed truth.

> And the seven thin and ill favoured kine that came up after them are seven years; and the seven empty ears blasted with the east wind shall be *seven years of famine*.[1]

With this prophetic warning as his guide, the Pharaoh established a vast food storage program in which sufficient food Was made available when "the famine was over all the face of the earth"[2] and became "sore in the land."[3] Joseph, who was placed in charge of the storage program, played an inspired role. He later told his brothers that *"God did send me before you to preserve life."*[4]

Seven years of famine are mentioned in other scriptural instances. For instance, when the prophet Gad gave King David the choice between famine, war, or pestilence as the punishment to come upon Israel, his query was "*Shall seven years of famine come unto thee in thy land?*"[5]

Seven years of famine came to the Palestine area in the days of Elisha, and that prophet warned the Shunamite woman that "*the Lord hath called for a famine; and it shall also come upon the land seven years*."[6]

The Mormons endured severe famines during the early days of the Utah period. The Saints have been continually counseled from that

---

1. Gen. 41:26-27. Joseph then told Pharaoh that "the thing is established by God, and God will shortly bring it to pass." (Gen. 41:32. For assurance that God brings famines see Hel. 12:1- 3; Mos. 1:17; 9:3; Eth. 9:28; 11:7;1 Ki. 17:1; Ezek. 5; Deut. 28; Ja. 5:17; etc.
2. Gen. 41:56. See Gen. 42-47. Note the economic conditions, in which money failed, during the famine (Gen. 47:15-26).
3. Gen. 43:1. A carving on an Egyptian tomb, now known as the "stele of famine," records another seven-year famine in Egypt:

   The tale is one of suffering and distress: "I am mourning on my high throne for the vast misfortune, because the Nile flood in my time has not come for seven years! Light is the grain; there is a lack of crops and of all kinds of food. Each man has become a thief to his neighbor. They desire to hasten and cannot walk. The child cries, the youth creeps along, and the old men; their souls are bowed down, their legs are bent together and drag along the ground, and their hands rest in their bosoms. The counsel of the great ones in the court is but emptiness. Torn open are the chests of provisions, but instead of contents there is air. Everything is exhausted." (From Ralph A. Graves, "Fearful Famines of the Past," *The National Geographic Magazine,* vol. xxxii, July 1917, p. 70.) (*Encyclopaedia Britannica, op. cit.,* vol. 9, pp. 58A.)
4. Gen. 45:5.
5. 2 Sam. 24:13.
6. 2 Ki. 8:1

time forward to store for a time of future famine and hardship. What should be emphasized is that the counsel and instruction given was that the saints should store a *seven year supply of food*.

Heber C. Kimball, for instance, warned in an 1857 discourse that "after your testimony *cometh the testimony of earthquakes, of famine, of fire and of desolation*. it shall come upon the world, and it shall begin at my house, saith the Lord, that is, *with that portion who rebel against Him in the midst of His house*. . . . These calamities are coming. . . . " The following are excerpts from his discourse:

> Brethren and sisters, this is the time in which to prepare. If you are not saved temporally in these Valleys, I shall not be. If you will take a course to bring distress on this people, we shall have to be distressed. . . .
>
> Brethren, go and build your storehouses before your grain is harvested, and lay it up, and *let us never cease until we have got a seven years' supply*. You may think that we shall not see times in which we shall need it. Do you not comprehend how comfortable it will be for us to know that we have *grain enough to last us seven years?* . . .
>
> Will you be slack, brethren, and let the evil come upon us, when we forewarn you of the future events that are coming: We are telling of what the prophets have said—of what the Lord has said to Joseph. Wake up, now, wake up, O Israel, and lay up your grain and your stores. I tell you that there is trouble coming upon the world. . . .
>
> Is it so in the United States? It is. They have got to eat that dish; *and when famine, pestilence, and starvation come upon us in a small degree, it will increase upon them fourfold,* packed down and running over, and they cannot help it. . . . *We will lay up the grain for seven years,* and thousands of them will worship us for a little johnny cake.[1]

Two months later, President Kimball again referred to the instruction to store up a seven years' supply:

> This is a part of our religion—to lay up stores and provide for ourselves and for the surrounding country; for the day is near when *they will come by thousands and by millions, with their fineries, to get a little bread*. That time is right by our door. . . .
>
> Say I, wake up, ye Saints of Zion, while it is called to-day, lest trouble and sorrow come upon you, as a thief in the night.
>
> Suppose it is not coming, will it hurt you to *lay up the products of the earth for seven years?* Will it hurt you, if you have your guns, swords, and spears in good condition, according to the law of the United States?[2]

---

1. Heber C. Kimball, JD 4:336-339. June 7, 1857.
2. Heber C. Kimball, JD 5:163-164. August 30, 1857.

Elder George A. Smith reminded the saints of the counsel to lay up seven years' provisions, explained how it was to be done, and warned of the folly of selling it when it should have been stored to meet future needs:

> . . . I wish to call the attention of the Conference to the text of President Young in relation to storing our wheat. This is a question of vast importance. A few years ago President Young gave counsel to the people of the Territory—most of whom agreed to it—to lay by seven years provisions. We were to have commenced three years ago, and were to have laid up one year's bread over and above the year's supply. The following year we were to add another year's supply, and so have continued until we had our seven years' supply laid up. . . . *I am aware that some of our brethren thought th¿s counsel extravagant;* they considered that it could not be necessary to lay up such a quantity of bread; and some of them, instead of getting out lumber and making good substantial bins for the preservation of their wheat, turned out their means for teams, and freighted their bread to the north, to the east, and to the west; and not only so, but in many instances they gave it away, if they could only get half price for hauling it. Hundreds and thousands of sacks of flour have been hauled away, *when it should have been stored up here against a day of want.*[1]

President Brigham Young, while speaking about the exemplary role which should be played by bishops, commented on the instruction to store for seven years:

> We have said much to the people with regard to laying up provisions to last them a few years. This is our duty now; it has been our duty for years. How many of our bishops have provisions laid up for one year, two years, or seven years? . Each bishop should be an example to his ward. If the bishop of a ward lays up wheat to last his family a year, two years, or seven years, as the case may be, his neighbors on the right and on the left will be very apt to do the same; they will very likely build good bins and try to fill them.[2]

President Young reminded the saints of the counsel to store for as much as seven years, and warned that they cannot expect God to continue to give them abundant harvests if they do not store their food:

> *Years ago, Brother Kimball counseled the people to lay up two year's provisions, and then enough for four, for six and for seven years.* I have it now, and I am dealing it out. Some people have so much faith that

1. George A. Smith, JD 12:141. October 9, 1867.
2. Brigham Young, JD 12:106. November 3, 1867.

> although the grasshoppers are around in such vast numbers, they are confident of an abundant harvest, because of the movements made to gather the poor this season. They say the Lord would not inspire His servants to bring the poor from the nations that they might starve. And so believing, they will go and sell the last bushel of wheat for comparatively nothing, trusting in God to provide for their wants. *My faith is not of this kind; it is reasonable. If the Lord gives good crops this season, and tells us to lay up from that abundance, I do not think He will increase His blessings upon us if we foolishly squander those He has already given us.* I believe He will bless the earth for His people's sake; and I will till it and try to get a crop from it; but *if I neglect to take advantage of the goodness of the Lord, or misuse or treat lightly His mercies, I need not expect that they will be continued upon me to the same extent.* Have not my sisters here, gleaned in the fields around for years past? And when they have had their gleanings thrashed out, *have they not taken the grain to The stores and sold it to our enemies, instead of laying it by?* And yet they will expect to be blessed continually with plenty! *I have not so much faith as this. I have a reasonable faith, a sustaining faith, one that I can build my hopes upon;* and I think I will not be disappointed. I labor and toil, but I do not waste my labor.[1]

While speaking of the need for the saints to provide for their own needs, Brigham Young commented on the need for an extensive supply of food, in preparation for a time when starving people will come to the saints for food. He warned that the saints must labor in their own behalf and bless themselves, not just expect God to supply their needs. Again, a seven year supply is mentioned:

> . . . is it any more inconsistent than to throw away and waste the substance the Lord has given us, and when we come to want, crying to Him for what we have wasted and squandered? The Lord has been blessing us all the time, and *He asks us why we have not been blessing ourselves.*
>
> Will this be instructive to you, my brethren, hereafter? *A great many have taken this counsel, and they are prepared. I had my seven years' breadstuffs on hand last year;* but I have to deal it out, and I will deal it out to the last bushel, and try my faith with my brethren. But are we deserving of praise from God or man? Who are deserving of praise? The persons who take care of themselves, or the ones who always trust in the great mercies of the Lord to take care of them? It is just as consistent to expect that the Lord will supply us with fruit when we do not plant the trees; or that, when we do not plow and sow and are saved the labor of harvesting, we should cry to the Lord to save us from want, as to ask Him to save us from the consequences of our own folly, disobedience and waste. It is said, by some, that the Lord is not going to tell His servants to gather His people here to

---

1. Brigham Young, JD 12:219. May 17, 1868.

starve. That is true; *but the Lord has said,* "Gather the poor from the nations;" and to the people here, *"Gather and save the produce I put within your reach, and prepare against a day of want. " Suppose a hundred thousand or a million starving people were coming here, and we had only grain to last for a couple of years, with famine around; they would offer their gold and their silver and their plate and their precious things for bread to eat, and you would hand it out until all was gone. Then you could sit down and look at the riches you had got, until all would perish together with hunger. This would be so, unless the people act more wisely than they do now.*[1]

Most Saints Lack Adequate Food Storage

And how obedient are the saints to the counsel to store food which has been given to them for over a century? Statistics are not readily available to answer the question. However, results of a study of LDS people in Utah, made by Utah State University, was presented in the welfare meeting of October General Conference in 1975. Bishop H. Burke Peterson, first counselor in the Presiding Bishopric presented the statistics, which were regarded as a representative sampling:

Five percent of church members had a year's supply of meat products, three percent had a year's supply of dried or canned fruits or vegetables, about 18 percent had a year's supply of grains and only three families in a hundred had a year's supply of canned or powdered milk. "On the average, about 30 percent of the church had a two-month supply of food. The remainder had little or none," Bishop Peterson said.[2]

Reports from the meeting indicated that "just more than half of the Church's 5,000 wards around the world have welfare production projects."[3] The Church welfare program is designed to assist only the needy—about four percent of the Church, and would be insufficient to meet the needs of a large portion of the Church in time of widespread emergency.[4] The position of the Church is that the individual members

1. Brigham Young, JD 12:243-244. July 25, 1868.
2. "Most LDS Unprepared, Welfare Meeting Told," Deseret News, October 4, 1975.
3. Ibid.
4. The report stated:

   There are 78 bishop's storehouses in the church to distribute commodities to the needy. Most of these are concentrated in the western states, but bishops and stake presidents should be planning for such storehouses throughout the world, he said.

   Bishop Peterson showed a chart indicating that demands on the bishop's storehouses have reached as high as $600,000 in 1975 and the need is increasing at the rate of 25 percent a year.

are responsible for meeting their own needs in future emergencies. Again referring to Elder Peterson's report:

> He said it was "extremely important" that local leaders and members place greater emphasis on home storage for a year's supply of food, clothing, and where possible, fuel and to grow gardens and make their own clothes.
>
> "In general, become as self-sufficient as possible *to prepare against the days to come,*" he said.
>
> Bishop Peterson said the church has a total of 671 production projects, including 143,000 acres under cultivation, but this is only meeting current needs.
>
> "*Family preparedness, with home production and storage, must be the way the majority of our church families take care of themselves,*" he said.
>
> The ward, stake and multi-stake production projects are only a "backup system" for helping those who are unable to care for themselves, he said.[1]

Prophecies of Famine in a Time of Future Conflict

Prophets of the restored Church have repeatedly warned of famines that will come in the last days. They have focused, in particular, on famine that will be experienced in America during a period of internal conflict prior to the return to Jackson County. Several of these prophecies allude to the coming of many people to obtain food from the saints in the tops of the mountains. Joseph Smith warned, for instance, that

> I am prepared to say by the authority of Jesus Christ, that not many years shall pass away before *the United States shall present such a scene of bloodshed as has not a parallel in the history of your nation; pestilence, hail, famine, and earthquakes will sweep the wicked of this generation from off the face of the land, to open and prepare the way for the return of the lost tribes of Israel from the north country.*[2]

> "We must prepare now if we are to have adequate commodities stored to handle major economic problems of the future," he said.
>
> Despite the heavy volume, the storehouses assisted only four percent of the church membership last year.
>
> One year's supply of commodities are on hand in the system at the present time, Bishop Peterson said, but this would be "quickly depleted by a major increase in demand. " (*Ibid.*)

---

1. *Ibid.*
2. HC 1:315. Letter of Joseph Smith to editor N.E. Seaton, January 4, 1833.

In July, 1839, the prophet Joseph told of a vision which he had received which warned of serious internal conflict within the United States in which even family members would struggle to the death with each other. His allusion to famine at the end of the vision may be indication that the people will be struggling to obtain food in a time of extreme scarcity and may explain why family members would take the lives even of loved ones:

> *There will be here and there a Stake [of Zion] for the gathering of the Saints. Some may have cried peace, but the Saints and the world will have little peace from henceforth. Let this not hinder us from going to the Stakes; for God has told us to flee, not dallying, or we shall be scattered, one here, and another there.* There your children shall be blessed, and you in the midst of friends where you may be blessed. The Gospel net gathers of every kind.
>
> *I prophesy, that that man who tarries after he has an opportunity of going, will be afflicted by the devil.* Wars are at hand; we must not delay; but are not required to sacrifice. We ought to have the building up of Zion as our greatest object. *When wars come, we shall have to flee to Zion.* The cry is to make haste. The last revelation says, Ye shall not have time to have gone over the earth, until these things come. It will come as did the cholera, war, fires, and earthquakes; *one pestilence after another, until the Ancient of Days comes, then judgment will be given to the Saints.*
>
> Whatever you may hear about me or Kirtland, take no notice of it; for if it be a place of refuge, the devil will use his greatest efforts to trap the Saints. You must make yourselves acquainted with those men who like Daniel pray three times a day toward the House of the Lord. *Look to the Presidency and receive instruction. Every man who is afraid, covetous, will be taken in a snare. The time is soon coming, when no man will have any peace but in Zion and her stakes.*
>
> *I saw men hunting the lives of their own sons, and brother murdering brother, women killing their own daughters, and daughters seeking the lives of their mothers. I saw armies arrayed against armies. I saw blood, desolation, fires. The Son of Man has said that the mother shall be against the daughter, and the daughter against the mother.* These things are at our doors. *They will follow the Saints of God from city to city.* Satan will rage, and the spirit of the devil is now enraged. I know not how soon these things will take place; but with a view of them, shall I cry peace? No! I will lift up my voice and testify of them. *How long you will have good crops, and the famine be kept off, I do not know; when the fig tree leaves, know then that the summer is nigh at hand.*[1]

---

1. HC 3:390-391. July 1, 1839. This was a portion of the Prophet's address to the Twelve. Note pertinent aspects of his warning: 1. When wars come, the Saints will have to flee to the stakes of Zion so they won't be scattered, 2. the judgments will continue until the coming of the Ancient of Days [to the Council at Adam-ondi-Ahman, early in the New Jerusalem era. See HC 3:386-387, 389, 391], 3. his message was that one should testify of the vision when one receives such a warning.

A powerful prophecy made at the end of the Civil War by Elder Orson Hyde, then President of the Quorum of the Twelve, asserts that scarcity of food will be the reason for future conflict within the United States. The prophecy was made in 1865 at Nephi, Utah:

> The eagle of war will now take up his flight and perch on the banks of the river Rhine, returning to his native heath when it will not be the white man of the north fighting for the liberation of the colored man of the south, *but will be the white man of the north and the white man of the south fighting for bread for their wives and children!*[1]

Brigham Young warned of famine that would occur in America and throughout the world when the testimony of the Elders ceases to be given [the times of the Gentiles are fulfilled] and God pours out his judgments:

> "Do you think there is calamity abroad now among the people?" Not much. *All we have yet heard and all we have experienced is scarcely a preface to the sermon that is going to be preached. When the testimony of the Elders ceases to be given, and the Lord says to them, "Come home; I will now preach my own sermons to the nations of the earth," all you now know can scarcely be called a preface to the sermon that will be preached with fire and sword, tempests, earthquakes, hail, rain, thunders and lightnings, and fearful destruction.* What matters the destruction of a few railway cars? You will hear of magnificent cities, now idolized by the people, sinking in the earth, entombing the inhabitants. The sea will heave itself beyond its bounds, engulphing mighty cities. *Famine will spread over the nations, and nation will rise up against nation, kingdom against kingdom, and states against states, in our own country and in foreign lands; and they will destroy each other, caring not for the blood and lives of their neighbours, of their families, or for their own lives.* They will be like the Jaredites who preceded the Nephites upon this continent, and will destroy each other to the last man, through the anger that the Devil will place in their hearts, because they have rejected the words of life and are given over to Satan to do whatever he listeth to do with them. You may think that the little you hear of now is grievous; yet *the faithful of God's people will see days that will cause them to close their eyes because of the sorrow that will come upon the wicked nations. The hearts of the faithful will be filled with pain and anguish for them.*[2]

---

1. This prophecy is contained in copies of personal papers of Elder Orson Hyde given to the author by Elder Hyde's granddaughter, Romania Woolley. Originals of these papers were contributed to the BYU library and copies were presented to the Church College of Hawaii.
2. JD 8:123. July 15, 1860.

Orson Pratt also warned of the future conflict which will take place in America, and said, concerning the food supply, that

> . . . There will be too much bloodshed, too much mobocracy, too much going forth in bands and destroying and pillaging the land to suffer people to pursue any local vocation with any degree of safety. *What will become of millions of the farmers upon that land ? They will leave their farms and they will remain uncultivated, and they will flee before the ravaging armies from place to place;* and thus will they go forth burning and pillaging the whole country; . . .[1]

In another discourse on the future period of internal conflict, Elder Pratt also spoke concerning the food supply:

> The time will come when *there will be no safety in carrying on the peaceable pursuits of farming or agriculture. But these will be neglected, and the people will think themselves well off if they can flee from city to city, from town to town and escape with their lives.* Thus will the Lord visit the people, if they will not repent.[2]

It takes little imagination to contemplate what would happen to the nation's food supply if this situation took place for even one season. To lose a national harvest would bring a famine of unprecedented proportions!

Elder Heber C. Kimball anticipated that the future famines, which will be part of the judgments to be poured out by God, "will be the most terrible and severe that have ever come upon the nations of the earth":

> . . . Every man who has a farm needs a storehouse—one made of rock and lime, that will guard your grain against the mice, rats, and all other four-legged vermin; also against the two-legged ones. *I have more fears of the two-legged ones than I have of the four-legged ones.*
>
> Plan to build a good storehouse, every man who has a farm, and never cease until you have accomplished it. And do not forget to pay your tithing before you put the grain into the storehouse. *Lay up enough for seven years, at a calculation for from five to ten in each family; and then calculate that there will be in your families from five to ten persons to where you now have one, because you are on the increase. . . .*
>
> When we have stored away our grain we are safe, independent of the world, in case of famine, are we not? Yes, we are; for, in that case, we will have the means for subsistence in our own hands. When the famines begin upon the earth, we shall be very apt to feel them first.

1. JD 20:151. March 9, 1879.
2. JD 12:344. December 27, 1868,

If judgments must need begin at the house of God, and if the righteous scarcely are saved, how will it be with the wicked ? Am I looking for famines? Yes, the most terrible and severe that have ever come upon the nations of the earth . . .[1]

Elder Kimball prophesied that there will come a time when the saints "will be obliged to depend upon our own resources," and the people of the U.S. will come to them for bread to eat:

Lay up your stores, and take your silks and fine things, and exchange them for grain and such things as you need, and *the time will come when we will be obliged to depend upon our own resources; for the time is not far distant when the curtain will be dropped between us and the United States*. When that time comes, brethren and sisters, you will wish you had commenced sooner to make your own clothing. I tell you, God requires us to go into home manufacture; and, prolong it as much as you like, you have got to do it.

You will also see the day that you will wish you had laid up your grain, if you do not do it now; for you will see the day, if you do not take care of the blessings God has given to you, that you will become servants, the same as the world will.

We have told you this before. You have been exhorted, year after year, to prepare for hard times: you have been told of this often enough. We have told you that when hard times come again you won't have the privilege that you had last time of having food dealt out to you gratuitously, but you will have to pay for all you get. This will come to pass. I suppose there are many who don't believe it. To such it is like a tune that strikes upon the drum of the ear, passes off, and is forgotten.

I will prove to you that I will put my faith with my works and *lay up stores for my family and for my friends that are in the United States, and I will be to them as Joseph was to the people in the land of Egypt. Every man and woman will be a saviour if they will do as I say.* You may write this down and send it to the States; for it will be published.

. . . It behoves us to be saving and to prepare for the time to come. The day will come when the people of the United States will come lugging the¿r bundles under their arms, coming to us for bread to eat. . . .

If you will do right—keep the commandments of God, I can say with all the propriety that any man, prophet, or apostle ever did, *you shall never want for food, or raiment, Or houses, or lands; and no power on the earth can injure you*. There is no power that shall prevent our prosperity; for we shall increase, while every other power upon the earth that is opposed to this work and Our God will go down. I just know it. Amen.[2]

---

1. JD 5:20, April 6, 1857.
2. JD 5:10-11. July 5, 1857. Note the conditional nature of the last paragraph of his prophecy. Will the saints be able to claim this blessing if they do not maintain the food supply they have been commanded to have on hand?

And it was Elder Kimball who prophesied that "*The day will come that you (strangers) will have to come to us for bread to eat; and we will be your saviours here upon Mount Zion.*"[1]

He also told how people would come to the tops of the mountains in this time of future peril. Speaking at the arrival of the second of the handcart companies, he prophesied that

> There will be *millions on millions* that will come much in the same way, only they will not have handcarts, for *they will take their bundles under their arms, and their children on their backs, and under their arms, and flee; and Zion's people will hal)e to send out relief to them, for they will come when the judgments come on the nations.*[2]

Famine, then, has been clearly represented in prophecy as being an instrument of God's judgments upon the wicked in the last days. Though the saints have been repeatedly commanded to have extensive supplies on hand, it appears that most have failed to do so. Can they lay claim upon God's mercies when famines come if they have failed to obey the counsel they have been given? According to the prophetic warnings cited above, the famines will be severe, and the burdens placed upon the saints will be great. It may well be that possession of adequate food storage, in obedience to the commandment, will be the factor that separates the righteous and wicked saints—the wise and foolish virgins—in the last days.

Summary

1. The Angel Moroni warned Joseph Smith that judgments are coming upon the earth by famine, sword, and pestilence. These three terms have been used repeatedly in the scriptures to symbolize the full extent of God's judgments.

2. Examples from the Old Testament and Book of Mormon demonstrate the use of these terms. In many of the situations listed, divine retribution was both swift and complete, leaving destruction and desolation in its wake.

3. Famine, sword, and pestilence serve both as the instruments of God's retribution and as his method for awakening his people to obedience as righteousness begins to slip away from them.

---

1. JD 5:9. July 5, 1857.
2. JD 4:106. September 28, 1856.

4. God has warned that the inhabitants of the earth will mourn because of his chastening hand which will be manifested through sword, famine, and plague until the consumption he has decreed has made a full end of all nations. The saints are to stand in holy places as these events transpire.

5. Past famines have killed millions of people, sometimes slaying one-third of the population.

6. Causes of famine include crop failure, war and civil disturbances, and natural catastrophes.

7. The personal physical effects of famine include loss of body weight, lethargy, emotional dullness, diarrhea, the spread of infectious diseases as body resistance is reduced, bloated belly, and hair turning grey.

8. Examples of human behavior in other famines were cited from the Bible and from Josephus. They showed the economic problems caused by a scarcity of food, cannibalism, robbery and murder, and a general decline in moral values.

9. The duration of famines sent by God was seven years in several scriptural situations. Early LDS Church leaders instructed the saints to store food sufficient for seven years in order to be prepared for future famines. They warned that the saints cannot expect God to bless them with abundant harvests and adequate food supply if the saints don't work to supply their own needs and if they don't preserve a seven-year supply instead of selling all their produce.

10. A survey reported in a 1975 general conference showed that most Latter-day Saints have not obeyed the counsel given to them to store food. Only about 30% of the Church had a supply adequate for even two months. Approximately three percent had a one-year's supply.

11. Prophecies by early Church leaders warn of future famine during the period of internal conflict in the United States, and indicate that lack of food may be a major reason for the strife of that era. Future famines are prophesied to be the most severe that have ever come upon the earth.

12. According to the prophetic statements cited, the saints will be the suppliers of food to others when famines come. Millions are expected to flee to the saints in the tops of the mountains to obtain food in that future era.

13. Obedience to the commandment to store food may be the factor that separates the righteous from the wicked saints—the wise and foolish virgins—in the last days.

XI
God Has Decreed Wars Upon the Wicked

Freedom is a fragile state, and a blessing enjoyed by relatively few in the world today.[1] Peace is also fragile, and depends upon man's righteousness. Jesus Christ, the "Prince of Peace,"[2] has power to give peace to man and to remove it from him. He grants peace to the righteous, and denies it to the wicked. The Psalmist wrote that "Great peace have they which love thy law: and nothing shall offend them,"[3] and the wise author of Proverbs observed that "When a man's ways please the Lord, he maketh even his enemies to be at peace with him."[4] Unfortunately, it is the message of both the scriptures and of the prophets that man's iniquity in the last days will cause peace to be removed from the earth and fear to come upon all mankind.

War to be Poured Out Upon the Nations

Wars are to come upon the earth in the last days. This is the message God has repeatedly revealed through his prophets. In 1831 a revelation stated:

> I have sworn in my wrath, and decreed wars upon the face of the earth, and *the wicked shall slay the wicked, and fear shall come upon every man;*
>
> *And the saints also shall hardly escape;* nevertheless, I, the Lord, am with them, and will come down in heaven from the presence of my Father and consume the wicked with unquenchable fire.
>
> And behold, this is not yet, but by and by.[5]

---

1. Since the early 50's, a New York based organization named Freedom House has monitored the level of freedom enjoyed in each of the nations of the earth. Its findings show that freedom is declining:

   Freedom House concluded that only 19.8 percent of the world's population lived in freedom, with 35.3% partly free and 44.9 not free. One year ago, it stated, 35% of the world's people were free. ("World Freedom Plunges, Research Group Notes," *Salt Lake Tribune*, December 28, 1975.)
2. Is. 9:6.
3. Ps. 119:165.
4. Prov. 1 6:7.
5. D&C 63:33-35.

The 1832 "Prophecy on War" warned that wars would continue until there was "a full end of all nations:"

> Verily, thus saith the Lord concerning the wars that will shortly come to pass, beginning at the rebellion of South Carolina, which will eventually terminate in the death and misery of many souls;
>
> And the time will come that *war will be poured out upon all nations,* beginning at this place.[1]

The prophecy then foretold the difficulties of the U.S. Civil War and alluded to the role of Great Britain in World Wars I and II, then continued into the future:

> *Then war shall be poured out upon all nations.*
>
> And it shall come to pass, after many days, slaves shall rise up against their masters, who shall be marshaled and disciplined for war.
>
> And it shall come to pass also that the remnants who are left of the land will marshal themselves, and shall become exceedingly angry, and shall vex the Gentiles with a sore vexation.
>
> *And thus, with the sword and by bloodshed the inhabitants of the earth shall mourn; . . . until the consumption decreed hath made a full end of all nations.*[2]

The Lord warned the saints that

> Ye hear of wars in foreign lands; but, behold, I say unto you, they are nigh, even at your doors, and not many years hence ye shall hear of wars in your own lands.[3]

The same revelation spoke of the era when the "times of the Gentiles be fulfilled."[4] That future period of God's judgments will be a time of intense warfare:

> *And in that day shall be heard of wars and rumors of wars, and the whole earth shall be in commotion, and men's hearts shall fail them,* and they shall say that Christ delayeth his coming until the end of the earth. . . . Men will harden their hearts against me, and *they will take up the sword, one against another, and they will kill one another.*[5]

---

1. D&C 87:1-2.
2. D&C 87:3-5, 6.
3. D&C 45:63. Note that the passage speaks of wars in the plural. Clearly it encompasses more than the U.S. Civil War.
4. D&C 45:25.
5. D&C 45:26, 33.

Another revelation warned the saints that "ye hear of wars in far countries, and you say that there will soon be great wars in far countries but *ye know not the hearts of men in your own land*."[1]

Five Future Conflicts Prophesied

The prophecies speak of five major conflicts, or periods of warfare, which are still in the future:

1. *A third world war,* in which Russia will be defeated and the United States will come off victorious after receiving divine aid.
2. *Internal conflict in the Americas,* characterized by mob violence and an uprising of the Lamanites.
3. *World War during the New Jerusalem period,* during which all nations except the saints will be at war.
4. *World-wide conflict as the nations which are controlled by the great and abominable church war among themselves,* in which the great and abominable church will be destroyed.
5. *Conflicts involving Israel,* which will culminate in the *Battle of Armageddon.*

These conflicts may tend to have a cause-and-effect relationship upon each other, and to merge chronologically. They may even overlap, with problems beginning in one part of the world as strife still rages elsewhere from a different conflict. They should be viewed as separate portions of the overall era when there will be "wars and rumors of wars among all the nations and kindreds of the earth."[2]

Two Types of War: Preparatory Wars and Wars of Complete Destruction

Early leaders of the Church explained that wars would occur during the last days, and that they would be of two different types:

Preparatory Wars—which would prepare the way for the preaching of the gospel, and

1. D&C 38:29.
2. 1 Ne. 14:15.

Wars of Complete Destruction—which will serve as punishment for the wicked and will result in great desolation.

These two types of warfare in the last days were discussed and documented in detail in *Prophecy—Key to the Future*[1] and will be considered here only briefly.

Orson Pratt contrasted the two types of war, stating that "*the one is a war preparatory to the proclamation of the Gospel; the other is a war of terrible destruction, which will not better the condition of those who escape*."[2]

The earliest period is the era of Preparatory Wars. In this period, the saints will still be scattered throughout the earth. Wars will serve to remove governments which are unreceptive to missionary labors and replace them with leaders which will allow the gospel message to be preached within their borders. World War II, the Korean War, and the war in Viet Nam, for instance, all served to open the way for the growth of the Church in Japan, IndoChina, and the Pacific area. The dividing line between the two periods will be the "fulfilling of the times of the Gentiles," when God will begin to gather out the saints and will commence pouring out his judgments upon the wicked in increased measure.

When the period of *Wars of Complete Destruction* commences, war will become God's instrument of terrible destruction and annihilation of the wicked as he cleanses the earth in preparation for his coming in glory. The Spirit will have withdrawn from the Gentile nations.

The third world war appears to take place during the period of preparatory wars. Though the other conflicts listed above may begin to develop during that era, it is anticipated that they will see their culmination as wars of complete destruction.

Prophecies of a Third World War

Joseph Smith made several prophetic statements which allude to future conflict which will apparently be of world war dimensions. In one of them, spoken on June 19, 1844, the prophet used the formation of a political unit known as the Independent American Party[1] to place

1. See *Prophecy—Key to the Future*, pages 4-10. Those pages should be read in this context for full understanding to be gained of the explanation given herein.
2. JD 7:186 July 10, 1859.

the context of the prophecy in the twentieth century instead of his own era. He foresaw the time when other nations will attempt to "divide up the lands of the United States." He saw that the U.S. will be weakened militarily by having spent her strength and means warring in foreign lands, and that the army will be sufficiently demoralized that half will give up.[2] This is his prophecy:

> There will be two great political parties in this country. One will be called the Republican, and the other the Democrat party. These two parties will go to war and *out of these two parties will spring another party which will be the Independent American Party. The United States will spend her strength and means warring in foreign lands until other nations will say, "Let's divide up the lands of the United States,"* then the people of the U.S. will unite and swear by the blood of their forefathers, that the land shall not be divided. Then *the country will go to war, and they will fight until one half of the US. army will give up, and the rest will continue to struggle.* They will keep on until they are very ragged and discouraged, and almost ready to give up—when *the boys from the mountains will rush forth in time to save the American Army from defeat and ruin.* And they will say, 'Brethren, we are glad you have come; give us men, henceforth, who can talk with God.' Then

---

1. Considerable stir was caused by the creation of the American Independent Party during the 1960's to support the political ambitions of Governor George Wallace. The name of his party was not exactly the same as that prophesied by Joseph Smith, and was therefore probably not the fulfillment of the prophecy. Several political groups literally named the Independent American Party also were organized during that era.

   One, organized in 1955 in New Orleans, Louisiana, with editor Phoebe Courtney as its motivating force, publishes an anti-Communist newspaper known as "The Independent American." Mrs. Courtney claimed divine inspiration as the motivating force for her organizing efforts. (See "Who is Behind the Independent American and Its Activities?," a 4-page letter from Phoebe Courtney, P.O. Box 4223, New Orleans, La., 70118, March 28, 1969.) Perhaps fulfillment of Joseph Smith's prophecy lies in her work, or maybe the future will hold more literal fulfillment—it is not the author's prerogative to say.

   The importance of the Independent American Party spoken of by Joseph Smith is only that of a chronological guide, to identify the time of fulfillment of the remainder of the prophecy.
2. Certainly the tremendous outlays of the Korean and Vietnamese Wars could fulfill this portion of the prophecy, though further fulfillment may still be forthcoming. These "no-win" wars seriously demoralized the U.S. military, and saw many thousands of desertions by U.S. soldiers. They led to the formation of the all-volunteer army. Perhaps they set the stage for a situation when a large portion of the American army could "give up"—a situation previously unknown in U.S. military history.

you will have friends, but *you will save the country when it's [sic] liberty hangs by a hair, as it were.*[1]

Another prophecy by Joseph Smith alluding to future warfare was made to the father of President John Taylor. Joseph had been conversing with Father Taylor concerning the battle of Waterloo, in which Father Taylor had participated. Joseph turned to Brother Taylor and said,

> Father Taylor, you will live to see, though I will not, greater battles than that of Waterloo. The United States will go to war with Mexico, and thus gain an increase of territory. The slave question will cause a division between the North and the South, and in these wars greater battles than Waterloo will occur. *But . . . when the great bear lays her paw on the lion the winding up scene is not far distant.*[2]

A statement purportedly made by Joseph Smith on May 6, 1843, also sheds light on a third world war setting:

> The Lord took of the best blood of the nations and planted them on the small islands now called England and Great Britain, and gave them great power in the nations for a thousand years and *their power will continue with them, that they may keep the balance of power and keep Russia from usurping her power over all the world. England and France are now bitter enemies, but they will be allied together and be united to keep Russia from conquering the world.*[3]

Numerous other statements by various Church leaders concerning aspects of a Third World War are cited in *Prophecy—Key to the Future,* pp. 10-15, and need not be repeated here. The object of this section is to comment on other materials not generally available.

Patriarchs throughout the Church have been warning of a Third World War for several decades in the blessings they have pronounced upon the saints. These prophetic warnings are portions of patriarchal

---

1. Mosiah Lyman Hancock, Life Story of Mosiah Lyman Hancock, p. 29.
2. N.B. Lundwall, Inspired Prophetic Warnings, p. 75. The author was citing the Juvenile Instructor, March 15, 1890, p. 162. The traditional interpretation of this statement has been that the bear is the symbol for Russia and the lion is the symbol for England. See p. 287.
3. Prophecy recorded by Edwin Rushton as having been made on May 6, 1843. For comment on this prophecy see *Prophecy—Key to the Future,* pp. 301-322. Note that England and France are depicted as holding the "balance of power" rather than actually being the major power which will oppose Russia. See reference to this prophecy on page 190.

blessings which are personal in nature, and not intended for general distribution throughout the Church.[1] Yet the import of their combined message is great, and should at least be alluded to in this context.

During the past fifteen years, the author has frequently been sought out by others who have related prophetic insights which they have been granted. Hundreds have alluded to patriarchal blessings or personal revelations preparing them for personal roles they will play when

1. Neither are patriarchal blessings official statements of Church doctrine. Doctrine, in the strictest and most specific sense, represents "official belief and position" of a religious organization. In this sense, among Latter-day Saints, it is the role of duly-constituted general authorities to annunciate doctrinal precepts which bind and command the Church. Such is the duty and prerogative of ordained general leadership who are to do so under the direction of revelation from on high.

But there are also other levels of doctrine. Passages exist in the revealed scriptures of the Church which, when shown to have specific patterns and relationships, take on new, more important meanings. The scriptures are canonized and regarded as doctrine, and such new insights, when properly demonstrated and documented, also stand as doctrine. Though they may not at first have been pronounced nor expounded by current Church authorities, yet those passages still constitute the revealed word of God, the highest authority of all. Man is obligated to search the scriptures, striving to understand their meaning completely, discovering in them the full meaning intended by God.

Yet another level exists. God has revealed that when men speak as they are moved upon by the Holy Ghost, then "whatsoever they shall speak when moved upon by the Holy Ghost shall be scripture, shall be the will of the Lord. shall be the mind of the Lord, shall be the voice of the Lord, and the power of God unto salvation. " (D&C 68:4) The Lord made this promise unto "all the faithful elders" of his church (D&C 68:2, 7). Though individual revelations through the Spirit are not given as instructions or commandments to the entire church, and are not to be regarded as the official doctrine of the church unless annunciated by duly constituted general authorities, yet such manifestations undeniably constitute revealed truth. Certainly insights revealed through the Holy Ghost are not to be denied, nor criticized, nor disregarded. Revealed truth is truth, no matter to whom it is revealed.

When extensive patterns of private revelation emerge, especially on matters of such far-reaching import as a world war which will affect the life of every citizen and saint, there comes a time when such patterns should be brought to the attention of all. They should not be represented as official doctrine nor as the stated position of the church, but as information of value which individuals should evaluate by comparison with existing facts and doctrine, thoughtful logic, and supplication for revealed verification. In this context, especially, Paul's instruction should be observed: ''Quench not the Spirit. Despise not prophesyings. Prove all things; Hold fast that which is good." (1 Thess. 5:19-21.)

God's judgments are poured out upon the earth. Dozens have told of patriarchal blessings which speak of a third world war. Frequently the Spirit has burned within us as these matters have been discussed. It has been right, and proper, that they bore testimony of these future events.[1]

Below are briefly summarized a few of these statements, regarded by the author as typical, relating to a future world war. For example, a blessing given in 1953 said,

> You will live to see the world go through *another world war,* where kingdom will rise against kingdom, and *Russia and her allies, in the due time of the Lord, will go down never to come up in such power again! And the United States, when and after the inside of the cup may be cleansed, will come off victorious,* and will after arise to great heights among the nations of the world.[2]

Another blessing prophesies the defeat of Russia and portrays the war as being typical of the period of preparatory wars, paving the way for missionary labors in that land:

> You will live to see the world go through *another world war, for the mother country will be attacked by a strong European power. This war will be largely in the air and under the surface of the ocean, and the waters will be unsafe for the ordinary traffic and the heavens will be unsafe, for deadly bombs will be sent to the affliction of the cities of this great country and, in turn we will afflict them with bombs* and you will live to see the mother country cleansed as the inside of a platter, for traitor after traitor will be suspicioned and detected and apprehended. You will live to see the *God of Heaven take over, as it were, and bring this war to a speedy victory to America and her allies. You will see Russia go down to defeat never to come up again as a major world power,* and you will live to see the *gospel go into that country after the war* has been brought to a termination, and a great and glorious work will be accomplished in that land.[3]

---

1. The author, for reasons not fully known to himself, has found himself cast in a role of receiving and analyzing information concerning future events. One sister, after sharing several prophetic dreams, later wrote that "It is strange, but I haven't had any more dreams on this subject since I spoke with you. It is almost as if the purpose has been filled by my telling you these things that day." (Letter dated October 16, 1967.)
2. It would appear, in the light of the events chronicled in this volume, that the rise of the United States to great heights which is mentioned in this context will be embodied in the work of the saints during the New Jerusalem era rather than the political scene as it is today.
3. Note the theme of divine intervention to bring the war to a victorious conclusion for America and her allies, which occurs repeatedly. Is this the same event as in Joseph Smith's prophecy recorded by Mosiah Hancock, cited earlier, when the "boys from the mountains will rush forth?"

In this day of nuclear armaments, is it not reasonable to assume that if the war reaches the level that Russia and the United States are bombing each other's homelands, these bombs will represent the latest in nuclear technology, with full atomic-bomb destructive power?

Another blessing, given in 1960, continues the "preparatory wars" theme of the way being opened for missionary labors in Russia:

> . . . Many changes shall take place in your day and time. *Nations shall fall and rise again with barriers removed that missionaries may go freely to the nation of Russia* and that as Ephraim has been gathered from the far parts of the earth, so shall *the dispersed of Judah be gathered* as the Lord has decreed. . . .[1]

Another blessing, given in 1956, warns of another world war. The theme of divine intervention is again mentioned:

> You will live upon the earth to see wars and commotions, and even much preparation for war, and you will see *bloodshed drench the earth* until your soul will be sick with seeing. You will live to see *another World War* and you may see service to your country before your passing, and *you will live to see the hand of providence come out on the side of free agency and the United States will be cleansed on the inside of the platter. . . . You will live to see the Russian Bear lay his heavy hand upon the British Lion, according to the prophecy of Joseph Smith.*[2]

And another:

> You will see nation rise against nation and kingdom against kingdom and see *a great and bloody war in which the U.S. and her forces will be arranged against Russia* and the God of Heaven will look on for awhile, apparently, and *then will take over and bring victory* to the side of the right, for the God of Heaven will never permit free agency to be trampled under foot and swept from the face of the earth.

And again:

> You will see *the nations of Europe torn into mighty fragments* and many of them uprooted, never again to come up as kingdoms. You will, therefore, see wars and bloodshed in your day, for the unrest of men that exists at the present time will ultimately develop into *swords and deadly*

---

1. There are still far more Jews in Russia than there are in Israel. They must be gathered as part of the future gathering of Israel.
2. Similarities between several of the excerpts cited are readily apparent, for some of the blessings were pronounced by the same individual.

bombs. You will live to see terrible earthquakes and one of these will rock the continent from ocean to ocean.

These excerpts should suffice to portray the pattern of prophetic warnings which exists from this source.

Other personal manifestations have contained insights which describe events of a future war. One such item, an account of future difficulties revealed to Elder Charles David Evans,[1] through an angelic visitor,[2] was printed in *The Contributor.* The manifestation describes what appears to be nuclear destruction, followed by radiation sickness. It tells of invasion by a foreign power, the sudden rise of a power in the west which counteracts the invasion,[3] and then gives the chronological indication that the war will precede the founding of the New Jerusalem:

> . . . *Dense clouds, blacker than midnight darkness, whose thunders reverberated with intonations which shook the earth, obscured the sunlight. Darkness reigned, unrivalled and supreme.*
>
> Again the light shone, revealing an *atmosphere tinged with a leaden hue, which was the precursor of an unparalleled plague* whose first symptoms were recognized by a *purple spot which appeared on the cheek, or on the back of the hand, and which, invariably, enlarged until it spread over the entire surface of the body, producing certain death.* Mothers, on sight of it, cast away their children as if they were poisonous reptiles. This plague, in grown persons, rotted the eyes in their sockets and consumed

---

1. Charles David Evans joined the Church in England in 1848 and came to the United States and Utah in 1854. He was bishop of the Salem Ward for a decade, was ordained a High Councilor in 1889 and was called as a patriarch in 1895, in which position he served until his death on May 14, 1908 at Payson, Utah. (Information furnished by his great granddaughter, Mrs. Joyce Lindstrom, in personal correspondence with the author, September 8, 1969. His biographical sketch is contained in Andrew Jenson's Latter-day Saint Biographical Encyclopedia, Vol. 4, p. 568.)
2. Elder Evans vividly describes the angelic being and his entrance into his bedroom at a midnight hour. The angel greeted him with these words:

   > Son, I perceive thou hast grave anxieties over the perilous state of thy country, that thy soul has felt deep sorrow for its future. I have therefore come to thy relief and to tell thee of the causes that have led to this peril Hear me attentively. ("A Dream," The Contributor, Representing the Young Men's Mutual Improvement Associations of the Latter-day Saints (Salt Lake City, Utah: Deseret News Publishing Company, 1894), Vol. 15, p. 639.

3. Can this, again, be the time when "the boys from the mountains will rush forth," as foretold in the Joseph Smith prophecy recorded by Mosiah Lyman Hancock, cited earlier?

the tongue as would a powerful acid or an intense heat. Wicked men, suffering under its writhing agonies, cursed God and died, as they stood on their feet, and the birds of prey feasted on their carcasses.

I saw in my dream the messenger again appear with a vial in his right hand, who addressing me said: "Thou knowest somewhat of the chemistry taught in the schools of human learning, behold now a chemistry sufficiently powerful to change the waters of the sea."

He then poured out his vial upon the sea and it became putrid as the blood of a dead man, and every living soul therein died. Other plagues followed I forbear to record.

A foreign power had invaded the nation which, from every human indication, it appeared would seize the government and supplant it with monarchy. I stood trembling at the aspect, when, lo, *a power arose in the west which declared itself in favor of the constitution in its original form; to this suddenly rising power every lover of constitutional rights and liberties throughout the nation gave hearty support. The struggle was fiercely contested,* but the stars and stripes floated in the breeze, and, bidding defiance to all opposition, waved proudly over the land. Among the many banners I saw, was one inscribed thus: "The government based on the Constitution, now and forever;" on another "Liberty of Conscience, social, religious, and political."

The light of the gospel which had but dimly shone because of abomination, now burst forth with a lustre that filled the earth. Cities appeared in every direction, *one of which, in the centre of the continent, was an embodiment of architectural science after the pattern of eternal perfections, whose towers glittered with a radiance emanating from the sparkling of emeralds, rubies, diamonds and other precious stones set in a canopy of gold* and so elaborately and skillfully arranged as to shed forth a brilliancy which dazzled and enchanted the eye, excited admiration and developed a taste for the beautiful, beyond anything man had ever conceived. . . .[1]

---

1. "A Dream," Ibid., pp. 640-641. Note the similarity of Elder Evan's description of the "plague" which comes from the dark clouds with the descriptions of survivors of the atomic bombing of Japan. Radiation breaks down the blood cells, causing people to bleed under the skin, in a manner similar to leukemia. Hence the purple spots like large bruises.

   Elder Evan's manifestation also reported the internal strife which is prophesied to come upon the nation:

   > . . . At this juncture I saw a banner floating in air whereupon was writ¿en the words Bankruptcy, Famine, Floods, Fire, Cyclones, Blood, Plague. Mad with rage men and women rushed upon each other. Blood flowed down the streets of cities like water. The demon of bloody hate had enthroned itself on the citadel of reason; the thirst for blood was intenser than that of the parched tongue for water. Thousands of bodies lay untombed in the streets. Men and women fell dead from the terror inspired by fear. Rest was but the precursor of the bloody work of the morrow. All Around lay the mournfulness of a past in ruins. Monuments erected to perpetuate the names of the noble and brave were ruthlessly destroyed by combustibles. A voice now sounded aloud these words,

Prophecies Showing Relationships Between World War III and Internal Conflict in the United States

The prophetic panorama seems to indicate that there will be a third world war, followed by internal strife in the United States, and then the return to Jackson County for the establishing of the New Jerusalem. Some prophetic warnings show chronological relationships between these events.

A vision granted to President Wilford Woodruff in 1878 seems to vividly depict this time period[1]. He was shown that great desolation would come upon the land from a terrible disease which would kill many people;[1] that Independence, Missouri [Jackson County] would be destroyed; internal strife [from lack of food?] and people struggling to come to the mountains; and finally the beginning of construction of the New Jerusalem; which establishes the chronological relationship and identifies the time of fulfillment.

President Woodruff recorded the vision in his personal journal,[2] which also contained numerous other prophetic insights. This is what he recorded:

> "Yet once again I shake not the earth only, but also heaven. nd this word yet once again signifies the removing of things that are shaken, as of things that are made; that those things that cannot be shaken may remain."
>
> Earthquakes rent the earth in vast chasms, which engulfed multitudes; terrible groanings and wailings filled the air; the shrieks of the suffering were indescribably awful. Water wildly rushed in from the tumultuous ocean whose very roaring under the mad rage of the fierce cyclone, was unendurable to the ear. Cities were swept away in an instant, missiles were hurled through the atmosphere at a terrible velocity and people were carried upward only to descend an unrecognized mass. Islands appeared where ocean waves once tossed the gigantic steamer. In other parts voluminous flames, emanating from vast fires, rolled with fearful velocity destroying life and property in their destructive course. The seal of the dread menace of despair was stamped on every human visage; men fell exhausted, appalled and trembling. Every element of agitated nature seemed a demon of wrathful fury. . . . (Ibid., p. 640).

---

1. Is this the same plague described by Charles David Evans? It appears to be. Is it radiation sickness? (Note characteristics which would seem to support that possibility: extreme thirst, sudden death leaving thousands unburied, the streets vacant but people using basements for refuge, world-wide devastation.) Is it the Lord's desolating scourge? Are the two the same?
2. Apostle Matthias F. Cowley, who prepared a biography of President Woodruff, based on his journals and other personal papers, cited the last

I went to bed at the usual hour, half past nine o'clock. *I had been reading the Revelations in the French language.* My mind was calm, more so than usual if that were possible. I composed myself for sleep, but felt a strange stupor come over me and I apparently became partially unconscious. Still I was not asleep nor awake, but had a strange far-away dreaming feeling.

The first thing I recognized was that I was in the Tabernacle at Ogden, Utah, sitting in the corner for fear they would call on me to preach, which, after singing the second song, they did by calling me to the stand. I arose to speak and said that I did not know that I had anything special to say except to bear my testimony of the truth of this work—when all at once it seemed I was lifted out of myself. I said, "Yes, I have something to say, it is this: Some of my brethren present have been asking me what is coming to pass. *I will tell you what will shortly come to pass—*"

Then I was in Salt Lake City walking through the streets. In parts of the city and upon the door of every house, I saw a badge of mourning, and I could not find a house but what was in mourning. I passed my own home and saw the same sign there. I asked the question, "Is that me who is dead?"

Something gave the answer, "No."

It seemed strange to me that *I saw no person on the streets in my wandering around the city. They seemed to be in their houses with their sick and dead.* I saw no funeral processions or anything of this kind, but the city was very still and quiet as if the people were praying. *It seemed as though the people had control over the disease, whatever it was,* I do not know, that was not shown to me.

I then looked in all directions over the territory,—east, west, north and south, and *found the same mourning in every place throughout the land.*

The next I knew I was *this side of Omaha.* It seemed I was above the earth looking down upon it as I passed along on my way east. *I saw the roads full of people, principally women, with just what they could carry in bundles on their backs, traveling to the mountains on foot.* And I wondered how they would get there with nothing but a small pack on their backs. It was remarkable to me that *there were so few men among them.* It did not seem as though trains were running; *the rails looked rusty and the roads abandoned.* In deed, I have no conception of how I traveled myself as I looked down upon the people.

I continued east through *Omaha and Council Bluffs, which were full of disease, and women were everywhere. The streets of Missouri and Illinois were in turmoil and strife. Men were killing one another, and women joined in the fighting Family against family were cutting each other to pieces in the most horrible manner imaginable.*

---

portion of the vision in his book Wilford Woodruff—History of His Life and Labors (Salt Lake City, Utah: Bookcraft, 1964), p. 505. It is noted that the account published in Wilford Woodruff differs slightly in wording, though not in message, from the account printed herein, a possible indication that various copies, or "versions," of this manifestation now exist.

Next I saw *Washington, D.C., and found the city a desolation. The White House was empty and the Halls of Congress likewise*. Everything was in ruin and the people seemed to have fled from the city and left it to take care of itself.

I was next in the city of *Baltimore,* in the square where the monument of 1812 stands in front of the St. Charles and other hotels. *The dead were everywhere. I saw their bodies piled up, filling the square. I saw women cut the throats of their own children for the sake of their blood. I saw them suck it from their veins to quench their own thirst, and then lie down in the streets and die.*

The waters of the city and the *Chesapeake Bay* were so stagnant, and such a stench arose from them on account of the putrefaction of the dead carcasses in them, that the very smell carried death with it.

Singularly again, I saw no men, except they were dead or dying in the streets. There were but very few women, and they were crazy and mad, or in a dying condition. Everywhere I went I saw the same all over the city. It was horrible beyond conception to behold.

I thought this was the end, but not so. Seemingly in an instant I was in *Philadelphia* where everything was still. No living soul was to be seen to greet me. It seemed as though the whole city was without inhabitants. In Arch and Chestnut streets, in fact, everywhere I looked the putrefaction of the dead bodies created such a stench that it was impossible for any creature to remain alive.

I next found myself on Broadway in *New York*. There it seemed as if the people had done all they could to overcome the disease. But in wandering down Broadway, I saw the bodies of beautiful women lying, some dead, and others in a dying condition, on the sidewalks. I saw men crawl out of the basements and violate the persons of some that were alive, then kill them and rob their dead bodies of the valuables they had on them. Then, before they could return to their basements, they themselves rolled over a time or two in agony and died.

On some of the streets *I saw mothers kill their own offspring and eat their flesh,* and then in a few minutes die themselves. And wherever I looked, I saw the same sights,—horror and desolation, rapine and death. *No horses, nor carriages, nor omnibusses, nor streetcars,—nothing but death and destruction everywhere*.

I then went to Central Park, and looking back, I saw a fire start, and just at that moment a mighty east wind sprang up and carried the flames west over the great city. And *it burned until there was not a single building left standing whole;* even down to the water's edge.—Warves and shipping—all seemed to be burned and swallowed up in common destruction. Nothing was left but desolation where a great city stood a short time before. Stench from the bodies that were burned was so great that it was carried a great distance across the Hudson River, and it spread disease and death wherever the fumes penetrated.

I cannot paint in words the horrors that seemed to encompass me about, it was beyond description or thought for me to conceive.

I supposed this was the end, *but I was given to understand that the same horrors that were here inacted were all over the world, east, west. north, and south.—That few were left alive,—still there were some.*

Immediately after, I seemed to be standing on the left bank of the Missouri River, opposite the city of *Independence,—but I saw no city. I saw the whole states of Illinois and Missouri and part of iowa, a complete wilderness of desert with no living human being there*.

I then saw a short distance from the river, twelve men draped in the robes of the Temple, standing in a square, or nearly so. I understood it to represent the twelve gates of the *New Jerusalem*. And *they with uplifted hands, were consecrating the ground and laying the cornerstone of the Temple*.

And while they were thus employed, I saw myriads of angels hovering over them and around them. And I heard the angels singing the most heavenly music. The words were: "*Now is established The Kingdom of God and His Christ, and He shall reign forever and ever! And the Kingdom shall never be thrown down, for the Saints have overcome!*"

I saw people coming from the river and from distant places to help build the Temple and the City. It seemed as though *there were hosts of angels helping to bring material for the construction of that building. Some were in Temple robes*, and the pillar-like cloud continued to hover over the spot.

Later, I found myself in the Ogden Tabernacle, where I was calling upon the people to listen to the beautiful strains of music from the angels, as the building seemed to be filled with them, and they were singing the words I heard before: "Now is the Kingdom of our God and His Christ established forever and ever!"

I rolled over on my bed and the clock struck twelve. The vision had occurred between 9:30 P.M. and midnight.

Even outside the Church many people have claimed manifestations and/or made prophecies of a third world war.[1] One such item, recorded by Mrs. Sols Guardisto, is of particular interest because it appears to show chronological and geographical relationships between the world war, the beginning of renewed religious persecution against the saints, disease and famine throughout the continent, and the gathering of the saints to places of refuge. Mrs. Guardisto visited the site of the Cardston Temple on two occasions in 1922, prior to the completion and dedication of the building. According to her account, each time she visited the site she received "powerful impressions" about the building and its role in the future. These she wrote in a letter which was placed in the possession of President Edward James Wood, the first president of that temple. He preserved the letter in his family file, and also made it available to others. A BYU masters thesis on the life

1. A discussion of such materials and an analysis of their validity and merits is beyond the scope of this volume. What is important, however, is the reader's realization that many such prophecies exist.

of President Wood, written by Melvin S. Tagg, a student in the College of Religious Instruction, records the manifestation in an appendix. In her[1] account, she told how she observed former Church leaders, then

---

1. Little is documented on the identity of Mrs. Guardisto. Though the author of the thesis which preserved her manifestation asserts that she later joined the Church, a check with the Church membership department yields no record of her membership. A letter to this author from J Forrest Wood, a descendant of Edward Wood, states

> It is a remarkable experience she seemed to have had and she does tell of things which have come about and other things which could come about. But any person who studies world conditions and the surrounding country about the temple could see its possibilities. I have asked our temple president here and also the wife of our former president; both of whom grew up here and remember well the story of her visit and experience. Both say they never knew of it being called a prophecy.
>
> I do not know her exact name. It is not shown on my copy. We have a copy here at the temple where I am recorder. It was given before the dedication of the temple. Melvin Tagg does not give the complete story; but his main facts are correct. All those directly connected with the story have passed away. I well remember of it and heard father speak many times about it. I have access to the records here in the temple but have never found anything more than I have given above. (Letter from Cardston, Canada dated 5 May, 1971.)

In an L.D.S.S.A. forum at the University of Utah Institute of Religion, October 10, 1969, the author queried President Hugh B. Brown about the manifestation and its author. He replied, "I knew the woman quite well and went through the temple with her. She claimed to have quite a remarkable manifestation but she didn't follow through. She ran off with another woman's husband. That doesn't disqualify the validity of the manifestation, but she didn't follow through. " (The author recorded his statement immediately after it was made.) Attempts to learn more of the woman through the avenues of genealogical research have not met with success.

The beginning of her letter indicates that the impressions she received were a new type of experience for her, yet she found them strong and compelling:

> We have been to the temple erected by your church, wherein the sacred rites are to be performed in accordance with your faith. The first time I was strongly impelled to describe to you my impressions. I did so, but before the completion of the letter I received some news which so affected me that, acting upon the spur of the moment, I destroyed the document in its entirety.
>
> The continued feeling within me of dissatisfaction as of something left undone, coupled with the desire upon the part of members of my household, who had not visited the temple, led to our second visit to Cardston, in which you so kindly consented to accompany us; notwithstanding the inclement weather and personal inconveniences to yourselves, which the journey necessarily entailed.

dead, who instructed her there in the temple and showed her future events. Then she recorded the impressions granted to her concerning

---

> It is because of this and many other evidences of your friendship that has given me the priviledge to presume to bother you with what, after all, may be only the foolish fantasies of a too impressionable mentality. To me it does not seem so, for never before in my lifetime has such powerful impressions been impinged upon my inner consciousness as during my visits thru the temple. Especially was this so at our second visit; the impressions of our first visit were repeated with such overwhelming intensity and variety of detail that I must positively inform you of my experiences.
>
> It seems to me it is a sacred duty on my part to do this, and knowing as I do that your friends will not lightly ridicule to outsiders what to me is a personal matter, I am going to give you in detail my experiences in the hope that if, as it may well be, it is something more than imagination, that you or others of your faith may wisely analyze and correctly use whatever may be gleaned from this letter. (Melvin Tagg, "A Remarkable Occurrence in the Cardston Temple," The Life of Ed ward James Wood [A Thesis Presented to the College of Religious Instruction, Brigham Young University, July 1959], p. 148.)

Note that the author, Mrs. Guardisto, had no ulterior motive in recording the manifestation; she did so only because she received the impression that it was her "sacred duty" to do so.

This is how she described the revelatory experience and her observance of former Church leaders:

> Time and again as I listened to the speaker explaining some phase of the building or its meaning, I would be seeing beyond him some illustration of a kaleidoscopic nature depicting what he was describing, only more completely and more vividly. The characters were so plain to me that I required all my self-control to keep silence from room to room. This continued and only ceased when we emerged into the frost and snow once more.
>
> There was no set plan for presenting these pictures or expressions to me. It seemed as if when I thought of something mental a picture instantly presented itself in explanation of some word of the conductor, which would have the same effect. I was not afraid, only awed by the wonder of it all and the fearful impressive feeling I received, which seemed to imbed every little detailed scene into my brain, from which I feel it will never be erased. Every now and again I would seem to receive a command, observe, remember and record, and vivid as all of it was, these incidents herein related are the ones upon which I received the instructions.
>
> The scenes which I observed of an historical character seemed chiefly to verify and amplify the speaker's outline of past history and so I do not feel impressed to record such, except to state that the same patriarchal characters whom I observed directing and influencing the early movements of the church, were the same down through every age and epoch and as the scene advanced to more modern times, I saw among

future international war and internal conflict in America:

> I can give no time as to the happenings except that the impressions I received was of actual present or immediate future.
>
> I saw first a brief but comprehensive sketch of the present state of the world, or, as you would term it, the Gentile Kingdoms. Each country in turn was shown, its anarchy, hunger, ambitions, distrusts and warlike activities, etc., and in my mind was formed from some source the words, "As it is today with the Gentiles."
>
> *I saw next international war again break out with its centre upon the Pacific Ocean, but sweeping and encircling the whole globe.* I saw that the *opposing forces were roughly divided by so-called Christianity on the one side, and by the so-called followers of Mohammed and Budda upon the other.* I saw that the great driving power within these so-called Christian Nations was the *Great Apostacy of Rome* in all its political, social and religious aspects. *I saw the world-wide dislocation and devastation of production and slaughter of people occur more swiftly and upon a larger scale than ever before. I saw an antagonism begin to express itself from those so-called Christian nations against your people. I saw those of a similar faith to yours in the Far-East begin to look toward Palestine for safety.*
>
> *I saw the international world war automatically break down, and national revolutions occur in every country and complete the work of chaos and desolation.* I saw *geological disturbances occur,* which helped in this work as if it were intended to do so. I saw the Cardston Temple preserved from all of this geological upheaval. *I saw the international boundary line disappear as these two governments broke up and dissolved into chaos. I saw race rioting upon this American continent on a vast scale.*
>
> *I saw hunger and starvation in this world granary of the American Continent sweep off vast numbers of these conflicting elements. I saw disease produced by hunger, strife and chaos complete the end of this present order or epoch.* How long these events were in reaching this consummation, I do not know. But, my impression was *from the outbreak of the international war, these things developed in a continuous procession, and almost*

---

these spiritual counsellors persons whose features I had previously observed as being in the material body on other historical occasions.

It seemed as though the Temple was filled with the actual spiritual bodies of these previous leaders of the Church, each seeming to have a definite work to do, automatically taking up in the spirit world the work that person was engaged in whilst in the flesh. In that Temple I saw persons who were leaders of your Church during its march across the American Desert, now engaged in helping those patriarchs under whose orders they seemed to be working. It was these leaders of your Church, or spiritual leaders, if I may use that term, who seemed instructed to show me the scenes here recorded. (Ibid., pp. 150-151)

ran concurrently, as it is with a sickness, the various symptoms are all in evidence at one and the same time, but in different stages of development.

My intensified thought was, "What of the Church, if such is to become the kingdom of the earth?" The thought was immediately answered by a subconscious statement, "As it is in the Church today," and I saw these higher spiritual beings throughout the length and breadth of the air, marshalling their spiritual forces and concentrating them upon the high officials of your Church on earth. I saw these spiritual forces working upon these officers, impressing and moving them, influencing and warning them. I saw these spiritual forces begin to unfold these things into the minds of your elders and other high officials, especially during their spiritual devotions and official duties, and those activities which exalt the mind of the individual or groups. I saw the impressions take hold and inspire the more receptive and spiritual men, until it was all clearly revealed to them in the way the spiritual patriarchs desired.

Again I seemed to hear the words, "As it will be." I saw the high officials in council, and under inspired guidance issue instructions to your people, *to reconsecrate their lives and energies to their faith.* To voluntarily discipline themselves by abstaining from all those forms of indulgence which weaken the body, sap the mentality, and deaden the spirit or waste their incomes. I saw further on, instructions given whereby the *places of refuge were prepared, quietly, but efficiently by in.spired elders. I saw Cardston and the surrounding foothills especially west and north—for miles being prepared for a refuge for your people, quietly but quickly.*

I saw artesian wells bored and other wells dug all over that territory, so that *when the open waters were polluted and poisoned* that the people of the Church and their cattle would be provided for. I saw the fuel resources of the district developed in many places, and vast piles of coal and timber stored for future use and building.

I saw the elders, still under Divine guidance, counselling and encouraging *the planting of every available acre of soil in this district, so that large supplies could be near the refuge.* I saw the Church property under cultivation of an intensified character, not for sale or profit, but for the use of the people. I saw the inspired officers giving instructions as to what would be the best crops to plant and cultivate, not for profit but *for use in storage at the time of chaos.* I saw the territory carefully surveyed and *mapped out for the camping of a great body of people* of the Church. I saw provisions also made for *a big influx of people who at present do not belong to the Church, but who will gather in their tribulation.* I saw vast quantities of surgical appliances, medicines, disinfectants, etc., stored in the Temple basement. I saw inspiration given the elders whereby the quality, quantity, and kind of things to be stored were judged, which might not be attainable in this territory during the time of chaos. I saw *defensive preparations made and stored as suggested by the power of inspiration.* I saw the elders working out the organizations of the camps upon maps. I saw the mining corridors used as places of storage underground; I saw the hills surveyed and corrals built in sequestered places for cattle, sheep, etc., quietly but quickly.

I saw the plans for the organization of the single men, and their duties, the scouts, the guards, the nurses, the cooks, the messengers, the children, the herders, the Temple guards, etc., etc., I saw all these preparations going on practically unknown to the Gentile world, except to the Great Apostacy, whose knowledge and hatred is far-reaching in this day of its temporary power. This was going on piece by piece as the elders were instructed so to do for the refuge.

I saw other officials obeying the inspired instructions carrying their messages and exhorting your people to follow out from time to time, the revelations given them. Whilst *all around throughout the Gentile world the chaos developed in its varying stages—faction against faction, nation against nation, but all in open or secret hostility to your people and their faith*. I saw your people draw closer and closer together as this became more intense and as the spiritual forces warned them through the mouth of your elders and other officers. I saw the spiritual forces influencing these members who had drifted away to reenter the fold. I saw a greater thing than ever before. *I saw vast quantities of necessaries supplied by members* whose spiritual eyes had been opened. I saw a *liquidation of properties and effects disposed of* quietly and quickly by members of the Church, as the spiritual influences directed them.

I saw the inspired call sent forth to all the Church to gather to the refuges of Zion. I saw the stream of your people quietly moving in the direction of their refuge. I saw your people moving more quickly and in larger numbers until all the stragglers were housed. I saw the wireless messages flashed from Zion's refuge to Zion's refuge in their several places, that all was well in the world. *And then the darkness of chaos closed around the boundaries of your people, and the last days of tribulations had begun*.[1]

Like other prophetic warnings recorded in this chapter, the above is not presented as "doctrine." The reader is invited to

---

1. Lest some might confuse the international war she observed with World War II, some of the identifying characteristics of the future conflict should be identified which were not typical of World War II:
   1. The forces tend to divide along religious lines Christians vs. Moslems and Buddhists. (Would this tend to identify those who will ally themselves with the Communists?)
   2. The church in Rome will be a driving power behind the Christian forces.
   3. Antagonism develops among the Christian nations against the Mormons.
   4. People in the Far East with a faith similar to Latter-day Saint belief will begin to look toward Palestine, or Israel for safety.
   5. The international war will break down, and national revolutions occur in every country.
   6. The international boundary line between the U.S. and Canada v~ disappear as the two governments break up and dissolve into chaos.

   None of these aspects characterize the scenario of World War II.

determine its validity for himself by seeking revealed confirmation, as should be done with any spiritual manifestation.

In summary concerning prophecies of a third world war, it should be observed that numerous prophetic warnings foretell its reality. They assert that America will be attacked by Russia and her allies, and that the war will have an extremely high casualty rate. Bombs will be dropped on both homelands, and it is reasonable to expect that nuclear warheads will be used. Some of the manifestations cited appear to describe the vast nationwide effects of radiation sickness and destruction. Many spies and traitors will be detected within the United States. The war will go badly for America, then God will intervene and bring the war to a victorious conclusion for America and her allies, while Russia and her allies will go down to defeat, never to rise in such power again. The way will be opened for missionary work to begin in Russia, which indicates that the war will be a "Preparatory War," before the "times of the Gentiles" are fulfilled. The war will be followed by a period of chaos in which governments will fall and anarchy will prevail, both in the United States and throughout the world.

Russia Rapidly Preparing for War
(See also: *An Update on Russia,* pp. 311-326)

For several decades, Russia has militantly prepared for future war. Its rush for military superiority has made it increasingly obvious that mere protection of the Russian homeland is not its goal. There will come a time when its massive forces will be employed for conquest, not just for defense.

Yet many Americans refuse to accept the indications of Russia's intentions. Former U.S. Secretary of Defense James Schlesinger described the apathetic attitude which is prevalent in the nation:

> *We as a nation are indulging in an ostrich syndrome, in burying our heads in the sand and not observing what is going on.*
>
> The Soviets have increased their military establishment to over four million men. . . . They have, in recent years, *produced four times as many subs and surface combatants as we have. They are producing 70 percent more tactical aircraft. In ground forces equipment, it is a production ratio of seven and eight to one. . . .*
>
> *What we have is a flight from reality.*[1]

1. Jack Anderson, "America's Flight From Reality," Deseret News, January 1 1976.

Yet knowledgeable sources are deeply concerned about Russia's military growth, and are increasingly vocal about the growing danger to the nation. Before leaving his office as Secretary of Defense in January. 1977, Donald Rumsfeld said

> *. . . The power balance trends of the last 10 to 15 years have been "decidedly adverse" to the United States.*
>
> Rumsfeld said expanded Soviet nuclear and conventional force strength has increased Soviet options. He suggested that continuation of these trends could tempt the Soviets to challenge the United States in an area of American national interest
>
> Intelligence reports made public at that time said that though *the Soviet military budget had grown by a third between 1965 and 1975, U.S. arms spending had dropped by a similar amount from the 1968 wartime high.*[1]

A report by the National Strategy Information Center has warned that there has never been greater military danger to the nation than at the present:

> *"In terms of explicit Soviet military capabilities . . . the over-all military threat to the United States has never been greater in this century. . . . "*
>
> *"The current and projected U.S. defense posture is inadequate to meet the threat posed by the Soviet Union," the report says. It estimated that Russian military spending has risen dramatically to the equivalent of at least $130 billion a year.*
>
> Meanwhile, the report says, "the United States has been disinvesting in defense through a subtle process of congressional budget cuts, inflation . . . and inadequate administration requests for defense expenditure."
>
> Since 1971, the center study says, *congressional budget cuts and inflation have reduced real U.S. defense resources by $45 billion.*[2]

Russia's annual percent of expenditure for armaments now exceeds Germany's peak when Adolf Hitler was preparing for the Nazi invasion of Europe:

> *For the past decade, Russia has been spending 20 percent of its gross national product annually on arms,* the former head of Defense Intelligence said this week.
>
> By contrast, Lt. Gen. Daniel 0. Graham, who retired November 3, told reporters this is well over three times as much as has been previously estimated by U.S. intelligence.

---

1. George Gedda, "Russians Gaining Power Balance?" *Salt Lake Tribune,* July 10, 1977.
2. "Defense Funds To Fall Short?" Deseret News, June 16, 1976.

Adolf Hitler's peak arms expenditure in his pre-World War ii program of "guns, not butter," only came to 19 percent of Germany's GNP. The United States this year is budgeting defense at a mere 5.4 percent.[1]

The Institute for Strategic Studies, in a "Strategic Survey, 1975," reported that

The numerical balance has moved against the West over the years and (the West's) qualitative edge could be eroded if present trends in Soviet weapons procurement continue. "The momentum of the Soviet arms buildup presents a major risk for detente and a cause for the *growing skepticism . . . over Soviet longer-term intentions*."[2]

Others around the world are warning that Russia's intentions are to wage war. China, particularly, has expressed this fear:

Russia is, for all practical purposes, on a war footing. The army has been increased to 4.3 million men. The crash naval building program has been accelerated.

Terrified Peking insists *the Russian military buildup is not primarily for diplomatic bargaining purposes and that Russia intends to make war.*

The Chinese, indeed, state that Leonid Breztnev is already waging war through small surrogate nations and that, moreover, he is winning them.[3]

From London comes this warning concerning the accelerated growth of the Russian navy, from the prestigious naval annual, "Jane's Fighting Ships:"

Russia has outspent and outbuilt the United States by 50 percent or more in warship construction for the past decade and now has an offensive navy which, in the judgment of an internationally authoritative handbook, *"has outrun the legitimate requirements of national defense. . . ."*

Warning that a navy of the scale Russia is now building can only be for "aggressive action," Capt. Moore contrasted the difficulties of the U.S. Navy in face of "the very vocal and sometimes downright dishonest efforts of a number of influential people who see their mission in life as the emasculation of America's defenses."[4]

---

1. Col. Robert D. Heinl Jr., "Russia Is Spending 20 Pct. On Military General Says," Deseret News, March 4, 1976.
2. "Both U.S., Russ 'Losing Influence,' " Deseret News, May 7, 1976.
3. Ernest Cuneo, "Russia Is On A War Footing," Deseret News, May 3, 19 76.
4. "Ominous New Russ Navy," Deseret News, September 20, 1975.

Editorial voices are also warning that Russia is rapidly outstripping the U.S. in the arms race. Though the U.S. previously held clear superiority, now the two forces are regarded as on approximately equal par. But within a few short years Russia will have gained clear and undisputed superiority. A typical editorial gives the following warning:

> It shouldn't have taken a change in defense chiefs to impress on Congress and the nation that *the U.S. is slipping behind Russia in military power.*
>
> Secretary of Defense Donald Rumsfeld sounded that warning this week, but declared the U.S. still has a "rough equivalence" with Russia.
>
> He warned, however, that *if present trends continue, the US. would definitely slip to No. 2 among world powers, with dangerous implications for international stability.*
>
> That's the same thing James R. Schlesinger was saying last year when he was fired by President Ford, apparently for being too strident in his opposition to deep cuts in the defense budget.
>
> That concern also has been voiced by Air-Force Gen. George S. Brown, chairman of the Joint Chiefs of Staff. "We believe that U.S. military strength . . . is sufficient today," says Gen. Brown. "*But we are greatly concerned about adverse military trends and what they portend for the future.*"
>
> Those concerns are buttressed by a recent study done by the Library of Congress on request of Iowa's Sen. John Culver, a liberal Democrat. *It showed the U.S. and Russia roughly equal in overall strategic nuclear power. But Russia is significantly ahead in conventional arms like tanks, attack submarines, and overall armed forces. . . .*
>
> Critics have pointed out—and rightfully—that overall defense isn't just a matter of comparing gun for gun and man for man. *The U.S., for example, has tremendous economic power and technological expertise which must be figured into the balance.*
>
> *The drawback here is that while such advantages may be brought to bear in a conventional war, they would be almost insignificant in a nuclear war.*
>
> *With Russia spending an estimated 40% more than the US. on defense expenditures,* now seems a poor time to try to cut U.S. spending for preparedness.[1]

Numerous comparisons of Russian and America military capacities are published, in an effort to warn of the nation's increasingly perilous position. The assessments change every few months, as the gaps in the arms race continue to widen, but this is a typical example:

1. "Is America Already No. 2 In Military Power Race?" *Deseret News,* March 9, 1976.

If you're convinced the Soviet Union isn't going to attack the United States no matter what, read no further.

If, on the other hand, you are concerned about the viability of our deterent posture compared to the Soviet Union's growing military strength, the following may give you pause.

Item: *The United States, for the first time in history, now lies virtually naked to both bomber and missile attack.*

All U.S. antiaircraft missiles (the Nikes and Bomarc rockets that guarded our cities for nearly two decades) have been removed. All U.S. antiballistic missile missiles (ABMs) are being dismantled.

In contrast, the Russians currently have about 12,000 antiaircraft missiles, along with one "Galosh" ABM site around Moscow.

The United States today has a mere 33 jet interceptors, and almost all are 10 to 20 years old. The Soviet Union reportedly has 2,600 jet interceptors, all first-line, modern craft.

Item: *The Soviet Union surpassed the U.S. in the number of missile launchers in 1971, and now leads by about 500.* The USSR surpassed the U.S. in the number of intercontinental ballistic missiles in 1969, and now is about 500 ahead. It attained virtual equality in the number of submarine-launched ballistic missiles last year.

The Russian missiles are substantially bigger and capable of carrying much larger, vastly more destructive warheads. The Soviet SS-9 ICBM, for example, carries a nuclear warhead equal to 25 million tons of TNT. And the new SS-18 can deliver an even bigger warhead or several smaller ones at once.

Together, Soviet missiles can deliver about 7 5 times the destructive force on American targets that U.S. missiles can deliver.

Moreover, the Russians have developed *a Fractional Orbital Bombardment System in which their ICBMs first are put in orbit, then brought down at will over a target.* The system gives the missiles virtually unlimited range. The U.S. has no similar capability.

Item: *New Soviet launch silos have a so-called "cold launch" capability.* This means the missiles can be blasted from their silos by compressed gas (the way American Polaris missiles are launched from their submarine tubes) and their rocket engines ignited only after the missiles clear the silo.

This technique leaves a missile silo unaffected by the flame and heat of the rocket exhaust, thus ready for instant reuse. Thus, the Soviet Union may give every appearance of adhering to the Strategic Arms Limitation Talks (SALT) restrictions, and still store additional missiles, ready for instant reloading.

American Minuteman and Titan II silos are damaged by a launching and have no such quick reload capability.

Item: *The Soviet Union now has an unsurpassed capability to conduct chemical warfare.* Secretary of Defense Donald Rumsfeld has termed this capability "*particularly worrisome since we do not possess a similar capability.*"

Item: *The Soviet Union has 4.4 million active members in its armed forces* and 6.8 million reservists for a total of 11.2 million. The U.S. has 2.1 million active members of the armed services and 1.8 million reservists, including National Guardsmen for a total of 3.9 million.

The Russians also have 42,000 tanks against our 9,000; at least 15,000 artillery pieces against our 6,000, and at least 35,000 armored and other fighting vehicles against our 22,000.

According to the Defense Department and other sources, *the Soviet Union is ahead of the U.S. in virtually every major area of military strength, though some American weapons remain technologically superior.*[1]

The concept of "overkill," or MAD ("mutual assured destruction," an assumption that neither major nuclear power can afford to initiate a nuclear war because the losses which both sides would ultimately sustain would be too devastating) is being challenged.[2] Observers are pointing out that the Russians have not accepted the validity of that theory, only the Americans believe it:

The essential and dangerous difference between American and Soviet response to the terrifying possibility of nuclear war is that *Americans really believe no exchange will ever occur,* because neither nation will risk its own destruction; but *the Soviets "have never accepted the 'overkill' concept or the concept of 'mutual assured destruction'. . . . The Soviet emphasis has rather been on survivability and indeed on the possibility of victory in a nuclear war."*[3]

A report received by the House Armed Services Committee in 1976, based on estimates of current Soviet civil defense capabilities and the present U.S. defense inadequacy, presented seriously lopsided differences:

The panel received truly alarming estimates . . . about the comparative casualties in the event of nuclear attack if the Soviets had evacuated their people during the crisis period and we were unable to do so: *the Soviets*

---

1. Peter Reich, "Russ Outstripping U.S. Defenses," Salt Lake Tribune, April 10, 1976.
2. One article defined "overkill" in this manner:

   Russia controls 5.3 billion tons of strategic nuclear firepower with intercontinental range. America controls 4.2 billion tons.

   These figures, from the Brookings Institution, mean that the Soviets could destroy every American man, woman and a child with a personal force equal to 231/2 tons of TNT. The Americans have 16 tons for each Russian.

   But it takes only a few ounces of TNT to kill a person.

   This is what the experts mean when they talk about "overkill." (Arthur L. Gavshon, "Technology Is Outpacing Politicians in N-Arms Race," *Deseret News,* August 5, 1977.)
3. Rowland Evans and Robert Novak, "Russian Roulette and Civil Defense," *Deseret News,* May 26, 1976.

> *would lose about 10½ million people; the United States would lose about 90 million people.*[1]

Military leaders have now recognized that "the Soviet Union has improved its civil defense to the point where it could receive very little damage in a nuclear war. . . . *Russian civil defense capabilities are so extensive the nation could cut its deaths in a nuclear war to about 10 million people—less than the number of dead in World War II. . . . The United States has virtually no civil defense capability and would take 10 times as many casualties in an attack.*"[2]

A study released in mid-1977 refined the casualty estimates for a nuclear holocaust, and emphasizes the folly of relying on a strategy that assumes each side is capable of virtually destroying the other. The Jones study measured potential fatalities under an arbitrary scenario in which the Soviets make a first-strike nuclear attack against U.S. strategic launchers and the U.S. immediately retaliates with an all-out nuclear strike specifically designed as a population killer. It predicts only 4 million Russian fatalities. In a reverse situation, however, U.S. losses are estimated at 72 million:

> The study claims that under "a full evacuation in accordance with Soviet Civil defense principles" *the number of fatalities from the American retaliatory attack would be as low as 4 million*—even lower, if the 24-hour walking time for evacuation is lengthened.

---

1. Ibid. The article noted that

> Soviet survival is based on rapid evacuation of the cities, on vast subterranean fallout shelters in the evacuated areas and on war plants capable of continuing operations after a nuclear exchange by virtue of "hardened" sites or geographic dispersal in remote areas.
>
> Lacking even skeleton programs for these "war-survival" measures (often called passive defense), the U.S. could find itself prohibitively out-psyched if deadlock between Moscow and Washington became the prelude to a possible nuclear exchange. Rather than risk such an exchange from a position of proven inferiority in terms of the ability to withstand it, the U.S. might be forced to yield. (Ibid.)

It also expressed concern that the U. S. civil defense program was funded with less than 10% of the $1 billion spent by the Soviets each year.

2. "Is Russia Bomb-proof?" Deseret News, July 20, 1976. The article then observed that

> The asymmetry in war survival capability is one of the factors which influence the Soviet belief that the correlation of world forces is shifting in favor of the USSR and hence one that bears importantly on Moscow's strategic and risk calculations and on assessments of the probable outcome of a nuclear war.

But the U.S. today has no plan whatever for "expedient shelters." Indeed civil defense has been lost under the liturgy of MAD, the concept of deterrence and the mythology of "overkill" (superfluous nuclear power).

Accordingly, in the reverse case—an American first strike against Soviet launchers, and Soviet retaliation designed only to kill people-the study predicts 72 million dead in the US. What is worse—if anything could be—is that even if the American people had access to "expedient shelters," the study predicts there would still be 20 million dead.

The catastrophic results both assume that 90 percent of the urban population has 24 hours to get out of town; that the evacuees take maximum advantage of residential housing for fall-out protection; and that the 10 percent left in the cities make "optimum use" of designated fall-out shelters (such as subways)—in tragic short supply here.

One reason for these ghoulishly high estimates is the *size of Soviet nuclear weapons, with much higher yields in both explosive force and in radiation than US. long-range missiles.*

The arithmetic is startling. A shelter that would protect a Soviet citizen one mile from the point of impact of an average-size American warhead (a Poseidon submarine-launched weapon) would give protection only at three miles from the point of impact of an average one megaton (million tons of TNT equivalent) Soviet warhead.

The study correctly suggests this conclusion: *"If this highly exaggerated model . . . cannot produce casualty levels far greater than those of past wars, then the 'population hostage' concept of mutual deterrence loses much of its credibility." The Soviet Union suffered 20 million fatalities in World War II, five times more than it suffered in the theoretical American nuclear strike aimed solely at Soviet people.*[1]

Russia, then, is rapidly preparing for war, both through accelerated weapons production and through an intensive civil defense program. The balance of power is rapidly shifting in favor of the Soviets, and it appears that the Russians could hold their casualties to levels they would regard as acceptable if they initiated a nuclear conflict (and past internal persecutions of the Russian citizenry indicate that the lives of their people are not held in high regard by the government).

If Russia gains a clear-cut military superiority, the stage may well be set for the fulfillment of the many prophecies cited earlier in this chapter.

Prophecies of Internal Conflict in the Americas

The scriptures speak expressly of a period of internal strife and conflict in the United States and the rest of the Americas.

---

1. Rowland Evans and Robert Novak, "In Nuclear Holocaust, How Many Deaths?" Deseret News, July 6, 1977.

Interestingly enough, the major scriptural prophecies of this future conflict were all spoken by the Savior himself as he visited the Nephites and Lamanites in America following his resurrection. Though they have been considered previously in this work,[1] yet they merit renewed attention with different emphasis, for the Lord gave in these prophecies an explanation of how the Lamanites would regain much of the Americas as the land for their inheritance. This is the Savior's prophetic message:

> But wo, saith the Father, unto the unbelieving of the Gentiles for notwithstanding they have come forth upon the face of this land, and have scattered my people who are of the house of Israel; and my people who are of the house of Israel have been cast out from among them, and have been trodden under feet by them;
>
> And because of the mercies of the Father unto the Gentiles, and also the judgments of the Father upon my people who are of the house of Israel, verily, verily, I say unto you, that after all this, and I have caused my people who are of the house of Israel to be smitten, and to be afflicted, and to be slain, and to be cast out from among them, and to become hated by them, and to become a hiss and a byword among them—
>
> And thus commandeth the Father that I should say unto you: *At that day when the Gentiles shall sin against my gospel, and shall be lifted up in the pride of their hearts above all nations, and above all the people of the whole earth, and shall be filled with all manner of lyings, and of deceits, and of mischiefs, and all manner of hypocrisy, and murders, and priestcrafts, and whoredoms, and of secret abominations; and if they shall do all those things, and shall reject the fulness of my gospel, behold, saith the Father, I will bring the fulness of my gospel from among them.*
>
> And *then* will I remember my covenant which I have made unto my people, O house of Israel, and *I will bring my gospel unto them.*
>
> And I will show unto thee, O house of Israel, that *the Gentiles shall not have power over you; but I will remember my covenant unto you, O house of Israel, and ye shall come unto the knowledge of the fulness of my gospel.*
>
> But if the Gentiles will repent and return unto me, saith the Father, behold they shall be numbered among my people, O house of Israel.
>
> *And I will not suffer my people, who are of the house of Israel, to go through among them, and tread them down, saith the Father.*
>
> *But if they will not turn unto me, and hearken unto my voice, I will suffer them, yea, I will suffer my people, O house of Israel, that they shall go through among them, and shall tread them down, and they shall be as salt that hath lost its savor, which Is thenceforth good for nothing but to be cast out, and to be trodden under foot of my people, O house of Israel.*
>
> *Verily, verily,* I say unto you, thus hath the Father commanded me—*that I should give unto this people this land for their inheritance.*[1]

1. See pp. 29-31, 52-54

Again, in 3rd Nephi 20, the Savior spoke of the internal strife in America which would serve to restore the Americas to the Lamanites as the land of their inheritance. It will be in the same era that the sword of God's justice will fall on "all the nations of the Gentiles."[2] He said that it was to occur in the era when God would complete the "fulfilling of the covenant" he has made to the House of Israel.[3] This was his prophecy:

> And *then* shall the remnants, which shall be scattered abroad upon the face of the earth, be *gathered in from the east and from the west, and from the south and from the north;* and they shall be brought to the knowledge of the Lord their God, who hath redeemed them.
>
> And the Father hath commanded me that *I should give unto you this land, for your inheritance.*
>
> And I say unto you, that if the Gentiles do not repent after the blessing which they shall receive, after they have scattered my people
>
> *Then shall ye, who are a remnant of the house of Jacob, go forth among them; and ye shall be in the midst of them who shall be many; and ye shall be among them as a lion among the beasts of the forest, and as a young lion among the flocks of sheep, who, if he goeth through both treadeth down and teareth in pieces, and none can deliver.*
>
> *Thy hand shall be lifted up upon thine adversaries, and all thine enemies shall be cut off.*
>
> And I will *gather my people together as a man gathereth his sheaves into the floor.*
>
> For I will make my people with whom the Father hath covenanted, yea, I will make thy horn iron, and I will make thy hoofs brass. And *thou shalt beat in pieces many people;* and I will consecrate their gain unto the Lord, and their substance unto the Lord of the whole earth. And behold, I am he who doeth it.
>
> And it shall come to pass, saith the Father, that *the sword of my justice shall hang over them at that day; and except they repent it shall fall upon them, saith the Father, yea, even upon all the nations of the Gentiles.*
>
> And it shall come to pass that I will establish my people, O house of Israel.
>
> And *behold, this people will I establish in this land,* unto the fulfilling of the covenant which I made with your father Jacob: and *it shall be a New Jerusalem And the powers of heaven shall be in the midst of this people: yea, even I will be in the midst of you.*[1]

---

1. 3 Ne. 1 6:8-1 6.
2. Recall the observation, reported earlier, that "I saw the international world war automatically break down, and national revolutions occur in every country and complete the work of chaos and desolation." See p. 199.
3. See 3 Ne. 20:11-12.

A third prophetic statement made by the Master during his appearance in the Americas describes the future conflict in more vivid detail. It shows the Lamanites as conquering their enemies, destroying the transportation, military strongholds, and also the cities:

> *And my people who are a remnant of Jacob shall be among the Gentiles, yea, in the midst of them as a lion among the beasts of the forest, as a young lion among the flocks of sheep, who, if he go through both treadeth down and teareth in pieces, and none can deliver.*
>
> Their hand shall be lifted up upon their adversaries, and all *their enemies shall be cut off.*
>
> Yea, wo be unto the Gentiles except they repent; for it shall come to pass in that day, saith the Father, that *I will cut off thy horses out of the midst of thee, and I will destroy thy chariots;*
>
> *And I will cut off the cities of thy land, and throw down all thy strongholds;*
>
> And I will cut off *witchcrafts* out of thy land, and thou shalt have no more soothsayers;
>
> Thy graven *images* I will also cut off, and thy standing *images* out of the midst of thee, and thou shalt no more worship the works of thy hands;
>
> And I will pluck up thy groves out of the midst of thee; *so will I destroy thy cities.*
>
> And it shall come to pass that all lyings, and deceivings, and envyings, and strifes, and priestcrafts, and whoredoms, shall be done away.
>
> For it shall come to pass, saith the Father, that at that day whosoever will not repent and come unto my Beloved Son, them will I cut off from among my people, O house of Israel;
>
> *And I will execute vengeance and fury upon them, even as upon the heathen, such as they have not heard.*[2]

The prophet Mormon, while recording the final destruction of the Nephites, suddenly looked ahead in time to the last days, and warned the Gentiles of that era that they must repent or be attacked by "a remnant of the seed of Jacob." He foresaw that if such occurs, "there is none to deliver."

> And then, O ye Gentiles, how can ye stand before the power of God, *except ye shall repent and turn from your evil ways?*
>
> Know ye not that ye are in the hands of God? Know ye not that he hath all power, and at his great command the earth shall be rolled together as a scroll?

---

1. 3 Ne. 20:13-22. Note that the final verse establishes the time of the conflict as prior to the establishing of the New Jerusalem.
2. 3 Ne. 21:12-21. Note verses 22-23, of the context, which again establish the events as preceding the establishment of the New Jerusalem.

> Therefore, repent ye, and humble yourselves before him, *lest he shall come out in justice against you lest a remnant of the seed of Jacob shall go forth among you as a lion, and tear you in pieces, and there is none to deliver.*[1]

The "Prophecy on War," given through Joseph Smith in 1832, alludes to this period, and warns that "*the remnants who are left of the land will marshal themselves, and shall become exceedingly angry, and shall vex the Gentiles with a sore vexation.*"[2]

The unworthy saints who pollute their inheritances in the last days during the era of the New Jerusalem, may also feel the wrath of the returning Lamanites if they do not live worthily. The Lord has warned that

> . . . They were set to be a light unto the world, and to be the saviors of men;
>
> And inasmuch as they are not the saviors of men, they are as salt that has lost its savor, and is thenceforth *good for nothing but to be cast out and trodden under foot of men.*
>
> But verily I say unto you, *I have decreed that your brethren which have been scattered shall return to the lands of their inheritances, and shall build up the waste places of Zion.*
>
> For after much tribulation, as I have said unto you in a former commandment, cometh the blessing.
>
> Behold, this is the blessing which I have promised *after your tribulations, and the tribulations of your brethren*—your redemption, and the redemption of your brethren, even *their restoration to the land of Zion,* to be established, no more to be thrown down.
>
> Nevertheless, *if they pollute their inheritances they shall be thrown down; for I will not spare them if they pollute their inheritances.*[3]

Modern prophets have said much about this period of internal conflict, indicating that it be a scene of local conflicts, mobocracy, and anarchy that will fill the land. Lack of food and the breakdown of local

1. Morm. 5:22-24. Concerning the remnant of the seed of Jacob see Al. 46:23-27; also D&C 109:65 and 113:10.
2. D&C 87:5.
3. D&C 103:9-14. See again D&C 85:7-12. Is it, then, apostate saints whom the Lord is referring to as the "Gentiles who shall sin against my gospel," and who "shall reject the fulness of my gospel?" Will they cause the remnant of Jacob to go through and tread them down? (See 3 Ne. 16:10, 14-15.)

manufacture, with resulting economic chaos, have been linked to this period. Already cited is Joseph Smith's vision in which he "*saw men hunting the lives of their own sons, and brother murdering brother, women killing their own daughters, and daughters seeking the lives of their own mothers. I saw armies arrayed against armies. I saw blood, desolation, fires.*"[1]

Reference was also made to Orson Hyde's warning that it "*will be the white man of the north and the white man of the south fighting for bread for their wives and children!*"[2]

Orson Pratt said, concerning the internal conflict, that

> *It will be a war of neighborhood against neighborhood, city against city, town against town, county against county, state against state,* and they will go forth, destroying and being destroyed and *manufacturing will, in a great measure, cease, for a time among the American nation.* Why? Because in these terrible wars, they will not be privileged to manufacture, there will be *too much bloodshed, too much mobocracy, too much going forth in bands and destroying and pillaging the land* to suffer people to pursue any local vocation with any degree of safety. *What will become of millions of the farmers upon that land ? They will leave their farms and they will remain uncultivated, and they will flee before the ravaging armies from place to place; . . .*[3]

He also warned,

> "What! This great and powerful nation of ours to be divided one part against the other and *many hundreds of thousands of souls to be destroyed by civil wars!*" Not a word of it would they believe. They do not believe *what is still in the future. . . .* The time will come when there will be *no safety in carrying on the peaceable pursuits of farming or agriculture. But these will be neglected, and the people will think themselves well off if they can flee from city to city, from town to town and escape with their lives.*[4]

Brigham Young taught that he heard Joseph Smith say,

> They shall have mobbing to their hearts content, if they do not redress the wrongs of the Latter-day Saints. *Mobs will not decrease, but will increase until the whole government becomes a mob, and eventually it will be state against state, city against city, neighborhood against neighborhood.*

---

1. HC 3:390-391. See p. 275.
2. Prophecy made at Nephi, Utah by Elder Orson Hyde. See p. 176.
3. JD 20:151. March 9, 1879.
4. JD 12:344. December 27. 1868.

He then amplified the statement, saying that "it will be Christian against Christian, and man against man, and *those who will not take up the sword against their neighbors, must flee to Zion.*[1]

President John Taylor warned that

> . . . God will lay his hand upon this nation, and they will feel it *more terribly than ever they have done before. There will be more bloodshed, more ruin, more devastation than ever they have seen before*. . . . There is yet to come a sound of war, trouble and distress, in which *brother will be arrayed against brother, father against son, son against father, a scene of desolation and destruction that will permeate our land* until it will be a vexation to hear the report thereof.[2]

Thus it is evident that the modern prophets have been fully aware of the coming internal conflict and have warned repeatedly of its devastating effect upon the nation.

Though their insights will not be repeated here, it should be noted that there are many Latter-day Saints today who have received prophetic indications of roles they will perform in this era. These indications have come in patriarchal blessings, personal manifestations, or both. It has been the author's privilege to talk with some of these individuals, at times interviewing them in depth. It is obvious that God is directing his people at many levels as this tumultuous period approaches.

The New Jerusalem Saints Will Assume Political Power as U.S. Government Ceases

The question is often asked if the nation of America will endure. The answer set forth by the prophets is yes! Political power and unity following the era of internal conflicts will eventually be restored, and the American nation will be again pre-eminent among the nations of the earth.

However, the prophets have clearly taught that there will be a complete change of government. Washington, D.C. will cease to be the capital. The present national bureaucracy will have its end. The internal conflict will sweep away the current system of governments and will pave the way for the political kingdom of God[3] and the millenni-

---

1. Deseret News, Vol. II, No. 9. May 1, 1861.
2. JD 20:318 October 6, 1879
3. A full treatment of statements concerning this political entity is beyond the scope of this work. See "The Establishment of the Kingdom of God," Prophecy—Key to the Future, pp. 67-81. for greater detail.

al kingdom through which Jesus Christ will rule and reign. The New Jerusalem will take its prophesied place as the dominant center of national and world affairs.

The loss of our national government is not a pleasant concept for patriotic Americans imbued with a love of their country, and we do not seek to hasten that day. Yet an eventual time of transition must come. Certainly the anticipation of righteous rule by inspired men of God, and eventually by the Saviour himself, outshines the predicted loss of our government as it is known today.

Prophetic statements by early Church leaders were repeatedly made to the effect that United States government will cease as the hand of God moves over the nation in judgment.

Joseph Smith, on several occasions, foretold the collapse of the federal government. On March 4, 1840, shortly after returning from a visit to Washington, D.C., Joseph wrote:

> . . . My heart faints within me when *I see, by the visions of the Almighty, the end of this nation,* if she continues to disregard the cries and petitions of her virtuous citizens, as she has done, and is now doing.[1]

Another such prophecy was uttered by Joseph as part of an amazing prediction concerning American politics which has since seen literal fulfillment.[2] On May 18,1843, Joseph prophesied the following to Judge Stephen A. Douglas:

> *I prophesy in the name of the Lord God of Israel,* unless the United States redress the wrongs committed upon the Saints in the state of Missouri and punish the crimes committed by her officers that *in a few years*

1. HC 4:89. March 4, 1840. The government continued to disregard the petitions of the Saints, leaving the conditional aspects of the prophecy unfulfilled.
2. On May 18, 1843, Joseph prophesied to a judge of the Illinois court, Stephen A. Douglas, that he (Douglas) would aspire to the presidency of the United States, warning him that if he ever turned against the Latter-day Saints, he would "feel the weight of the hand of the Al mighty." Douglas became the presidential candidate of the Independent Democratic Party, the predominant party of the day, in 1860. He espoused a position critical of the saints. Though it appeared that Douglas would gain an easy presidential victory, his party was suddenly split and he lost to the little-known Republican candidate, Abraham Lincoln.

   For further details on the remarkable prophecy made by Joseph Smith and its literal fulfillment, see the author's book, The Prophecies of Joseph Smith, pp. 336-338.

the government will be utterly overthrown and wasted, and there will not be so much as a potsherd left.[1]

On December 16, 1843, Joseph Smith again prophesied the destruction of the national government, as follows:

> While discussing the petition to Congress, *I prophesied, by virtue of the holy Priesthood vested in me, and in the name of the Lord Jesus Christ,* that, if Congress will not hear our petition and grant us protection, *they shall be broken up as a government.*[2]

Other Church leaders also warned that the U.S. Government would come to an end. President Brigham Young, for instance, said:

> *The nations will consume each other,* and the Lord will suffer them to bring it about. It does not require much talent or tact to get up opposition in these days. You see it rife in communities, in meetings, in neighborhoods, and in cities. *That is the knife that will cut down this government. The axe is laid at the root of the tree, and every tree that bringeth not forth good fruit will be hewn down.*[3]

Orson Pratt, while describing the future conflict within the United States. said.

> If a war of this description should take place, who could carry on his business in safety? Who would feel safe to put his crops in the ground, or to carry on any enterprise? *There would be fleeing from one State to another, and general confusion would exist throughout the whole Republic.*

---

1. HC 5:394. May 18,1843. The prophecy was a conditional one, with the conditions remaining unfulfilled. The saints were never redressed for their losses in Missouri, nor were the Missourians punished for their offenses. With the conditions unmet, it appears that the judgments upon the government can still be expected to take place.
2. HC 6:116. December 16, 1843. An interpretation that Joseph "doubtless had reference to the party in power," the Democratic party, rather than the national government, is set forth in an editorial comment on that page of the History of the Church. While it gives interesting comment on the politics of the day, it in no way documents the unjustified assumption that Joseph meant other than what he actually said, that "Congress...shall be broken up as a government." In the light of Joseph's other statements cited herein and the statements by other Church leaders also cited, the validity of the footnote with its assumption, is doubtful.

   Again, the prophecy is a conditional one in which the conditions were not met. Congress did not grant protection to the saints, who so desperately needed it.
3. JD 8:143. August 12, 1860.

> *Such eventually is to be the condition of this whole nation,* if the people do not repent of their wickedness; and *such a state of affairs means no more or less than the complete overthrow of the nation, and not only of this nation, but the nations of Europe.*[1]

Elder Pratt aptly described the transition of rule from the U.S. Government to the saints, depicting the saints as maintaining stability when present government ceases:

> God has sent forth his warning message in the midst of this nation, but they have rejected it and treated his servants with contempt; the Lord has gathered out his people from their midst, and has planted them here in these mountains; and *he will speedily fulfill the prophecy in relation to the overthrow of this nation, and their destruction. We shall be obliged to have a government to preserve ourselves in unity and peace; for they, through being wasted away, will not have the power to govern;* for state will be divided against state, city against city, town against town, and the whole country will be in terror and confusion; mobocracy will prevail and their [sic] will be no security, through this great Republic, for the lives or property of the people. *When that time shall arrive, we shall necessarily want to carry out the principles of our great constitution and as the people of God, we shall want to see those principles magnified, according to the order of union and oneness which prevails among the people of God.* We can magnify it, and all will be united without having democrats or republicans and all kinds of religions; we can magnify it according to the spirit and letter of the constitution, though we are united in politics, religion, and everything else.[2]

President Wilford Woodruff also foresaw and foretold the eventual fall of U.S. Government. He wrote that

> *The American nation will be broken in pieces like a potter's vessel* and will be cast down to hell if it does not repent,—and this, because of murders, whoredoms, wickedness, and all manner of abominations, *for the Lord has spoken it.*[3]

---

1. JD 18:341. February 25, 1877.
2. DEN, Vol. 8, No. 265. October 2, 1875
3. Matthias F. Cowley, Wilford Woodruff—History of His Life and Labors (Salt Lake City, Utah: Bookcraft, 1964), p. 500. Summer, 1877. While closing his journal for the previous year, Elder Woodruff wrote his observation that "To a great extent, virtue has departed from the land, and honesty has been driven from the various departments of government. Men seek to aggrandize themselves rather than to serve the interests of the people. Death and destruction are sown in the land which Is ripening for the harvest. " (Ibid., p. 490.)

In an epistle to the world, written by Wilford Woodruff on February 22,1879, he prophesied,

> . . . *I will say, in the name of Jesus Christ*, the Son of the living God, that "Mormonism" will live and prosper, Zion will flourish, and the Kingdom of God will stand in power and glory and dominion as Daniel saw it, *when this nation is broken to pieces as a potter's vessel and laid in the dust, and brought to judgment*, or God never spoke by my mouth.1

In the same epistle he warned that the period would be a time of international anarchy, when legal barriers would fall and laws would not be observed:

> . . . I wish to warn all nations of the judgments of God which are at their doors. *Thrones will be cast down, nations will be overturned, anarchy will reign, all legal barriers will be broken down, and the laws will be trampled in the dust. You are about to be visited with war, the sword, famine, pestilence, plague, earthquakes, whirlwinds, tempests, and with the flame* of devouring fire; by fire and with the sword will God plead with all flesh, and *the slain of the Lord will be many.* The anger of the Lord is kindled and His sword is bathed in heaven, and is about to fall upon Idumea, or the world. And who is able to abide these things? And who will stand when He appeareth? The fig trees are leaving, and the signs of all heaven and earth indicate the coming of the Son of Man. *The seals are about to be opened, the plagues to be poured forth. Your rivers and seas will be turned to blood and to gall. And the inhabitants of the earth will die of plagues.* And the unbelief of great Babylon, with the whole Christian world, will not make the truths of God without effect. . . .[2]

In a letter to the leaders of the Church, written from Arizona on September 15, 1879, Elder Woodruff wrote that "*the lawyers, judges, and the nation are hastening to their doom as fast as time will permit, and they are sure of their fate.*"[3]

---

1. *Ibid.*, p. 508.
2. *Ibid.*, p. 511 .
3. *Ibid.*, p. 528. Elder Woodruff knew well the future events which will transpire in America, having seen them in vision. As early as October 18, 1848, he wrote:

   > . . . the visions of my mind have been opened so that I saw clearly my duty to my God, to my wife, to my children, to the Saints, and to the world at large. I have also seen the awful and certain judgments of God, which like a gathering storm are ready to burst upon the whole Gentile world, especially this nation which has heard the sound of the gospel but rejected it, together with the testimony of the servants of God; has stoned and killed the prophets; has become drunk with the blood of martyrs and Saints; and finally has driven the entire Church with the priesthood and keys of eternal life out of its midst into the wilderness and mountains of Israel." (Ibid., p. 333. See also pp. 152-153.)

On January 26, 1880, a vision to Elder Woodruff again showed him the destruction of the nation. He wept, as would anyone who loves his country:

> I went to bed filled with prayer and meditation. I fell asleep and remained in slumber until about midnight, when I awoke. The Lord then poured out His spirit upon me and opened the vision of my mind so that I could comprehend in a great measure the mind and will of God concerning the nation and concerning the inhabitants of Zion. *I saw the wickedness of the nation, its abominations and corruptions and the judgments of God and the destruction that awaited it.* Then I also comprehended the great responsibility which rested upon the Quorum of the Apostles. My head became a fountain of tears, and my pillow was wet with the dews of heaven. Sleep departed from me. The Lord revealed unto me the duty of the Apostles and of all the faithful elders of Israel.[1]

In a discourse delivered in 1880, Elder Woodruff asserted that the destruction of the American nation, together with other nations of the world, "is sure":

> When I contemplate the condition of our nation, and see that wickedness and abominations are increasing, so much so that the whole heavens groan and weep over the abominations of this nation and the nations of the earth, *I ask myself the question, can the American nation escape? The answer comes, No; its destruction, as well as the destruction of the world, is sure;* just as sure as the Lord cut off and destroyed the two great and prosperous nations that once inhabited this continent of North and South America, because of their wickedness, so will he them destroy, and *sooner or later they will reap the fruits of their own wicked acts, and be numbered among the past.*[2]

---

1. Ibid., pp. 530-531. The account records that "The revelation was submitted to the Quorum of the Twelve Apostles just prior to the April conference of that year. It was accepted by that body as the word of the Lord, according to Elder Woodruff's journal, under date of April 4th, 1880." (*Ibid.*, p. 531.)

   Two days after the vision, on January 28, 1880, another vision was granted to him:

   > "On January 28th I was again given a vision. It concerned the destiny of our nation and of Zion. My pillow was again wet by a fountain of tears as I beheld the judgments of God upon the wicked. I was strongly impressed that the Apostles and elders should warn the inhabitants of the earth." (*Ibid.*)

2. JD 21:301. August 1, 1880. Wilford Woodruff's prophecy of December 16, 1878, should be recalled in this context. He saw terrible destruction throughout the world, with Washington, D.C. a desolation. Congress and the White House were empty, and the people had fled from the city. (See pp. 194-196.)

Others also have seen the end of the American nation in vision. One was apostle Moses Thatcher, who told a congregation in 1882, "I have seen the *end of this nation,* and it is terrible."[1]

But as the present political system crumbles under the prophesied chaos and anarchy, both law and order, and Constitutional government are expected to be preserved among the saints.

Brigham Young taught that the saints would save the Constitution at a "critical juncture":

> Will the Constitution be destroyed? No: it will be held inviolate by this people; and, as Joseph Smith said, "The time will come when *the destiny of the nation will hang upon a single thread. At that critical juncture, this people will step forth and save it from the threatened destruction." It will be so.*[2]

The following year he taught that

> . . . When the Constitution of the United States hangs, as it were, upon a single thread, *they will have to call for the "Mormon Elders to save it from utter destruction; and they will step forth and do it.*[3]

President Young taught that the maintaining of Constitutional principles by the saints would be under their own government, the Kingdom of God, not under U.S. Government as it is known today:

> *When the day comes in which the Kingdom of God will bear rule,* the flag of the United States will proudly flutter unsullied on the flag staff of liberty and equal rights, without a spot to sully its fair surface; the glorious flag our fathers have bequeathed to us will then be unfurled to the breeze *by those who have power to hoist it aloft and defend its sanctity.*[4]

President John Taylor observed in 1879,

> . . . And then *the day is not far distant when this nation will be shaken from centre to circumference.* And now, you may write it down, any of

1. *Franklin Ward Historical Record,* Franklin, Idaho, June 16, 1882.
2. JD 7:15. July 4, 1854.
3. JD 2:182. February 18, 1855.
4. JD 2:317. July 8, 1855. See D&C 105:32-34. Though some have interpreted these statements as having been fulfilled in the U.S. Civil War Brigham Young made it clear that such was not a proper interpretation. Following that war he said, "How long will it be before the words of the prophet Joseph will be fulfilled? He said if the Constitution of the United States were saved at all it must be done by these people. It will not be many years before these words come to pass." (JD 12:204. April 8, 1868.)

> you, and *I will prophesy it in the name of God*. And then will be fulfilled that prediction to be found in one of the revelations given through the Prophet Joseph Smith. *Those who will not take up their sword to fight against their neighbor must needs flee to Zion for safety. . . . When the people shall have torn to shreds the Constitution of the United States the Elders of Israel will be found holding it up to the nations of the earth and proclaiming liberty and equal rights to all men,* and extending the hand of fellowship to the oppressed of all nations. This is part of the programme, and as long as we do what is right and fear God, he will help us and stand by us under all circumstances.[1]

George Q. Cannon also asserted that the time will come when liberty and Constitutional government will only be found among the saints:

> . . . the day will come—and this is another prediction of Joseph Smith's—I want to remind you of it, my brethren and sisters, *when good government, constitutional government liberty will be found among the Latter-day Saints, and it will be sought for in vain elsewhere;* when the Constitution of this land and republican government and institutions will be upheld by this people who are now so oppressed and whose destruction is now sought so diligently. *The day will come when the Constitution, and free government under it, will be sustained and preserved by this people. . . .*[2]

The scenario is drawn, then, with the numerous statements cited above, of a future time of internal conflict in which lawlessness and anarchy will reach such devastating proportions that national and local government will fail. There will be greater stability among the saints during this era, and people will be drawn to it to escape the chaos of other areas. A new government will be established among the saints and that political Kingdom of God will espouse and uphold the principles of Constitutional government. Eventually it will be the only governing power with stability in the nation, and it will grow in power and influence as the New Jerusalem rises to unparalleled pre-eminence.

Will this nation, then, endure? Yes, but only after a tragic reduction of population, complete economic disruption and upheaval, disintegration of governmental control and finally of the government itself. There will be much suffering, much fear, much sorrow, and much chastening. The nation which will emerge will be as the butterfly

1. JD 21:8. August 31, 1879.
2. JD 23:104. November 20, 1881. For other statements on this subject see the author's book, Prophecy—Key to the Future, "Appendix 1, The United States Constitution Will Hang By A Thread," pp. 297-300.

which has struggled to emerge from its cocoon. It will become a thing of beauty, leaving behind the withered shell which once housed and encompassed it.

International Conflict During the New Jerusalem Era—A Fourth World War

It is expected that the period of internal conflict will mark the time for the saints to wend their way back to Jackson County, Missouri to establish the New Jerusalem. Orson Pratt expressed the expectation held by the saints concerning the future time of return:

> *When the time shall come that the Lord shall waste away this nation, he will give commandment to this people to return and possess their own inheritance* which they purchased some forty-four years ago in the state of Missouri.[1]

The area is expected to have been swept clean in the destruction of the world war or internal conflicts which will precede the return. As he related his vision of future judgments he received in 1878, Wilford Woodruff related that "I seemed to be standing on the left bank of the Missouri River, opposite the city of *Independence; but I saw no city. I saw the whole states of Illinois and Missouri and part of Iowa, a complete wilderness of desert with no living human being there.*[2]

Heber C. Kimball, in his extended prophecy to Amanda H. Wilcox, said that Jackson County "will be swept so clean of its inhabitants that . . . there will not be left so much as a yellow dog to wag his tail."[3]

---

1. DEN, Vol. 8, No. 265, October 2, 1875. For a broader description of the return to and establishment of the New Jerusalem, and events to take place therein, see Prophecy—Key to the Future, pp. 84-126.
2. Revelation to Wilford Woodruff, December 16, 1878. See pp. 293-296.
3. Prophetic Sayings of Heber C. Kimball to Amanda H. Wilcox. The "yellow dog" statement, it appears, was originally made by Joseph Smith, as identified in the following letter written by George Burkett to his children in December, 1870, from Eden City (Ogden Valley, Weber County), Utah. Earlier in the letter, Elder Burkett indicated that members of Zion's Camp went to his home when cholera broke out among them [see HC 2:112] It was probably at that time that the statement was made by Joseph Smith, which Elder Burkett quotes:

   Do not be in a hurry of going to Jackson County for the land has to be cleared and the power of God to rest upon it before we think of returning there.

Indeed, the Lord has revealed that he will clear the way for the returning saints by removing their enemies:

> For behold, *I do not require at their hands to fight the battles of Zion;for, as I said in a former commandment, even so will I fulfil—I will fight your battles.*
>
> Behold, the destroyer I have sent forth to destroy and lay waste mine enemies; and not many years hence they shall not be left to pollute mine heritage, and to *blaspheme my name upon the lands which I have consecrated for the gathering together of my saints.*[1]

Yet it appears that the saints will still have to be prepared militarily and to function as an army in their return:

> And after these lands are purchased, *I will hold the armies of Israel guiltless in taking possession of their own lands, which they have previously purchased with their moneys, and of throwing down the towers of mine enemies that may be upon them, and scattering their watchmen, and avenging me of mine enemies* unto the third and fourth generation of them that hate me.
>
> *But first let my army become very great, and let it be sanctified before me, that it may become fair as the sun, and clear as the moon, and that her banners may be terrible unto all nations:*
>
> That the kingdoms of this world may be constrained to acknowledge that the kingdom of Zion is in very deed the kingdom of our God and his Christ; therefore, let us become subject unto her laws.[2]

There will be other cities and towns in nearby areas which will be standing, but desolate, and as the tribes of Israel gather to the New Jerusalem area they will inherit them. They will outnumber the church members, "for more are the children of the desolate than the

---

I heard Joseph Smith say in my house when in Clay Co. that when we returned there, there would not be a dog to wag its tail, or move its tongue against us, none but the pure in heart will go up there and the Lord will prepare the people. They shall be clear as the sun, fair as the moon and terribly valiant as an army with banners; there are virgins and hundred and forty four thousand that shall stand on Mount Zion, these are the bride the Lamb's wife.

Acopy of this portion of the letter was given to the author February 11 , 1965 by Geraldine Nelson (Mrs. Merrell Nelson), of Logan, Utah. She is a third great-granddaughter of George Burkett.

---

1. D&C 105:14-15
2. D&C 105:30-32.

children of the married wife, saith the Lord."[1] The Saviour has promised them that

> . . . thou shalt break forth on the right hand and on the left, and *thy seed shall inherit the Gentiles and make the desolate cities to be inhabited.*[2]

The New Jerusalem will be a place of refuge for people from throughout the world, who will come to escape the warfare that will be raging around them. Indeed, the Lord has revealed that its inhabitants "shall be the only people that shall not be at war one with another":

> And with one heart and with one mind, gather up your riches that ye may purchase an inheritance which shall hereafter be appointed unto you.
>
> And it shall be called the New Jerusalem, a land of peace, *a city of refuge, a place of safety for the saints of the Most High God;*

---

1. 3 Ne. 22:1. See also D&C 133:26-34; 2 Ne. 29:12-14. Orson Pratt supported this interpretation when he said,

   The city of Zion, with its Sanctuary and Priesthood, and the glorious fulness of the Gospel, will constitute a standard which will put an end to jarring creeds and political wranglings, by uniting the republics. states, provinces, territories, nations, tribes, kindreds, tongues, people, and sects of North and South America in one great and common bond of brotherhood; while truth and knowledge shall make them free, and love cement their union. (JD 24:31-32. October 26, 1879.)
2. 3 Ne. 22:3. Note the important chronological sequence outlined in the preceding verses:
   1. The remnant of Jacob will tread down the cities of the Gentiles (3 Ne. 21:12-19).
   2. The wicked (apostate) will be cut off from among the Lord's people (3 Ne. 21:20-21).
   3. The church will help the remnant of Jacob build the New Jerusalem (3 Ne. 21:23).
   4. The Lord's people, scattered across the land, will gather to the New Jerusalem (3 Ne. 21:24).
   5. The Lord will appear to them (3 Ne. 21:25).
   6. The gospel will be preached to the (Lamanite) remnant (3 Ne. 21:26).
   7. The work will commence among the lost tribes of Israel (3 Ne. 21:26).
   8. The major period of gathering scattered Israel will commence, among all nations (3 Ne. 21:27-29).
   9. Those gathering will inhabit the desolate cities (3 Ne. 22:1-3).

> And the glory of the Lord shall be there, and *the terror of the Lord also shall be there, insomuch that the wicked will not come unto it,* and it shall be called Zion.
>
> And it shall come to pass among the wicked, that *every man that will not take his sword against his neighbor must needs flee unto Zion for safety.*
>
> And there shall be gathered unto it out of every nation under heaven; *and it shall be the only people that shall not be at war one with another.*
>
> And it shall be said among the wicked: *Let us not go up to battle against Zion, for the inhabitants of Zion are terrible; wherefore we cannot stand.*
>
> And it shall come to pass that the righteous shall be gathered out from among all nations, and shall come to Zion, singing with songs of everlasting joy. . . .
>
> For when the Lord shall appear he shall be terrible unto them, that *fear may seize upon them, and they shall stand afar off and tremble.*
>
> *And all nations shall be afraid because of the terror of the Lord, and the power of his might.* Even so. Amen.1

Here then, is a significant prophecy of international conflict-not a third world war, for that war will have ended previously. Is it not, then, a fourth world war—a devastating conflagration which only the New Jerusalem will escape because the power of God is there?

Other revelations speak of it. The Lord spoke of wars which were to come upon the earth, then warned of one specific war during which the saints will be assembled on the land of Zion and desolation comes upon the wicked:

> I, the Lord, am angry with the wicked; I am holding my Spirit from the inhabitants of the earth.
>
> *I have sworn in my wrath, and decreed wars upon the face of the earth, and the wicked shall slay the wicked, and fear shall come upon every man;*
>
> *And the saints also shall hardly escape; nevertheless, I, the Lord, am with them, and will come down in heaven from the presence of my Father and consume the wicked with unquenchable fire.*
>
> And behold, this is not yet, but by and by.
>
> Wherefore, seeing that I, the Lord, have decreed all these things upon the face of the earth, *I will that my saints should be assembled upon the land of Zion;*
>
> And that every man should take righteousness in his hands and faithfulness upon his loins, and lift a warning voice unto the inhabitants of the earth; and *declare both by word and by flight that desolation shall come upon the wicked.*[2]

---

1. D&C 45:65-71, 74-75.
2. D&C 63:32-37. Note that this description in no way matches the events of the Third World War. It is in a different geographical and chronological setting.

The Savior, after telling how the New Jerusalem would be cleansed of apostates and false prophets and apostles,[1] foretold the flight of people from all nations to the New Jerusalem and the fear the nations of the earth will have of the New Zion:

> For, behold, I say unto you that Zion shall flourish, and the glory of the Lord shall be upon her;
>
> And she shall be an ensign unto the people, and *there shall come unto her out of every nation under heaven.*
>
> And the day shall come when *the nations of the earth shall tremble because of her, and shall fear because of her terrible ones.* The Lord hath spoken it. Amen.[2]

Again, a later revelation depicts the New Jerusalem as a place of defense when God's wrath is poured out upon the whole earth:

> Verily I say unto you all: Arise and shine forth, that thy light may be a standard for the nations;
>
> And that the gathering together upon the land of Zion, and upon her stakes, *may be for a defense, and for a refuge from the storm, and from wrath when it shall be poured out without mixture upon the whole earth.*[3]

A prophecy in the Book of Revelation appears to refer to this Fourth World War, when every nation except the New Jerusalem will be at war. John foresaw war emanate from near the River Euphrates, in which a terrible army uses fire and smoke and brimstone[4] which slays a third of mankind:

> And the sixth angel sounded, and I heard a voice from the four horns of the golden altar which is before God,
>
> Saying to the sixth angel which had the trumpet, *Loose the four angels which are bound in the great river Euphrates.*
>
> *And the four angels were loosed, which were prepared for an hour. and a day, and a month, and a year, for to slay the third part of men.*
>
> *And the number of the army of the horsemen were two hundred thousand thousand: and I heard the number of them.*

---

1. See D&C 64:35-40.
2. D&C 64:41-43. Note again the world-wide scope of the warning.
3. D&C 115:5-6. Note again the world-wide implications of the prophecy.
4. Rev. 9:17-18. Nuclear weapons again? Imagine what terrible weaponry is required to slay one-third of mankind! See the commentary on the chronological relationship of this war, followed by the gathering of Israel to Palestine, then followed by the Battle of Armageddon in Prophecy—Key to the Future, p. 185. The commentary is related to Rev. 9:13-11:19.

> And thus I saw the horses in the vision, and them that sat on them, having breastplates of fire, and of jacinth, and brimstone: and the heads of the horses were as the heads of lions; and out of their mouths issued fire and smoke and brimstone.
>
> *By these three was the third part of men killed, by the fire, and by the smoke, and by the brimstone,* which issued out of their mouths.[1]

Orson Pratt, that great student and expounder of prophecy, was fully aware of this period of warfare which will come upon the earth during the New Jerusalem era. He spoke of it on several occasions. Characteristic of his comments is the following:

> By-and-by the Spirit of God will entirely withdraw from those Gentile nations, and leave them to themselves. *Then they will find something else to do besides warring against the Saints in their midst—besides raising their sword and fighting against the Lamb of God; for then war will commence in earnest,* and such a war as probably never entered into the hearts of men in our age to conceive of. *No nation of the Gentiles upon the face of the whole earth but what will be engaged in deadly war, except the Latter-day Kingdom.* They will be fighting one against another. And when that day comes, *the Jews will flee to Jerusalem, and those nations will almost use one another up,* and those of them who are left will be burned; for that will be the last sweeping judgment that is to go over the earth to cleanse it from wickedness.[2]

He also taught,

> It is not only a Gospel to be preached to all the nations of the earth, but in connection with it *you will have to make proclamation connected with it, to all people, to fear God and give glory to him, for the hour of his judgment is come.* And as these judgments come, *kingdoms and thrones will be cast down and overturned. Empire will war with empire, kingdom with kingdom, and city with city, and there will be one general revolution throughout the earth, the Jews fleeing to their own country,* desolation coming upon the wicked, with the swiftness of whirlwinds and fury poured out.[3]

And also:

> When that day shall come [when the missionaries will be called home] there shall be wars, not such wars as have come in centuries and years that

1. Rev. 9:13-18.
2. JD 7:188. July 10, 1859. For additional exposition of the theme of a Fourth World War, and other statements by Elder Pratt, see Prophecy-Key to the Future, "Universal Conflict and the Fall of the Christian Nations," pp. 159-166.
3. JD 14:65-66. March 26, 1871

are past and gone, but *a desolating war.* When I say desolating, I mean that *it will lay these European nations in waste. Cities will be left vacated, without inhabitants. The people will be destroyed by the sword of their own hands. Not only this but many other cities will be burned;* for when contending armies are wrought up with the terrible anger, without the Spirit of God upon them, when they have not that spirit of humanity that now characterizes many of the wars amongst the nations, when they are left to themselves, there will be no quarter given, no prisoners taken, but *a war of destruction, of desolation, of the burning of the cities and villages, until the land is laid desolate.*[1]

Thus it is seen that a pattern of scripture and modern exposition indicates there will be a period of world-wide warfare at the day the New Jerusalem has been established in Jackson County, Missouri. Indeed, the inhabitants there "shall be the only people that shall not be at war one with another." In that era, the New Jerusalem will be "a city of refuge, a place of safety," and "every man that will not take his sword against his neighbor must needs flee unto Zion for safety." This gathering will be "out of every nation under heaven." Truly this future event—a fourth world war—is one of the most significant signs of the times which will precede the Savior's glorious return.

Conflict as the Great and Abominable Church Collapses—Part of Fourth World War

A previous chapter[2] has discussed in detail the extensive persecution which is to be experienced by the saints at the hands of a "great and abominable church." As was recorded therein, that persecution will continue until nations embracing that church war among themselves and bring about the collapse of that Satan-inspired entity. That broad panorama of prophecy need not be repeated in this context. What is important here is some comment on the chronological relationships of these events.

Comment was made on the "great and marvelous work" and the Lord's "strange act" which will cause men to join either the church of God or the church of the devil.[3] That divisive event was prophesied in several Book of Mormon passages, which also indicate its chronological relationships to other future events. 1 Ne. 22:8-12 indicates that

---

1. JD 20:150-151. March 9, 1879.
2. See "Sixth Warning: The Great and Abominable Church Will Persecute the Saints," pp.71-97.
3. See pp. 75-83.

the divisive event will precede the gathering of Israel to the lands of their inheritance (which 3 Ne. 21:22-29 shows will be after the construction of the New Jerusalem). 2 Ne. 25:15-18 also speaks of the divisive event in a context preceding the gathering of Israel, but linking it with the coming of a false Messiah.1

2 Ne. 27:26 speaks of "a marvelous work and a wonder," and the chapter places it in the context of the era when "the multitude of all the nations" shall "fight against Mount Zion"[2] but early enough that the Gentiles of "this land" will still be "drunken with iniquity and all manner of abominations."[3] 2 Ne. 28:32-29:14 again shows that the "marvelous work" will precede the time when the house of Israel "shall be gathered home to the lands of their possessions."4 3 Ne. 21:9-23 also places the "marvelous work" prior to the uprising of the remnant of Jacob and the building of the New Jerusalem. The Lord's "strange act" is to precede the fall of the U.S. Government, for the Lord in his fury shall "vex the nation."[5] The Canadian manifestation of Sols Guardisto tells of the religious animosity and persecution which will arise against the Church during the Third World War.

All of these allusions combine to show that the persecutions of the saints by the great and abominable church will begin early in the future series of last days events—prior to the internal conflict in the United States and before the return to Jackson County, Missouri. Animosity will continue against the Church during the New Jerusalem period, and "the nations of the earth shall tremble because of her, and shall fear because of her terrible ones."[6] The wicked will want to war against the New Jerusalem but will be afraid to do so,[7] and the Lord will fight battles for the saints.[8]

But there is to come a time when the persecution will cease, and the great and abominable church will be destroyed in a period of intense international warfare. That warfare will involve the Church,

---

1. See pp. 133-140 These pages and the balance of Chapter IX give strong indication that there will be difficulty with the coming of a false Messiah in the early days of the New Jerusalem.
2. 2 Ne. 27:3.
3. 2 Ne. 27:1.
4. 2 Ne. 29:14. This gathering, presumably, includes the uprising of the remnant of Jacob in which the Lamanites will reclaim the Americas as the land of their inheritance. See 3 Ne 16:15-16;20:14-18;21:12-22.
5. D&C 101:89-95.
6. D&C 64:43.
7. D& c 45:67, 70.
8. D&C 105:14.

for John prophesied of ten kings that "*shall make war with the Lamb, and the Lamb shall overcome them.*"[1]

Nephi saw that the wrath of God would come upon the great and abominable church, resulting in international warfare, while the saints will still be scattered throughout the earth:

> And it came to pass that I looked and beheld the whore of all the earth, and she sat upon many waters; and she had dominion over all the earth, *among all nations, kindreds, tongues, and people.*
>
> And it came to pass that *I beheld the church of the Lamb of God, and its numbers were few, because of the wickedness and abominations of the whore who sat upon many waters; nevertheless, I beheld that the church of the Lamb, who were the saints of God, were also upon all the face of the earth; and their dominions upon the face of the earth were small, because of the wickedness of the great whore whom I saw.*
>
> And it came to pass that I beheld that the great mother of abominations *did gather together multitudes upon the face of all the earth, among all the nations of the Gentiles, to fight against the Lamb of God.*
>
> And it came to pass that I, Nephi, beheld the power of the Lamb of God, that it descended upon the saints of the church of the Lamb, and *upon the covenant people of the Lord, who were scattered upon all the face of the earth;* and they were armed with righteousness and with the power of God in great glory.
>
> And it came to pass that I beheld that the *wrath of God was poured out upon the great and abominable church, insomuch that there were wars and rumors of wars among all the nations and kindreds of the earth.*[2]

Then he described the fall of the great and abominable church as the nations under its power war among themselves:

> *And the blood of that great and abominable church, which is the whore of all the earth, shall turn upon their own heads; for they shall war among themselves, and the sword of their own hands shall fall upon their own heads, and they shall be drunken with their own blood.*
>
> *And every nation which shall war against thee, O house of Israel, shall be turned one against another,* and they shall fall into the pit which they digged to ensnare the people of the Lord. *And all that fight against Zion shall be destroyed, and that great whore, who hath perverted the right ways of the Lord, yea, that great and abominable church, shall tumble to the dust* and great shall be the fall of it.
>
> For behold, saith the prophet, the time cometh speedily that Satan shall have no more power over the hearts of the children of men; for the day soon cometh that all the proud and they who do wickedly shall be as stubble; and the day cometh that they must be burned.

---

1. Rev. 17:12-14
2. 1 Ne. 14:11-15

> For the time soon cometh that the fulness of the wrath of God shall be poured out upon all the children of men; *for he will not suffer that the wicked shall destroy the righteous.*
>
> Wherefore, he will preserve the righteous by his power, even if it so be that the fulness of his wrath must come, and *the righteous be preserved, even unto the destruction of their enemies by fire.* Wherefore, the righteous need not fear; for thus saith the prophet, they shall be saved, even if it so be as by fire.
>
> Behold, my brethren, I say unto you, that these things must shortly come; yea, even *blood, and fire, and vapor of smoke must come;* and it must needs be upon the face of this earth; and it cometh unto men according to the flesh if it so be that they will harden their hearts against the Holy One of Israel.
>
> For behold, *the righteous shall not perish; for the time surely must come that all they who fight against Zion shall be cut off.*[1]

Its demise will be an event of major proportions, for Nephi prophesies that "*great must be the fall thereof.*"[2] He also prophesied that "*all that fight against Zion shall be destroyed,* and that great whore, who hath perverted the right ways of the Lord, yea, *that great and abominable church, shall tumble to the dust and great shall be the fall of it.*[3]

According to John's prophecy, the ten kings who will fight against the church will turn upon the capital city of the abominable church "and shall make her desolate and naked, and shall eat her flesh, and burn her with fire."[4]

Nephi learned from an angel the time of this terrible destruction of the great and abominable church, and indicated that it would still precede the major period of Israel's gathering:

> . . . When the day cometh that the wrath of God is poured out upon the mother of harlots, which is the great and abominable church of all the earth, whose foundation is the devil, *then, at that day, the work of the Father shall commence, in preparing the way for the fulfilling of his covenants, which he hath made to his people who are of the house of Israel.*[5]

The prophet clearly linked the gathering of Israel to the lands of their inheritance, the warring of the nations of the great and abominable church, and fighting against Zion by the nations into one chronological era as he expounded the prophecies.[6]

---

1. 1 Ne. 22:13-19.
2. 2 Ne. 28:18.
3. 1 Ne. 22:14.
4. Rev. 17:16.
5. 1 Ne. 14:17.
6. 1 Ne. 22:8-14.

The conclusion becomes inevitable, then: the conflict which brings the fall of the great and abominable church is the same which will rage in the days of the New Jerusalem, when every nation will be at war except the inhabitants of that protected city. Though two separate patterns of prophecy seem to speak of these conflicts, the chronological relationships show that both are the same period of international conflict, and both represent important aspects of the Fourth World War.

The Battle of Armageddon

This momentous conflict, the most prophesied event in all scripture, will take place in Israel in the last days. It draws its name from Megiddo,[1] a mountain located in the plain of Esdraelon, a triangular valley about sixty miles northwest of Jerusalem. This mountain is a strong defensive position which dominates the valley and commands the north-south route through Palestine. It has been the site of innumerable battles in the past, and the archaeological remains of several fortresses dating back to Old Testament times are still very much in evidence there.

John the Revelator foretold this great future conflict. He spoke of three "unclean spirits" that will "come out of the mouth of the dragon, and out of the mouth of the beast, and out of the mouth of the false prophet."[2] He then described their mission:

> . . . They are the spirits of devils, working miracles, which go forth unto the kings of the earth and of the whole world, *to gather them to the battle of that great day of God Almighty. . . .*
>
> And he gathered them together into a place called in the Hebrew tongue *Armageddon*.[3]

Israel has lived its precarious existence for more than two decades, fighting several wars, and the world has talked continuously about the approaching conflict of Armageddon, often assuming that the conflict at hand was the beginning of that battle. Though Israel will probably endure continued conflict and tension with its neighbors in the years to come,[4] those who are well acquainted with the message of the scriptures recognize that numerous major events (plus a host of minor

1. Har-Magedon is the Greek transliteration of the Hebrew for "mountain of Megiddon."
2. Rev. 16:13.
3. Rev. 16:14, 16.
4. See "Prophecies Concerning Israel's Political Affairs," Prophecy—Key to the Future, pp. 192-194.

events which have been prophesied) must precede that final conflict. These include:

1. A third World War.[1]
2. The fulfilling of the times of the Gentiles.[2]
3. Internal conflict in the United States and other nations.[3]
4. The establishment of the New Jerusalem and the political kingdom of God.[4]
5. The appearance of Christ in the New Jerusalem.[5]
6. A fourth World War.[6]
7. The return of the Ten Tribes from the north.[7]
8. The calling of 144,000 high priests.[8]
9. Christ's appearance at the council at Adam-ondi-Ahman.[9]
10. The gathering of all the tribes of Israel to the land of Israel.[10]
11. The rule of David the Prince.[11]
12. The construction of the temple in Jerusalem.[12]

Then, and not until then, will the Battle of Armageddon be waged. This book focuses on America's future, rather than events in Israel and elsewhere, and will not attempt to describe the Battle of Armageddon in detail (a project which could be a complete book). Yet that prophesied conflict is of such major import that it deserves at least summary consideration in this chapter on wars which have been prophesied.

Greed will be the motive for the war, and Ezekiel prophesied that Israel's enemies will come

> *To take a spoil, and to take a prey;* to turn thine hand upon the *desolate places that are now inhabited,* and upon the *people that are gathered out of*

1. See PP. 185-209, *Prophecy—Key to the Future,* pp. 1-16.
2. See *Prophecy—Key to the Future,* pp. 17-34.
3. See pp. 193-202 209-215, *Prophecy—Key to the Future,* pp 67-105.
4. See pp. 215-223, *Prophecy—Key to the Future,* pp. 67-105
5. See *Prophecy—Key to the Future,* 112-117.
6. See pp. 223-233, *Prophecy—Key to the Future,* pp. 15
7. See *Prophecy—Key to the Future,* pp. 11 7-1 21.
8. See *Prophecy—Key to the Future,* pp. 121-125.
9. See *Prophecy—Key to the Future,* pp. 167-176.
10. See *Prophecy—Key to the Future,* pp. 127-139, 177-179, 182-189.
11. See *Prophecy—Key to the Future,* pp. 17 9-1 82.
12. See *Prophecy—Key to the Future,* pp. 189-192.

> *the nations,* which have gotten cattle and goods, that dwell in the midst of the land.[1]

The leader of the attacking army is to be ''Gog, the chief prince of Meshech and Tubal."[2] His army will be called "Magog";[3] and will be comprised primarily of people from countries surrounding Israel.[4]

The war, which will continue for three-and-a-half years,[5] will take a heavy toll. Two-thirds of the people of Israel will be slain,[6] and five-sixth's of the attacking army, including its leader, Gog, will fall on the mountains of Israel.[7] The battle will rage in Jerusalem. Zechariah prophesies that "the city shall be taken, and the houses rifled, and the women ravished; and half of the city shall go forth into captivity, and the residue of the people shall not be cut off from the city."[8] Even a portion of the temple will be overrun by the invaders.[9] Two prophets in Jerusalem will prophesy during the 3½ years, and will have power to withhold rain from the earth and smite with plagues. They will be killed in the conflict. Their bodies will lie unattended in the streets for 3½ days, then life will return to them and they will be caught up to heaven.[10]

During the battle great judgments will be poured out. Not only will the rain be withheld by the two prophets, but God will send pestilence, an over-flowing rain, great hailstones, fire and

---

1. Ezek. 38:12.
2. Ezek. 38:2-3. These geographical terms date back to the "table of nations" found in Genesis 10, and refer to the settling places of the descendants of Noah, who spread across the face of the land following the flood. Meshech and Tubal appear to refer to portions of modern Turkey and southern Russia near the Caspian Sea. It should be remembered that two world wars will transpire before the Battle of Armageddon which will greatly alter the boundaries and stature of the nations of the earth. Present-day attempts to assert that Gog will be of a certain nationality are of little value.
3. Ezek. 39:6.
4. See "Nations Which Will Attack Palestine," *Prophecy—Key to the Future,* pp. 198-202.
5. Rev 11:2. Note that the time for the Battle of Armageddon is to be longer than that of the fourth World War, or universal conflict, which John prophesies will last for about thirteen months (Rev. 9:15).
6. Zech. 13:7-9.
7. Ezek. 39:1-6.
8. Zech. 14:2.
9. Rev. 11:1-2.
10. Rev. 11:3-12.

brimstone.[1] A great earthquake will level a tenth of the city of Jerusalem, and destroy the cities of other nations at the same time.[2]

Israel will fare poorly in the struggle, and will appear doomed to defeat, when Christ will suddenly appear on the Mount of Olives. The mountain will cleave in two, allowing an avenue of escape for the beleaguered Israelites.[3] They will rally as God lends his strength in the fray.[4]

Ezekiel prophesied the eventual fall of the invading army:

> Therefore, thou son of man, prophesy against Gog, and say, Thus saith the Lord God; Behold, I am against thee, O Gog, the chief prince of Meshech and Tubal:
>
> And I will turn thee back, and *leave but the sixth part of thee,* and will cause thee to come up from the north parts, and will bring thee upon the mountains of Israel:
>
> And I will smite thy bow out of thy left hand, and will cause thine arrows to fall out of thy right hand.
>
> *Thou shalt fall upon the mountains of Israel, thou, and all thy bands, and the people that is with thee: I will give thee unto the ravenous birds of every sort, and to the beasts of the field to be devoured.*
>
> Thou shalt fall upon the open field: for I have spoken it, saith the Lord God.[5]

Birds of prey will eat the flesh of the fallen armies,[6] and seven months will be required to bury the dead.[7] It will be a time of great mourning in Israel.[8]

The great Battle of Armageddon, tragic as it will be, will still serve to lead man to the knowledge and acceptance of God's great power. They will see the miraculous aid God will grant unto Israel, and know of his glorious appearance on the Mount of Olives. As the Savior said, after revealing the great judgments that will come upon the invaders,

> Thus will I magnify myself, and sanctify myself; and I will be known in the eyes of many nations, and they shall know that I am the Lord.[9]

---

1. Ezek. 38:22; Rev. 16:21; Zech. 14:12, 15.
2. Rev. 11:13; 16:19.
3. Zech. 14:4-5, D&C 45:47-50.
4. Zech. 12:8.
5. Ezek. 39:1-5.
6. Ezek. 39:17-20;Rev. 19:17-18.
7. Ezek. 39:9-16.
8. Zech. 12:10-14.
9. Ezek 38:23. This concept, that God will "magnify himself" or "make bare his arm" in the eyes of all nations, is frequently expressed in connection with the Battle of Armageddon and at times becomes a "code word" for that event in scriptural allusions.

And also:

> And I will set my glory among the heathen, and *all the heathen shall See my judgment that I have executed,* and my hand that I have laid upon them.
>
> So the house of Israel shall know that I am the Lord their God from that day and forward.
>
> *And the heathen shall know* that the house of Israel went into captivity for their iniquity; because they trespassed against me, therefore hid I my face from them, and gave them into the hand of their enemies: so fell they all by the sword.
>
> According to their uncleanness and according to their transgressions have I done unto them, and hid my face from them.
>
> Therefore thus saith the Lord God; Now will I bring again the captivity of Jacob, and have mercy upon the whole house of Israel, and will be jealous of my holy name;
>
> After that they have borne their shame, and all their trespasses whereby they have trespassed against me, when they dwelt safely in their land, and none made them afraid.
>
> *When I have brought them again from the people, and gathered them out of their enemies' lands, and am sanctified in them in the sight of many nations;*
>
> *Then shall they know that I am the Lord their God,* which caused them to be led into captivity among the heathen: but I have gathered them unto their own land, and have left none of them any more there.
>
> *Neither will I hide my face any more from them:* for I have poured out my spirit upon the house of Israel, saith the Lord God.

Summary

1. God has sworn to send wars upon the earth in the last days "until the consumption decreed hath made a full end of all nations." These conflicts will serve as judgments upon those who do evil and who harden their hearts. "The wicked shall slay the wicked, and fear shall come upon every man."

2. The scriptures and the prophets have warned of five future major conflicts, or periods of warfare:

- A. A Third World War.
- B. Internal conflict in the Americas.
- C. A Fourth World War during the New Jerusalem period.
- D. World-wide conflict related to the fall of the great and abominable church.
- E. The Battle of Armageddon.

---

1. Ezek. 39:21-29

3. There are to be two types of warfare in the last days:

A. Preparatory Wars, which prepare the way for the preaching of the gospel, and
B. Wars of Complete Destruction, which punish the wicked and result in great desolation.

4. A Third World War, between Russia and her allies and America and her allies has been repeatedly prophesied. Prophesied characteristics of this future war are to include the following:

A. An initial attack by Russia.
B. Each of the major powers will bomb the other's homeland.
C. Much of the war will be fought in the air and in the sea.
D. The war will be a great and bloody war.
E. The United States will appear to be losing the war in its initial stages.
F. Many spies and traitors will be apprehended in the United States.
G. A major portion of the U.S. Army will give up.
H. God will intervene and enter the conflict, helping America to achieve the victory.
I. A major force will suddenly rise in America's west to counteract enemy invasion.
J. Russia will go down to defeat, never to rise in such power again.
K. Missionaries will go into Russia, preaching the gospel to the house of Israel there.

5. The probability of nuclear warfare during this conflict, as the major powers bomb their enemy's homelands, is great. Some of the prophetic warnings describe scenes and events which appear to be atomic warfare with the resulting effects of radiation.

6. Russia is presently on a war footing and has developed a major military force. The balance of military power is rapidly shifting in Russia's favor, and she has established momentum which military experts assert will give her definite superiority within a few years.

7. Of particular concern is Russia's extensive civil defense preparations, as compared to very limited civil defense capability in the United States. According to recent studies, a Russian nuclear attack on

America might be reasonably expected to produce 72,000,000 casualties, while losses in an American attack on Russia could be limited to as few as 4,000,000. The strategic assumption that Russia would not risk a nuclear attack on the U.S. because of losses she would suffer in retaliatory strikes is being abandoned.

8. Some prophetic warnings establish the relationship between World War III and later internal conflict in the United States, indicating that national revolutions will result as the international war breaks down, and that the strife and destruction of the world war will establish conditions of shortages, famine, economic instability, and antagonism which will lead to the internal conflict.

9. Chronological relationships in the prophetic warnings indicate that internal conflict in the United States (and hence World War III which will precede the internal conflict) will occur prior to the return to the New Jerusalem.

10. The Savior prophesied that the remnant of Jacob [the Lamanites] will reclaim much of the Americas as the land of their inheritance as they rise up to destroy transportation, military strongholds, and cities.

11. The internal conflict in the United States has been depicted as local strife and anarchy, with mob rule and pillaging bands making it impossible for the nation to continue the pursuit of manufacturing, farming, and commerce effectively. Even family members will slay one another. The spectre of widespread famine is clearly raised in the prophetic warnings, and may explain the reason for much of the strife.

12. Early Church leaders repeatedly prophesied the complete destruction of U.S. Government and the end of this nation as it presently exists. As the internal conflict brings government control to an end, it is prophesied that the saints will be able to maintain a higher level of stability. They will form a government, a political "Kingdom of God," which will maintain liberty and constitutional principles, and will increase in influence as people rally to its standard. There will be a transfer of rule to the saints, in preparation for Christ's millennial rule.

13. During the period of third World War and/or internal conflicts, areas will be swept clean of their populations, leaving them desolate.

Independence, Missouri is prophesied to be one such area. The saints will return and there build a great city, the New Jerusalem. Desolate areas nearby will also be inhabited.

14. The saints will be organized in military fashion during the return to Jackson County. Their army will become very great, and will be regarded with fear and terror by the other nations.

15. The New Jerusalem will serve as a place of refuge to which people from throughout the world will flee to escape the destruction of a fourth World War. God's power will be upon the city protecting it, but it will be the only place that is not at war as a fourth World War rages.

16. John the Revelator prophesied of a war which would last for thirteen months and which would slay the third part of men. His prophecy indicates some type of geographical link with the River Euphrates.

17. The saints will be persecuted by the great and abominable church, even prior to the return to Jackson County. The wrath of God will finally be turned against that wicked organization during the fourth World War. Nations assembled to fight against the saints will turn on each other and wage war, causing the great church to collapse. Ten kings who had previously warred against the saints will destroy the capitol city of the great and abominable church.

18. The Battle of Armageddon is a conflict which will take place in the land of Israel following the fourth World War, the return of the Jews and Ten Tribes to their homeland, and the construction of the Jerusalem temple. It will take place during the rule of David the Prince. The battle draws its prophetic name from Megiddo, a fortress in the plain of Esdraelon. This war is the most prophesied event in all scripture.

19. The enemy army, Magog, will be led by a general named Gog. His army will advance on Jerusalem and capture most of the city. A sudden appearance by the Savior on the Mount of Olives will aid the Israelites, enabling them to rally and win the war. Two-thirds of Israel will be slain while Gog and five-sixths of his army will fall on the mountains of Israel.

20. The Battle of Armageddon will show the heathen nations that the Lord is God. They will be receptive to missionary work after learning of the Lord's divine intervention during the conflict.

XII

Pestilence and the Lord's Desolating Scourge

The two preceding chapters, with this one, examine the three major instruments of God's judgments upon the wicked: famine, sword, and pestilence. Less is said of the third of these instruments than of the other two, but the prophesied impact of the ravages of pestilence upon the wicked nations of the world obviously will be tremendous.

The Lord has said unto the nations of the earth,

> *How oft have I called upon you* by the mouth of my servants, and by the ministering of angels, and by mine own voice, and by the voice of thunderings, and by the voice of lightnings, and by the voice of tempests, and by the voice of earthquakes, and great hailstorms, *and by the voice of famines and pestilences of every kind,* and by the great sound of a trump, and by the voice of judgment, and by the voice of mercy all the day long, and by the voice of glory and honor and the riches of eternal life, and would have saved you with an everlasting salvation, but ye would not?
>
> *Behold, the day has come, when the cup of the wrath of mine indignation is full.*[1]

Sickness and pestilence, then, are tools with which God chastens his people and chastises the wicked of the earth.

Warnings of Pestilence in the Last Days

The Lord has revealed that pestilence is to be expected in the last days:

> Behold, I speak for mine elect's sake; for nation shall rise against nation, and kingdom against kingdom; *there shall be famines, and pestilences, and earthquakes, in divers places.*
>
> And again, *because iniquity shall abound, the love of many shall wax cold;* but he that shall not be overcome, the same shall be saved.[2]

---

1. D&C 43:25-26.
2. JS 1:29-30.

Repeated warnings of future disease and pestilence have been given in numerous private manifestations and through patriarchs of the Church. Such warnings are intended as private counsel and not as official Church doctrine. Yet here again, as with prophetic warnings of a third World War and of internal conflict within the United States, the saints should certainly be aware that this widespread pattern of personal revelation exists. The following brief excerpts from patriarchal blessings are typical of the pattern:

> You will live upon the earth to see scourge after scourge of sickness poured out upon the world, and *the saints will hardly escape, for many will fall by the plague*—even on your right hand and on your left.

Also:

> You will see the scourge of sickness poured out from time to time and you will *see the wicked swept from under Heaven in the twinkling of an eye, time and time again,*

And again:

> . . . you will live as long as life is desirable, and the scourges of the day in which you live will pass by you, as the scourge did in the days of the Israelites in Egypt, and not slay you. *You will see famines stalk abroad on the land. You will see the pestilence of earthquakes and upheavals in the earth*

Another warns,

> You will live to see the nations of the earth scourged for their sins. You will *live to see epidemics go forth that will baffle the skill of doctors and will sweep the inhabitants of the earth into the spirit world by thousands.* . . . You will have the blessings of the earth through your long life and hunger will never be forced upon you by *the scourge or the scourges of hunger that will afflict man.*

Yet another tells of the Ten Tribes coming from the north to Zion, and says, "You will see the *earth cleansed by a scourge of sickness before their coming* to make room for a dwelling place for them."

These brief excerpts should suffice as an indication that a broad pattern of personal warnings exists. God is moving at many levels and in many ways to prepare his people for the days of trouble and distress which are coming.

The Lord's Desolating Scourge

A scriptural pattern of prophecy exists which warns of a specific disease identified in modern revelation as "the Lord's desolating scourge." One revelation, given even before the restoration of the Church, warns of the judgment that will go forth upon the earth if men harden their hearts against the gospel:

> . . . *A desolating scourge shall go forth* among the inhabitants of the earth, and *shall continue to be poured out from time to time,* if they repent not, *until the earth is empty, and the inhabitants thereof are consumed away* and utterly destroyed by the brightness of my coming.[1]

An 1831 revelation spoke of sickness that will come after the time of the Gentiles have been fulfilled:

> . . . There shall be men standing in that generation, that shall not pass until *they shall see an overflowing scourge, for a desolating sickness shall cover the land.*
>
> But my disciples shall stand in holy places, and shall not be moved; but *among the wicked, men shall lift up their voices and curse God and die.*[2]

A year later, in September, 1832, the Lord revealed that

> . . . I, the Almighty, have laid my hands upon the nations, *to scourge them* for their wickedness.
>
> *And plagues shall go forth, and they shall not be taken from the earth until I have completed my work,* which shall be cut short in righteousness—[3]

Of particular concern to Church members is the realization that several revelations warn of the possibility of this terrible scourge being visited upon the saints because of disobedience. A warning to the Church in 1832 was sobering:

> . . . Your minds in times past have been darkened because of unbelief, and because you have treated lightly the things you have received-
>
> *Which vanity and unbelief have brought the whole church under condemnation.*
>
> *And this condemnation resteth upon the children of Zion, even all.*

1. D&C 5:19. Concerning this warning, the Lord promised that "my word shall be verified at this time as it hath hitherto been verified." (D&C 5:20)
2. D&C 45:31-32.
3. D&C 84:96-97.

> *And they shall remain under this condemnation until they repent and remember the new covenant, even the Book of Mormon and the former commandments which I have given them, not only to say, but to do according to that which I have written—*
>
> That they may bring forth fruit meet for their Father's kingdom; *otherwise there remaineth a scourge and judgment to be poured out upon the children of Zion.*
>
> For shall the children of the kingdom pollute my holy land? Verily, I say unto you, Nay.[1]

A year later, the Lord warned the saints that his scourge would come upon the world, and cautioned the saints that if they were not obedient, they would be afflicted with pestilence and plague:

> For behold, and lo, vengeance cometh speedily upon the ungodly as the whirlwind; and who shall escape it?
>
> *The Lord's scourge shall pass over by night and by day, and the report thereof shall vex all people; yea, it shall not be stayed until the Lord come;*
>
> For the indignation of the Lord is kindled against their abominations and all their wicked works.
>
> Nevertheless, Zion shall escape *if* she observe to do all things whatsoever I have commanded her.
>
> But *if* she observe not to do whatsoever I have commanded her, *I will visit her according to all her works, with sore affliction, with pestilence, with plague, with sword, with vengeance, with devouring fire.*[2]

A remark made by President Heber C. Kimball is significant in this context:

> If the Saints will repent, the Lord's wrath will be turned away, but *they will not repent until it is too late.*[3]

Biblical passages also speak of this terrible desolating scourge. Reference has previously been made to Isaiah's prophecy,[4] in which he speaks of men who will think to escape the scourge by making a "covenant" with death and hell. But he warns,

> And your covenant with death shall be disannulled, and your agreement with hell shall not stand; *when the overflowing scourge shall pass through, then ye shall be trodden down by it.*

---

1. D&C 84:54-59. See also D&C 112:24-26, 1 Pet. 4:17. Note that the last two verses allude to Zion, possibly associating the time of the scourge to the return to that land.
2. D&C 97:22-26.
3. Orson F. Whitney, Life of Heber C. Kimball (Salt Lake City, Utah: Bookcraft, 1967), p. 446.
4. See pp. 147-150.

> From the time that it goeth forth it shall take you: for morning by morning shall it pass over, by day and by night: and *it shall be a vexation only to understand the report*.[1]

Isaiah concludes his reference to the scourge with the observation that "I have heard from the Lord God of hosts *a consumption, even determined upon the whole earth*."[2]

Another chapter of Isaiah pronounces a "woe" to "the land shadowing with wings," a reference Church commentators have ascribed to America because of important illusions in the context.[3] In his prophecy, the population is compared to a grapevine. Isaiah pronounces this warning of destruction to come upon the land in the era people are to be gathered[4] to Mount Zion:

> For afore the harvest, when the bud is perfect, and the sour grape is ripening in the flower, *he shall both cut off the sprigs with pruning hooks, and take away and cut down the branches.*
>
> *They shall be left together unto the fowls of the mountains, and to the beasts of the earth: and the fowls shall summer upon them, and all the beasts of the earth shall winter upon them.*[5]

Elder Orson Pratt, while expounding Isaiah's prophecy, said that God will visit the American continents

> . . . with judgments that are terribly severe that will cause them to *lie by hundreds and thousands unberied [sic], from one end of the land to the other,* to be meat for the fowls of the air and the beasts of the earth. Why? Because *the judgments will be swift, giving no time for burial.*
>
> Inquires one—"Do you really believe that such judgments are coming upon our nation?" I do not merely believe. but I know it.[6]

The devastating effects of the terrible disease(s) which will be poured out will not be felt just in America. It should be recalled that

1. Is. 28:18-19. Note the strong parallel in the wording between this passage and D&C 97:23.
2. Is. 28:22.
3. See JD 17:318-319, JD 2:295. Note characteristics of the land in the prophecy: it sends out messengers [missionaries] to "a nation scattered and peeled" [scattered Israel], it lifts an ensign on the mountains, and it has a Mount Zion. Yet it is not Palestine, but "beyond the rivers of Ethiopia." What other nation but America could this be? No other possibility even presents itself.
4. See Is. 18:7. This verse, then, helps to fix the time of the prophetic fulfillment.
5. Is. 18:5-6.
6. JD 17:319. February 28, 1875.

Wilford Woodruff, when he saw the scene in vision, "Was given to understand that *the same horrors that were here enacted were all over the world, east, west, north, and south.—That few were left alive,—still there were some.*[1]

John the Revelator prophesied a series of plagues which are to come upon the earth in the beginning of the seventh thousand years of the earth's existence.[2] They will constitute the first of three "woes" which he pronounced:

> The first angel sounded, and there followed hail and fire mingled with blood, and they were cast upon the earth: and the *third part of trees was burnt up, and all green grass was burnt up.*
>
> And the second angel sounded, and as it were a great mountain burning with fire was cast into the *sea: and the third part of the sea became blood;*
>
> *And the third part of the creatures which were in the sea, and had life, died*; and the third part of the ships were destroyed.
>
> And the third angel sounded, and there fell a great star from heaven, burning as it were a lamp, and *it fell upon the third part of the rivers, and upon the fountains of waters;*
>
> And the name of the star is called Wormwood: and the third part of the waters became wormwood; and many men died of the waters, *because they were made bitter.*
>
> And the fourth angel sounded, and the third part of the sun was smitten, and the third part of the moon, and the third part of the stars; so as *the third part of them was darkened,* and the day shone not for a third part of it, and the night likewise.
>
> And I beheld, and heard an angel flying through the midst of heaven, saying with a loud voice, Woe, woe, woe, to the inhabiters of the earth by reason of the other voices of the trumpet of the three angels, which are yet to sound!
>
> And the fifth angel sounded, and I saw a star fall from heaven unto the earth: and to him was given the key of the bottomless pit.
>
> And he opened the bottomless pit; and there arose a smoke out of the pit, as the smoke of a great furnace; and the *sun and the air were darkened by reason of the smoke of the pit.*
>
> *And there came out of the smoke locusts upon the earth: and unto them was given power,* as the scorpions of the earth have power.
>
> And it was commanded them that they should not hurt the grass of the earth, neither any green thing, neither any tree; but *only those men which have not the seal of God in their foreheads.*
>
> And to them it was given that they should not kill them, but that *they should be tormented five months: and their torment was as the torment of a scorpion, when he striketh a man.*

---

1. Revelation to Wilford Woodruff December 16, 1878. See pp. 194-196.
2. See D&C 77:12-13. These plagues are to follow the sealing of the 144.000 (see Rev. 7:2-8) and hence. the return of the Ten Tribes.

> *And in those days shall men seek death, and shall not find it; and shall desire to die, and death shall flee from them.*
>
> And the shapes of the locusts were like unto horses prepared unto battle; and on their heads were as it were crowns like gold, and their faces were as the faces of men.
>
> And they had hair as the hair of women, and their teeth were as the teeth of lions.
>
> And they had breastplates, as it were breastplates of iron; and the sound of their wings was as the sound of chariots of many horses running to battle.
>
> And they had tails like unto scorpions, and there were stings in their tails: and *their power was to hurt men five months.*
>
> And they had a king over them, which is the angel of the bottomless pit, whose name in the Hebrew tongue is Abaddon, but in the Greek tongue hath his name Apollyon.
>
> One woe is past; and, behold, there come two woes more hereafter.

Descriptions of the Scourge

Various new diseases may be poured out upon the earth in the last days. For instance, the possibility of radiation sickness from nuclear war is also very real.[2] There remain, however, several descriptions in the scriptures and other manifestations which allude to a horrible disease which cannot at present be identified. One such description is in the Doctrine and Covenants, Section 29, which is linked with the fall of the great and abominable church:

> But, behold, I say unto you that before this great day shall come the sun shall be darkened, and the moon shall be turned into blood, and the stars shall fall from heaven, and there shall be greater signs in heaven above and in the earth beneath;
>
> *And there shall be weeping and wailing among the hosts of men;*
>
> And there shall be a great hailstorm sent forth to destroy the crops of the earth.
>
> And it shall come to pass, because of the wickedness of the world, that I will take vengeance upon the wicked, for they will not repent; for the cup of mine indignation is full; for behold, my blood shall not cleanse them if they hear me not.
>
> *Wherefore, I the Lord God will send forth flies upon the face of the earth, which shall take hold of the inhabitants thereof, and shall eat their flesh, and shall cause maggots to come in upon them;*
>
> *And their tongues shall be stayed that they shall not utter against me; and their flesh shall fall from off their bones, and their eyes from their sockets;*

---

1. Rev. 8:7-9:12.
2. See pp . 191-193.

And it shall come to pass that the beasts of the forest and the fowls of the air shall devour them up.

And the great and abominable church, which is the whore of all the earth, shall be cast down by devouring fire, according as it is spoken by the mouth of Ezekiel the prophet, who spoke of these things, which have not come to pass but surely must, as I live, for abominations shall not reign.[1]

A similar description, of flesh falling from the bones and eyes falling from their sockets, is found in Zechariah's prophecy of the judgment that will come upon nations which fight against Jerusalem during the Battle of Armageddon:

. . . This shall be the plague wherewith the Lord will smite all the people that have fought against Jerusalem; *Their flesh shall consume away while they stand upon their feet, and their eyes shall consume away in their holes,* and their tongue shall consume away in their mouth. . . .

And so shall be the plague of the horse, of the mule, of the camel, and of the ass, and *of all the beasts* that shall be in these tents, as this plague.

The prophet Isaiah also describes the period of the Battle of Armageddon, as does Zechariah. He warns that "by fire and by his sword will the Lord plead with all flesh: and the slain of the Lord shall be many."[3] Then, like Zechariah's 14th chapter, he tells how people will go up to Jerusalem following that battle. In doing so, he apparently alludes to the aftermath of the plague, saying:

. . . They shall go forth, and look upon the carcases of the men that have transgressed against me: *for their worm shall not die, neither shall their fire be quenched;* and they shall be an abhorring unto all flesh.[4]

In the manifestation shown to Charles D. Evans, he was shown a disease with similar symptoms. He saw that

This plague in grown persons *robbed the eyes in their sockets and consumed the tongue as would a powerful acid or an intense heat.* Wicked men suffering under its writhing agonies cursed God and died, or they stood on their feet and birds of prey feasted on their carcasses.[5]

Past Manifestations of the Disease

It appears that the same terrible disease, or one similar to it, has been manifested in past situations in which it was regarded as the

1. D&C 29:14-21.
2. Zech. 14:12, 15.
3. Is. 66:16.
4. Is. 66:24.
5. Charles D. Evans, *op. cit.* See p. 292

result of God's judgments upon the wicked. Specifically, various cases of the affliction have been reported through the years in connection with the mobocrats who assassinated Joseph Smith. One such account was left by Martha James Cragun, who encountered one of the mobocrats. Jack Reed. in August 1881:

> About the last of September I heard that Jack Reed was very sick of a strange ailment. He was taken ill in a few days after having made the statement that he took part in the affair at Carthage—but no one had told me of his sickness until I heard it from one of my Indian friends who said he had worms in his flesh. I determined to see him if I could and try to get him to verify the statement he had made at the meeting. The man had no family and Mr. McGuire was his attendant. I asked Mr. McGuire if he would allow Mrs. Whitmore and myself to visit Mr. Reed. *He said that Mr. Reed was a sight that no white woman could be allowed to look upon. He was literally eaten alive by worms. His eye balls had fallen out, the flesh on his cheeks and neck had fallen off and though he could breathe he could take nourishment only through an opening in his throat, and said McGuire, "Pieces of flesh as large as my two hands have fallen off from different parts of his body. . . ."* One called "Jack Longstreet" became Reed's first attendant in company with McGuire. To these men Reed confessed that his participation in the murder of the Prophets was the cause of his affliction. *He said to Longstreet: "It is the Mormon curse that is upon me. I cannot live—I must utterly rot before I die." He said that Brigham Young had pronounced that curse upon all that mob, and he had known thirteen of them to die just as he was dying*.1

Parley P. Pratt, an early apostle, also recorded a similar fate for some of the mobocrats. He wrote of several examples:

> A colonel of the Missouri mob, who helped to drive, plunder and murder the Mormons, died in the hospital at Sacramento, 1849. Beckwith had the care of him; *he was eaten with worms—a large black headed kind of maggot—which passed through him by myriads, seemingly a half pint at a time! Before he died these maggots were crawling out of his mouth and nose! He literally rotted alive! Even the flesh on his legs burst open and fell from the bones!* They gathered up the rotten mass in a blanket and buried him, without awaiting a coffin!
>
> A Mr.____, one of Missouri mob, died in the same hospital about the same time, and under the care of Mr. Beckwith. *His face and jaw on one side literally rotted, and half of his face actually fell off! One eye rotted out, and half of his nose, mouth and jaw fell from the bones!* The doctor scraped the bones, and unlocked and took out his jaw from the joint round

1. N.B. Lundwall, comp., "Thirteen Mobocrats Meet a Common Fate," The Fate of the Persecutors of the Prophet Joseph Smith (Salt Lake City, Utah: Bookcraft, 1952), pp. 295-296. See also pp. 298, 304, 334-335, 337, which cite other examples.

> to the centre of the chin. *The rot and maggots continued to eat till they ate through the large or jugular vein of his neck, and he bled to death!* He, as well as Townsend, stank so previous to their death that they had to be placed in rooms by themselves, and it was almost impossible to endure their presence, and the flies could not be kept from blowing them while alive![1]

Even in ancient times, a similar fate was recorded as coming upon the wicked. The historian Josephus recorded the fatal sickness of the evil King Herod (son of Antipater), as follows:

> But now Herod's distemper greatly increased upon him after a severe manner, and *this by God's judgment upon him for his sins;* for a fire glowed in him slowly, which did not so much appear to the touch outwardly, as it augmented his pains inwardly; for it brought upon him a vehement appetite to eating, which he could not avoid to supply with one sort of food or other. *His entrails were also exulcerated, and the chief violence of his pain lay on his colon; an aqueous and transparent liquor also had settled itself about his feet, and a like matter afflicted him at the bottom of his belly. Nay, further, his privy-member was putrified, and produced worms;* and when he sat upright, he had a difficulty of breathing, which was very loathsome, on account of the stench of his breath, and the quickness of its returns; he had also convulsions in all parts of his body, which increased his strength to an insufferable degree.[2]

With the limited descriptions available, it is impossible to determine if these examples from the past are the same as those prophesied for the future judgments. Yet one broad principle is evident: disease and pestilence are used as instruments of God's retribution upon the wicked. The record of the past shows that they have been

1. Autobiography of Parley P. Pratt (Salt Lake City, Utah: Deseret Book Company, sixth edition, 1966), p. 425.
2. The Life and Works of Flavius Josephus (New York: Holt, Rinehart and Winston, n.d.), "Antiquities of the Jews," Book XVII, paragraph 5, p. 514. In his "Wars of the Jews," Bk. I, paragraph 5, p. 664, he gave a similar description:

   After this, the distemper seized upon his whole body, and greatly disordered all its parts With various symptoms; for there was a gentle fever upon him, and an intolerable itching over all the surface of his body, and continual pains in his colon, and dropsical tumours about his feet, and an inflammation of the abdomen, and a putrefaction of his privy member. that produced worms. Besides which he had a difficulty of breathing upon him, and could not breathe but when he sat upright, and had a convulsion of all his members, insomuch that the diviners said those diseases were a punishment upon him for what he had done to the Rabbins.

used on a limited basis, but prophecies of the future warn that their effect will be widespread as increased wickedness prevails.

Summary

1. The Lord has called the people of the earth by many methods, including preaching, angels, earthquakes, famines, and pestilence, offering the people everlasting salvation, but they would not receive it. The day has now come when the cup of his wrath and indignation is full.

2. The Lord has warned that there shall be wars, famines, pestilences, and earthquakes in the last days. Because iniquity shall abound, the love of many shall grow cold.

3. Many private manifestations and patriarchal blessings warn of future plagues and pestilences which will occur, taking a heavy toll of casualties. Some of these manifestations link the sicknesses to famines.

4. The Lord has warned repeatedly of a terrible last days disease called the "Lord's desolating scourge." It will cover the land, and will continue to be poured out from time to time until the Lord comes in glory.

5. The Lord has warned his Church that if the members do not repent and obey his commandments, he will scourge them with pestilence, plague, the sword, and with devouring fire.

6. In his vision of the terrible plague which would come upon America, Wilford Woodruff saw that "few were left alive," and that the horrors he saw were to happen all over the world.

7. Isaiah prophesied that destruction will come to America in the era people are to be gathered to Mount Zion. John the Revelator also prophesied a series of plagues which are to come upon the earth in the beginning of the seventh thousand years of the earth's existence.

8. John prophesied that

A. A third part of the trees and grass will be burned.
B. One-third of the animals of the sea will be destroyed.

C. One-third of the fresh waters will become bitter, and many men will die from them.
D. Locusts [or other entities depicted as locusts] will torment those who are not God's servants for five months.
E. The affliction in those days will be so severe that men will seek death and desire to die.

9. Scriptural descriptions of a terrible last days' disease depict a sickness in which the flesh will fall from men's bones and eyeballs fall from their sockets, while maggots infest them. The disease described is linked chronologically with the third world war, with the fall of the great and abominable church and also with the Battle of Armageddon. Thus it appears to be a constantly-recurring plague.

10. Descriptions of deaths of some of the men who participated in the assassination of Joseph Smith seem to fit the pattern of the prophesied disease, as does Josephus' account of the death of wicked King Herod. It is possible there is a specific disease which God visits upon the wicked. It may be the same plague that will be manifested in the last days.

III

Personal Preparation For the Last Days

XIII

Choosing a Course for the Future

America stands at the crossroads! Though the last fifteen years was a period of serious moral decay for the nation, it is still possible to cause changes that will bring blessings, rather than cursing, upon the land. But now is the time for action, for if the national rush towards sin and corruption continues at the previous pace, wickedness will soon abound to the degree that the judgments of the last days will be poured out without measure upon us all.

Questions such as these are frequently asked:

"What should my attitude be towards the future?"

"What can *I* do to help America escape the terrible judgments which have been prophesied?"

"What should *I* do to protect myself and my family from the suffering which will accompany the judgments?"

"How can *I* prepare for the cataclysmic events which lie ahead?"

This final chapter is written to suggest specific actions that citizens of America and faithful Latter-day Saints can undertake to prepare for the future. It should be observed that every principle suggested is based on counsel and insight God has revealed in the scriptures. He has foreseen, forewarned, and revealed the course his saints should follow in the last days. The principles suggested will be presented in a numbered list, designed to serve as a tangible summary which can be taken and literally applied.

Adopt Attitudes Based on Gospel Principles

The gospel of Jesus Christ provides instruction and insight, telling man how he should conduct himself during the perilous era of the last days. If he will adopt the eternal perspectives revealed in the gospel plan, he will "build his house upon a rock," rather than upon sand,[1] and have stability and meaning to life as the judgments are poured out.

1. See Mt. 7:24-27.

This section will suggest attitudes and understandings which should prove beneficial.

1. Gain eternal perspective: God directs the affairs of man. There is comfort in the knowledge that God, who created the earth and made man after his own image,[1] sees and knows all things.[2] "All things are before him,"[3] and he "governeth and executeth all things."[4] Though he allows man to exercise his free agency,[5] he maintains ultimate control over the actions and fate of both individuals and nations.[6] He has promised to guide and shape the course of those who live righteously, and has instructed the saints to "let your hearts be comforted; *for all things shall work together for good to them that walk uprightly.*"[7]

2. Gain eternal perspective: God desires to bless and reward man. God seeks the eternal progress and well-being of his people. He has revealed that "this is my work and my glory—to bring to pass the immortality and eternal life of man."[8] The Savior has told the saints they are "*ye whom I delight to bless with the greatest of all blessings, ye that hear me;*"[9] and he has said:

> I, the Lord, am merciful and gracious unto those who fear me, and *delight to honor those who serve me* in righteousness and in truth unto the end.
>
> *Great shall be their reward and eternal shall be their glory.*[10]

He has said to his people that the fulness of the earth is theirs to use and enjoy, and that "it pleaseth God that he hath given all these things unto man."[11] He would extend his richest blessings to all mankind if they would only accept his overtures:

---

1. D&C 20:17-18.
2. D&C 38:1-3.
3. D&C 88:41.
4. D&C 88:40.
5. D&C 58:28; 104:17.
6. For extensive listings of examples concerning this principle, see the author's book *Prophets and Prophecies of the Old Testament,* p. 91.
7. D&C 100:15. As Paul taught, "All things work together for good to them that love God." (Ro. 8:28) See also D&C 90:24; 105:40; 111:11.
8. Moses 1:39.
9. D&C 41:1. But the same verse contains a strong warning to the saints: saying that "Ye that hear me not will I curse, that have professed my name, with the heaviest of all cursings."
10. D&C 76:5-6. Verses 7-10 promise choice blessings to these individuals.
11. D&C 59:16-21.

> O, ye nations of the earth, how often would I have gathered you together as a hen gathereth her chickens under her wings, but ye would not!
>
> How oft have I called upon you . . . by the voice of mercy all the day long, and by the voice of glory and honor and the riches of eternal life, and *would have saved you with an everlasting salvation, but ye would not!*[1]

3. Gain eternal perspective: Last days' judgments are part of man's mortal probation. The prophet Alma explained the probationary nature of mortal life, saying that

> . . . There was a space granted unto man in which he might repent; therefore *this life became a probationary state; a time to prepare to meet God;* a time to prepare for that endless state which has been spoken of by us, which is after the resurrection of the dead.[2]

God has revealed to the saints that they must be tested and refined through that testing process:

> . . . I have decreed in my heart, saith the Lord, that *I will prove you in all things, whether you will abide in my covenant, even unto death, that you may be found worthy.*
>
> For if ye will not abide in my covenant ye are not worthy of me.[3]

Indeed, remaining faithful in tribulation appears to be a necessary requirement for gaining the highest of eternal rewards. A revelation from the Lord teaches that

> . . . Blessed is he that keepeth my commandments, whether in life or in death; and *he that is faithful in tribulation. the reward of the same is greater in the kingdom of heaven.*
>
> Ye cannot behold with your natural eyes, for the present time, the design of your God concerning those things which shall come hereafter, and *the glory which shall follow after much tribulation.*
>
> *For after much tribulation come the blessings.* Wherefore the day cometh that ye shall be crowned with much glory; the hour is not yet, but is nigh at hand.[4]

4. Gain eternal perspective: God chastens those he loves. Our Heavenly Father loves his children who are here on earth. His son.

1. D&C 43:24-25. See Mt. 23:37.
2. Al. 12:24. See also 2 Ne. 2:21; 9:27; 33:9; Al. 42:4; Hel. 13:38; D&C 29:42-44.
3. D&C 98:14-15.
4. D&C 58:2-4. See also D&C 103:11-14.

Jesus Christ, also loves his people—those who are "children of Christ" through the gospel covenant.[1] Like any loving parent, they seek to teach and encourage man, sometimes correcting his conduct and directing him towards the proper course of behavior.

This correcting process will be a part of the judgments of the last days and will ultimately prove to be a blessing for the saints who heed the warning message. The Master has revealed,

> Verily, thus saith the Lord unto you whom I love, and *whom I love I also chasten that their sins may be forgiven,* for with the chastisement *I prepare a way for their deliverance* in all things out of temptation. . . .[2]

He has said that

> *My people must be tried in all things,* that they may be prepared to receive the glory that I have for them, even the glory of Zion; and *he that will not bear chastisement is not worthy of my kingdom.*[3]

The chastening process has previously been experienced in the Church in connection with the failure to properly establish the New Jerusalem. Yet "Zion shall be redeemed, although she is chastened for a little season."[4] The early problem concerning Jackson County, in which the saints were driven out by their enemies, provided the basis for a revelation in which the Lord explained the relationship between chastening and the sanctification process:

> Verily I say unto you, concerning your brethren who have been afflicted, and persecuted, and cast out from the land of their inheritance—
>
> *I, the Lord, have suffered the affliction to come upon them, wherewith they have been afflicted, in consequence of their transgressions;*
>
> Yet I will own them, and they shall be mine in that day when I shall come to make up my jewels.
>
> Therefore, they must needs be chastened and tried, even as Abraham, who was commanded to offer up his only son.
>
> *For all those who will not endure chastening, but deny me, cannot be sanctified.*[5]

The saints must obtain confidence that the chastening which will come will ultimately bless them if they endure it in faith. As the Lord told Joseph Smith concerning the great tribulations he suffered:

---

1. See Mos. 5:5-7
2. D&C95:1.
3. D&C 136:31.
4. D&C 100:13. See D&C 103:4.
5. D&C 101:1-5.

> . . . Know thou, my son, that *all these things shall give thee experience, and shall be for thy good.*
>
> The Son of Man hath descended below them all. Art thou greater than he?

5. Gain eternal perspective: Death is sweet to those who die in the Lord. All men must die. Death is an essential element of the eternal plan of salvation, for it is also birth into the next phase of man's probationary existence, the spirit world. For the righteous, it constitutes entrance into Paradise, where man can progress more rapidly than in mortality, and where he will experience greater joy than here on earth. Yes, man should make it his goal to live his mortal life well and fulfill his life's mission with honor, but his more advanced goal is to leave this "frail existence" and to partake of the increased blessings available in the spirit world.

As the time approaches for the earth to end its temporal existence, God will increase the pace of entrance into the next phase of life, sweeping millions of mortals, both righteous[2] and wicked, into the spirit existence through the varied judgments of the last days. For the righteous, death will be a blessing and a much-desired release from sorrow and tribulation as these events occur. The wicked will also seek death, but will be without hope and will fear it.[3]

The saints can bless and prepare themselves by learning about death and life after death. Joseph Smith taught that "it is important that we should understand . . . our departure hence . . . and *it is a subject we ought to study more than any other.*"[4]

Concerning those who die, the Lord has revealed that

> . . . *If they die they shall die unto me, and if they live they shall live unto me.*
>
> Thou shalt live together in love, insomuch that thou shalt weep for the loss of them that die, and more especially for those that have not hope of a glorious resurrection.

1. D&C 122:7-8. See verses 1-7.
2. The belief that the righteous will be completely spared from the judgments of the last days is incorrect, and in direct contradiction to dozens of the scriptural passages previously cited in this book. God alluded to the death of many of the righteous when he revealed that "the day of my visitation cometh speedily, in an hour when ye think not of; and where shall be the safety of my people, and refuge for those who shall be left of them?" (D&C 124:10.)
3. Rev. 9:6. See also Morm. 2:13-15;6:7.
4. HC 6:50. October 9. 1843.

> And it shall come to pass that *those that die in me shall not taste of death, for it shall be sweet unto them;*
>
> *And they that die not in me, wo unto them, for their death is bitter.*[1]

God has promised that

> . . . All they who suffer persecution for my name, and endure in faith, though they are called to lay down their lives for my sake yet they shall partake of all this glory.
>
> Wherefore, *fear not even unto death;* for in this world your joy is not full, but in me your joy is full.
>
> Therefore, *care not for the body, neither the life of the body; but care for the soul, and for the life of the soul.*
>
> And seek the face of the Lord always, that in patience ye may possess your souls, and ye shall have eternal life.[2]

His instruction has been to

> *Let no man be afraid to lay down his life for my sake; for whoso layeth down his life for my sake shall find it again.*
>
> And whoso is not willing to lay down his life for my sake is not my disciple.[3]

6. Gain eternal perspective: There must be a transition to Christ's millennial kingdom. While the prospect of upheaval and chaos in America is extremely unpleasant to contemplate, yet the realization that it will serve as the transition to the Savior's personal rule on earth places it in the necessary perspective. Jesus has revealed,

> Wherefore, hear my voice and follow me, and *you shall be a free people, and ye shall have no laws but my laws when I come,* for I am you lawgiver. and what can stay my hand?[4]

His promise is that "I will be your ruler when I come; and behold, I come quickly, and ye shall see that my law is kept."[5] Concerning the saints, he has promised that "the Lord shall be in their midst, and his glory shall be upon them, and *he will be their king*

---

1. D&C 42:44-47
2. D&C 101:35-38. See Al. 24:7-27.
3. D&C 103:27-28. See also D&C 101:10-16; 63:2-4, 49-51; 84:80-84; Mt. 6:25-34; 10 38-39; 16:24-27; 3 Ne. 12:30.
4. D&C 38:22.
5. D&C 41:4.

and their lawgiver."[1] "The Lord, even the Savior, shall stand in the midst of his people, and shall reign over all flesh."[2]

The judgments which will come upon America will serve to cleanse her, eliminating much of the wicked and criminal element which would not abide by the Savior's rule. The ultimate result will be a change from the present telestial level to the blessings of the terrestrial level which the earth will enjoy during the millennium.[3]

7. Gain eternal perspective: The earth is approaching the end of its temporal existence. It is difficult to understand the events of the last days unless those events are viewed in the light of God's eternal plan. The Lord has revealed that the earth only is to exist under present mortal conditions for a very short period, for he has referred to "the seven thousand years of its continuance, or its temporal existence."[4] Sometime in the beginning of the final thousand years, Christ is to come in-glory and rule for a millennium in righteousness.[5] The earth will then undergo a dramatic change,[6] passing away[7] and then being recreated, or resurrected, as a celestial earth.[8] It will be removed from its present location and "placed in the cluster of the celestial kingdoms,"[9] and there complete its eternal mission, serving as an everlasting home for exalted, celestialized beings.[10]

---

1. D&C45:59.
2. D&C 133:25.
3. "The earth will be renewed and receive its paradisiacal glory." (Article of Faith 10)
4. D&C 77:6.
5. D&C 29:11 .
6. As Elder Orson Pratt explained

   Not only will the elements melt with fervent heat, but the great globe itself will pass away. It will cease to exist as an organized world. It will cease to exist as one of the worlds that are capable of being inhabited. Fire devours all things, converting the earth into its original elements; it passes away into space.

   But not one particle of the elements which compose the earth will be destroyed or annihilated. They will all exist and be brought together again by a greater organizing power than is known to man. The earth must be resurrected again, as well as our bodies; its elements will be re-united, and they will be brought together by the power of God's word. (JD 18:346-347. February 25, 1877.)
7. D&C 29:26; 88:25-26.
8. D&C 88:18-19.
9. Brigham Young, JD 17:117. June 28, 1874.
10. D&C 88:19-20.

Seen from this perspective, mortal existence upon the earth is a transitory experience—only a brief but important interlude in God's eternal plan. Problems of the world today, such as the "population explosion," the danger of exhausting world food and mineral supplies, and similar concerns, take on a different perspective when viewed with the realization that God's plan does not call for this earth to continue as a mortal habitation much longer than another thousand years. We can have confidence in the Lord's indication that "the earth is full, and *there is enough and to spare;* yea, I have prepared all things."[1]

8. Gain eternal perspective: Look forward to the blessings of the millennial era. As the sorrows of last days' tribulation approach, there is comfort in looking past them to the glorious blessings of the millennial era. The revelations teach that "*he that liveth when the Lord shall come, and hath kept the faith, blessed is he*."[2] It will be a time of peace and harmonious living, and God has revealed that "*they shall not hurt nor destroy* in all my holy mountain; for the earth shall be full of the knowledge of the Lord."[3] Satan will be bound,[4] and men "shall *not labour in vain,* nor bring forth for trouble."[5] After the Savior comes "that same *sociality* which exists among us here will exist among us there, only it will be coupled with eternal glory."[6] The Lord has promised that "you shall be a *free people,* and ye shall have no laws but my laws."[7] The great Jehovah has sworn that in that era "I will pour out my *spirit upon all flesh,*"[8] and "in that day when the Lord shall come, he shall *reveal all things*."[9] Indeed, it will be the "time to come in the which nothing shall be withheld."[10] During the millennial era "there shall be *no sorrow because there is no death,*"[11] and "for the space of a thousand years the *earth shall rest*."[12]

Look forward, past the strife and sorrow of the days of chastisement and cleansing. Focus on the joys of the millennial era, live to be worthy to partake of them, and kindle a hope that the glorious day will soon come.

---

1. D&C 104:17
2. D&C 63:50.
3. Is. 11:9; 65:25.
4. Rev. 20:1-3. See D&C 101:28.
5. Is. 65:23.
6. D&C 130:2.
7. D&C 38:22.
8. Joel 2:28.
9. D&C 101:32.
10. D&C 121:28.
11. D&C 101:29
12. Moses 7:64.

Spiritual Preparations for Survival

It must be remembered that the cataclysmic events of the last days are God's judgments upon the wicked. He will send them upon men, and the inhabitants of the earth shall "*be made to feel the wrath, and indignation, and chastening hand of an Almighty God*"[1] in "*the day when the wrath of God shall be poured out upon the wicked without measure*."[2]

Man's wickedness will bring the judgments. Individual righteousness is the only valid shield against them. National righteousness is the only deterrent that will prevent their being poured out upon the land.

Personal preparedness through righteous living, being obedient to God's commandments, and being attuned to receive guidance from the Holy Ghost hold the key to survival during the troubled times to come. In these areas the Lord has given much counsel in the scriptures.

9. Cleanse yourself from sins which will bring judgments: Repent. Counsel given by revelation has a vital message for God's people today. The Lord has commanded the saints to

> *Cleanse your hearts and your garments, lest the blood of this generation be required at your hands.*
>
> Be faithful until I come, for I come quickly; and my reward is with me to recompense every man according as his work shall be.

His commandment has been emphatic:

> . . . *I command you to repent—repent, lest I smite you* by the rod of my mouth, and by my wrath, and by my anger, *and your sufferings be sore*—how sore you know not, how exquisite you know not, yea, how hard to bear you know not.[4]

His warning is that the judgments will extend to every man who fails to cleanse his life:

> . . . Surely *every man must repent or suffer,* for I, God, am endless.
>
> Wherefore I revoke not the judgments which I shall pass, but woes shall go forth, weeping, wailing and gnashing of teeth, yea, to those who are found on my left hand.[5]

1. D&C 87:6.
2. D&C 1:9.
3. D&C 112:33-34
4. D&C 19:15.
5. D&C 19:4-5.

The commandment to repent is given especially to the saints, with the admonition, "Wherefore, *let the church repent of their sins,* and I, the Lord, will own them, otherwise they shall be cut off."[1] The unrepentant saints will lack the inspiration and strength of testimony needed to sustain them when the trials come, for the Lord has warned that "he that repents not, from him shall be taken even the light which he has received; for my Spirit shall not always strive with man. . . ."[2] But for those who will repent of all their sins, his promise is that "I will go before you and be your rearward; and I will be in your midst, and you shall not be confounded."[3]

Here, then, is the grand key to survival—those who will not repent will reap God's judgments, but those who will repent will receive God's guidance and protection in the perilous period ahead. But even the repentant must maintain themselves beyond sin, for the Lord has commanded,

> Abide ye in the liberty wherewith ye are made free; *entangle not yourselves in sin, but let your hands be clean, until the Lord comes*.[4]

10. Escape judgments through obedience: Keep God's commandments. Obedience to God's commandments will also provide the avenue for escape from the judgments to come. A revelation warns that

> . . . The indignation of the Lord is kindled against their abominations and all their wicked works.
>
> Nevertheless, *Zion shall escape if she observe to do all things whatsoever I have commanded her.*[5]

While warning of sin, pride, covetousness, and detestable things among the saints, the Lord stressed that repentance and obedience are the keys to escaping his judgments:

> Verily I say unto you, that *I, the Lord, will chasten them and will do whatsoever I list, if they do not repent and observe all things whatsoever I have said unto them.*
>
> And again I say unto you, *if ye observe to do whatsoever I command you, I, the Lord, will turn away all wrath and indignation* from you, and the gates of hell shall not prevail against you.[6]

1. D&C 63:63. See D&C 84:55-59.
2. D&C 1:33.
3. D&C 49:26-27
4. D&C 88:86.
5. D&C 97:24-25.
6. D&C 98:21-22.

Obedience to every commandment God reveals will be the test which the saints must meet, as the Lord proves them with the trials of the last days:

> . . . I give unto you a commandment, that ye shall forsake all evil and cleave unto all good, that *ye shall live by every word which proceedeth forth out of the mouth of God.*
>
> For he will give unto the faithful line upon line, precept upon precept; and *I will try you and prove you herewith.*
>
> And whoso layeth down his life in my cause, for my name's sake, shall find it again. even life eternal.[1]

Just as God's guidance is pledged for the repentant, he has promised to shape events for the benefit of the obedient in the last days:

> Keep all the commandments and covenants by which ye are bound; and *I will cause the heavens to shake for your good,* and Satan shall tremble and Zion shall rejoice upon the hills and flourish.[2]

But loss of the faith and the triumph of their enemies await those who fail to render obedience:

> Be diligent in keeping all my commandments, *lest judgments come upon you, and your faith fail you, and your enemies triumph over you.*[3]

11. Be free from the sins of the generation: Sanctify yourselves. Sanctification is the process whereby men "yield their hearts unto God,"[4] so that the Holy Ghost helps them to deny themselves of all ungodliness and thus become holy individuals[5] able to stand spotless before God.[6] Their garments are "washed white through the blood of the Lamb" and sin becomes abhorrent to them.[7]

In the last days context, the Lord has warned that "all those who will not endure chastening, but deny me, cannot be sanctified."[8] Concerning the day of his coming in glory, he has revealed that "the day soon cometh that ye shall see me, and know that I am; for the veil of darkness shall soon be rent, and *he that is not purified shall not abide the day.*[9]

---

1. D&C 98:11-13. See D&C 45:2, 6.
2. D&C 35:24.
3. D&C 136:42.
4. Hel. 3:35.
5. Moro. 10:32-33.
6. 3 Ne. 27:20.
7. Al. 13:11-12.
8. D&C 101:5.
9. D&C 38:8.

Their being sanctified will enable the saints to be found free from the blood and sins of this wicked generation. The Lord has revealed,

> *Behold, I will hasten my work in its time.*
>
> And I give unto you, who are the first laborers in this last kingdom, a commandment that you assemble yourselves together, and organize yourselves, and prepare yourselves, and *sanctify yourselves; yea, purify your hearts, and cleanse your hands and your feet before me, that I may make you clean;*
>
> *That I may testify unto your Father, and your God, and my God, that you are clean from the blood of this wicked generation;* . . .[1]

The sanctification process causes an actual change and renewing of the body.[2] John the Revelator has told of 144,000 men who will be called from the tribes of Israel and "sealed . . . in their foreheads. "[3] These men will labor during the judgments of the last days to bring converts into the church.[4] As Elder Orson Pratt explained, God "will purify their bodies until they shall be quickened, and renewed and strengthened, and they will be partially changed. . . . This will prepare them for further ministrations among the nations of the earth, . . . they can stand forth in the midst of these desolations and plagues and not be overcome by them."[5]

Attaining sanctification, then, will shield the saints from the judgments, allow them to be accounted free from the blood and sins of the generations, and prepare them to receive the full eternal benefits of the Lord's atoning sacrifice.

12. Prepare Spiritually: Be guided by the Holy Ghost. Ability to receive inspiration and guidance of the Spirit will be necessary for survival of the saints during the judgments of the last days. The Lord has revealed that

> . . . At that day, when I shall come in my glory, shall the parable be fulfilled which I spake concerning the ten virgins.
>
> *For they that are wise and have received the truth, and have taken the Holy Spirit for their guide, and have not been deceived*—verily I

1. D&C 88:73-75. See verses 85, 138; 109:42; 112:33.
2. See D&C 84:33; 88:67-68.
3. Rev. 7:3.
4. For more detailed information on the 144,000 see the author's book, Prophecy—Key to the Future, pp. 121-125, 141-142.
5. JD 15:365-366. March 9, 1873.

say unto you they shall not be hewn down and cast into the fire, but shall abide the day.[1]

Recognizing promptings of approaching danger; receiving guidance on methods of obtaining food and other necessary items; being directed in where to live and travel; discerning between friends and enemies, truth and error, true and false prophets—all these abilities will be indispensible when the period of "the desolation of abomination" begins. But being continually receptive to the Spirit does not come easily. It requires a conditioning of the mind and will—a humbling and cleansing of the self:

> Let him that is ignorant *learn wisdom by humbling himself and calling upon the Lord his God,* that his eyes may be opened that he may see, and his ears opened that he may hear;
>
> *For my Spirit is sent forth into the world to enlighten the humble and contrite. and to the condemnation of the ungodly.*[2]

"Ye receive the Spirit through prayer,"[3] drawing near unto God so that he in turn draws near unto you.[4] The power of the Holy Spirit is then bestowed by God "on those who love him, and purify themselves before him."[5] There is the need to develop a relationship of faith and trust in the promptings which come:

> . . . *Put your trust in that Spirit which leadeth to do good*—yea, to do justly, to walk humbly, to judge righteously; and this is my Spirit.
>
> Verily, verily, I say unto you, *I will impart unto you of my Spirit, which shall enlighten your mind, which shall fill your soul with joy;*
>
> *And then shall ye know, or by this shall you know, all things whatsoever you desire of me,* which are pertaining unto things of righteousness, in faith believing in me that you shall receive.[6]

The Holy Ghost is a comforter,[7] who will teach and bring necessary things to remembrance.[8] He will testify of the Christ,[9] guide into all truth,[10] and will reveal things to come[11]—all of which are blessings which will be sorely needed by the saints during the era of future strife and chaos.

---

1. D&C 45:56-57.
2. D&C 136:32-33.
3. D&C 63:64. See 14:8.
4. D&C 88:63-65.
5. D&C 76:116.
6. D&C 11:12-14.
7. Jn. 14:26.
8. Ibid.
9. Jn. 15:26.
10. Jn. 16:13.
11. Ibid.

13. Recognize last days events: Watch for signs of the times. The Lord instructed his people to be alert to signs that prophesied events are about to take place. After giving his great prophecy of last days events to his disciples on the Mount of Olives, he told them,

> Now learn a parable of the fig tree; when his branch is yet tender, and putteth forth leaves, ye know that summer is nigh:
>
> So likewise ye, when ye shall see all these things, know that it is near, even at the doors.[1]

One of the identifying characteristics of those who fear and serve the Lord is their awareness of the signs of the times. As the Savior observed,

> . . . He that feareth me shall be looking forth for the great day of the Lord to come, *even for the signs of the coming of the Son of Man*. . . . And he that watches not for me shall be cut off.[2]

An understanding of the signs of the times is promised to the saints:

> And he that believeth shall be blest with signs following, even as it is written.
>
> *And unto you it shall be given to know the signs of the times, and the signs of the coming of the Son of Man;* . . .[3]

The Lord's instruction is to

> Gird up your loins and be watchful and be sober, *looking forth for the coming of the Son of Man,* for he cometh in an hour you think not.[4]

The purposes of knowing the prophesied signs of the times, and then being aware of their fulfillment as the events transpire, are fourfold. First, that knowledge prevents deception and confusion:

> Wherefore, *be not deceived,* but continue in steadfastness, looking forth for the heavens to be shaken, and the earth to tremble and to reel to and fro as a drunken man, and for the valleys to be exalted, and for the

---

1. Mt. 24:32-33. See D&C 35:16.
2. D&C 45:39, 44.
3. D&C 68:10-11
4. D&C 61:38.

mountains to be made low, and for the rough places to become smooth.[1]

Second, observing the fulfillment of the signs of the times reminds the saints of their need to maintain personal worthiness:

> . . . *Take heed to yourselves,* lest at any time your hearts be overcharged with surfeiting, and drunkenness, and cares of this life, and so that day come upon you unawares.
>
> For as a snare shall it come on all them that dwell on the face of the whole earth.
>
> *Watch ye therefore, and pray always, that ye may be accounted worthy to escape all these things that shall come to pass, and to stand before the Son of Man.*[2]

Third, knowing the prophesied events and the order in which they will transpire allows one to prepare for them and to accept them when they take place. The Lord, speaking of the tribulations of the last days, has told the saints to "remember this, *which I tell you before, that you may lay it to heart, and receive that which is to follow.*"[3]

Finally, knowing the prophecies and recognizing the signs of the times allows the saints to bear witness of God's hand in future events:

> Behold, verily I say unto you, for this cause I have sent you—that you might be obedient, and *that your hearts might be prepared to bear testimony of the things which are to come; . . .*[4]

The author has observed "the ostrich syndrome" among the saints from time to time. There are those who say "I don't want to know about the prophecies of last days—they frighten me." Others have said, "The prophecies are negative in their approach. We should 'think positive'—let's only talk about happy things." Their philosophies are not the Lord's way, and are in direct opposition to his oft-repeated instructions. They neither prepare themselves, nor fulfill the commandments that they should warn and prepare others. They would do well to heed the Lord's warning that "*he that watches not for me shall be cut off.*"[5]

---

1. D&C 49:23.
2. Lk. 21:34-36. See also Mt. 24:42; 25:13;Mk. 13:35-37;Lk. 12:37-40; Eph. 6:18;1 Thess. 5:6;1 Pet. 4:7;Rev. 16:15.
3. D&C 58:5. See D&C 106:4-5.
4. D&C 58:6.
5. D&C45:44.

14. Teach doctrines of the last days: Seek knowledge for protection. A major element in the spiritual preparation of the saints is the necessity of their being properly informed concerning the prophecies of the last days. The Lord has emphasized that this people need to understand what is prophesied to come to pass, and they need to be able to discern the signs of the times by recognizing the preparations for these events among the nations of the earth. This instruction was given by revealed commandment:

> *And I give unto you a commandment that you shall teach one another the doctrine of the kingdom.*
>
> Teach ye diligently and my grace shall attend you, that you may be instructed more perfectly in *theory,* in *principle,* in *doctrine,* in the *law of the gospel,* in *all things that pertain unto the kingdom of God,* that are expedient for you to understand;
>
> Of things both in heaven and in the earth, and under the earth; *things which have been, things which are, things which must shortly come to pass; things which are at home, things which are abroad; the wars and the perplexities of the nations, and the judgments which are on the land; and a knowledge also of countries and of kingdoms—*
>
> *That ye may be prepared in all things* when I shall send you again to magnify the calling whereunto I have called you, and the mission with which I have commissioned you.[1]

Not only are the saints commanded to teach each other about the things which are to come to pass, they are also commanded to personally "treasure up wisdom" to protect themselves against the wickedness of men in the last days:

> And again, I say unto you that the *enemy in the secret chambers seeketh your lives.*
>
> Ye hear of wars in far countries, and you say that there will soon be great wars in far countries, but ye know not the hearts of men in your own land.
>
> I tell you these things because of your prayers; wherefore, *treasure up wisdom in your bosoms, lest the wickedness of men reveal these things unto you by their wickedness,* in a manner which shall speak in your ears with a voice louder than that which shall shake the earth; but if ye are prepared ye shall not fear.
>
> And that ye might *escape the power of the enemy, and be gathered unto me a righteous people,* without spot and blameless [2]

15. Prepare the saints for the hour of judgment: Warn your neighbor. After commanding the saints to teach one another about

1. D&C 88:77-80. See also D&C 88:118; 97:12-14.
2. D&C 38:28-31.

"things which must shortly come to pass" and about the "judgments which are on the land,"[1] the Lord specified the warning duty required of all his people:

> Behold, I sent you out to *testify and warn the people,* and *it becometh every man who hath been warned to warn his neighbor.*[2]

The context of this passage clearly indicates that the warning spoken of by the Savior is not merely the preaching of general gospel principles. That warning is

> . . . *to prepare the saints for the hour of judgment which is to come;* that their souls may *escape the wrath of God, the desolation of abomination* which awaits the wicked, both in this world and in the world to come.[3]

In the dedicatory prayer for the Kirtland Temple, which was given to the Prophet Joseph Smith by revelation, deep concern is expressed for the need to prepare the saints against coming judgments.

> Put upon thy servants the testimony of the covenant, that when they go out and proclaim thy word they may seal up the law, and *prepare the hearts of thy saints for all those judgments thou art about to send,* in thy wrath, upon the inhabitants of the earth, because of their transgressions, *that thy people may not faint in the day of trouble.*[4]

And also:

> We know that thou hast spoken by the mouth of thy prophets terrible things concerning the wicked, in the last days that thou wilt pour out thy judgments, without measure;
> Therefore, O Lord, *deliver thy people from the calamity of the wicked;* enable thy servants to seal up the law, and bind up the testimony, that *they may be prepared against the day of burning.*[5]

The Lord has commanded the saints repeatedly to

> *Prepare ye, prepare ye for that which is to come,* for the Lord is nigh;
> And the anger of the Lord is kindled, and his sword is bathed in heaven, and it shall fall upon the inhabitants of the earth.[6]

1. See again D&C 88:79.
2. D&C88:81.
3. D&C 88:84-85.
4. D&C 109:38.
5. D&C 109:45-46.
6. D&C 1:12-13. See also D&C 31:8; 33:10; 65:1-3; 85:3; 88:92; 133:4-5, 10, 19.

He has told them that

> . . . I give unto you a commandment, that *every man,* both elder, priest, teacher, and also member, go to with his might, with the labor of his hands, *to prepare and accomplish the things which I have commanded.*
>
> *And let your preaching be the warning voice, every man to his neighbor,* in mildness and in meekness.[1]

The commandment of the Lord, then, is that the saints admonish and warn one another, helping each other to prepare for the difficult times to come. This, obviously, is the motive for this book.

16. Preach repentance to non-members: Warn of coming judgments. The Lord has commanded that warning of coming judgments be a major part of the missionary message to the world at large in the last days. Two messages, repentance and the warning of coming judgments, are to go hand in hand as the major themes of missionary labor. The Lord told the elders, for instance, "*Behold, I Sent you out to reprove the world of all their unrighteous deeds, and to teach them of a judgment which is to come.*"[2] He commanded that all the church should preach that two-fold message:

> And verily I say unto you, the rest of my servants, go ye forth as your circumstances shall permit, in your several callings, unto the great and notable cities and villages, *reproving the world in righteousness of all their unrighteous and ungodly deeds, setting forth clearly and understandingly the desolation of abomination in the last days.*[3]

The Lord has instructed those laboring in the missionary effort to "open your mouths and they shall be filled, saying: *Repent, repent, and prepare ye the way of the Lord,* and make his paths Straight; for the kingdom of heaven is at hand; . . ."[4] Another revelation instructs those who are called to preach the gospel to

> . . . *Cry repentance* unto a crooked and perverse generation, *preparing the way* of the Lord for his second coming.
>
> For behold, verily, verily, I say unto you, the time is soon at hand that I shall come in a cloud with power and great glory.

1. D&C 38:40-41.
2. D&C 84:87.
3. D&C 84:117. The same dual message, of calling to repentance and prophesying of future judgments, characterized the work even in the days of Enoch. See Moses 6:27.
4. D&C 33:10.

..And it shall be a great day at the time of my coming, for all nations shall tremble.

But before that great day shall come, the sun shall be darkened, and the moon be turned into blood; and the stars shall refuse their shining, and some shall fall, and *great destructions await the wicked.*

Wherefore, *lift up your voice and spare not,* for the Lord God hath spoken; therefore *prophesy,* and it shall be given by the power of the Holy Ghost.[1]

And also:

Lift up your voices and spare not. *Call upon the nations to repent,* both old and young, both bond and free, *saying: Prepare yourselves for the great day of the Lord;*

For if I, who am a man, do lift up my voice and call upon you to repent, and ye hate me, what will ye say when the day cometh when the thunders shall utter their voices from the ends of the earth, speaking to the ears of all that live, saying—Repent, and prepare for the great day of the Lord?[2]

Thus the two-fold message of latter-day missionaries is clearly set forth by the Lord. They are to call to repentance, and prepare the people for the Lord's coming by warning of the judgments of the last days.

Warning of future events is required of those who are obedient to the Lord, and is not to be omitted from the missionary message:

Behold, verily I say unto you, for this cause I have sent you, that you might be obedient, and that your hearts might be prepared *to bear testimony of the things which are to come; . . .*[3]

And that requirement extends to "every man":

Wherefore, seeing that I, the Lord, have decreed all these things upon the face of the earth, I will that my saints should be assembled upon the land of Zion;

And that every man should take righteousness in his hands and faithfulness upon his loins, and *lift a warning voice unto the inhabitants of the earth;* and declare both by word and by flight that desolation shall come upon the wicked.[4]

17. Bind the law and seal the testimony: Testify against the wicked. The Lord has revealed that this wicked generation has ripened

1. D&C 34:6-10.
2. D&C 43:20-21.
3. D&C 58:6.
4. D&C 63:36-37.

in iniquity until it is now "*white already to be burned*."[1] It is now the eleventh hour, and the last time missionaries will be

> . . . Ye are called to lift up your voices as with the sound of a trump, to *declare my gospel unto a crooked and perverse generation*.
>
> For behold, the field is white already to harvest;and it is the *eleventh hour,* and the *last time* that I shall call laborers into my vineyard.
>
> *And my vineyard has become corrupted every whit; and there is none which doeth good save it be a few;* and they err in many instances because of priestcrafts, all having corrupt minds.[2]

This "crooked and perverse generation"[3] has become so wicked the Lord is withholding his spirit from the inhabitants of the earth.[4] The saints have been instructed to

> . . . Watch, for the adversary spreadeth his dominions, and darkness reigneth;
>
> And the anger of God kindleth against the inhabitants of the earth *and none doeth good, for all have gone out of the way.*[5]

Concerning the rest of the world besides the saints, the Lord has revealed that

> . . . *All flesh is corrupted before me; and the powers of darkness prevail upon the earth,* among the children of men, in the presence of all the hosts of heaven—
>
> Which causeth silence to reign, and all eternity is pained, and *the angels are waiting the great command to reap down the earth,* to gather the tares that they may be burned;and, behold, *the enemy is combined*.[6]

God has decreed that "this gospel of the kingdom shall be preached in all the world *for a witness unto all nations;* and then shall the end come."[7] The Lord has said that the missionaries are "called to prune my vineyard with a *mighty pruning,* yea, even for the last time."[8] This witness, or "pruning," will serve to convert and gather out the righteous who remain, but it will also condemn the wicked. Speaking of those who will have believed on his words and will have been born again, the Lord said, "Their testimony shall also go forth *unto the condemnation of this generation* if they harden their hearts against them."[9]

---

1. D&C 31:4.
2. D&C 33:2-4.
3. D&C 34:6.
4. D&C 63:32.
5. D&C 82:5-6.
6. D&C 38:11-12.
7. Mt. 24:14.
8. D&C 24:19.
9. D&C 5:18.

The Lord's servants are to seal up the righteous to partake of the blessings of eternal life and to be protected against Satan's power in the last days.[1] They have a similar responsibility to seal up the wicked unto judgment and condemnation. A revelation from the Savior states that

> . . . They who go forth, bearing these tidings unto the inhabitants of the earth, *to them is power given to seal both on earth and in heaven, the unbelieving and rebellious;*
>
> Yea, verily, *to seal them up unto the day when the wrath of God shall be poured out upon the wicked without measure*—[2]

This "sealing up" process is a fundamental aspect of the labor of the missionaries in the last days. The Lord has commanded,

> . . . Tarry ye, and labor diligently, that you may be perfected in your ministry to go forth among the Gentiles for the last time, as many as the mouth of the Lord shall name, *to bind up the law and seal up the testimony,* . . .[3]

Then the Lord's answer to the wicked at the last day shall be that they have been sealed up unto darkness by the Lord's servants:

> Behold, and lo, there are none to deliver you; for ye obeyed not my voice when I called to you out of the heavens; ye believed not my servants, and when they were sent unto you ye received them not.
>
> Wherefore, *they sealed up the testimony and bound up the law,* and ye were delivered over unto darkness.[4]

Thus the Lord's servants have been commanded to leave a witness against those who reject them by shaking off the dust from their feet,[5] and they eventually stand as witnesses of the house, village or city which cast them out.[6] The Lord has said, concerning enemies who come against the saints to drive them out.

> . . . *Ye shall curse them;*
>
> *And whomsoever ye curse, I will curse, and ye shall avenge me of mine enemies.*
>
> And my presence shall be with you even in avenging me of mine enemies, unto the third and fourth generation of them that hate me.[7]

---

1. See D&C 68:11-12; 109:38; 124:124; 131:5.
2. D&C 1:8-9. See D&C 124:93;128:8-11.
3. D&C 88:84.
4. D&C 133:71-72.
5. D&C 24:15-17; 60:15; 99:4-5.
6. D&C 75:18-22; 84:92-97.
7. D&C 103:24-26.

Bearing testimony against the wicked is an awesome responsibility, and one not to be taken lightly, nor used indiscriminately without careful restraint! Yet it is a duty commanded of God, and an integral part of his plan. It is necessary in the last days, just as it was in Alma's time[1] and in the era of the New Testament church.[2] As the gap between righteousness and iniquity widens, the necessity for testimony against the wicked will rapidly increase.

18. Go ye out from Babylon: Be separate from the wicked. The Lord has commanded, "Prepare ye, prepare ye, O my people,"[3] and then has told the saints to "*go ye out from Babylon. Be ye clean that bear the vessels of the Lord.*"[4] In another revelation his counsel is to "*go ye out from among the wicked. Save yourselves.*"[5] Another warning proclaims the Lord's message that "all the proud and they that do wickedly shall be as stubble; and I will burn them up, for I am the Lord of Hosts; and *I will not spare any that remain in Babylon.*"[6] The Lord's instruction has been given to "*Go ye out from among the nations, even from Babylon, from the midst of wickedness, which is spiritual Babylon.*"[7]

That saint who wishes to be spiritually and temporally prepared would do well to examine the environment in which he lives and works. He should evaluate his situation, prayerfully assessing whether his surroundings and associates are conducive to his living the gospel, or whether his environment is leading him and his family away from that which is righteous and good. It would be to his benefit, also, to evaluate what the situation would be if difficult conditions were to arise such as severe food shortages, international war or internal conflict, or persecution of the Church. In such extreme situations, would he be able to continue in his present surroundings, or would he be subjected to severe pressures, and perhaps even have to "take his sword against his neighbor"[8] in defense of his family, his home, his supplies, and his liberty? Every Latter-day Saint who is in tune with the Holy Spirit is entitled to revealed guidance concerning where he should work and reside. Such promptings come to many. Indeed, over the past decade the author has conversed with numerous individuals who had moved to new environments because of personal inspiration which they have received.

---

1. Al. 14:11.
2. Lk. 11:49-51.
3. D&C 133:4.
4. D&C 133:5.
5. D&C 38:42.
6. D&C64:24.
7. D&C 133:14.
8. D&C45:68.

The present activity and direction of the Church, however, should be considered when making a decision concerning where to live. In this day of "lengthened stride" towards missionary work, the gospel message is being taught world-wide. The place where the saints are most needed is in the outlying stakes and missions, where they can be most actively involved with the rapid growth, rather than being clustered in the center of the Church. No general "gathering" call has been given, and it still appears "*necessary that ye should remain for the present time in your places of abode,* as it shall be suitable to your circumstances."[1] It is still a time of preparation prior to the gathering, but a time to assist the saints and to "*strengthen them and prepare them* against the time when they shall be gathered."[2]

Even at the height of the future difficulties, when the Church will be the subject of intense persecution, the saints will still be scattered throughout the world. In his vision of that future era, Nephi saw that "the church of the Lamb, who were the saints of God, were also *upon all the face of the earth; . . .*"[3]

The scriptures indicate that there will be two times, and types, of gathering. The first will be to various places of refuge among the stakes of Zion, as the nation endures the agonies of world war and internal conflict. Then, after the Missouri area has been swept clean,[4] the New Jerusalem will be built. The scriptures reveal that there will be a general assembling to that area. No advantage is to be gained by undirected moves which are out of chronological synchronization with these periods. To move to the New Jerusalem area, prior to its cleansing, for instance, could be disastrous.

In the first gathering period, the saints will have need to assemble in various places of refuge[5] throughout the Americas, the "land of Zion,"[6] among the stakes:

---

1. D&C 48:1.
2. D&C31:8.
3. 1 Ne. 14:12. Nephi added, however, that "their dominions upon the face of the earth were small, because of the wickedness of the great whore whom I saw." (Ibid.)
4. See Wilford Woodruff's vision, p. 196, also pp. 223-225.
5. See pp. 200-201.
6. In this passage the term "Zion" appears to be used in the broad sense, as expressed by Joseph Smith in the April, 1844 conference: ..."I will make a proclamation that will cover a broader ground. The whole of America is Zion itself from north to south, and is described by the prophets, who declare that it is the Zion where the mountain of the Lord should be, and that it should be in the center of the land." (HC 6:318-319. April 8. 1844.)

> . . . That the gathering together upon *the land of Zion, and upon her stakes, may be for a defense, and for a refuge from the storm,* and from wrath when it shall be poured out without mixture upon the whole earth.[1]

The Lord speaks of "*Zion, and in her stakes, and in Jerusalem*" as "those places which I have appointed for refuge."[2] He revealed that his will is that the saints "gather together, and stand in holy places."[3] The Savior says that as the overflowing scourge of sickness is poured out, "My disciples shall stand in holy places, and shall not be moved."[4] The Lord has cautioned that this gathering should be accomplished "*not in haste, lest there should be confusion, which bringeth pestilence.*"[5] His caution to the saints is to "let not your gathering be in haste, nor by flight; but *let all things be prepared before you.*"[6] It appears that the saints will need to be alert to this approaching time of gathering to places of refuge, and not tarry or procrastinate when the need arises.

A prophetic statement made by President Heber C. Kimball seems to indicate that the separation, or "sifting time," will even involve the saints of the Utah area. In 1856 he said,

> We think we are secure here in the chambers of the everlasting hills, where we can close those few doors of the canyons against mobs and persecutors, the wicked and the vile, who have always beset us with violence and robbery, but I want to say to you, my brethren, the time is coming when *we will be mixed up in these now peaceful valleys to that extent that it will be difficult to tell the face of a Saint from the face of an enemy to the people of God. Then, brethren, look out for the great sieve, for there will be a great sifting time, and many will fall;* for I say unto you there is a *test*, a *TEST*, a TEST coming, and who will be able to stand?[7]

The scriptures also speak of a second gathering, a later assembling of the saints, at the site of the New Jerusalem in Missouri:

---

1. D&C 115:6.
2. D&C 124:36.
3. D&C 101:22. Verses 20-22 allude to the stakes as being the "holy places." See also verses 64-68
4. D&C 45:32. See 87:8.
5. D&C 63:24.
6. D&C 101:68.
7. Orson F. Whitney, Life of Heber C. Kimball (Salt Lake City, Utah: Bookcraft, 1967), p. 446. This statement was preserved by Elder Edward Stevenson. President A.F. McDonald recorded, concerning Heber C. Kimball, that "he clearly foreshadowed the time of trial the Saints are now passing through, and to a period still before us. He often used the language, 'A test, a test is coming. ' '' (Ibid. p. 447.)

> . . . The decree hath gone forth from the Father that they shall be gathered in unto *one place upon the face of this land,* to prepare their hearts and be prepared in all things against the day when *tribulation and desolation are sent forth upon the wicked.*[1]

The Lord has revealed his desire "that my covenant people may be *gathered in one* in that day when I shall come to my temple."[2] He described the New Jerusalem as a "city of refuge, a place of safety for the saints of the Most High God,"[3] and said that

> . . . It shall come to pass among the wicked, that *every man that will not take his sword against his neighbor must needs flee unto Zion for safety.*
>
> *And there shall be gathered unto it out of every nation under heaven;* and it shall be the only people that shall not be at war one with another.[4]

Yet even in that day, when world-wide conflict will make it imperative that the saints be "gathered in one," there will still be those who will have been "commanded to tarry"[5] who will be scattered throughout the world.[6]

To be prepared to gather to appropriate places of refuge as the difficulties come upon the world will require individual alertness to personal promptings and responsiveness to Church directions, plus adequate preparation for mobility, coupled with the realization that many saints will find it necessary to "*declare both by word and by flight that desolation shall come upon the wicked.*"[7] It will be necessary to grasp and accept the implications of a separation of the obedient from the disobedient and unjust. It will also place tremendous responsibility upon Church authorities to properly prepare the saints and to help them develop adequate places of refuge, and also to be sufficiently responsive to divine guidance that they can give proper and timely directives in a time when many lives are at stake and the potential for human suffering is enormous.

19. Seek divine strength, guidance and protection: Pray always. There is tremendous strength and power gained through effec-

1. D&C 29:8.
2. D&C 42:36.
3. D&C 45:66.
4. D&C 45:68-69.
5. D&C 133:4.
6. See again 1 Ne. 14:12. Also Prophecy—Key to the Future, pp. so-9
7. D&C 63:37.

tive prayer and the Lord has commanded that his people utilize that strength for their own benefit during the difficult events of the last days.

Elder Heber C. Kimball spoke of the importance of each individual being personally receptive to divine guidance and possessing a firm testimony in connection with the events of the last days. He said,

> This Church has before it many close places through which it will have to pass before the work of God is crowned with victory. To meet the difficulties that are coming, *it will be necessary for you to have a knowledge of the truth of this work for yourselves. The difficulties will be of such a character that the man or woman who does not possess this personal knowledge or witness will fall.* If you have not got the testimony, live right and call upon the Lord and cease not till you obtain it. If you do not you will not stand.
>
> Remember these sayings, for many of you will live to see them fulfilled. *The time will come when no man nor woman will be able to endure on borrowed light. Each will have to be guided by the light within himself. If you do not have it, how can you stand?* Do you believe it? . . .
>
> *You will have all the persecution you want and more too,* and all the opportunity to show your integrity to God and truth that you could desire.[1]

On another occasion he remarked, "*Unless a man knew that Jesus was the Christ, he could not stand in this Church.* He said that the Lord

---

1. Orson F. Whitney, Life of Heber C. Kimball, op. cit., pp. 449-450, 451. In this same discourse, delivered in 1867, he said:

> You have the First Presidency, from whom you can get counsel to guide you, and you rely on them. The time will come when they will not be with you. Why? Because they will have to flee and hide up to keep out of the hands of their enemies. You have the Twelve now. You will not always have them, for they too will be hunted and will have to keep out of the way of their enemies. You have other men to whom you look for counsel and advice. Many of them will not be amongst you, for the same reason. You will be left to the light within yourselves. If you don't have it you will not stand; therefore seek for the testimony of Jesus and cleave to it, that when the trying time comes you may not stumble and fall. (Ibid., p. 450.)

The saints endured this type of experience during the anti-Mormon persecutions of the 1880's. Whether a similar situation will occur in connection with the persecutions prophesied for the future remains to be seen. The fulfillment of Heber C. Kimball's prophecy that "the time would come when the government would stop the Saints from holding meetings. When this was done the Lord would pour out His judgments," (Ibid., p. 442) has not yet been realized. Does it imply future persecution from Governmental sources, and foreshadow a similar situation to the 1880's period?

would allow all manner of abominations to come to Zion, in order to purify His people."[3]

The Savior has commanded that Divine supplication be made for many things, but foremost is individual prayer for protection and strength so that one can endure till Christ comes. The revealed instruction has been given to "*Pray always that you enter not into temptation,* that you may abide the day of his coming, whether in life or in death."[2] A similar revelation conveyed the Savior's admonition to "*Pray always, that ye may not faint, until I come*. Behold, and lo, I will come quickly, and receive you unto myself."[3] Diligent obedience is required if the saints are to be able to rely on prayer to assist them when troubled times come. Said the Lord concerning earlier saints,

> They were slow to hearken unto the voice of the Lord their God; therefore, *the Lord their God is slow to hearken unto their prayers, to answer them in the day of their trouble*.[4]

The Lord had delivered the same warning to the people of King Noah in Book of Mormon times:

> . . . Except this people repent and turn unto the Lord their God, they shall be brought into bondage; and none shall deliver them, except it be the Lord the Almighty God.
>
> Yea, and it shall come to pass that *when they shall cry unto me I will be slow to hear their cries; yea, and I will suffer them that they be smitten by their enemies.*
>
> And except they repent in sackcloth and ashes, and cry mightily to the Lord their God, *I will not hear their prayers, neither will I deliver them out of their afflictions: . . .*[5]

Truly no course but righteous obedience can safely be followed in the perilous times to come.

Another scriptural warning speaks of prayer being made ineffective because of unwillingness to share with the needy. As the shortages and famines of the last days occur, this may become a matter of serious import, affecting both the temporal and spiritual salvation of many:

---

1. Ibid., p. 441. This statement was made in 1856.
2. D&C 61:39.
3. D&C 88:126.
4. D&C 101:7.
5. Mos. 11:23-25. See also Mos. 7:29, 33; 9:3, 17-18; 21:14-15

> . . . *If ye turn away the needy, and the naked, and visit not the sick and afflicted, and impart of your substance, if ye have, to those who stand in need*—I say unto you, if ye do not any of these things, behold, *your prayer is vain, and availeth you nothing,* and ye are as hypocrites who do deny the faith.

The saints would do well to pray for the nation and its leaders, seeking that it might follow a course of righteousness, and making supplication that impending judgments be delayed until the Lord's work of gleaning the righteous is accomplished. As in Book of Mormon times, such prayers can delay the judgments, a process which may presently be happening:

> Yea, and I say unto you that *if it were not for the prayers of the righteous, who are now in the land, that ye would even now be visited with utter destruction;* yet it would not be by flood as were the people in the days of Noah, but it would be by famine, and by pestilence, and the sword.
>
> *But it is by the prayers of the righteous that ye are spared; now therefore, if ye will cast out the righteous from among you then will not the Lord stay his hand;* but in his fierce anger he will come out against you; then ye shall be smitten by famine, and by pestilence, and by the sword; and the time is soon at hand except ye repent.[2]

Yet prayer alone cannot save the nations—only their repentance and acceptance of the gospel can avert the judgments. The Lord has said.

> Behold, verily, verily, I say unto you, that the people in Ohio call upon me in much faith, *thinking I will stay my hand in judgment upon the nations, but I cannot deny my word.*
>
> Wherefore lay to with your might and call faithful laborers into my vineyard, that it may be pruned for the last time.
>
> *And inasmuch as they do repent and receive the fulness of my gospel, and become sanctified, I will stay mine hand in judgment.*[3]

Like the prophets and disciples of old, the saints should seek to "leave a blessing upon this land in their prayers."[4] Yet there will come

---

1. Al. 34:28.
2. Al. 10:22-23. See pp. 114-121. Concerning the time in the last days when the Lord will "in his fury vex the nation," the Lord has instructed the saints to "Pray ye, therefore, that their ears may be opened unto your cries, that I may be merciful unto them, that these things may not come upon them." (D&C 101:92.)
3. D&C 39:16-18.
4. See D&C 10:46-52

a time, when the persecution against the saints becomes intense, that they may be

> Calling upon the name of the Lord day and night, saying: *O that thou wouldst rend the heavens,* that thou wouldst come down, that the mountains might flow down at thy presence. . . .
>
> O Lord, *thou shalt come down to make thy name known to thine adversaries,* and all nations shall tremble at thy presence—
>
> When thou doest terrible things, . . .[1]

20. Prepare for return of the united order: Be ready to share. With the strong prophetic warnings concerning future famine which have been given, there is reason to ponder how the needs of large portions of the population can be met. Surely there is need for the saints to "warn their neighbor," encouraging those around them to anticipate the possibility of future shortages. But the question "Must I share in a time of extreme need?" often arises.

The third world war and internal conflict within the United States will serve as a transition period, in preparation for the return of the saints to establish the New Jerusalem. The Lord has revealed that by the time of that return, the saints must again be living the united order, for that unity is a

> . . . Union required by the law of the celestial kingdom;
>
> And *Zion cannot be built up unless it is by the principles of the law of the celestial kingdom;* otherwise I cannot receive her unto myself.[2]

Just how, and when, the principle of consecration under the united order is to be reinstated is not known by the author, but it is obvious that a major need may arise if famine and extreme shortages come upon the saints. Such a scenario might set the stage, creating sufficient need that the saints might overcome the obstacle of selfishness which prevented the united order from becoming their way of life in the past.[3]

The Lord has said that the united order is to be "for the benefit of my church, and *for the salvation of men until I come*."[4] While speaking of the united order, he revealed that it was to serve to make the church independent in the time of tribulation:

---

1. D&C 133:40, 42-43. See Al. 33:10; D&C 109:50-52.
2. D&C 105:4-5.
3. See D&C 105:1-10.
4. D&C 104:1.

> Behold, this is the preparation wherewith I prepare you, and the foundation, and the ensample which I give unto you, whereby you may accomplish the commandments which are given you;
>
> That through my providence, *notwithstanding the tribulation which shall descend upon you, that the church may stand independent* above all other creatures beneath the celestial world; . . .

And he also said.

> . . . *It is my purpose to provide for my saints,* for all things are mine.
>
> But it must needs be done in mine own way, and behold *this is the way that I, the Lord, have decreed to provide for my saints,* . . .[2]

Sometime in the future, then, the saints can expect the Lord to again command them, saying, "I require all their surplus property to be put into the hands of the bishop of my church in Zion."[3] And they will again be instructed that

> . . . *Inasmuch as they receive more than is needful for their necessities and their wants, it shall be given into my storehouse;*
>
> *And the benefits shall be consecrated unto the inhabitants of Zion,* and unto their generations, inasmuch as they become heirs according to the laws of the kingdom.
>
> Behold, *this is what the Lord requires of every man in his stewardship,* even as I, the Lord, have appointed *or shall hereafter appoint* unto any man.
>
> And behold, *none are exempt from this law who belong to the church of the living God.*[4]

They can anticipate the instruction that

> Zion must arise and put on her beautiful garments.
>
> Therefore I give unto you this commandment, that *ye bind yourselves by this covenant,* and it shall be done according to the laws of the land.
>
> Behold, here is wisdom also in me for your good.
>
> And you are to be equal, or in other words, *you are to have equal claims on the properties,* for the benefit of managing the concerns of your stewardships, *every man according to his wants and his needs, inasmuch as his wants are just—*
>
> *And all this for the benefit of the church of the living God, that every man may improve upon his talent, that every man may gain other talents,* yea, even an hundred fold, to be cast into the Lord's storehouse, to become the common property of the whole church—[5]

---

1. D&C 78:13-14.
2. D&C 104:15-16.
3. D&C 119:1.
4. D&C 70:7-10.
5. D&C 82:14-18.

The Lord has stressed the attitude with which the saints must function when the principles of the united order are restored, emphasizing that every man must be "seeking the interest of his neighbor, and doing all things with an eye single to the glory of God,"[1] and warning that "in your temporal things you shall be equal, *and this not grudgingly,* otherwise the abundance of the manifestations of the Spirit shall be withheld."[2]

When this eternal principle[3] is restored, the Lord has warned of severe penalties which will come upon those who harden their hearts against it. His instruction is that they "shall be dealt with according to the laws of my church, and shall be delivered over to the buffetings of Satan until the day of redemption."[4] The person who breaks the covenant of the united order, according to the Lord, "shall be cursed in his life, and shall be trodden down by whom I will,"[5] and shall eventually "lift up his eyes in hell, being in torment."[6] Those who won't abide by the law of the united order in the days of the New Jerusalem "shall not be found worthy to abide among you."[7]

Thus a vital aspect of the spiritual preparation of the saints is that they condition themselves to the future acceptance of the principles of the united order. Their willingness to share for the common good may hold the key to both spiritual and temporal salvation in the days to come.

21. Resolve to attain eternal goals: Endure to the end. Much has been written about the judgments God will pour out in the last days. Comment has been made about the testing of the saints, and concerning the possibility of the saints receiving chastening from the Almighty. It appears that there will be many trials to be endured, and that the future will not be easy. In the face of such a possibility, it is imperative that the Lord's people fix their sights clearly upon the attaining of their eternal goals. They must commit to themselves, to their families, and to their Father in Heaven that no matter what comes, they will endure to the end, overcoming their trials and obstacles. They will set a course to obtain their salvation and exaltation, and not be swayed from it by the trials of the last days.

---

1. D&C 82:19
2. D&C 70:14.
3. See D&C 82:20; 104:1; 119:4.
4. D&C 82:21. See 104:9.
5. D&C 104:5. See verses 2-9; 105:6.
6. D&C 104:18.
7. D&C 119:5. See also verse 6.

The Lord has promised that "*if you keep my commandments and endure to the end you shall have eternal life,* which gift is the greatest of all the gifts of God."[1]

He has warned of the condemnation that will await the fearful and unbelieving,[2] while promising that "*he that endureth in faith and doeth my will, the same shall overcome,* and shall receive an inheritance upon the earth when the day of transfiguration shall come "[3]

"The Lord giveth no commandments unto the children of men, save *he shall prepare a way for them* that they may accomplish the thing which he commandeth them."[4] The Father has given the saints "*power to overcome all things* which are not ordained of him—"[5] The saints have been instructed to "pray continually, that ye may not be tempted above that which ye can bear."[6] There is power granted to every man, then, to fulfill the commandments, overcome the challenges and resist the temptations which may come.

The hardships may become intense. The saints may have to "endure" in the fullest sense of the word. They may cry out in sorrow, as did the prophet Alma, "How long shall we suffer these great afflictions, O Lord? O Lord, give us strength according to our faith which is in Christ, even unto deliverance."[7] They may feel God has abandoned them, and cry out to him in anguish, as did the prophet Joseph:

> O God, where art thou? And where is the pavilion that covereth thy hiding place?
>
> How long shall thy hand be stayed, and thine eye, yea thy pure eye, behold from the eternal heavens the wrongs of thy people and of thy servants, and thine ear be penetrated with their cries?
>
> Yea, O Lord, how long shall they suffer these wrongs and unlawful oppressions, before thine heart shall be softened toward them, and thy bowels be moved with compassion toward them?[8]

Yet the eternal goal cannot be abandoned, and "blessed are they who are faithful and endure, whether in life or in death, for they shall inherit eternal life."[9] They must be like the Lamanite converts of old: "They never did look upon death with any degree of terror, for their

1. D&C 14:7.
2. D&C 63:17-18.
3. D&C 63:20.
4. 1 Ne. 3:7. See 1 Ne. 17:3,50-51.
5. D&C 50:35.
6. Al. 13:28.
7. Al. 14:26.
8. D&C 121:1-3.
9. D&C 50:5.

hope and views of Christ and the resurrection; therefore, *death was swallowed up to them by the victory of Christ over it*."[1] And they must be like the missionaries who labored in Book of Mormon times, whose afflictions "were swallowed up in the joy of Christ."[2] As one prophet expressed his confidence in prayer, "*I will cry unto thee in all mine afflictions, for in thee is my Joy.*"[3]

Yes, the saints would do well to fix their path upon the eternal goal, and resolve that they will endure to the end, no matter what trials they must overcome.

Temporal Preparations for Survival

22. Anticipate physical needs: Store food, clothing, fuel. The saints have been counseled repeatedly to store the supplies needed to preserve life in times of shortage and want.[4] Theirs is the responsibility to prepare for their own personal and family needs, and also to anticipate the needs of many who will gather together in times of future distress. As Heber C. Kimball explained, "*This is a part of our religion—to lay up stores and provide for ourselves and for the surrounding country;* for the day is near when they will come by thousands and by millions, with their fineries, to get a little bread."[5]

Many events can cause shortages and scarcity of necessary commodities. Besides the obvious dangers of crop failure and war, consider other possibilities: strikes, transportation breakdown, economic upheaval, energy shortages, disruption of farming, quarantine against pestilence, etc. The supply of basic commodities is directly dependent upon manpower, equipment, and profit. If it becomes unprofitable to manufacture, distribute, or sell commodities, the items will either disappear from the stores or exorbitantly increase in price until the average family cannot afford to purchase them.

Serious difficulties can develop overnight. Food stores were suddenly left bare in many parts of the nation, for instance, as the "Cuban crisis" developed. The "great depression" erupted in a matter of hours

1. Al. 27:28.
2. Al. 31:38.
3. Al. 33:11.
4. See pages 169-174.
5. JD 5;163-164. August 30. 1857.

as the stock market collapsed. The "energy crisis" emerged abruptly, with no meaningful advance warning to the general public.

Because of the possibility of rapid changes, and because of the prophetic warnings of future hardships, it is vital that an effective preparedness program be established in every family unit.

Several brief suggestions might prove helpful:

A. *Anticipate emergency situations*. Think what would happen in a variety of situations such as a prolonged power failure, an extended transportation strike which would leave stores bare, a major disaster such as an earthquake, etc. What would you need if you were unable to buy anything from local merchants? Record your observations and analyze them in terms of preparatory actions required.

B. *Inventory present needs and supplies*. No meaningful storage program can be developed without proper assessment of needs and the setting of realistic goals and timetables. No comprehensive, long-range storage program can be maintained without a record-keeping system. The inventory should include food, clothing, fuel, and household necessities. Anticipate family growth and needs for years to come.

C *Store medical and sanitation supplies*. If severe shortages occurred, people would soon feel particular need for basic medicinal goods to ward off the typical minor ailments with which families are beset. There would also be need for disinfectants, first aid supplies, home pesticides, etc.

D. *Buy home maintenance supplies*. If difficult times come, there is a definite possibility of extended periods in which basic services such as power and fuel supply are maintained, but in which many necessary items are unavailable from merchants. There is wisdom in storing a basic supply of nuts and bolts, nails, faucet washers, toilet parts, electrical switches, light bulbs, etc. Every home should have basic tools for repair and construction available.

E. *Involve the neighborhood in storage activities*. Latter-day Saints have been commanded to warn their neighbors and to prepare them for coming judgments.[1] In no situation is this command more imperative than in the area of storage of survival commodities. In a time of real shortage, unprepared neighbors could cause serious dilemmas of both a moral and temporal nature.

F. *Avoid the "hoarding" mentality*. In times of scarcity, the "have nots" tend to accuse the "haves" of hoarding. The publicity they gen-

1. D&C 88:81, 84.

erate can sometimes place a viable storage program in an unfavorable light, causing discouragement and even persecution. Systematically-spaced buying, rather than "panic buying," tends to dispel this attitude. Prior emphasis and community publicity on the advantages of food storage and preparedness will help place the practice in better prospective.

G. *Plant a garden*. Prepare to be self-supporting to as great a degree as possible. Successful gardening requires skill and experience which cannot be learned overnight, and it often requires long-range soil development. Tools should be acquired. Seeds should be stored. Records should be kept.

H. *Obtain a survival library*. Many books explain helpful techniques for self-sufficient living. Building a basic library on food storage and preservation, gardening, home repair, and outdoor survival is a wise precaution.

I. *Provide emergency heating and cooling facilities*. Emergency ability to maintain warmth in even one room could be the means of averting severe discomfort and suffering in a fuel shortage or power outage. There should also be provision for emergency cooking on the stove or fireplace. A supply of wood or coal should be on hand. There should be some provision for the emergency refrigeration of foodstuffs in case of prolonged power failure.

J. *Insulate homes*. Advance effort to properly insulate homes would be of particular value in times of fuel shortages. Adding insulation, upgrading window quality, installing weather stripping and storm doors—all are effective preparedness measures as well as hedges against rapidly-rising fuel costs.

K. *Repair, paint homes*. A vital aspect of preparedness is having the home in good repair. Plumbing, heating, electrical items, the roof, exterior surfaces—every aspect of a home should be maintained in good condition. Homes should be painted. Once hard times come, it is difficult to meet the costs of such repairs.

L. *Replace worn appliances*. Old stoves, refrigerators, toilets, and other necessary appliances should be upgraded while supplies are plentiful.

M. *Provide for home security from theft*. Scarcity of food and other necessary supplies would cause a serious increase in the danger of theft. Preparation should be made to maintain the security of the home.

N. *Safe storage of important records*. In the event of major disruptions or emergencies, there might be increased need for ready access to vital family records. Such records should be cataloged and preserved in a safe place, protected from fire and water damage and from theft. There might also be a need for ready access to addresses of family members and other important directions for distant geographical areas.

O. *Maintain mobility and travel potential*. In case of serious emergency, families might find it necessary to travel relatively long distances to reach shelter in the homes of other family members or acquaintances. An automobile should be maintained in good working order, and an adequate supply of gas should be safely stored in portable containers. An emergency travel kit should be planned and prepared. Maps should be on hand.

P. *Pre-arranged emergency travel plan*. The chance of having to rapidly leave one area and travel to another increases as the possibility of future war increases. Contingency decisions should be made, and all family members should be made aware of them.

23. Anticipate the possibility of nuclear war: Strengthen civil defense. Numerous prophecies of the last days warn of the danger of a Third World War and clearly assert that such a conflict will come to pass.[1] Current media reports frequently cite evidence of Russia's continuing increase in offensive weaponry, on a scale which indicates the intent of "aggressive action." Of particular concern are other news reports indicating America's vulnerability to attack, which predict the probable destruction of over a third of the U.S. population should a sudden nuclear assault occur.

In the author's opinion, there is vital need to strengthen the nation's civil defense program, making greatly increased provision for protection from nuclear attack. The fallout shelter program should be reemphasized, with renewed effort to locate new shelters, restock existing shelters, and inform and educate the public. It is the author's belief that thoughtful citizens should exert their influence at the local, the state, and the national level, calling for immediate action to strengthen the land against attack.

Much has been said about America's offensive capability, and there are those who monitor it closely. In the light of Russia's rapid increase in military might, it is imperative that a strong offensive force be maintained. But that offensive force will not prevent attack on America's homeland, nor preserve the people if an attack occurs. There is immediate need to strengthen the nation's defense capability as well as offensive capacity.

---

1. See pp. 182-240, and *Prophecy—Key To The Future*, pp. 10-15.

On an individual level, it would be wise for families to carefully consider the need for a family fallout shelter. With many federal shelters now unstocked, citizens are increasingly vulnerable and often have no alternative but to make personal provision for protection against fallout. They need to re-educate themselves concerning the dangers of nuclear radiation, and discover that a two-week shelter stay would be far less than adequate protection against radiation sickness if one of Russia's huge new warheads were exploded nearby, with its larger radiation output and resulting extended period of radioactive decay.

Remember, the warning of prophecy is that a Third World War will occur, and that it will include the bombing of America's homeland, with severe loss resulting.

24. Anticipate the danger of economic upheaval: Be free from debt. As the world enters the trauma of the last days, economic stability may become increasingly fragile. Shortages of supplies may occur. Production may cease. Transportation and distribution systems may become inoperative. There continues to be the dual dangers of inflation and depression. War always influences the economy.

With the potential for economic instability looming ever more ominous as perilous times approach, there is wisdom in proceeding cautiously in matters of personal finance. These suggestions are offered:

A. *Be free from debt.* This counsel has been given to Latter-day Saints by their leaders on many occasions. It is wise instruction. In times of difficulty, indebtedness becomes financial bondage, and those who are in debt are not in full control of either their lives or their property. Set a course which will repay all indebtedness as soon as possible. That may not be the most profitable course for "good" times, but the freedom and security it offers for troubled times far outweighs the profit lost.

B. *Place preparation for security before pleasure and profit.* In establishing personal priorities, recognize the value of proper food storage, home care, and other basics of personal security over the many luxury items which are available. Preparation for future family well-being should take precedence over boats, campers, and speculative financial ventures.

C. *Be self-sustaining.* Every effort should be made for able-bodied individuals to provide for their own needs, and to resist the temptation to draw from government welfare programs. Those who do not provide for their own needs are not free, and are locked into unproductive situations which will not allow them to make adequate preparations for the future, nor enjoy life fully in the present. There is no effective substitute for personal effort and the development of individual skills and abilities.

D. *Provide for financial emergencies.* A family needs a cushion of readily-available capital to serve as protection against sudden emergencies. An amount equal to six month's income is often recommended. There is also need for the protection available through insurance programs.

E. *Recognize that money has value only in a working economy.* Money is only a means of exchange and has no value in and of itself. It can be used to obtain goods and services in normal times, but may be worthless in times of economic distress. There is wisdom in obtaining needed and desired items before periods of instability arise.

24. Anticipate communication disruption: Make long range emergency plans. Communication and transportation networks could be seriously disrupted or destroyed in the event of war or internal strife. Many of today's families are scattered across the nation. There is wisdom in establishing a family emergency plan, specifying what steps the family would take to be reunited or maintain family ties in the event of major problems in the nation, fixing dates and places for future meetings, proposing alternate communication systems, etc. A formal family organization would strengthen the emergency plans.

Interacting with Others in the Last Days Environment

The duties of the American citizen are many, and require diligent service and loyalty to the principles of freedom if liberty is to be preserved. A present role of the saints is to be a stabilizing influence in the many communities in which they reside across the land.

25. Fulfill the responsibilities of citizenship: Obey the laws of the land. As the perilous days of the "Saturday night of time" draw closer, it is vital that obedience be rendered to the laws of the land and that governmental stability be maintained. The Lord has revealed his counsel on this matter, instructing his people to

> Let no man break the laws of the land, for *he that keepeth the laws of God hath no need to break the laws of the land.*

> Wherefore, *be subject to the powers that be,* until he reigns whose right it is to reign, and subdues all enemies under his feet.[1]

He has commanded the saints to support laws which maintain man's freedom, rights and privileges:

> . . . Verily I say unto you concerning the laws of the land, it is my will that my people should observe to do all things whatever I command them.
>
> *And that law of the land which is constitutional, supporting that principle of freedom in maintaining rights and privileges,* belongs to all mankind, and is justifiable before me.
>
> Therefore, I, the Lord, justify you, and your brethren of my church, in befriending that law which is the constitutional law of the land;
>
> And as pertaining to law of man, whatever is more or less than this cometh of evil.
>
> *I, the Lord God, make you free, therefore ye are free indeed, and the law also maketh you free.*[2]

A declaration of belief regarding governments and laws was adopted by the Church in 1835, which asserts that "we believe that governments were instituted of God for the benefit of man; and that he holds men accountable for their acts in relation to them, . . ."[3] That declaration holds that governments should make and administer laws "for the good and safety of society,"[4] and that governments are to frame and hold inviolate laws which accomplish three purposes:

1. secure to each individual the free exercise of conscience,[5]
2. secure to each individual the right and control of property, and
3. secure to each individual the protection of life.[6]

That declaration also holds that "*to the laws all men owe respect and deference, as without them peace and harmony would be supplanted by*

1. D&C 58:21-22.
2. D&C 98:4-8.
3. D&C 134:1.
4. Ibid.
5. Note that the Lord said this was his purpose in establishing the U.S. Constitution, "That every man may act in doctrine and principle pertaining to futurity, according to the moral agency which I have given unto him, that every man may be accountable for his own sins in the day of judgment. " (D&C 101:78. See verses 79-80.)
6. D&C 134:2.

anarchy and terror; . . ."[1] Such a period of anarchy, or internal conflict, is clearly indicated by many prophetic warnings concerning America's future.[2] It appears obvious that anarchy will be averted, in that future period, only to the degree that America's citizens maintain peace and stability through obedience to law and loyal allegiance to existing governments.

What can each individual do to support his country and render obedience to the laws of the land? The author listed the following suggestions in the program to a patriotic bicentennial pageant which he wrote and directed. They were presented under the title, "What Can *I* Do To Preserve My Freedoms?"

1. I'll study the Constitution and the basic documents of America with my family.
2. I'll fly the flag, and respect it as the symbol of our country.
3. I'll make national holidays a special time to teach my children their national heritage.
4. I'll pledge to keep myself and my family free from sin and the evils of the land.
5. I'll have respect for law and order, and for those who administer the law.
6. I'll know what my children are studying in school, and encourage school officials to promote patriotism and loyalty.
7. I'll work to keep our community and country clean and beautiful.
8. I'll do an honest day's work, and be honest and above reproach in all my dealings.
9. I'll study the scriptures and know the prophetic promises and warnings revealed concerning this great land.
10. I'll teach my children the value of work, and strengthen their qualities of self-reliance and personal initiative.
11. I'll support clubs and organizations which are working to build character and establish positive values.
12. I'll actively resist crime and corruption, and be alert to dangers such as vandalism, drugs, and pornography.
13. I'll strengthen my family relationships and make my family unit a solid building block of society.
14. I'll prepare for the possibility of difficult times ahead by having an emergency supply of food and clothing and being free from debt.

---

1. D&C 134:6.
2. 193-202, 209-223. Also, *Prophecy—Key to the Future*, pp. 40-66.

15. I'll speak out for what I believe, but be sure my statements are characterized by dignity, decency, maturity of thought, and knowledge of the facts.

16. I'll study and properly prepare myself for a vocation so I can be a productive member of the community.

17. I'll be aware of the rising strength of potential enemies to our freedom, and be alert to changes in the international balance of power.

18. I'll work to help good men be elected, and seek to have governmental officials accountable for their actions.

19. I'll read and learn what actually happens when people fall into bondage, so I can understand the freedoms we sometimes take for granted.

20. I'll know the political candidates who can shape my way of life, and support only those I feel will serve competently and righteously.

21. I'll support programs and policies which make government the servant of the people, rather than people the servants of government.

22. I'll study the effects of opposing ideologies on our peace and liberty so I can recognize these theories and those who teach them.

23. I'll list the principles and policies which I believe will help preserve our freedom, and then work to support them.

24. I'll subscribe to a patriotic publication and try to be well-informed on current events.

25. I'll study the major local, state, and national political issues, and know where I stand concerning them.

26. I'll be aware of our national defense capabilities, and work to keep my country prepared.

27. I'll obey the scriptural commandments to warn others of the judgments that are coming if the people of this nation allow wickedness to prevail.

28. I'll preach the gospel by word and by example, for I know that the righteousness of the people is the key to this nation's destiny.

29. I'll pray each day for our country and for its leaders, asking God to let His blessings and protection continue with us.[1]

---

1. Program, *This Is My Country,* presented by the Bountiful, Utah Stake, March 12 and 13, 1976, in the Bountiful Regional Center.

26. Elect good leaders: Uphold honest and wise men. In this era when the nation has plunged rapidly towards wickedness which may bring God's judgments, it is essential that the tide be stemmed, by choosing men of integrity for positions of governmental leadership. God has revealed that

> . . . *When the wicked rule the people mourn.*
>
> Wherefore, honest men and wise men should be sought for diligently, and good men and wise men ye should observe to uphold; otherwise whatsoever is less than these cometh of evil.[1]

The declaration of belief regarding governments and laws states that

> We believe that all governments necessarily require civil officers and magistrates to enforce the laws of the same; and that *such as will administer the law in equity and justice should be sought for and upheld* by the voice of the people if a republic, or the will of the sovereign.[2]

Latter-day Saints believe they should work within the governmental system to accomplish necessary ends. Criminals should be "delivered up and dealt with according to the laws of the land."[3] Those who have been wronged should "importune for redress, and redemption, by the hands of those who are placed as rulers and are in authority over you—according to the laws and constitution of the people, . . ."[4] The saints are to be tolerant of others, and even of imperfections in the actions of their elected leaders, remembering the Lord's counsel:

> . . . Verily I say unto you, and this is wisdom, make unto yourselves friends with the mammon of unrighteousness and they will not destroy you .
>
> *Leave judgment alone with me,* for it is mine and I will repay.[5]

27. Prepare for future persecutions: Learn how to deal with enemies. Another major message of prophecy is that the saints must endure severe persecution in a time yet future.[6] The Lord has seen fit to give very specific instructions concerning how the saints should deal with those who oppose them. His people should be aware of these instructions and be prepared to abide by them if the need arises. He had told them to

---

1. D&C 98:9-11 .
2. D&C 134:3.
3. D&C 42:79. See verses 84-86.
4. D&C 101:76-77. See verses 81-92.
5. D&C 82:22-23. See 58:20.
6. See pp. 71-95.

> . . . *Organize yourselves according to the laws of man; That your enemies may not have power over you;* that you may be preserved in all things; that you may be enabled to keep my laws; that every bond may be broken wherewith the enemy seeketh to destroy my people.[1]

Revealed counsel has been given to "Be patient in afflictions, *revile not against those that revile*. Govern your house in meekness, and be steadfast."[2] The Lord has also commanded, "Behold, it is said in my laws, or forbidden, to get in debt to thine enemies."

Zion's Camp was taught other principles to help them be safe from their enemies. The Lord instructed them to "Talk not of judgments, neither boast of faith nor of mighty works, but *carefully gather together,* as much in one region as can be, consistently with the feelings of the people; . . ."[3] They were also told to

> . . . Sue for peace, not only to the people that have smitten you, but also to all people:
>
> *And lift up an ensign of peace,* and make a proclamation of peace unto the ends of the earth;
>
> *And make proposals for peace unto those who have smitten you,* according to the voice of the Spirit which is in you, and all things shall work together for your good.[4]

While he was a prisoner in Liberty Jail, the prophet Joseph Smith set forth the duties of the saints in relation to their persecutors. He said it was their "imperative duty" to

1. Be sure all the saints were informed and given knowledge of the sufferings and abuses which had been endured.[5]
2. Be sure a record was kept of all damages sustained, both of character, personal injuries, and real property.[6]
3. Be sure a record was kept of the names of all persons involved in instances of oppression.[7]
4. Be sure to obtain evidence in the form of statements and affidavits.[8]
5. Be sure to gather copies of all libelous publications.[9]
6. Publish the above to all the world and present them to heads of government.[10]

---

1. D&C 44:4-5.
2. D&C 31:9.
3. D&C 105:24.
4. D&C 105:38-40.
5. D&C 123:1.
6. D&C 123:2.
7. D&C 123:3.
8. D&C 123:4.
9. D&C 123:4-5.
10. D&C 123:6.

All of the preceding is

> . . . Enjoined on us by our Heavenly Father, before we can fully and completely claim that promise which shall call him forth from his hiding place; and also that *the whole nation may be left without excuse before he can send forth the power of his mighty arm.*[1]

Doctrine and Covenants section 98 contains a comprehensive explanation of how to deal with enemies who persecute the saints. The Lord has said,

> Now, I speak unto you concerning your families—*if men will smite you, or your families, once,* and ye bear it patiently and revile not against them, neither seek revenge, ye shall be rewarded;
>
> But if ye bear it not patiently, it shall be accounted unto you as being meted out as a just measure unto you.
>
> And again, *if your enemy shall smite you the second time,* and you revile not against your enemy, and bear it patiently, your reward shall be an hundred-fold.
>
> And again, *if he shall smite you the third time,* and ye bear it patiently, your reward shall be doubled unto you four-fold;
>
> *And these three testimonies shall stand against your enemy if he repent not, and shall not be blotted out.*
>
> And now, verily I say unto you, if that enemy shall escape my vengeance, that he be not brought into judgment before me, then *ye shall see to it that ye warn him in my name, that he come no more upon you, neither upon your family,* even your children's children unto the third and fourth generation.
>
> And then, if he shall come upon you or your children, or your children's children unto the third and fourth generation, *I have delivered thine enemy into thine hands;*
>
> And then if thou wilt spare him, thou shalt be rewarded for thy righteousness; and also thy children and thy children's children unto the third and fourth generation.
>
> *Nevertheless, thine enemy is in thine hands;* and if thou rewardest him according to his works thou art justified; *if he has sought thy life, and thy life is endangered by him, thine enemy is in thine hands and thou art justified.*[2]

The declaration of belief regarding governments and laws states that

> *We believe that men should appeal to the civil law for redress of all wrongs and grievances,* where personal abuse is inflicted or the right of

1. *Ibid.* He added that "there is much which lieth in futurity, pertaining to the saints, which depends upon these things." (D&C 123:15.)
2. D&C 98:23-31.

> property or character infringed, where such laws exist as will protect the same; but we believe that *all men are justified in defending themselves, their friends, and property, and the government, from the unlawful assaults and encroachments of all persons in times of exigency,* where immediate appeal cannot be made to the laws, and relief afforded.[1]

Two passages from the Book of Mormon explain the motives under which it is appropriate to engage in combat with enemies. The first deals with the Nephites as they united to resist the Lamanites who were attacking under the leadership of their wicked chief captain, Zerahemnah:

> Nevertheless, the Nephites were inspired by a better cause, for *they were not fighting for monarchy nor power but they were fighting for their homes and their liberties, their wives and their children, and their all, yea, for their rites of worship and their church.*
>
> And they were doing that which they felt was the *duty which they owed to their God;* for the Lord had said unto them, and also unto their fathers, that: *Inasmuch as ye are not guilty of the first offense, neither the second, ye shall not suffer yourselves to be slain by the hands of your enemies.*
>
> And again, the Lord has said that: *Ye shall defend your families even unto bloodshed.* Therefore for this cause were the Nephites contending with the Lamanites, *to defend themselves, and their families, and their lands, their country, and their rights, and their religion* [2]

The second describes the motives of the Nephites as they united under the leadership of General Moroni:

> *Now the Nephites were taught to defend themselves against their enemies, even to the shedding of blood if it were necessary;* yea, and they were also taught *never to give an offense, yea, and never to raise the sword except it were against an enemy, except it were to preserve their lives.*
>
> *And this was their faith, that by so doing God would prosper them in the land,* or in other words, if they were faithful in keeping the commandments of God that *he would prosper them in the land; yea, warn them to flee, or to prepare for war, according to their danger;*
>
> And also, that *God would make it known unto them whither they should go to defend themselves against their enemies,* and by so doing, the Lord would deliver them; and this was the faith of Moroni, and his heart did glory in it; not in the shedding of blood but *in doing good, in preserving his people, yea, in keeping the commandments of God, yea, and resisting iniquity.*[3]

---

1. D&C 134:11
2. Al. 43:45-47
3. Al. 48:14-16.

If enemies attempt to drive the saints from the land of Zion,[1] the Lord has instructed his people that

> . . . *Ye shall curse them;*
> *And whomsoever ye curse, I will curse* and ye shall avenge me of mine enemies.
> And my presence shall be with you even in avenging me of mine enemies, unto the third and fourth generation of them that hate me.[2]

During all the events of the future, the saints should remember the Lord's decree that they will prevail against their enemies so long as they keep his commandments:

> Behold, *they shall,* for I have decreed it, *begin to prevail against mine enemies from this very hour.*
> And by hearkening to observe all the words which I, the Lord their God, shall speak unto them, *they shall never cease to prevail* until the kingdoms of the world are subdued under my feet, and the earth is given unto the saints, to possess it forever and ever.
> *But inasmuch as they keep not my commandments, and hearken not to observe all my words, the kingdoms of the world shall prevail against them.*[3]

In Conclusion

Thus ends this account of God's message concerning the events of the last days. It is scriptural. It is accurate in its interpretation. It is true. It is written in partial fulfillment of the inspired prayer of Joseph Smith, in which he asked the Savior to

> *Put upon thy servants the testimony of the covenant,* that when they go out and proclaim thy word they may *seal up the law, and prepare the hearts of thy saints for all those judgments thou art about to send,* in thy wrath, upon the earth, because of their transgressions, *that thy people may not faint in the day of trouble.*[4]

---

1. See D&C 64:41-43; 45:66-75.
2. D&C 103:24-26. See verses 2-3. This commandment differs from the Savior's instruction to "love your enemies" (see Mt. 5:38-45), but is in accordance with other passages of scripture: Al. 33:10; D&C 109:50-53; 133:40, 42-43. It conforms to the Lord's commandment that the saints should leave a witness against the wicked in the last days. (See pp. 273-276.)
3. D&C 103:6-8.
4. D&C 109:38.

It has not been an easy book to write. Neither has it been a pleasant one, for it speaks of tragic events which will bring much sorrow and suffering upon the land and people I love. But the Spirit gave repeated instruction that it come forth, and I have sought to obey. If it were in my power to turn away the prophesied calamities, I would do so, and save the nation from the impending judgments. I recognize that deliverance will only be granted to the Lord's people who live in righteousness, and I seek to be numbered among them. My sentiments were well expressed in the prayer of dedication offered by the prophet Joseph:

> *O Lord, we delight not in the destruction of our fellow man;* their souls are precious before thee;
>
> *But thy word must be fulfilled.* Help thy servants to say, with thy grace assisting them: Thy will be done, O Lord, and not ours.
>
> We know that thou hast spoken by the mouth of thy prophets *terrible things concerning the wicked, in the last days—that thou wilt pour out thy judgments, without measure;*
>
> Therefore, O Lord, *deliver thy people from the calamity of the wicked;* enable thy servants to seal up the law, and bind up the testimony, that they may be prepared against the day of burning.[1]

Ye saints, remember that "All victory and glory is brought to pass unto you through your diligence, faithfulness, and prayers of faith."[2] Put on the whole armor of God, "That ye may be able to withstand the evil day,"[3] and look forward to the day when the Church will arise and "Shine forth fair as the moon, clear as the sun, and terrible as an army with banners; and be adorned as a bride. . . ."[4] "Fear not to do good,"[5] and trust in the Lord as he brings about the establishment of his Zion and prepares the pure in heart. Find joy in the anticipation of his peaceable kingdom, and remember that he has instructed the saints to

> . . . Let your hearts be comforted concerning Zion; for all flesh is in mine hands; *be still and know that I am God.*[6]

Summary

1. This chapter has been written to assist those desiring to adopt an effective course for the future. It summarizes scriptural counsel for

1. D&C 109:43-46.
2. D&C 103:36.
3. D&C 27:15-18. See Eph. 6:10-17
4. D&C 109:73-74
5. D&C 6:33-34.
6. D&C 101:16.

proper attitudes and conduct, and attempts to point out a viable path that will safely lead through the perilous times to come.

2. It is wise to adopt attitudes concerning the last days which are based on eternal perspective. Attempting to envision the events to come from God's point of view can help man to properly orient his life. Eight observations were made:

A. God directs the affairs of man.
B. God desires to bless and reward man.
C. Last day's judgments are part of man's mortal probation.
D. God chastens those he loves.
E. Death is sweet to those who die in the Lord.
F. There must be a transition to Christ's millennial kingdom.
G. The earth is approaching the end of its temporal existence.
H. Look forward to the blessings of the millennial era.

3. Scriptural counsel was cited concerning spiritual preparations for survival. The saints have been instructed to

A. Cleanse themselves from sins which bring judgments: Repent.
B. Escape judgments through obedience: Keep God's commandments.
C. Be free from the sins of the generation: Sanctify themselves.
D. Prepare spiritually: Be guided by the Holy Ghost.
E. Recognize last day's events: Watch for signs of the times.
F. Teach doctrines of the last days: Seek knowledge for protection.
G. Prepare the saints for the hour of judgment: Warn their neighbor.
H. Preach repentance to non-members: Warn of coming judgments.
I. Bind the law and seal the testimony: Testify against the wicked.
J. Go ye out from Babylon: Be separate from the wicked.
K. Seek divine strength, guidance and protection: Pray always.
L. Prepare for return of the united order: Be ready to share.
M. Resolve to attain eternal goals: Endure to the end.

4. Temporal preparations for survival were also recommended, which included the following principles and instructions:

A. Anticipate physical needs: Store food, clothing, fuel.
B. Anticipate the reality of nuclear war: Strengthen civil defense.
C. Anticipate the danger of economic upheaval: Be free from debt.
D. Anticipate communication disruption: Make long-range emergency plans.

5. Scriptural counsel for interacting with others in the last days was presented, together with many suggestions for being an effective citizen. This counsel was summarized under the following categories:

A. Fulfill the responsibilities of citizenship: Obey the laws of the land.
B. Elect good leaders: Uphold honest and wise men.
C. Prepare for future persecution: Learn how to deal with enemies.

6. As the events of the last days unfold, the saints must be willing to say "Thy will be done, O Lord, and not ours," and then "be still and know" that God is governing the affairs of men.

List of Quotations

BOOK OF MORMON

I Nephi

1 Nephi (Cont.)

2 Nephi

2 Nephi (Cont.)

BIBLE

OLD TESTAMENT

Appendix
An Update on Russia

Since the earliest editions of *Inspired Prophetic Warnings* were published, major changes have occurred in the world's political scene, particularly concerning the dissolution of the Union of Soviet Socialist Republics and the emergence of the European Union. This appendix is written to bridge that time gap and provide insights concerning Russia as it exists at the time of this edition (2004).

Brief Histories of Russia During the Past Century

In its *Countries of the World* section on "Russia," the *Encyclopedia Britannica Almanac 2003* provided this summary:

> The Russian Revolution that overthrew the czarist regime in 1917 marked the beginning of a government of soviets ("councils"). The Bolsheviks brought the main part of the former empire under communist control and organized it as the Russian Soviet Federated Socialist Republic (RSFSR; coextensive with present-day Russia). The Russian SFSR joined other soviet republics in 1922 to form the USSR. Although it fought with the Allies in World War II, after the war tensions with the West led to the decades-long Cold War.
>
> Upon the dissolution of the USSR in 1991, the Russian SFSR was renamed and became the leading member of the Commonwealth of Independent States. It adopted a new constitution in 1993. During the 1990s, it struggled on several fronts, beset with economic difficulties, political corruption, and independence movements.
>
> Putin was elected president in 2000, with economic reform, governmental reorganization, cut-backs in the military, and rooting out corruption and favoritism as his chief goals. Putin targeted reforms in government structure and the judicial system in an effort to coordinate federal and local government and eliminate long-standing abuses. In 2001 the Duma passed legislation making it possible to buy land for the first time since the establishment of Soviet power.
>
> Although foreign debt, capital flight, and a balance of payments deficit were a drag on the economy, production improved significantly. Oil production boomed and a significant increase in the GDP led to a welcome budget surplus. A flat income tax of 13% was levied, aimed at wiping out inequities and increasing government income.
>
> After 11 Sep 2001, Putin offered the US help in combating terrorism. Both the US and Russia pledged to reduce the number of nuclear weapons over the ensuing decade. In May 2002 the landmark NATO-Russian Council established an alliance to work toward common security goals. Russia worked to improve foreign relations on many fronts—with surrounding countries, members of the former Soviet Union, China, the US, and West-

ern Europe. Critics still found reason for concern in the treatment of the media and in the unresolved conflict with the break-away Chechen Republic.[1]

The same source, in its *Rulers and Regimes of the Middle East* section, provided the following list of the "Chairmen (or First Secretaries) of the Communist Party of the Soviet Union" and "Presidents of Russia," under the heading "Rulers of Russia":

Ruler	***Reign***
Chairmen (or First Secretaries) of the Communist Party of the Soviet Union	
Vladimir Lenin	1917-24
Joseph Stalin	1924-53
Georgy Malenkov	1953
Nikita Khrushchev	1953-64
Leonid Brezhnev	1964-82
Yury Andropov	1982-84
Konstantin Chernenko	1984-85
Mikhail Gorbachev	1985-91
Presidents of Russia	
Boris Yeltsin	1990-99
Vladimir Putin[2]	2000-

A more detailed coverage of Russian history, beginning right after the end of World War II in 1945, is provided in the *Time Almanac 2004*. It details the events which led up to the 1991 collapse of the USSR and the resignation of Mikhail S. Gorbachev as general-secretary of the Communist Party on August 23, when he clashed with Boris Yeltsin (who had been elected to the newly created position of President of Russia on July 10, 1991):

> The USSR built a cordon of Communist states running from Poland in the north to Albania and Bulgaria in the south, including East Germany, Czechoslovakia, Hungary, and Romania, which composed the territories the Soviet troops occupied at the war's end. With its eastern front solidified, the Soviet Union launched a political offensive against the non-Communist West, moving first to block the Western access to Berlin. The Western powers countered with an airlift, completed unification of West Germany, and organized the defense of western Europe in the North

1. *Encyclopedia Britannica Almanac* 2003 (Chicago: Encyclopedia Britannica, Inc.), p. 614.
2. *Ibid.*, p. 705.

Atlantic Treaty Organization (NATO). Stalin died on March 6, 1953, and was succeeded the next day by G. M. Malenkov as premier.

The new power in the Kremlin was Nikita S. Khrushchev, first secretary of the party. Khrushchev formalized the eastern European system into a Council for Mutual Economic Assistance (Comecon) and a Warsaw Pact Treaty Organization as a counterweight to NATO. The Soviet Union exploded a hydrogen bomb in 1953, developed an intercontinental ballistic missile by 1957, sent the first satellite into space (Sputnik I) in 1957, and put Yuri Gagarin in the first orbital flight around Earth in 1961. Khrushchev's downfall stemmed from his decision to place Soviet nuclear missiles in Cuba and then, when challenged by the U.S., backing down and removing the weapons. He was also blamed for the ideological break with China after 1963. Khrushchev was forced into retirement on Oct. 15, 1964, and was replaced by Leonid I. Brezhnev as first secretary of the party and Aleksei N. Kosygin as premier.

U.S. president Jimmy Carter and Brezhnev signed the SALT II treaty in Vienna on June18, 1979, setting ceilings on each nation's arsenal of intercontinental ballistic missiles. The U.S. Senate refused to ratify the treaty because of the invasion of Afghanistan by Soviet troops on Dec. 27, 1979. On Nov. 10, 1982, Soviet radio and television announced the death of Leonid Brezhnev. Yuri V. Andropov, who had formerly headed the KGB, became his successor, but died less than two years later, in Feb. 1984. Konstantin U. Chernenko, a 72-year-old party stalwart who had been close to Brezhnev, succeeded him.

In the months following Chernenko's assumption of power, the Kremlin took on a hostile attitude toward the West of a kind rarely seen since the height of the cold war 30 years before. Led by Moscow, all the Soviet bloc countries except Romania boycotted the 1984 Summer Olympic Games in Los Angeles—tit-for-tat for the U.S.-led boycott of the 1980 Moscow Games, in the view of most observers. After 13 months in office, Chernenko died on March 10, 1985. He had been ill much of the time and left only a minor imprint on Soviet history. Chosen to succeed him as Soviet leader was Mikhail S. Gorbachev, who led the Soviet Union in its long-awaited shift to a new generation of leadership. Unlike his immediate predecessors, Gorbachev did not also assume the title of president but wielded power from the post of party general secretary.

The Soviet Union took much criticism in early 1986 over the April 24 meltdown at the Chernobyl nuclear plant and its reluctance to give out any information on the accident.

In June 1987, Gorbachev obtained the support of the Central Committee for proposals that would loosen some government controls over the economy and in June 1988, an unusually open party conference approved several resolutions reforming the Soviet system. These included a shift of some power from the party to local soviets, and a ten-year limit on the terms of elected government and party officials. Gorbachev was elected president in 1989. The elections to the Duma were the first competitive elections in the Soviet Union since 1917. Dissident candidates won a surprisingly large minority although pro-government deputies maintained a strong lock on the Supreme Soviet.

Dissolution of the USSR

The possible beginning of the fragmentation of the Communist Party took place when Boris Yeltsin, leader of the Russian SSR who urged faster reform, left the Communist Party along with other radicals. In March 1991, the Soviet people were asked to vote in a referendum on national unity engineered by Gorbachev. The resultant victory for the federal government was tempered by the separate approval in Russia for the creation of a popularly elected presidency of the Russian republics. The bitter election contest for the Russian presidency, principally between Yeltsin and a Communist loyalist, resulted in a major victory for Yeltsin. He took the oath of office for the new position on July 10, 1991.

Reversing his relative hard-line position, Gorbachev together with leaders of nine Soviet republics signed an accord called the Union Treaty, which was meant to preserve the unity of the nation. In exchange the federal government would have turned over control of industrial and natural resources to the individual republics. An attempted coup d'Ètat took place on Aug. 19, 1991, orchestrated by a group of eight senior officials calling itself the State Committee on the State of Emergency. Boris Yeltsin, barricaded in the Russian Parliament building, defiantly called for a general strike. The next day huge crowds demonstrated in Leningrad, and Yeltsin supporters fortified barricades surrounding the Parliament building. On August 21 the coup committee disbanded, and at least some of its members attempted to flee Moscow. The Soviet Parliament formally reinstated Gorbachev as President. Two days later he resigned from his position as general-secretary of the Communist Party and recommended that its Central Committee be disbanded. On August 29 the Parliament approved the suspension of all Communist Party activities pending an investigation of its role in the failed coup.[3]

The events which followed, under the presidential leadership of Boris Yeltsin and his successor, Vladimir Putin, are also summarized in the *Time Almanac* historical explanation:

At the time of the attempted coup, the republic's president, Boris Yeltsin, was the most popular political figure in the former Soviet Union. A leading reformer, he became the first directly elected leader in Russian history and received 60% of the vote for president of the Russian Republic. Yeltsin championed the cause for national reconstruction and the adoption of a Union Treaty with the other republics to create a free-market economic association. On Dec. 12, 1991, the Russian Parliament ratified Yeltsin's plea to establish a new commonwealth of independent nations open to all former members of the Soviet Union. The new union was created with the governments of Ukraine and Belarus who along with Russia were the three original cofounders of the Soviet Union in 1922. After the end of the Soviet Union, Russia and ten other Soviet republics joined in a Commonwealth of Independent States on Dec. 21, 1991.

---

3. *Time Almanac 2004* (Des Moines, Iowa: Time Almanac, 2003), pp. 852-53.

At the start of 1992, Russia embarked on a series of dramatic economic reforms, including the freeing of prices on most goods, which led to an immediate downturn. A national referendum on confidence in Yeltsin and his economic program took place in April 1993. To the surprise of many, the president and his shock-therapy program won by a resounding margin. In September, Yeltsin dissolved the legislative bodies left over from the Soviet era. The impasse between the executive and the legislature resulted in an armed conflict on Oct. 3. Yeltsin prevailed largely through the support of the military and other forces.

The southern republic of Chechnya's president accelerated his region's drive for independence in 1994. In December, Russian troops closed the borders and sought to squelch the independence drive. The Russian military forces met firm and costly resistance. In May 1997, the two-year war formally ended with the signing of a peace treaty that adroitly avoided the issue of Chechen independence.

In March 1998 Yeltsin dismissed his entire government and replaced Prime Minister Viktor Chernomyrdin with the young and little known fuel and energy minister Sergei Kiriyenko. On Aug. 28, 1998, amid the Russian stock market's free fall, the Russian government halted trading of the ruble on international currency markets. This financial crisis led to a long-term economic downturn and to political upheaval. President Boris Yeltsin then sacked Prime Minister Kiriyenko and reappointed Chernomyrdin. The Duma rejected Chernomyrdin and on Sept. 11 elected foreign minister Yevgeny Primakov as prime minister. The repercussions of Russia's financial emergency were felt throughout the Commonwealth of Independent States.

Impatient with Yeltsin's chronic illnesses and increasingly erratic behavior, the Duma attempted to impeach him in May 1999 on five charges: provoking the 1991 fall of the Soviet Union, using force to dissolve the Parliament in 1993, starting the ill-conceived 1994–1996 war in Chechnya, ruining the nation's military, and impoverishing the Russian people through ruinous economic policies—the charge regarding Chechnya was considered the only one with a chance of approval. But the impeachment motion was quickly quashed and soon Yeltsin was on the ascendancy again. In keeping with his capricious style, Yeltsin dismissed Prime Minister Yevgeny Primakov and replaced him with Interior Minister Sergei Stepashin. Just three months later, however, Yeltsin ousted Stepashin and replaced him with Vladimir Putin on Aug. 9, 1999, announcing that in addition to serving as prime minister, the former KGB agent was his choice as a successor in the 2000 presidential election.

In a decision that took Russia and the world by surprise, Boris Yeltsin resigned on Dec. 31, 1999, and Vladimir Putin became the acting president. One of Putin's first acts was to grant Yeltsin immunity from prosecution (Yeltsin and family members had been accused of corruption and financial misconduct). On March 26, 2000, Putin won the presidential election with about 53% of the vote. Since then Putin has moved to centralize power in Moscow and has attempted to limit the power and influence of both the regional governors and wealthy business leaders. Although Russia remains economically stagnant, Putin has brought his nation a measure of political stability it never had under the mercurial and erratic Yeltsin.

Just three years after the bloody 1994–1996 Chechen-Russian war ended in devastation and stalemate, the fighting started again in 1999, with Russia launching air strikes and following up with ground troops. By the end of November, Russian troops had surrounded Chechnya's capital, Grozny, and about 215,000 Chechen refugees had fled to neighboring Ingushetia. Russia maintained that a political solution was impossible until Islamic militants in Chechnya had been vanquished. In Feb. 2000, after almost five months of fighting, Russian troops captured Grozny, the Chechen capital. The control of Grozny was a political as well as a military victory for Putin, whose hard-line stance against Chechnya has greatly contributed to his political popularity. Despite repeated Russian claims of victory, the war continued to drag on in 2002.

In 1999, the former Russian satellites of Poland, Hungary, and the Czech Republic joined NATO, raising Russia's hackles. The desire of Lithuania, Latvia, and Estonia, all of which were once part of the Soviet Union, to join the organization in the future has further alarmed Russia.

In Aug. 2000 the Russian government was severely criticized for its handling of the *Kursk* disaster, a nuclear submarine accident that left 118 sailors dead.

Russia was initially alarmed in 2001 when the U.S. announced its rejection of the Anti-Ballistic Missile Treaty of 1972, which for 30 years had been viewed as a crucial force in keeping the nuclear arms race at bay. But Putin was eventually placated by Bush's reassurances, and in May 2002, the U.S. and Russian leaders announced a landmark pact to cut both countries' nuclear arsenals by up to two-thirds over the next ten years.

On Oct. 23, Chechen rebels seized a crowded Moscow theater and detained 763 people, including 3 Americans. Armed and wired with explosives, the rebels demanded that Russian government end the war in Chechnya. Government forces stormed the theater the next day, after releasing a gas into the theater, which killed not only all the rebels but more than 100 hostages.

During the fall 2002–winter 2003 diplomatic wrangling at the United Nations over Iraq, Russia sided with the majority of western European nations in calling for more weapons inspections and diplomacy before resorting to war. Russia's UN ambassador stated: "We see no reason whatsoever to interrupt the inspections and any resolution which contains ultimatums and which contains automaticity for the use of force is not acceptable to us."

In March Chechens voted in a referendum that approved a new regional constitution making Chechnya a separatist republic within Russia. Agreeing to the constitution meant abandoning claims for complete independence. While Moscow has presented the referendum as a way of bringing peace to the war-ravaged region, it is unclear how much power Russia would actually grant the separatist republic. A spate of Chechen suicide bombings followed throughout the year.

In April 2003 reformist politician Sergei Yushenkov became the third outspoken critic of the Kremlin to be assassinated in the last five years. Just hours before he was gunned down, Yushenkov had officially registered his new political party, Liberal Russia.[4]

4. *Ibid.*, pp. 853-54.

On May 1, 2004, ten former communist-occupied countries isolated during the Cold War were admitted to the European union. They are: the Czech Republic, Estonia, Hungary, Latvia, Lithuania, Poland, Slovakia and Slovenia, along with the islands of Cyprus and Malta. Including this group of countries in its membership increased the European Union to 25 countries with a combined population of 450 million citizens.

LDS Missionary Work in Russia

Several prophecies from years past have indicated that missionary work would eventually be carried out in Russia. For instance, Orson Pratt said,

> Even in Russia, that place where they would almost put you to death if you brought a printed work of religious nature into the empire,—in that country, where they will not suffer you to propagate the Bible unmolested, whose religion is established by law, *has the Gospel of Jesus Christ to be preached. Yes, the Church of the Saints is to be established there;* and after it is established, there they are to gather together in multitudes, like other nations, to fight against it.[5]

President David O. McKay, speaking at a devotional assembly at Brigham Young University in May, 1960, taught that the gospel would be preached in Russia. He said:

> Russia enveloped with communism—a new religious freedom must come. God will overrule it, for *that people must hear the truth, and truth in simplicity. Truly there is much for the Church to do in the coming century.*[6]

Elder Melvin J. Ballard, in a conference address in April, 1930, had said:

> I am sure also that God is moving in Russia. Much as we are disturbed over the tyranny and the oppression that is waged against religion in that land today, it is not a new thing, for that has been the order for ages. But I can see God moving also in preparing the way for other events that are to come. The field that has gone to wild oats needs to be plowed up and harrowed and prepared for a new seed. So in Russia. It may seem appalling to us, but it is God breaking up and destroying an older order of things, and *the process will be the accomplishment of God's purposes within a very short period of time, which normally may have taken generations. But*

---

5. JD, 7:185-86. See *Prophecy—Key to the Future,* p. 14, and *Inspired Prophetic Warnings,* pp. 189-90.
6. *Church News,* May 28, 1960. See *Prophecy—Key to the Future,* p. 12.

that people will come back, for I bear witness that there are thousands of the blood of Israel in that land, and God is preparing the way for them.[7]

As the heavy Communist grip on the entire USSR and surrounding nations began to loosen in the late 1980s, and the Iron Curtain began to disintegrate, the Lord and his Church were preparing to carry the missionary message into Russia. One by one, the boundaries of existing missions were extended and new missions were opened. The *Deseret News 2003 Church Almanac*[8] records the number of Church members in the various countries which previously had been under heavy Russian and Communist influences, as of the end of 2001:

Country	Members	Country	Members
Albania	1,001	Latvia	544
Armenia	850	Lithuania	640
Belarus (formerly White Russia)	394	Mongolia	3,521
Bulgaria	1,765	Poland	1,255
Croatia	345	Romania	1,985
Czech Republic	1,732	Russia	15,128
Estonia	621	Serbia & Montenegro	203
Georgia	100	Slovakia	105
Hungary	3,605	Slovenia	250
Kazakhstan	5,508	Ukraine	7,990
		Total	**47,362**

Though it is still in its beginning stages, it is obvious that missionary work in the former USSR, and in other countries which were under Russian influence until the fall of the Iron Curtain, is well underway and further Church growth is to be expected there.

Russia Still a Major Military Power and Potential Threat to the Americas

As this edition of *Inspired Prophetic Warnings* goes to press, the United States has just completed one year in its occupation of Iraq. The following chart[9] reflects the continuing status of Russia's military might as being the fifth strongest in the world, as of 2002:

7. CR, April, 1930, p. 157. See *Prophecy—Key to the Future,* p. 14.
8. *Deseret News 2003 Church Almanac: The Church of Jesus Christ of Latter-day Saints* (Salt Lake City: The Deseret News, 2002), pp. 274-426.
9. *Encyclopedia Britannica Almanac 2003,* pp. 736-37.

Nations with Largest Armed Forces

Countries with a military strength of at least 200,000 active personnel. Personnel numbers are in thousands ('000). Dollars refer to US currency. Source: The Military Balance, 2001-02, *The International Institute of Strategic Studies*

Rank	Country	Military Personnel* Active	Military Personnel* Reserves	Defense Spending ($ Billions)	Army Main Battle Tanks	Navy Major Warships/ Carriers	Navy Sub-Marines	Air Force Strategic Combat Aircraft	Nuclear Weapons
1.	China	2,310.0	>500	42.0	8,000	62/0	69	2,900	yes
2.	**US**	**1,367.7**	**1,200.6**	**291.2**	**7,620**	**116/12**	**73**	**4,147**	**yes**
3.	India	1,263.0	535.0	14.7	3,414	26/1	16	738	
4.	N. Korea	1,082.0	4,700.0	2.1	3,500	3/0	26	621	
5.	**Russia**	**977.1**	**2,400.0**	**60.0**	**21,820**	**34/1**	**56**	**4,380**	**yes**
6.	S. Korea	683.0	4,500.0	12.8	2,330	39/0	19	555	
7.	Pakistan	620.0	513.0	3.7	>2,300	8/0	10	353	
8.	Turkey	515.1	378.7	10.8	4,205	23/0	13	505	
9.	Iran	513.0	350.0	7.5	1,565	3/0	6	283	
10.	Vietnam	484.0	>3,000	1.0	1,315	6/0	2	189	
11.	Myanmar	444.0	0.0	2.1	100	0/0	0	113	
12.	Egypt	443.0	254.0	2.9	3,860	11/0	4	580	
13.	Iraq	424.0	650.0	1.4	2,200	0/0	0	316	
14.	Taiwan	370.0	1,658.0	17.6	>926	32/0	4	482	
15.	Syria	321.0	354.0	0.8	4,700	2/0	0	589	
16.	Germany	308.4	363.5	28.8	2,521	14/0	14	434	
17.	Thailand	306.0	200.0	2.5	333	12/1	0	153	
18.	Ukraine	303.8	1,000.0	1.1	3,937	3/0	1	543	
19.	Indonesia	297.0	400.0	1.5	0	17/0	2	108	
20.	Brazil	287.6	1,115.0	17.9	178	18/1	4	281	
21.	France	273.7	419.0	35.0	809	34/1	10	473	yes
22.	Ethiopia	252.5	0.0	0.5	>300	0/0	0	51	
23.	Japan	239.8	47.7	45.6	1,050	54/0	16	297	
24.	Italy	230.4	65.2	21.0	1,349	21/1	7	329	
25.	UK	211.4	247.1	34.6	636	31/3	16	427	yes
26.	Poland	206.0	406.0	3.3	1,677	3/0	3	212	

As can be seen from the above chart, Russia's army is still in formidable force, and capable of waging both local and international wars. They continue to produce advanced weaponry and to publicize their military and armament accomplishments. The four news releases cited below are typical of their current efforts, activities and accomplishments.

Russia deploys fresh batch of strategic nuclear missiles

MOSCOW—Russia has deployed a fresh batch of its top-of-the-line strategic nuclear missiles after a break caused by a funding shortage, and military officials presented ambitious plans Monday for building weapons even more potent.

Russian Defense Minister Sergei Ivanov inaugurated the new set of Topol-M missiles at the Tatishchevo missile base in the central Saratov region Sunday, describing them as a "21st-century weapon" unrivaled in the world.

"This is the most advanced state-of-the-art missile in the world," Defense Minister Sergei Ivanov said in remarks broadcast by Russian television stations Monday. "Only such weapons can ensure and guarantee our sovereignty and security and make any attempts to put military pressure on Russia absolutely senseless."

Ivanov on Monday reported the deployment to President Vladimir Putin, saying the military will continue modernizing all components of the nation's nuclear forces.

The Interfax-Military News Agency said six Topol-Ms were deployed Sunday.

The first 10 such missiles entered duty in December 1998 and two more sets followed in the next two years. The military had planned to continue the deployment in regular annual installments, but got the fourth batch of Topol-Ms out only Sunday.

The Topol-M missiles, capable of hitting targets more than 6,000 miles away, have so far been deployed in silos. Its mobile version, mounted on a heavy off-road vehicle, is set to become operational next year, the Strategic Missile Forces chief, Col.-Gen. Nikolai Solovtsov, said in televised remarks.

The daily Izvestia said that the Topol-M lifts off faster than its predecessors and maneuvers in a way that makes it more difficult to spot and intercept. It is also capable of blasting off even after a nuclear explosion close to its silo, the newspaper reported.

The deployed Topol-Ms have been fitted with single nuclear warheads, but there are plans to equip each missile with three individually targeted warheads, Izvestia said. The missile's mobile version will carry from four to six warheads, the Interfax-Military News Agency quoted an unidentified General Staff officer as saying . . .

Putin said in October that Russia had several dozen Soviet-built SS-19 missiles that remained factory-fresh because they were stockpiled without fuel. The General Staff officer who spoke to Interfax said these missiles would enter service beginning in 2010 and remain on duty through 2030.

Next year, design work will start on a next-generation heavy nuclear missile, which will enter service after 2009, the officer said. The new missile will be capable of carrying 10 nuclear warheads with a total weight of up to 4.4 tons, compared to Topol-M's combat payload of 1.32 tons, he added.

Russia's strategic aviation chief, Lt.-Gen. Igor Khvorov, said Monday that the air force was drawing up requirements for a new strategic bomber that could become operational in 2014-2016, the Interfax-Military News Agency said.[10]

Russia boasts anti-Star Wars weapon Thursday

MOSCOW—Russia has successfully tested a hypersonic anti-Star Wars weapon capable of penetrating any prospective missile shield, a senior general said Thursday.

The prototype weapon proved it could maneuver so quickly as to make "any missile defense useless," Col.-Gen. Yuri Baluyevsky, the first deputy chief of the General Staff of the Russian armed forces, told a news conference.

He said that the prototype of a new hypersonic vehicle had proved its ability to maneuver while in orbit, thereby making it able to to dodge an enemy's missile shield.

---

10. Associated Press, *Deseret Morning News,* Monday, December 22, 2003.

"The flying vehicle changed both the altitude and direction of its flight," Baluyevsky said. "During the experiment conducted yesterday, we proved that it's possible to develop weapons that would make any missile defense useless."

Baluyevsky's comment followed a statement by President Vladimir Putin, who said Wednesday after attending rocket launches from the Plesetsk launch pad in northern Russia that experiments conducted during the military maneuvers had proven that Russia could build new strategic weapons that would be unrivaled in the world . . .

As part of the massive military maneuvers described as the largest in more than two decades, the military launched a Molniya-M booster rocket with a Kosmos military satellite from the northern Plesetsk launch pad and two ballistic missiles—a Topol from Plesetsk and an RS-18 from the Baikonur cosmodrome in Kazakhstan.[11]

Russia plans major N-maneuvers

MOSCOW—Russia's nuclear forces reportedly are preparing their largest maneuvers in two decades, an exercise involving the test-firing of missiles and flights by dozens of bombers in a massive simulation of an all-out nuclear war.

President Vladimir Putin is expected to personally oversee the maneuvers, which are apparently aimed at demonstrating the revival of the nation's military might and come ahead of Russian elections in March.

The business newspaper Kommersant said the exercise was set for mid-February and would closely resemble a 1982 Soviet exercise dubbed the "seven hour nuclear war" that put the West on edge.

Official comments on the upcoming exercise have been sketchy. The chief of Russia's Strategic Missile Forces, Col.-Gen. Nikolai Solovtsov, was quoted by the Interfax-Military News Agency as saying the planned maneuvers would involve several launches of intercontinental ballistic missiles in various regions of Russia, but he wouldn't give further details . . .

Kommersant said the maneuvers would involve Tu-160 strategic bombers test-firing cruise missiles over the northern Atlantic. Analysts describe such an exercise as an imitation of a nuclear attack on the United States.

Other groups of bombers will fly over Russia's Arctic regions and test-fire missiles at a southern range near the Caspian Sea, the newspaper said.

As part of the exercise, the military is planning to conduct several launches of intercontinental ballistic missiles, including one from a Russian nuclear submarine in the Barents Sea, the Kommersant report said.

The military also plans to launch military satellites from the Baikonur cosmodrome in Kazakhstan and the Plesetsk launch pad in northern Russia—a simulation of the replacement of satellites lost in action, Kommersant said.

Russia's system warning of any enemy missile attack and a missile defense system protecting Moscow will also be involved in the exercise, it added.

---

11. Associated Press, *Deseret Morning News*, Thursday, February 19, 2004.

Pavel Felgenhauer, an independent military analyst, said the military has regularly held nuclear exercises that were timed to coincide with the annual test-firing of aging Soviet-built missiles.

"It has been a routine affair, but it can be expanded if they want a show," he said.

Ivan Safranchuk, head of the Moscow office of the Center for Defense Information, a Washington-based think-tank, said the maneuvers would further strengthen Putin's popularity ahead of the March 14 presidential election he is expected to win easily.

Putin has repeatedly pledged to rebuild Russia's military might and restore pride to the demoralized service . . .

Putin's support for the United States following the Sept. 11, 2001 terror attacks bolstered relations with Washington and helped broker a new U.S.-Russian nuclear arms reduction deal and a Russia-NATO partnership agreement in 2002.

But the U.S.-Russian honeymoon has soured lately over Moscow's criticism of the war in Iraq, U.S. concerns about authoritarian trends in the Kremlin's domestic policy, and Russia's perceived attempts to assert its authority over ex-Soviet neighbors.[12]

At the present time, the danger of nuclear war between Russia and the USA is still regarded as an ever-present threat, and is still a matter for public outcry and on going concern. Typical of this concern is the following warning by an outspoken anti-war activist:

Caldicott says nukes still pose a global threat

Anti-nuclear activist Helen Caldicott warns of a continuing global threat posed by U.S. and Russian nuclear stockpiles.

Caldicott said Saturday at Portland, Maine, in a speech sponsored by peace groups that the former Cold War rivals still have thousands of nuclear weapons aimed at each other and a single mistake could result in mutual annihilation.

"Anything that happens in the world that triggers anxiety could blow us all off the face of the Earth," Caldicott said. "No one knows about it now. In the '80s, people were scared out of their brains."

The 65-year-old Australian activist and author spoke mainly about problems of command and control, especially inside Russia's aging nuclear program.

She said problems with nuclear weapons programs could lead to a mistaken belief that the country is under attack, prompting a decision to launch a retaliatory strike.[13]

Russia is still a country in a state of flux. There is a continuing power struggle between old-line communists and those who are trying to democratize the country. When private ownership of property and

12. Isachenkov, Vladimir. Associated Press, *Deseret Morning News*, Saturday, January 31, 2004.
13. *Deseret Morning News*, Monday, April 26, 2004.

businesses was introduced, major holdings flowed into the balance sheets of the privileged few, leaving the national economy in serious jeopardy. As one author recently observed,

> Russia has its own set of uncertainties.
>
> In a recent article in the Washington Times, the ambiguities surrounding the new Russia were addressed by Ariel Cohen, a research fellow at the Heritage Foundation.
>
> "Russia has not rid itself of its communist heritage . . .
>
> "Russia seeks security, prestige and prosperity. It is still trying to decide what it wants to be—an empire, a republic or a Slavic Union.
>
> "One thing is certain: It cannot be all of these things. And other post-Soviet Countries cannot become prosperous democracies if they insist on being authoritarian."
>
> Russia's struggles are taking place within an economy that is close to being in chaos. . . . there is precious little room for wasteful expenditures—and not room for strategic blunder.[14]

The article goes on to state:

> **Russia Still a Threat, Says Defense Intelligence Agency**
>
> The Pentagon's official line portrays America's Cold War enemy as just another friendly nation. However, its own intelligence agency says Russia remains a nuclear threat.
>
> President Bush's administration is endeavoring to sell Russian leaders, European allies, members of Congress and the American people on replacing the half-century-old strategy of mutual assured destruction with an anti-missile defensive shield.
>
> Top administration officials from the president to Vice President Dick Cheney to Secretary of State Colin Powell to Defense Secretary Donald Rumsfeld to National Security Adviser Condoleezza Rice are characterizing Russia not as a foe to be feared but as a peaceful partner to be welcomed.
>
> While that is taking place in the spotlight of the world state, back at home the Pentagon's Defense Intelligence Agency is looking down the road 20 years and seeing something considerably different—and menacing.
>
> **Russia's Crumbling Conventional Forces**
>
> What has furrowed the brows of DIA intelligence experts is a good-news, bad-news combination.
>
> The good news, from the Pentagon perspective, is that Russia's conventional weapons—heavy artillery, tanks and highly mobile assault troops that under the old Soviet Union threatened to overrun all of Western Europe—are fast becoming relics of the past.

14. Perry John L., "Russia Still a Threat, Says Defense Intelligence Agency, *NewsMax.com*. Saturday, August 25, 2001.

That outdated land-warfare equipment, and accompanying air support, are deteriorating in a hurry. Remnants of the once-vaunted Red Army are now underpaid, wretchedly housed and deeply demoralized.

The bad news is—because of that same good news, from where the Pentagon sits—Russia is clinging doggedly to, and betting its long-term military strategy upon, its still-enormous arsenal of nuclear-tipped intercontinental ballistic missiles.

There is only one conceivable target for those thousands of holocaust weapons of mass destruction—the cities of America.

The Old Doomsday Horror

One of the nightmares of U.S. strategists is the possibility that one or more embittered, frustrated, leftover militarists from the Soviet era will manage to launch a flight of ICBMs at the United States.

That was at the core of concerns expressed by a designated long-range worrier at the DIA during the fourth annual Space and Missile Defense conference conducted at Huntsville, Ala., on Aug. 21.

Looking ahead to the major strategic threats facing the United States over the coming two decades was Ken Knight, deputy for global projections at the DIA.

As reported by the authoritative *DefenseNews.com,* which tracks developments in the military scene worldwide, Knight gave this overview of existing and emerging serious threats:

An Unrelenting Missile Menace

• Although it is not easy to predict with pinpoint certainty how those threats will be expressed, there is no question that the strategic nuclear threat once posed by the Soviet Union still endures, and will on into the future.

• Nor is the threat confined to the aging ICBMs that can be retargeted on a moment's notice at U.S. cities.

• Cruise missiles designed to blast ships at sea now compose more than one-fifth of all the nations' combined inventories of cruise missiles.

• Within 19 years, there will be an entirely different orientation, with nearly half of the world inventory of cruise missiles being designed to strike targets on land.

Newer Threats Emerging

• By no means will all the threats be in the form of missiles. The United States is in serious danger of strategic threats to its banking system, financial structure and electric power grids.

• Does the American military have any clear-cut counter-strategies for dealing with those newer threats? None at this time.

Not only is the United States without specific defenses for those vulnerabilities, but, what could be even worse, "The role of the U.S. military in deterring such threats is in flux," Knight said.[15]

Other major problems face Russia, including a major Aids epidemic:

---

15. *Ibid.*

Ex-Soviet bloc faces Aids on African scale

The Aids epidemic in the former Soviet Union, which is growing faster than anywhere else in the world, threatens the same sort of devastation as in sub-Saharan Africa and could soon menace the rest of Europe, the International Aids conference in Barcelona heard yesterday.

Many of those facing the tragedy of soaring HIV infection in eastern Europe accuse the west of having abandoned them once communism crumbled, said Kasia Malinowska-Sempruch, director of International Harm Reduction Development, which is part of the Open Society Institute chaired by George Soros.

"As a native of Poland, not only am I terrified at the prospect of the rapidly growing HIV epidemic, but I'm frustrated and angry as well," she said in one of the conference's keynote speeches yesterday. "The world celebrated with us when the Berlin Wall fell, and then left us alone to deal with the consequences.

"We are richer in terms of human rights and some essential personal freedoms, but we are poorer in many other ways."

HIV infections have been doubling every year for the past three years in the former eastern bloc. Infections occur mainly in drug users, but will spread through the population by transmission to their partners. Out of 4 million drug users, a million are infected.

The situation is particularly bad in the Ukraine where close to 1% of the 48 million population is estimated to have HIV.

"Economic despair, social dislocation and easy access to heroin and other opiates have all contributed to an explosion of drug use," said Dr. Malinowska-Sempruch. Trafficking from Afghanistan has meant a ready supply of drugs.

"If the world is unable or unwilling to turn its attention to this region and offer help in dealing with this looming disaster, the consequences will be horrific," she added.

But a 27-country survey by the Lithuanian branch of her network, spanning central Europe to the former Soviet Union, has found that less than 1% of those infected are getting the three-drug cocktail recommended by the World Health Organization.

"High prices of medication and low levels of public commitment are fueling our HIV crisis. We have already overtaken North America in numbers of people with HIV. If we do not act soon, we may become another Africa," said Emilis Subata, the Lithuania coordinator.

"All the social and human factors are in place for a major, major epidemic," said Dr. Malinowska-Sempruch. "We have seen how HIV spreads from one country to another very, very quickly. Poland has kept it in check but now that Ukraine has such high levels of infection I'm sure they are going to start noticing that in the border areas there are more infections."

---

16. Boseley, Sarah, "Ex-Soviet bloc faces Aids on African scale," *The Guardian*, Wednesday, July 10, 2002.

Drug users are too afraid to seek help, because they fear being sent to jail, she said.

"By favouring confinement over treatment in Eastern Europe and former Soviet Union, authorities are condemning drug users to overcrowded prisons where needles are shared and HIV rates are surging at an even faster rate than among the population at large."[16]

A Danger of Future Russian Alliances

In the tumultuous years which lie ahead, Latter-day Saints must remember the prophecy made by the Prophet Joseph Smith on June 19, 1844, just eight days before his martyrdom. As he looked down through time, the Prophet said that "*The United States will spend her strength and means worrying in foreign lands until other nations will say, "'Let's divide up the lands of the United States, . . .*'" and he warned of a terrible struggle which this nation must yet face.[17] This prophecy warns of nations who will combine their military forces against the United States in a time when America will be perceived as being in a seriously weakened state.

We can't ignore the prophecies warning of a future conflict involving Russia, but at this point, attempts to forecast any future military alliances Russia might embrace is speculative, at best.

Several possible future Russian alliances spring to mind when one examines the Armed Forces chart on p. 319: an anti-U.S. alliance with (1) China, (2) India, (3) North Korea or South Korea, or both, and/or (4) an alliance with forces from nations with strong Moslem ties (a glance at the chart suggests countries such as Pakistan, Turkey, Iran, Iraq and Syria). This latter type of alliance seems to best conform with the prophecy by Sols Guardisto which says, "I saw next international war again break out with its centre upon the Pacific Ocean, but sweeping and encircling the whole globe. I saw that the opposing forces were roughly divided by so-called Christianity on the one side, and *by the so-called followers of Mohammed and Budda upon the other.*"[18]

Watch for some sort of alliance which is not yet visible but which may be formed in the years which lie ahead. Remember, on a personal level: "If ye are prepared, ye shall not fear."[19]

---

17. Prophecy recorded by Mosiah Lyman Hancock. See *Prophecy—Key to the Future,* pp. 10-11, and *Inspired Prophetic Warnings,* pp. 186-91.
18. See p. 199.
19. D&C 38:30.

Index

D

E

F

G

H

I

J

K

L

M

N

O

P

R

About the Author

Duane S. Crowther is well known and highly qualified as an author, theologian, teacher, and lecturer. He graduated with high honors from Brigham Young University with a BA in music education. He also holds a master's degree from Brigham Young University in Old and New Testament, an MBA from the University of Phoenix, and he has completed course work for a PhD in music education at the University of Utah.

A creative and prolific author, Mr. Crowther has written more than fifty books, including such well-known favorites as *Prophecy—Key to the Future*, *Life Everlasting*, *The Prophecies of Joseph Smith*, *Inspired Prophetic Warnings*, *Gifts of the Spirit*, *Prophets and Prophecies of the Old Testament*, *The Godhead*, *Jesus of Nazareth: Savior and King*, *How to Understand the Book of Mormon*, *How to Write Your Personal History*, *Key Choral Concepts*, and *You Can Read Music*. He is the author and narrator of more than three dozen cassette talk tapes, in addition to numerous magazine articles and music compositions.

In his professional life, he has served as a Latter-day Saint seminary instructor and principal; taught university classes for Brigham Young University, the University of Utah, and the University of Phoenix; and still teaches music, Old and New Testament history, and writing skills classes in public school adult education programs. He was president and senior editor of Horizon Publishers and Distributors, Inc., in Bountiful, Utah.

Mr. Crowther has written and produced national award-winning patriotic pageants. He has lectured at numerous business and writer's seminars, BYU Education Week, youth conferences, and other Church gatherings. He has hosted and escorted tours to Israel, Mexico, Central America, Hawaii, and other locales.

His has been a life of continued and varied service within the Church. He served two full-time and three stake missions. He has been a district president, branch president, high priests group leader, stake mission president, seventy's quorum president, and elders quorum president. He also has served as a Sunday School and YMMIA superintendent and president; ward music chairman; stake music and drama director; a member of several stake boards; a director of numerous regional, stake, and ward choirs; and a teacher and teacher trainer. A gifted and knowledgeable teacher, he has served as a gospel doctrine instructor for more than twenty-five years. Other Church assignments have included callings as a temple worker and as a guide on Temple Square. He and his wife presently serve as temple workers in the Bountiful Utah Temple, and he is currently serving as a high priests instructor, the boy scout troop committee chairman, the stake employment specialist, and his ward's chorister. He is a Master M-Man and an Eagle Scout.

Mr. Crowther is married to Jean Decker, who also is an author, editor, teacher, and musician. The parents of eight children and grandparents of twenty-eight grandchildren, the Crowthers reside in Bountiful, Utah.

0 26575 09837 2